Hollow Fields

VOLUME 1

MADELEINE ROSCA
STORY & ART

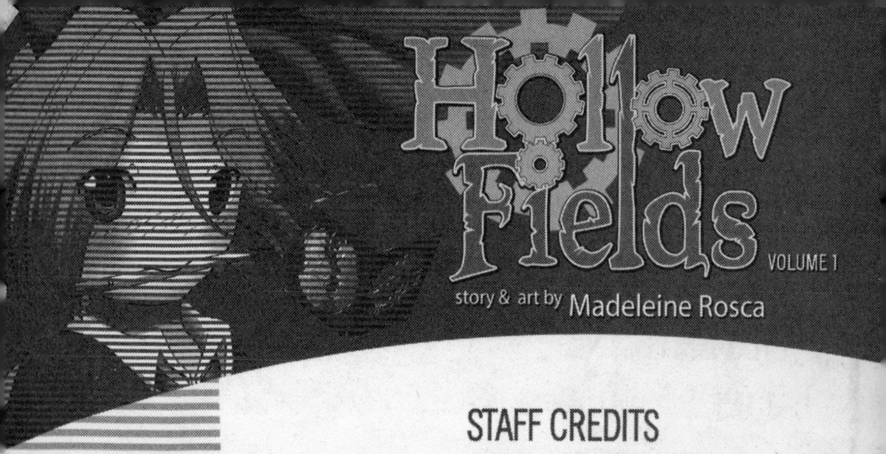
Hollow Fields
VOLUME 1
story & art by Madeleine Rosca

STAFF CREDITS

toning	**Armand Roy Canlas**
lettering	**Jon Zamar**
graphic design	**Jon Zamar**
	Nate Legaspi
cover design	**Nicky Lim**
assistant editor	**Adam Arnold**
editor	**Jason DeAngelis**
publisher	**Seven Seas Entertainment**

This is a work of fiction. Names, characters, places, and incidents are the products of the author's imagination or are used fictitiously. Any resemblance to actual events, locales, or persons, living or dead, is entirely coincidental.

Visit us online at www.gomanga.com.

ISBN 978-1-933164-24-3

Printed in Canada

First printing: June, 2007

10 9 8 7 6 5 4 3 2 1

TABLE OF CONTENTS

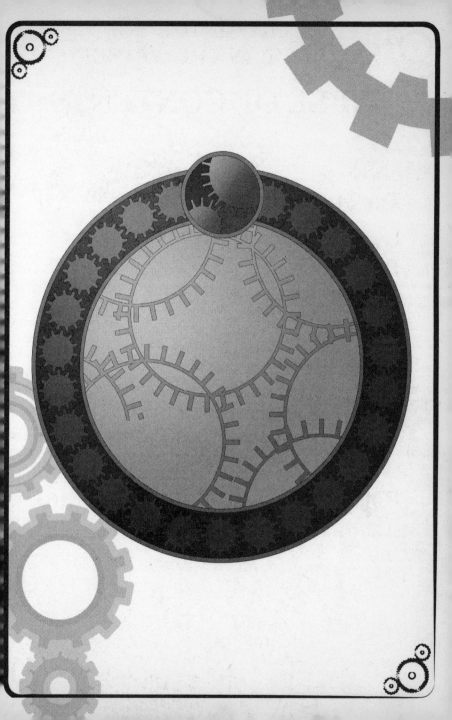

CHAPTER ONE
The Maid in the Machine

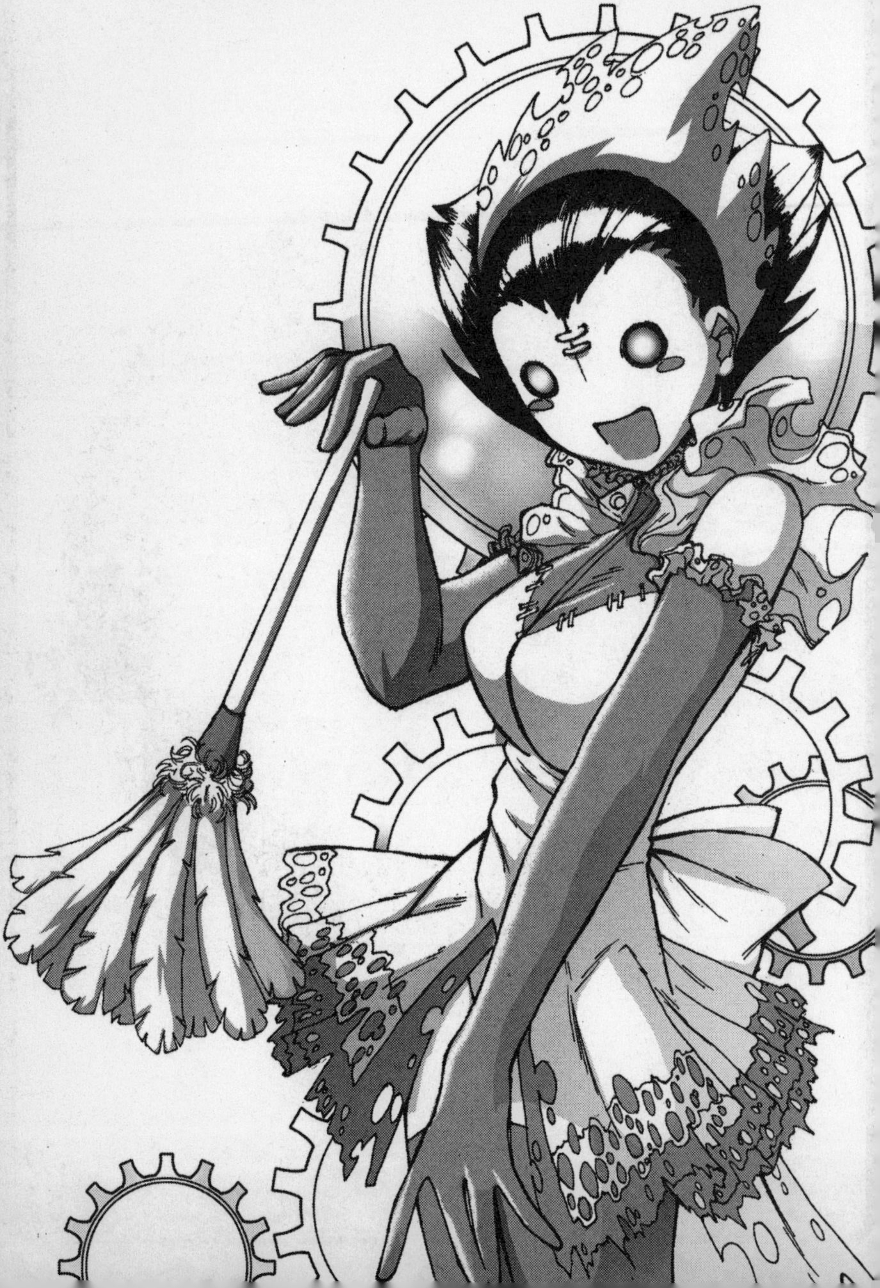

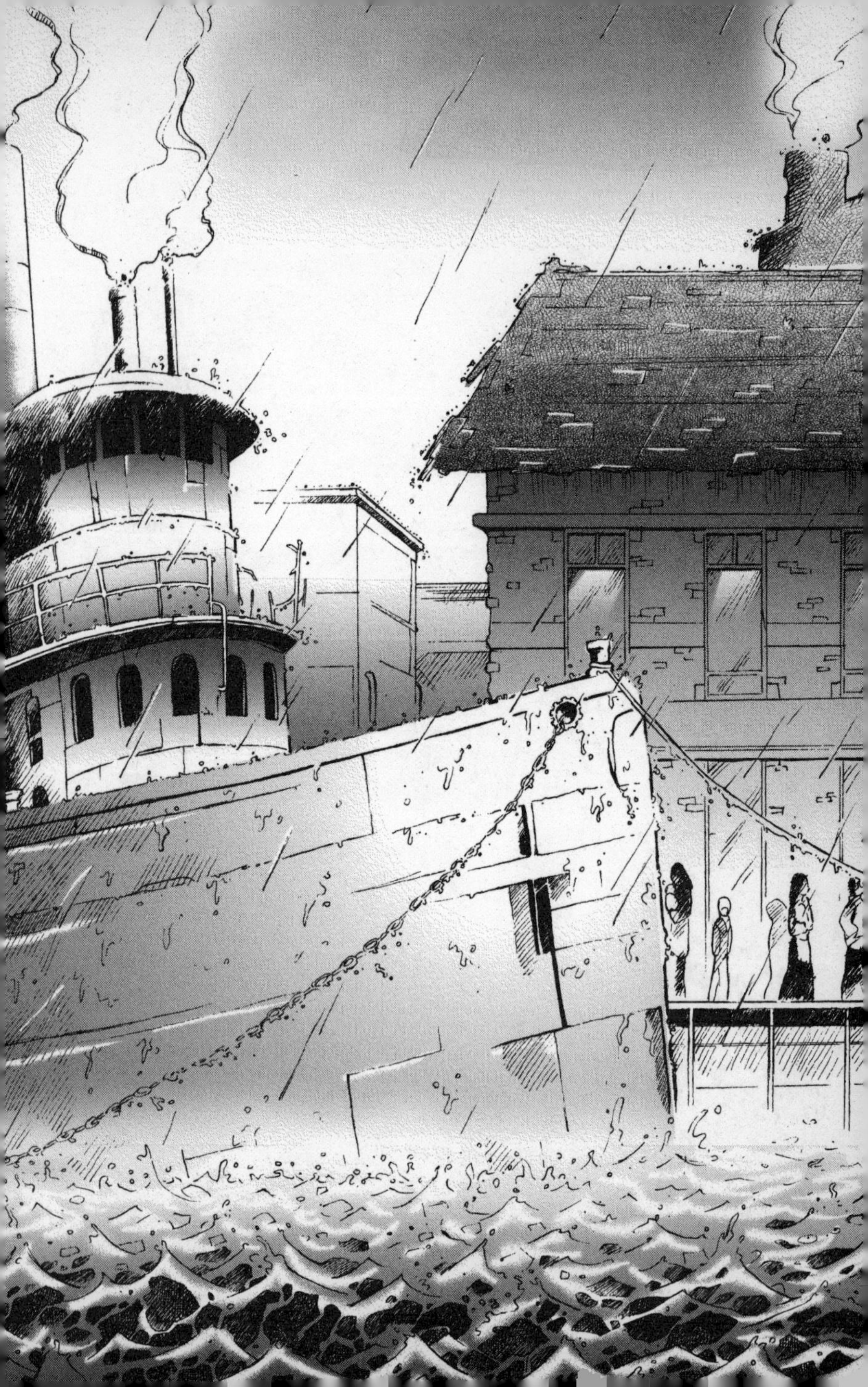

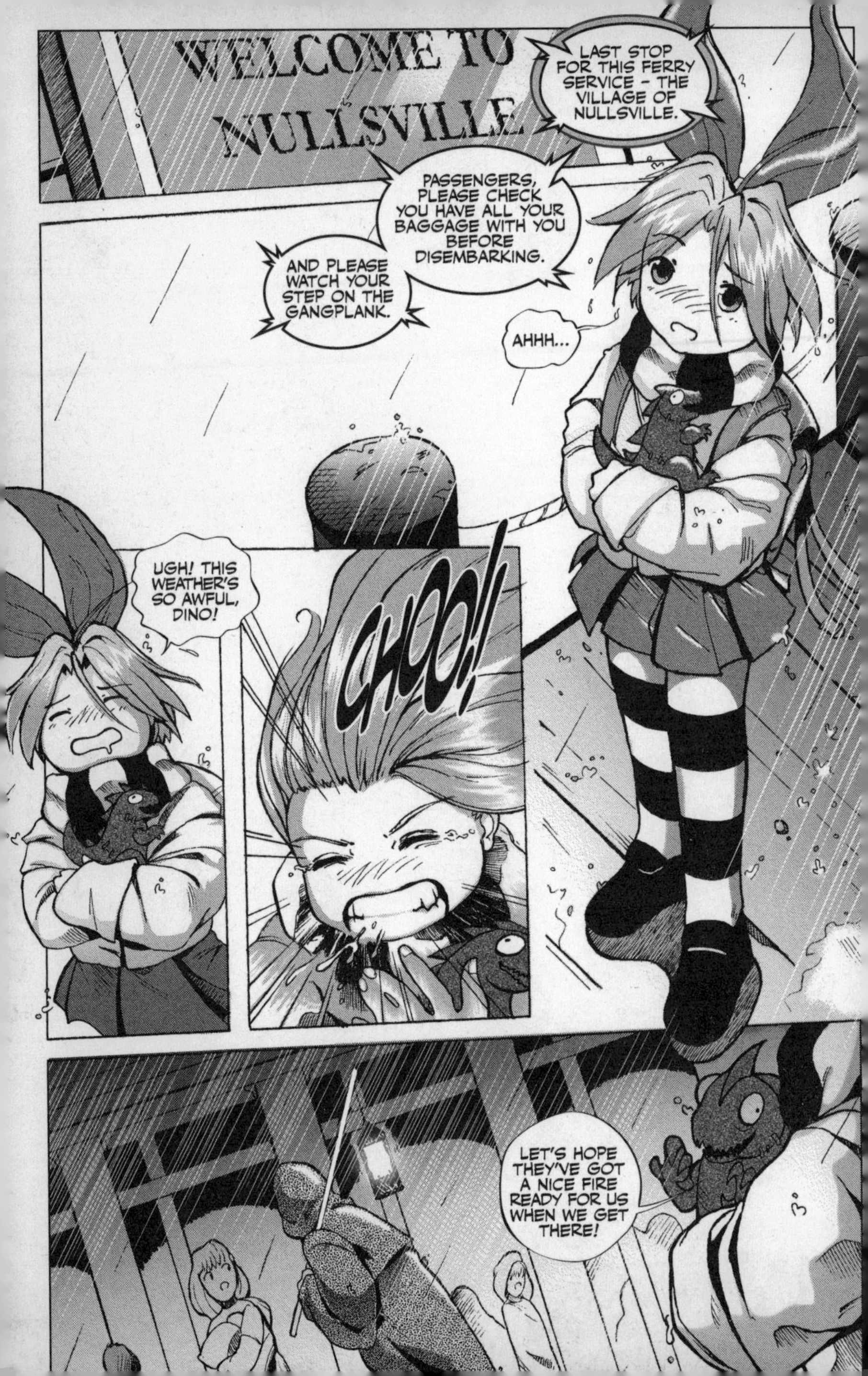
WELCOME TO NULLSVILLE
LAST STOP FOR THIS FERRY SERVICE - THE VILLAGE OF NULLSVILLE.
PASSENGERS, PLEASE CHECK YOU HAVE ALL YOUR BAGGAGE WITH YOU BEFORE DISEMBARKING.
AND PLEASE WATCH YOUR STEP ON THE GANGPLANK.
AHHH...
CHOO!!
UGH! THIS WEATHER'S SO AWFUL, DINO!
LET'S HOPE THEY'VE GOT A NICE FIRE READY FOR US WHEN WE GET THERE!

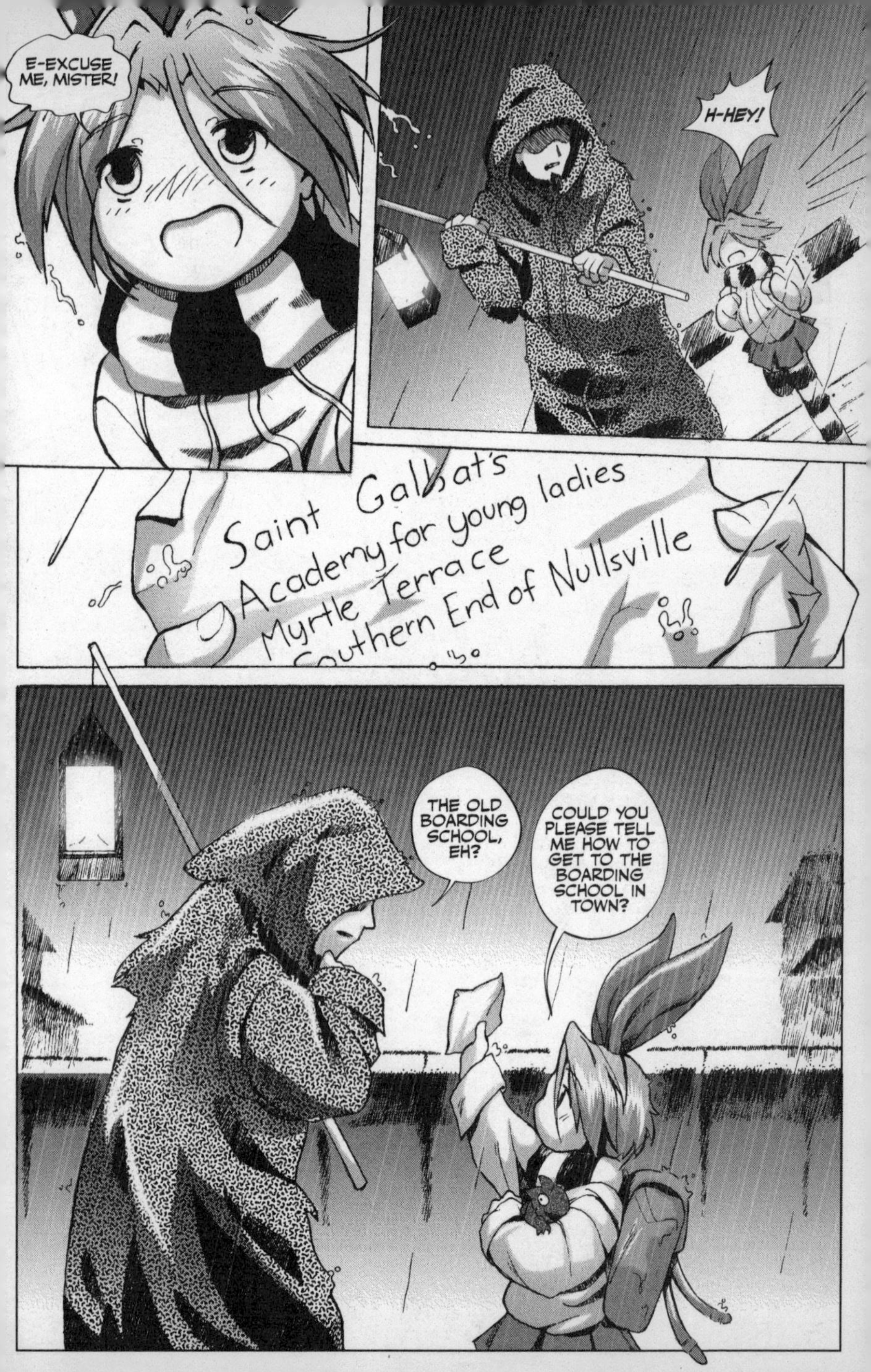
H-HEY!
E-EXCUSE ME, MISTER!
Saint Galbat's
Academy for young ladies
Myrtle Terrace
Southern End of Nullsville
COULD YOU PLEASE TELL ME HOW TO GET TO THE BOARDING SCHOOL IN TOWN?
THE OLD BOARDING SCHOOL, EH?

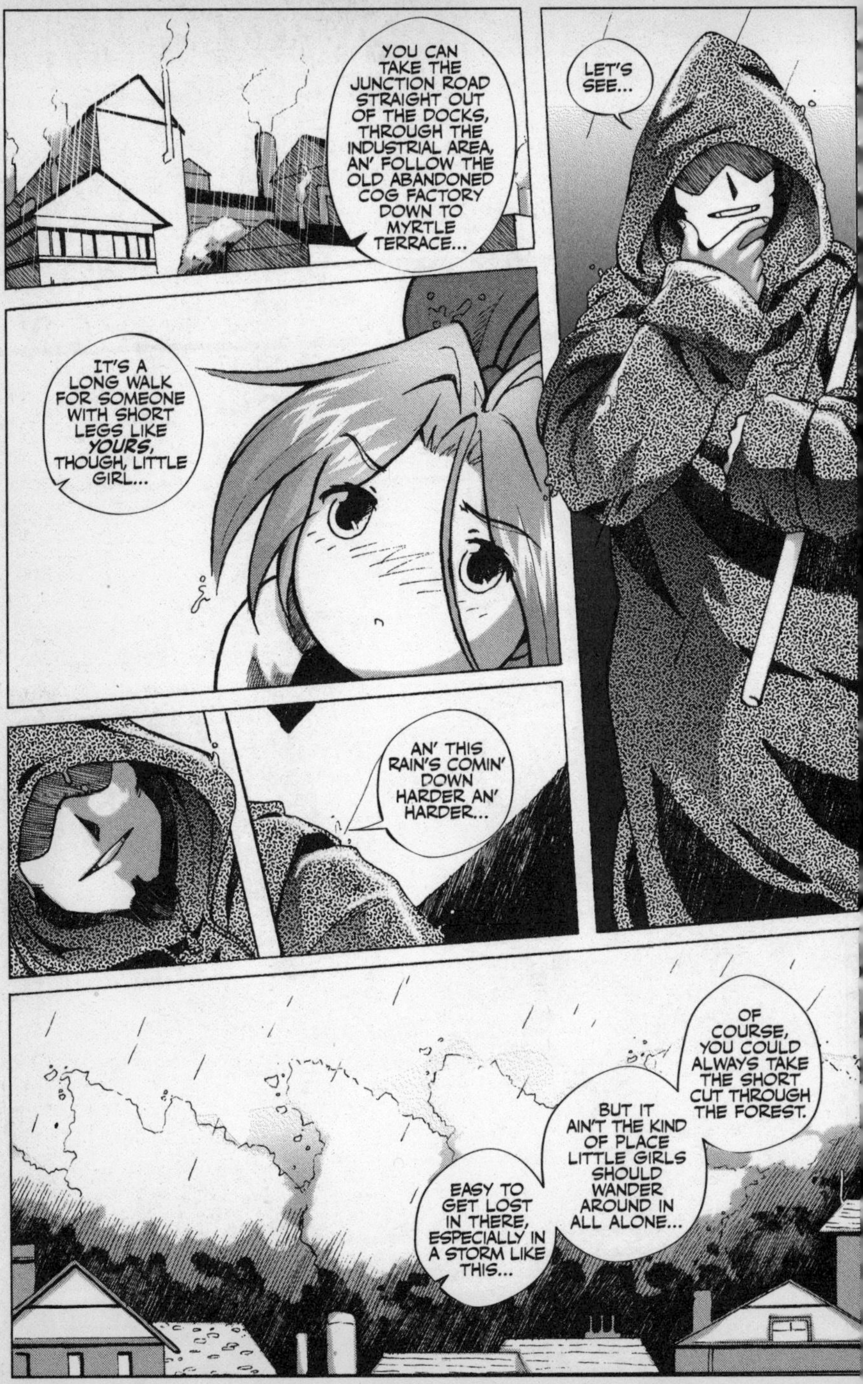

LET'S SEE...
YOU CAN TAKE THE JUNCTION ROAD STRAIGHT OUT OF THE DOCKS, THROUGH THE INDUSTRIAL AREA, AN' FOLLOW THE OLD ABANDONED COG FACTORY DOWN TO MYRTLE TERRACE...
IT'S A LONG WALK FOR SOMEONE WITH SHORT LEGS LIKE *YOURS*, THOUGH, LITTLE GIRL...
AN' THIS RAIN'S COMIN' DOWN HARDER AN' HARDER...
OF COURSE, YOU COULD ALWAYS TAKE THE SHORT CUT THROUGH THE FOREST.
BUT IT AIN'T THE KIND OF PLACE LITTLE GIRLS SHOULD WANDER AROUND IN ALL ALONE...
EASY TO GET LOST IN THERE, ESPECIALLY IN A STORM LIKE THIS...

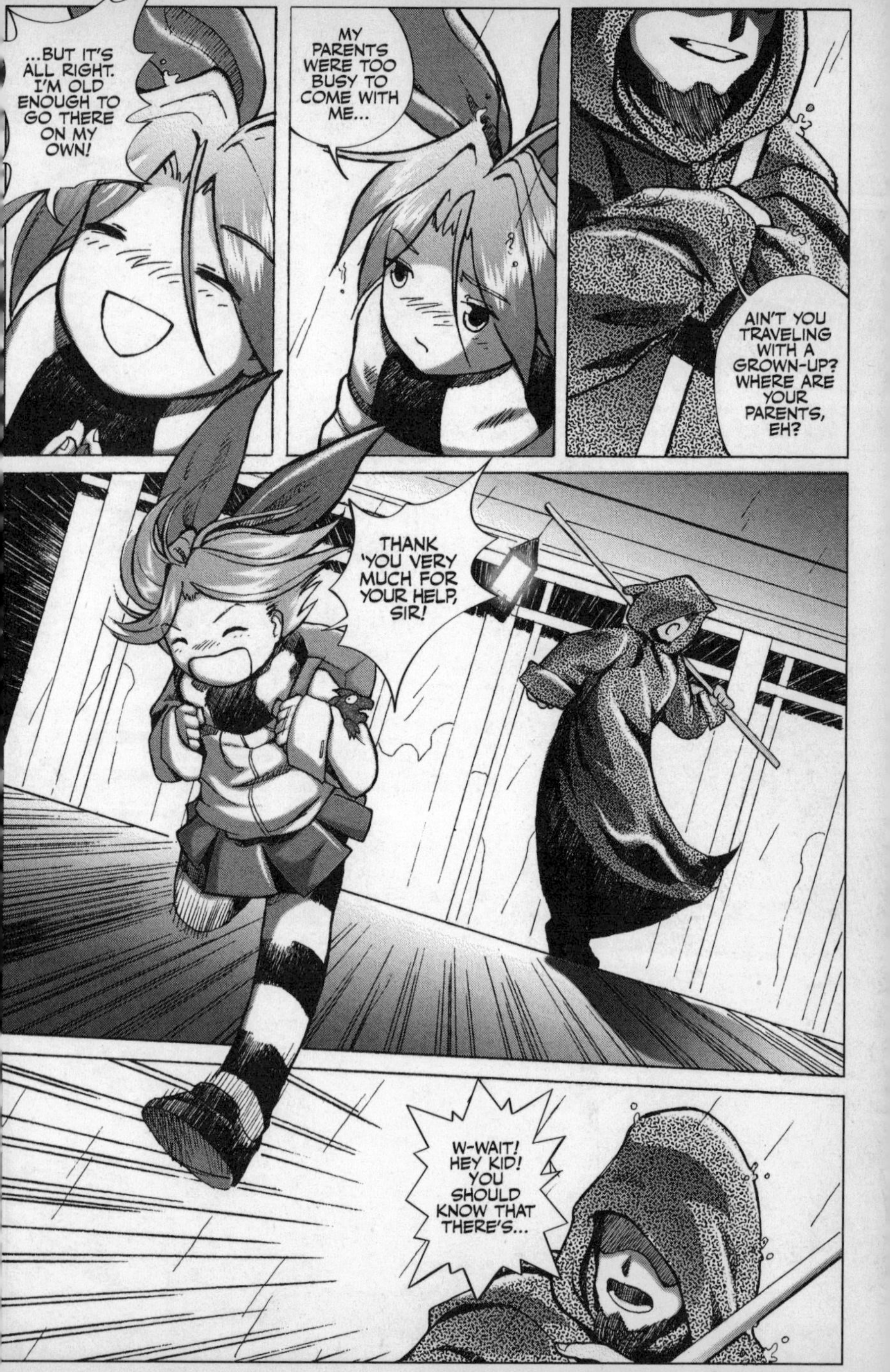
AIN'T YOU TRAVELING WITH A GROWN-UP? WHERE ARE YOUR PARENTS, EH?
MY PARENTS WERE TOO BUSY TO COME WITH ME...
...BUT IT'S ALL RIGHT. I'M OLD ENOUGH TO GO THERE ON MY OWN!
THANK 'YOU VERY MUCH FOR YOUR HELP, SIR!
W-WAIT! HEY KID! YOU SHOULD KNOW THAT THERE'S...

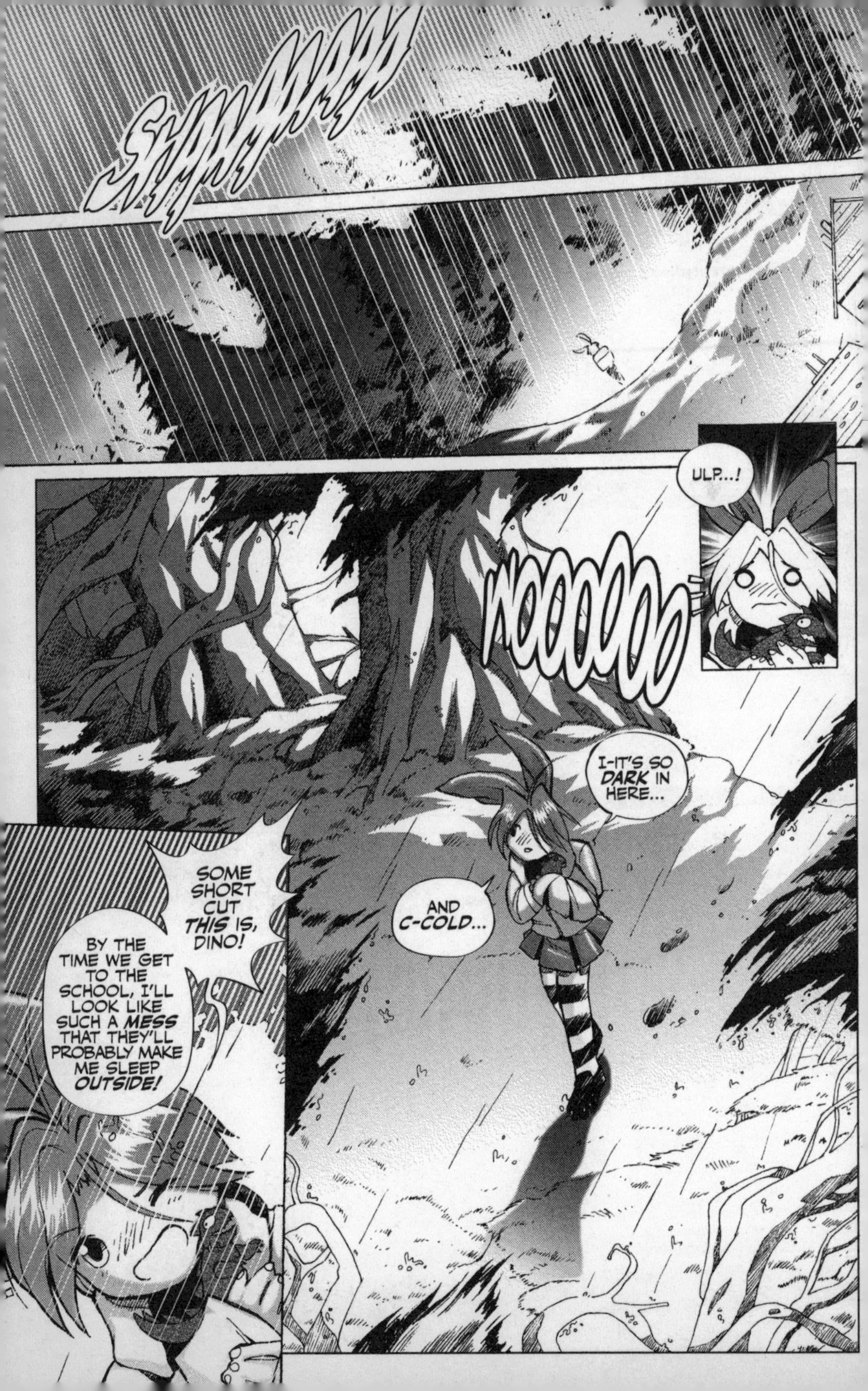
ULP...!
I-IT'S SO DARK IN HERE...
AND C-COLD...
SOME SHORT CUT THIS IS, DINO!
BY THE TIME WE GET TO THE SCHOOL, I'LL LOOK LIKE SUCH A MESS THAT THEY'LL PROBABLY MAKE ME SLEEP OUTSIDE!

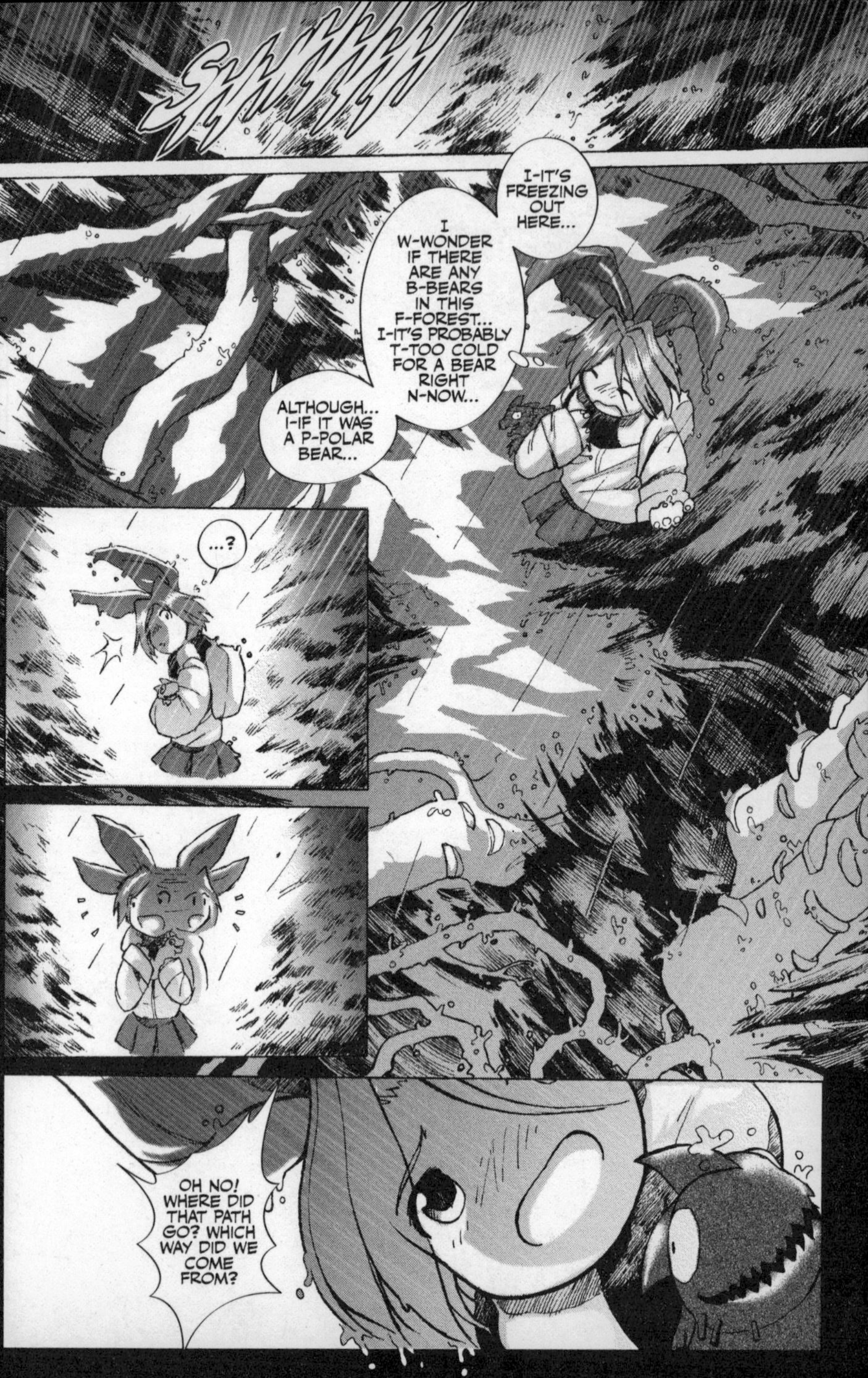
I-IT'S FREEZING OUT HERE...
I W-WONDER IF THERE ARE ANY B-BEARS IN THIS F-FOREST... I-IT'S PROBABLY T-TOO COLD FOR A BEAR RIGHT N-NOW...
ALTHOUGH... I-IF IT WAS A P-POLAR BEAR...
...?
OH NO! WHERE DID THAT PATH GO? WHICH WAY DID WE COME FROM?

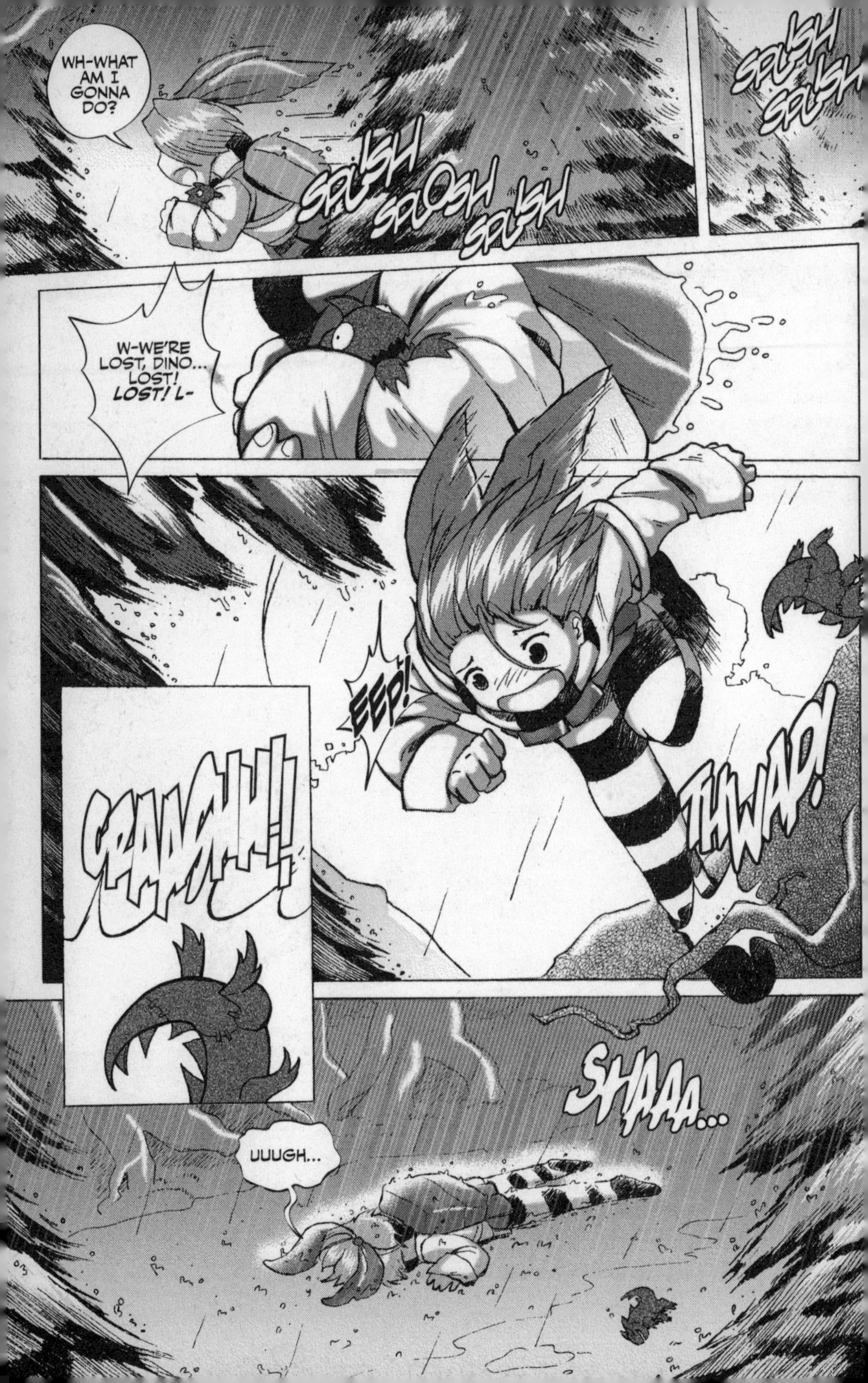
WH-WHAT AM I GONNA DO?
SPLUSH SPLOSH SPLUSH
SPLUSH SPLUSH
W-WE'RE LOST, DINO... LOST! LOST! L-
EEP!
THWAP!
CRANCH!!
SHAAA...
UUUGH...

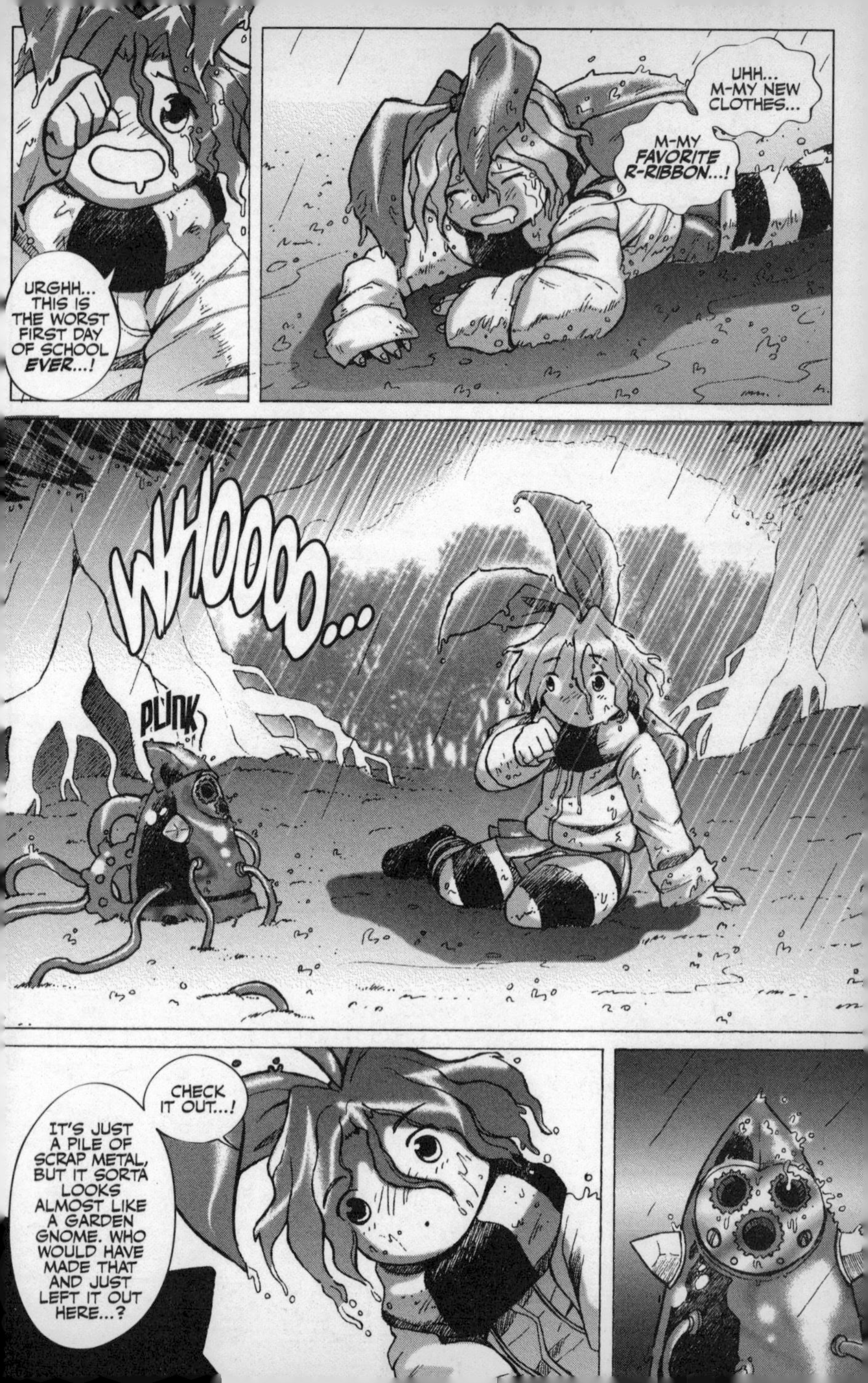
UHH... M-MY NEW CLOTHES...
M-MY FAVORITE R-RIBBON...!
URGHH... THIS IS THE WORST FIRST DAY OF SCHOOL **EVER**...!
WHOOOO...
PLINK
CHECK IT OUT...!
IT'S JUST A PILE OF SCRAP METAL, BUT IT SORTA LOOKS ALMOST LIKE A GARDEN GNOME. WHO WOULD HAVE MADE THAT AND JUST LEFT IT OUT HERE...?

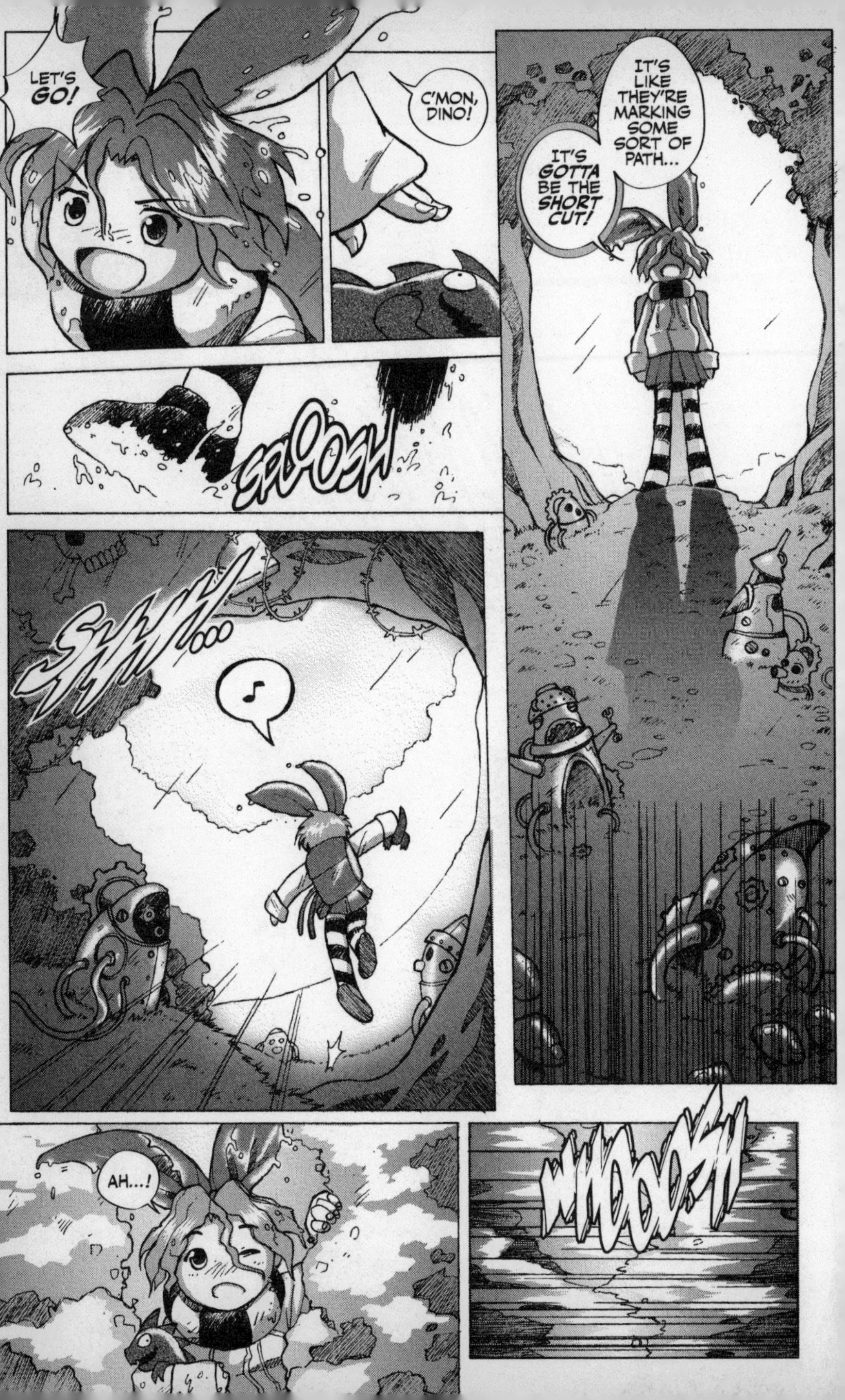
IT'S LIKE THEY'RE MARKING SOME SORT OF PATH...
IT'S GOTTA BE THE SHORT CUT!
C'MON, DINO!
LET'S GO!
SPLOOSH
SHWM...
♪
WHOOOSH
AH...!

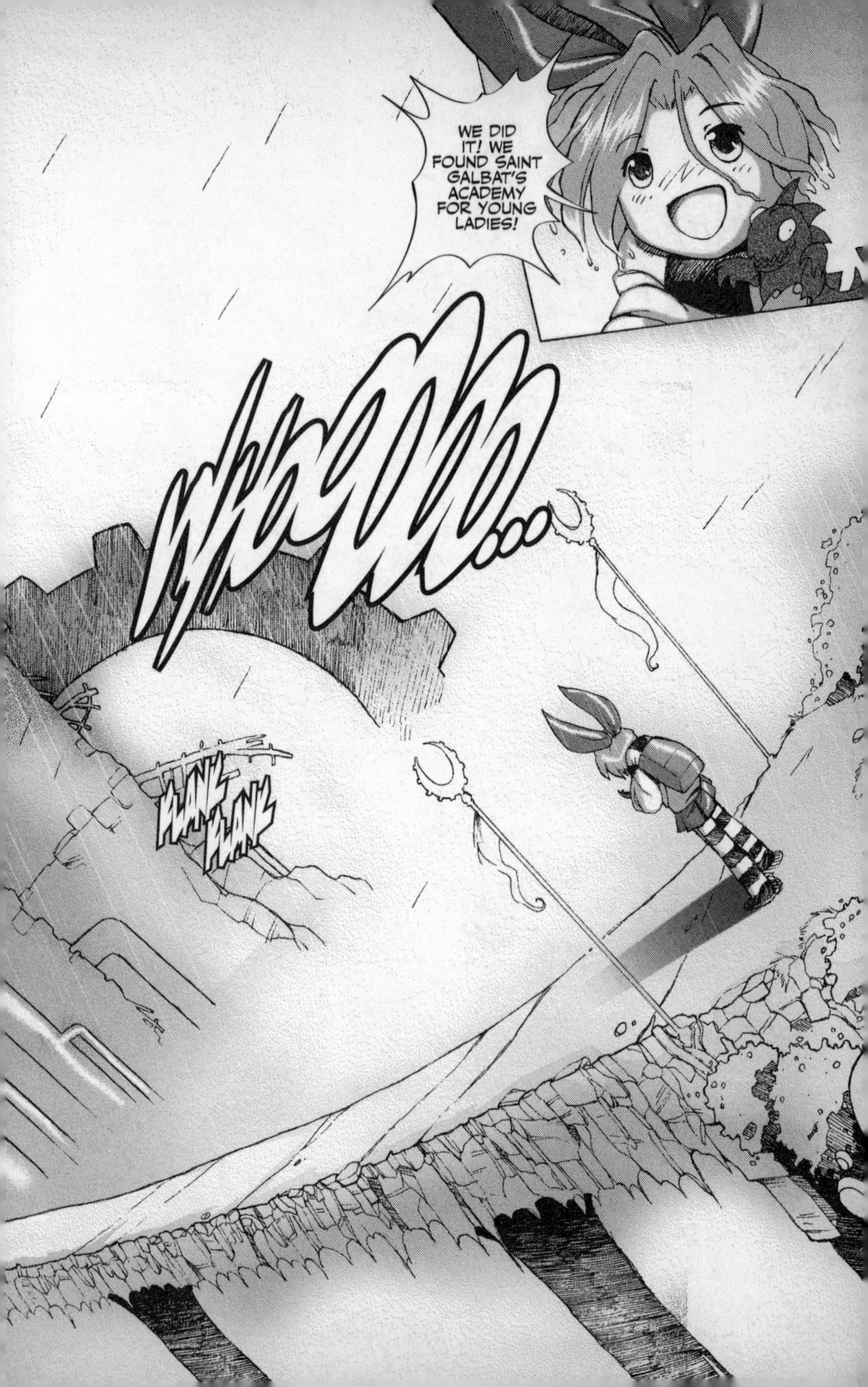
WE DID IT! WE FOUND SAINT GALBAT'S ACADEMY FOR YOUNG LADIES!
FLANK FLANK

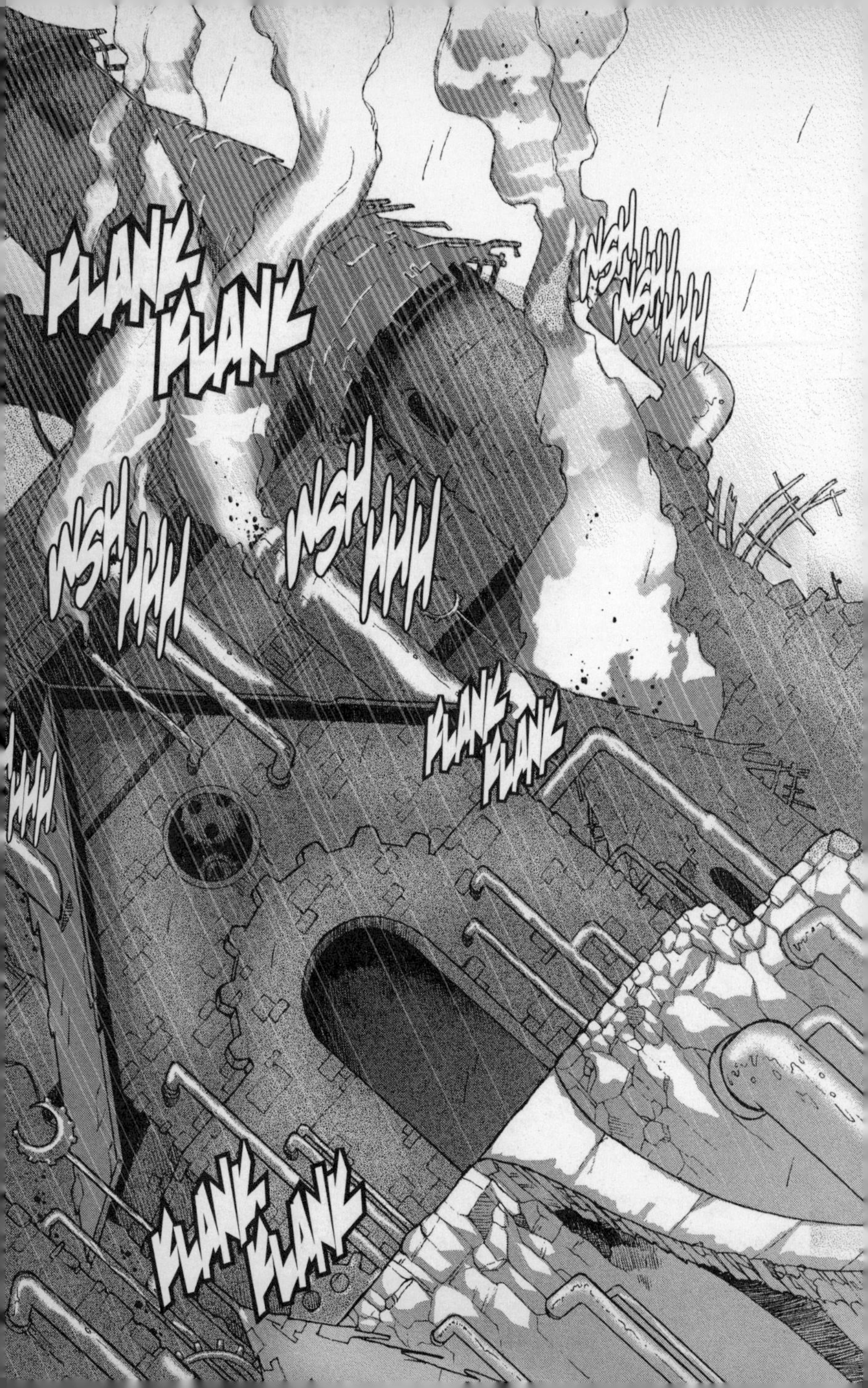
WSHHHH WSHHHH
KLANK KLANK
WSHHHH
WSHHHH
KLANK KLANK
KLANK KLANK

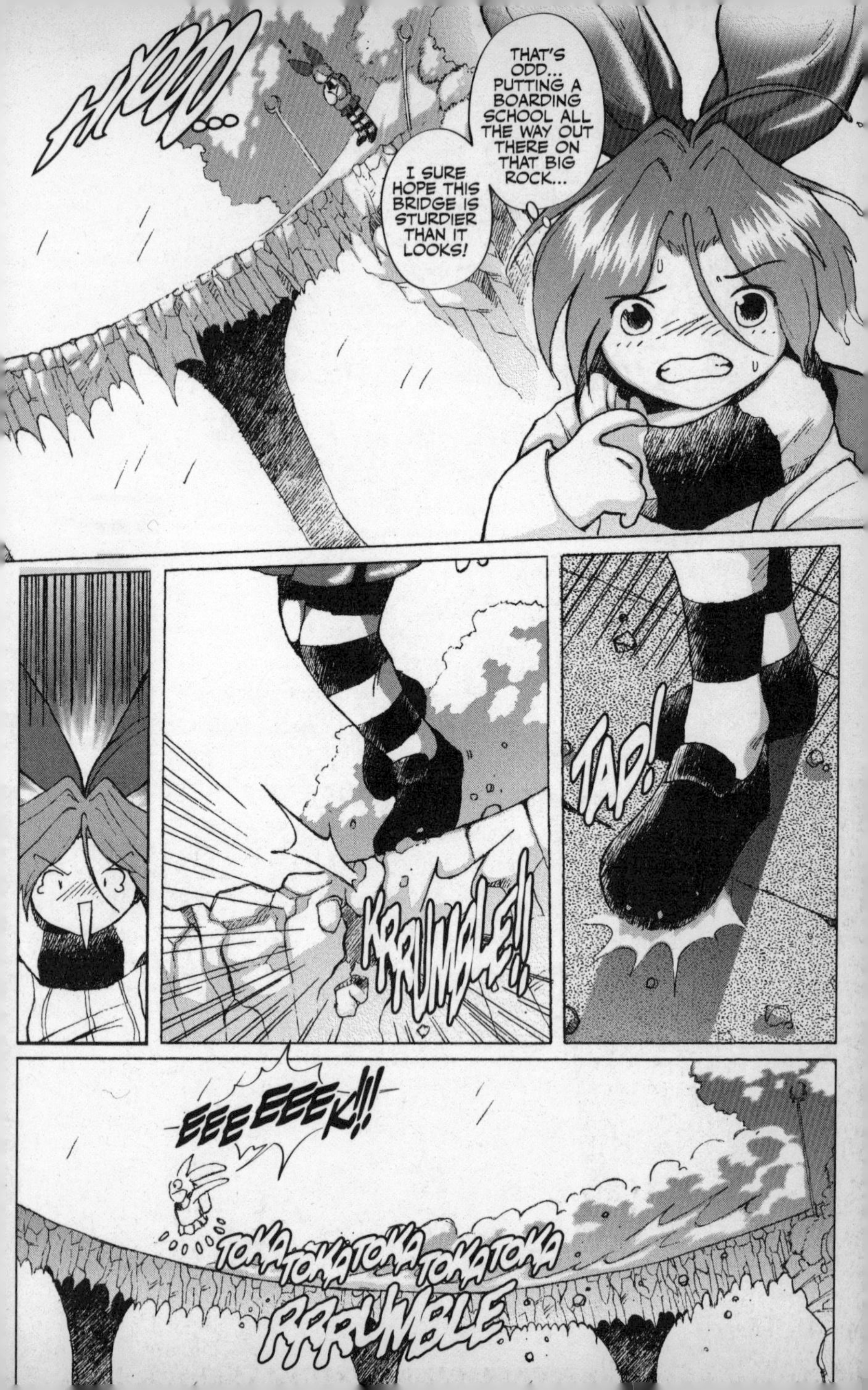
HYOOO...
THAT'S ODD... PUTTING A BOARDING SCHOOL ALL THE WAY OUT THERE ON THAT BIG ROCK...
I SURE HOPE THIS BRIDGE IS STURDIER THAN IT LOOKS!
TAP!
KRRUMBLE!!
EEEEEEK!!!
TOKA TOKA TOKA TOKA TOKA
RRRUMBLE

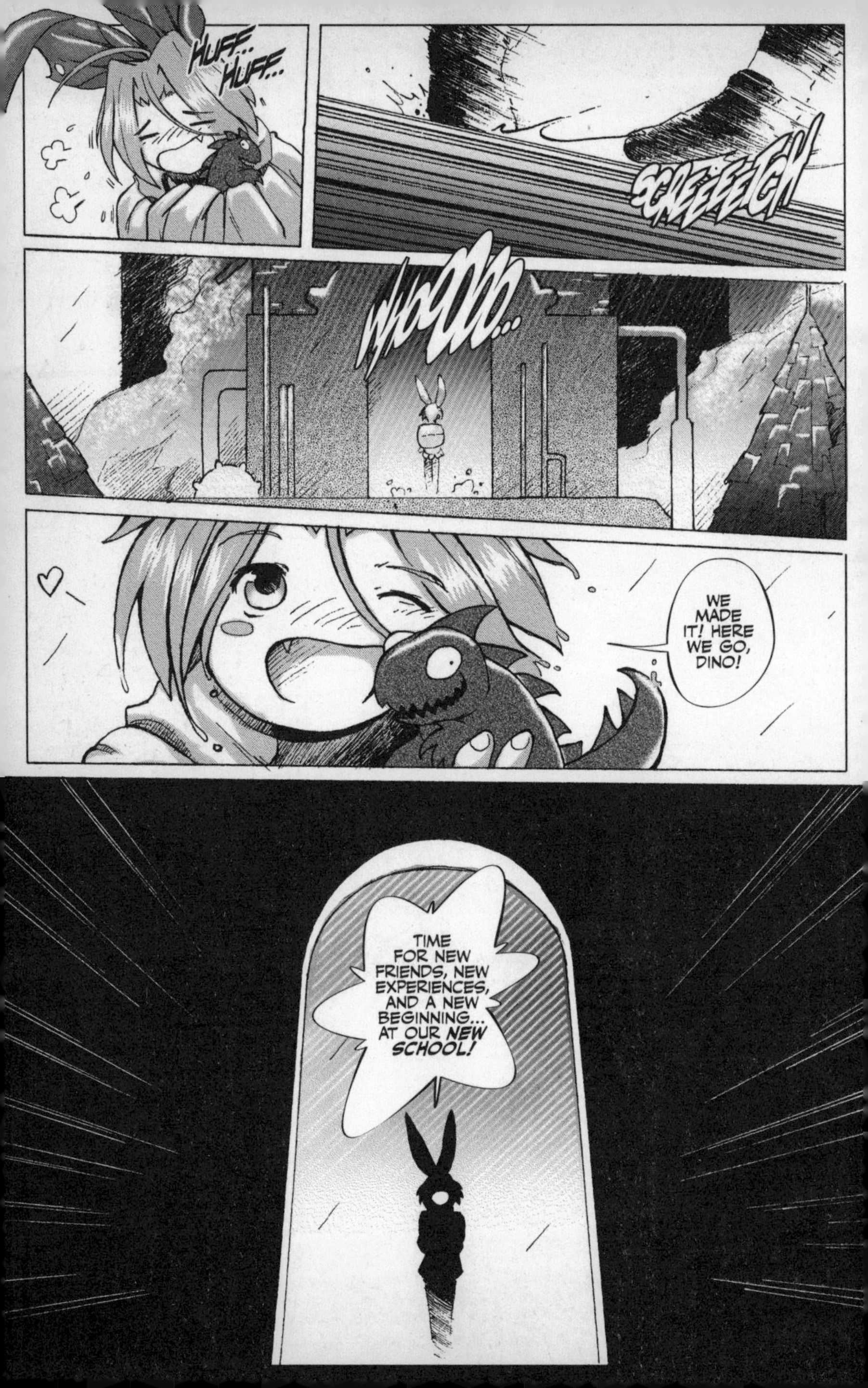
SCREEEETCH
HUFF... HUFF...
WHOOOOO...
WE MADE IT! HERE WE GO, DINO!
TIME FOR NEW FRIENDS, NEW EXPERIENCES, AND A NEW BEGINNING... AT OUR NEW SCHOOL!

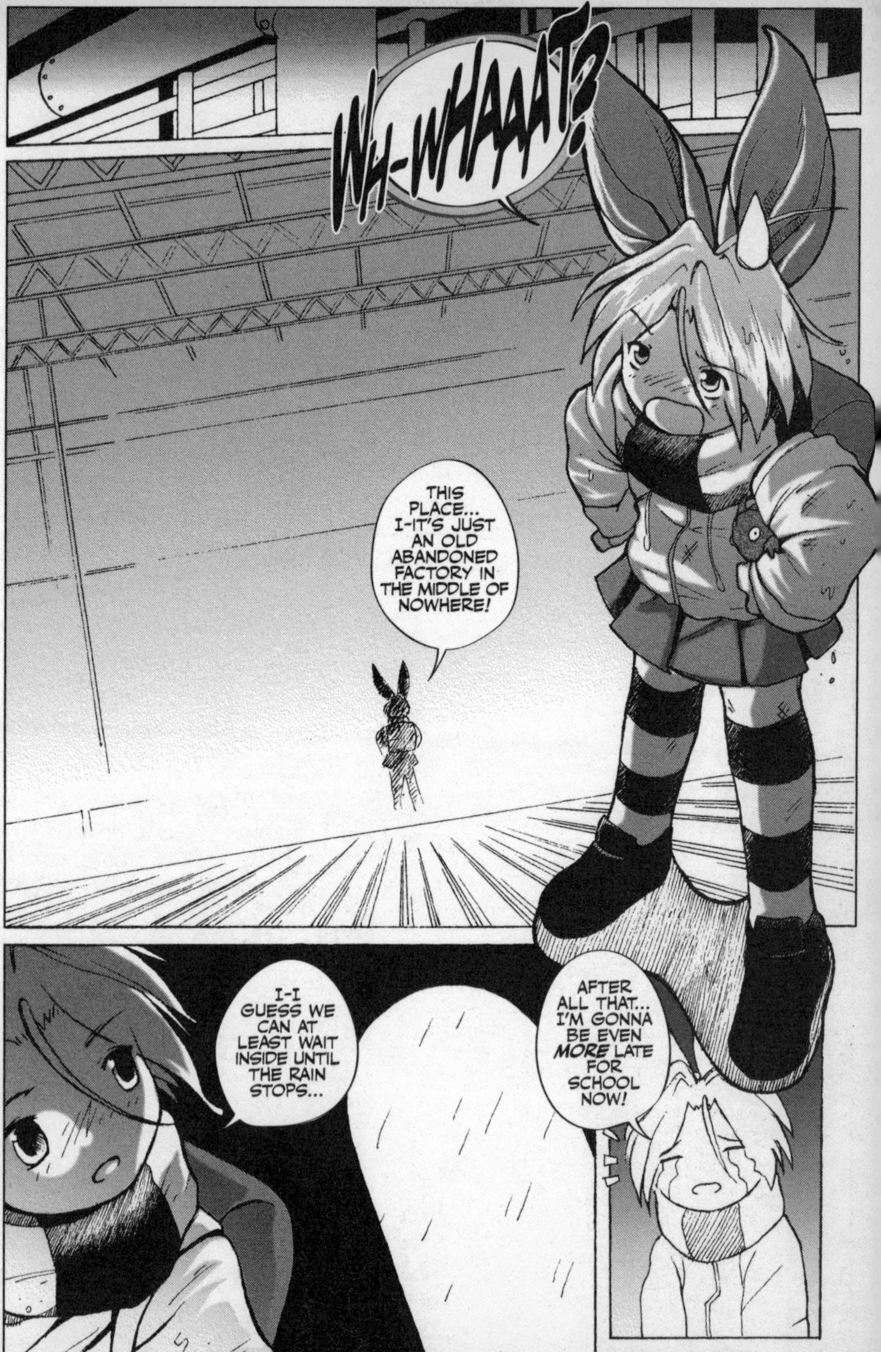
WH-WHAAAT?!
THIS PLACE... I-IT'S JUST AN OLD ABANDONED FACTORY IN THE MIDDLE OF NOWHERE!
AFTER ALL THAT... I'M GONNA BE EVEN MORE LATE FOR SCHOOL NOW!
I-I GUESS WE CAN AT LEAST WAIT INSIDE UNTIL THE RAIN STOPS...

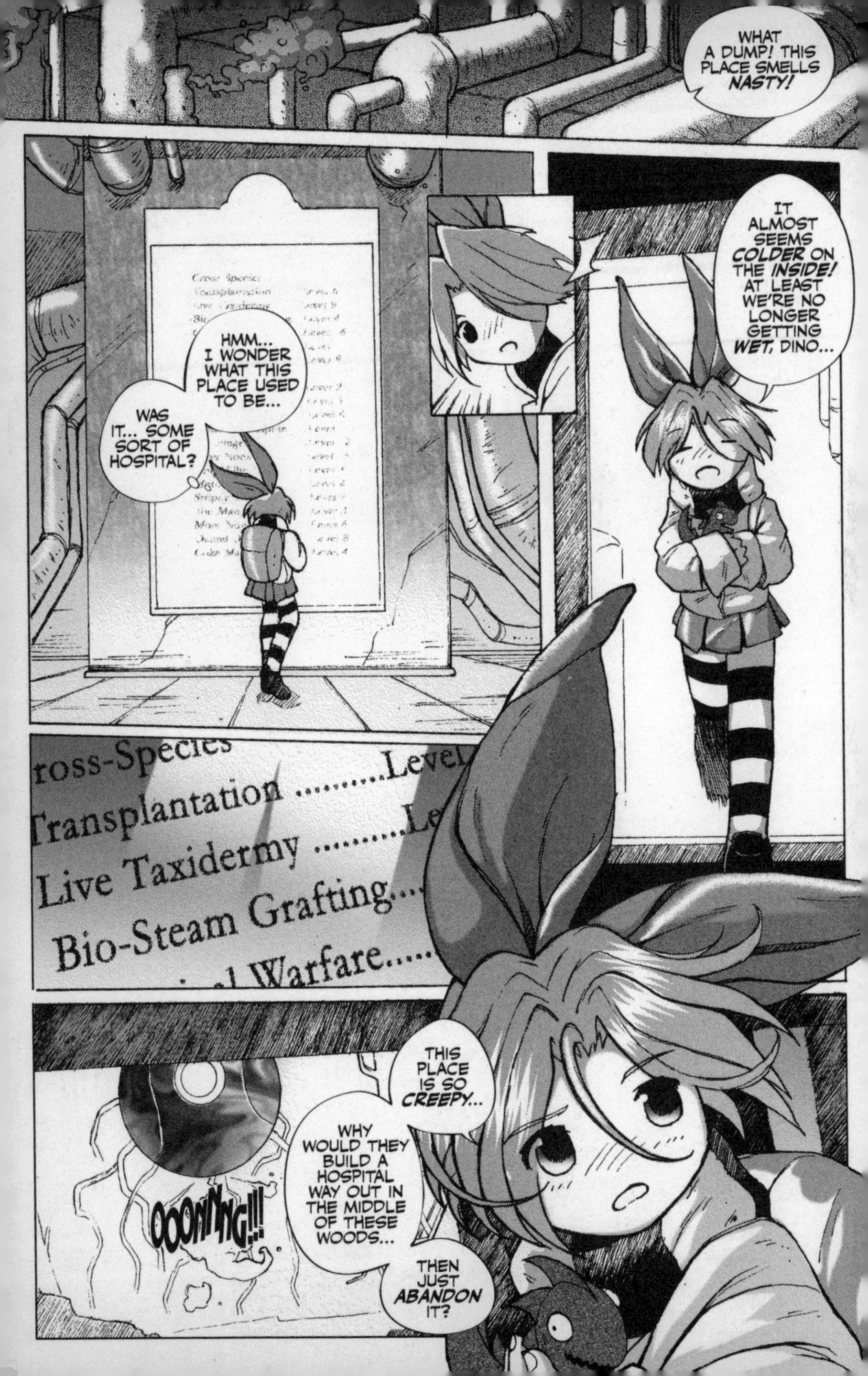
WHAT A DUMP! THIS PLACE SMELLS NASTY!
IT ALMOST SEEMS COLDER ON THE INSIDE! AT LEAST WE'RE NO LONGER GETTING WET, DINO...
HMM... I WONDER WHAT THIS PLACE USED TO BE...
WAS IT... SOME SORT OF HOSPITAL?
ross-Species
Transplantation ....Level
Live Taxidermy ....Le
Bio-Steam Grafting....
l Warfare.....
THIS PLACE IS SO CREEPY...
WHY WOULD THEY BUILD A HOSPITAL WAY OUT IN THE MIDDLE OF THESE WOODS...
THEN JUST ABANDON IT?
OOONNNG!!!

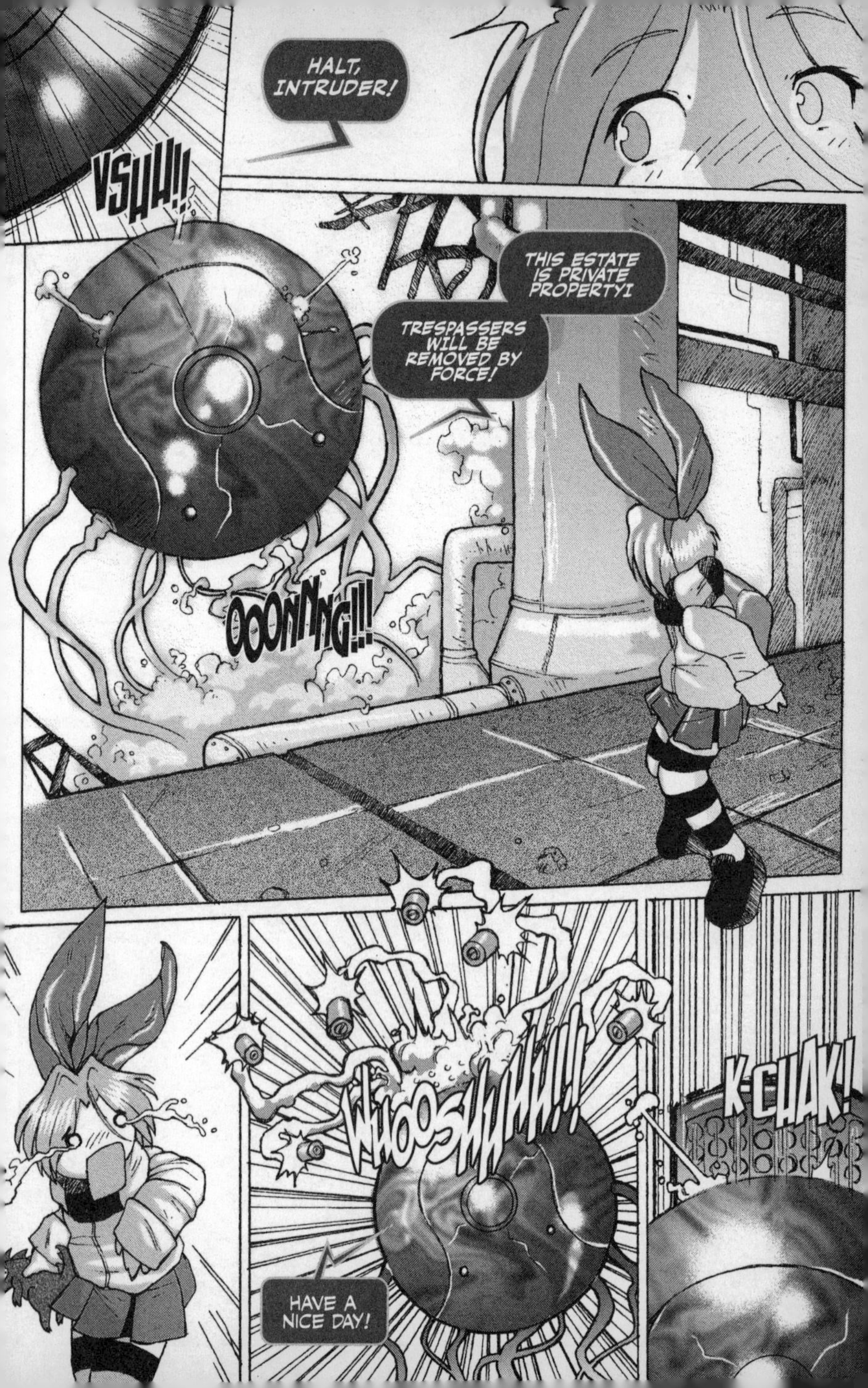
HALT, INTRUDER!
VSHH!!!
THIS ESTATE IS PRIVATE PROPERTY!
TRESPASSERS WILL BE REMOVED BY FORCE!
OOONNNG!!!
K-CHAK!
WHOOSHHH!!!
HAVE A NICE DAY!

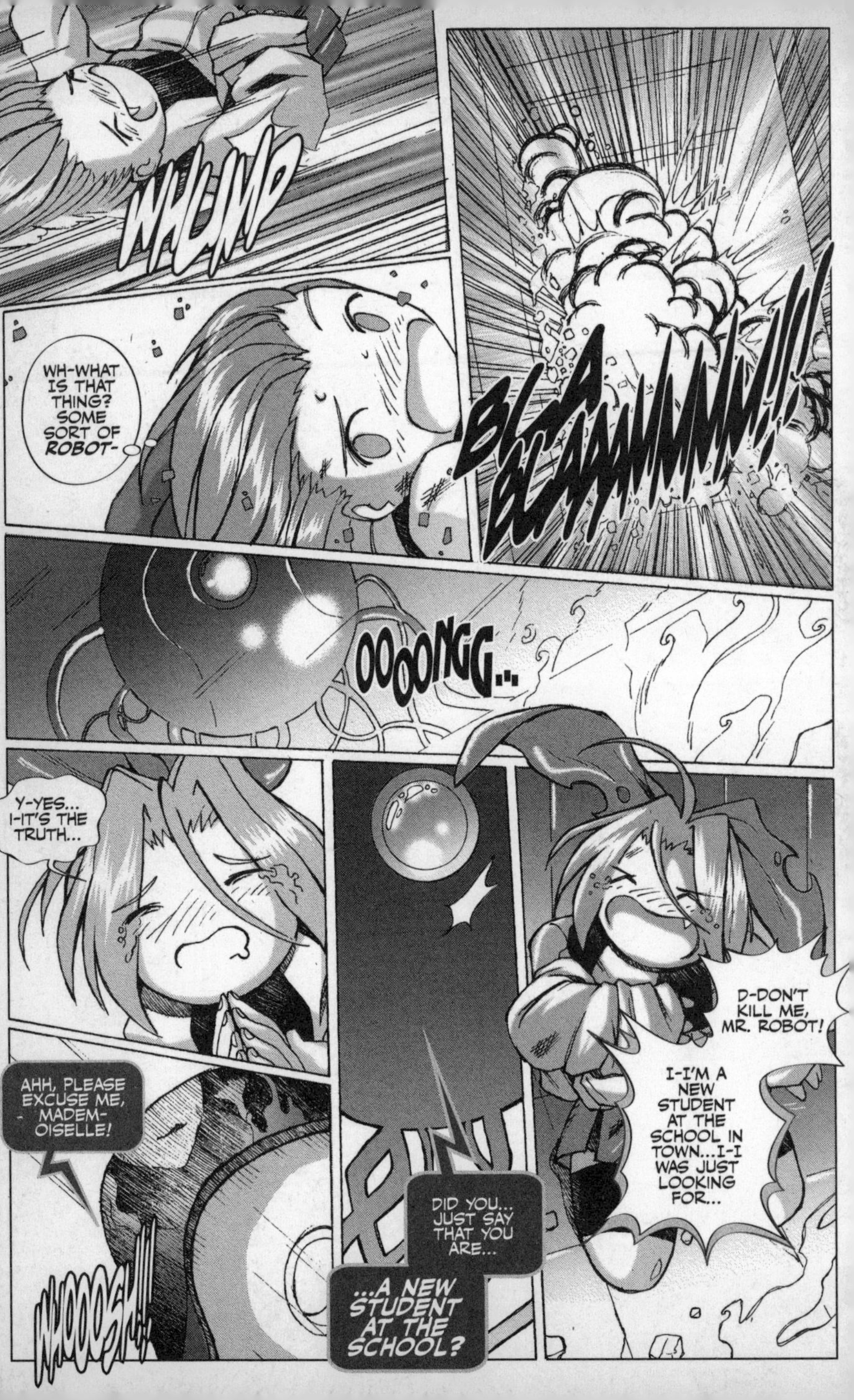
BLAAAMMMM!!!
WHUMP
WH-WHAT IS THAT THING? SOME SORT OF ROBOT-
OOOONGG...
D-DON'T KILL ME, MR. ROBOT!
I-I'M A NEW STUDENT AT THE SCHOOL IN TOWN...I-I WAS JUST LOOKING FOR...
DID YOU... JUST SAY THAT YOU ARE...
...A NEW STUDENT AT THE SCHOOL?
Y-YES... I-IT'S THE TRUTH...
AHH, PLEASE EXCUSE ME, MADEMOISELLE!
WHOOSH!!!

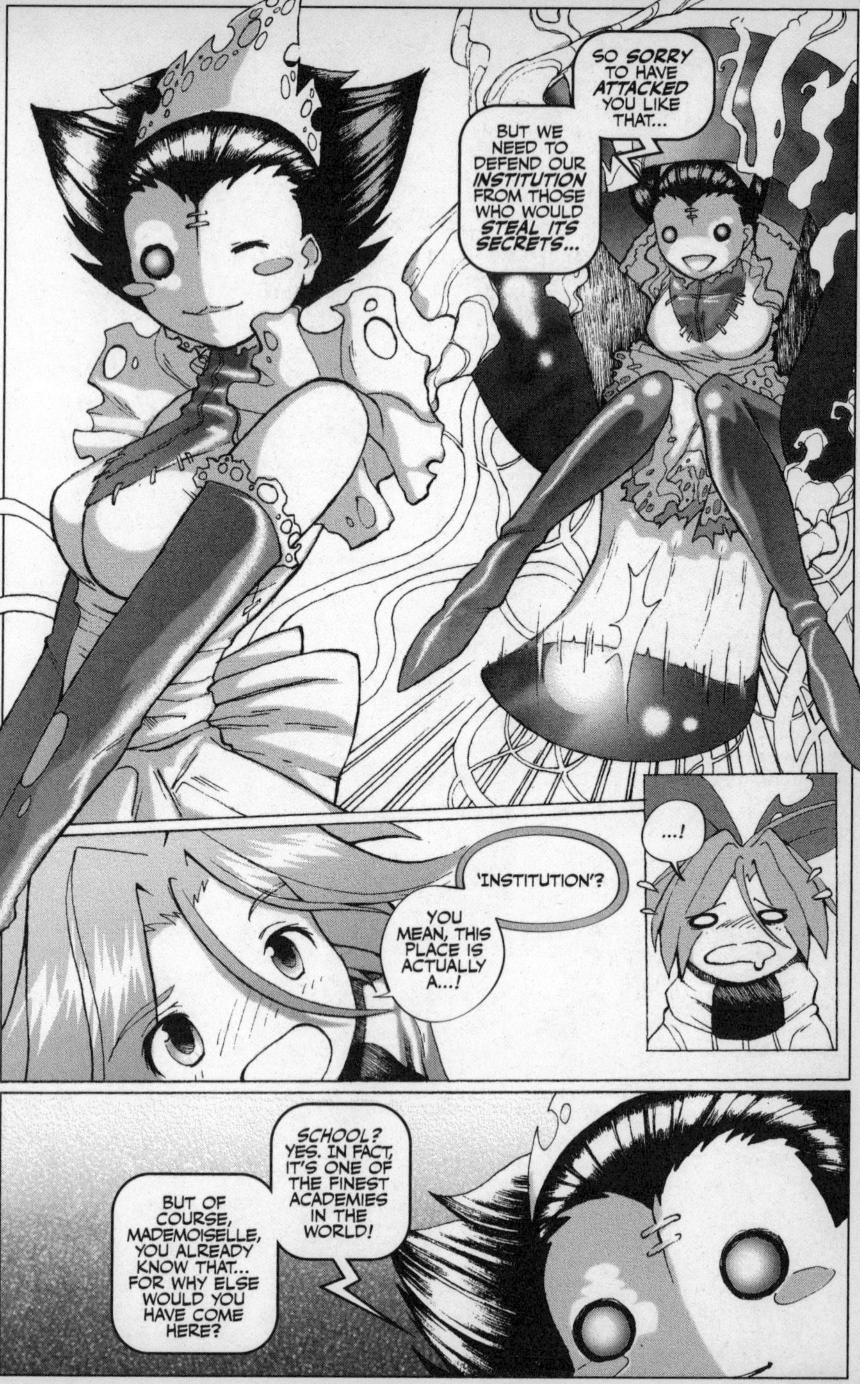
SO SORRY TO HAVE ATTACKED YOU LIKE THAT...
BUT WE NEED TO DEFEND OUR INSTITUTION FROM THOSE WHO WOULD STEAL ITS SECRETS...
...!
'INSTITUTION'?
YOU MEAN, THIS PLACE IS ACTUALLY A...!
SCHOOL? YES. IN FACT, IT'S ONE OF THE FINEST ACADEMIES IN THE WORLD!
BUT OF COURSE, MADEMOISELLE, YOU ALREADY KNOW THAT... FOR WHY ELSE WOULD YOU HAVE COME HERE?

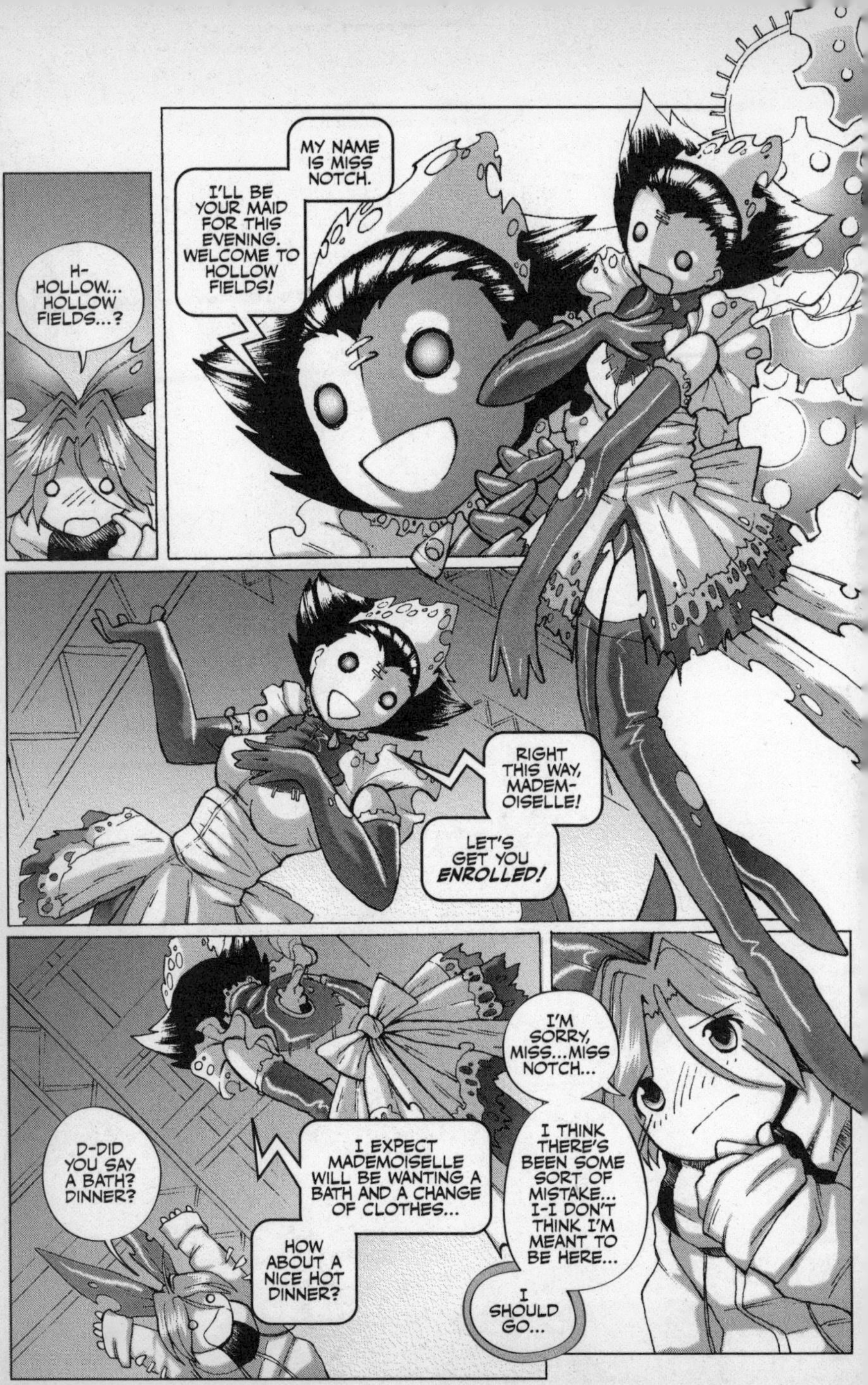
MY NAME IS MISS NOTCH.
I'LL BE YOUR MAID FOR THIS EVENING. WELCOME TO HOLLOW FIELDS!
H-HOLLOW... HOLLOW FIELDS...?
RIGHT THIS WAY, MADEM-OISELLE!
LET'S GET YOU *ENROLLED!*
I'M SORRY, MISS...MISS NOTCH...
I THINK THERE'S BEEN SOME SORT OF MISTAKE... I-I DON'T THINK I'M MEANT TO BE HERE...
I SHOULD GO...
I EXPECT MADEMOISELLE WILL BE WANTING A BATH AND A CHANGE OF CLOTHES...
HOW ABOUT A NICE HOT DINNER?
D-DID YOU SAY A BATH? DINNER?

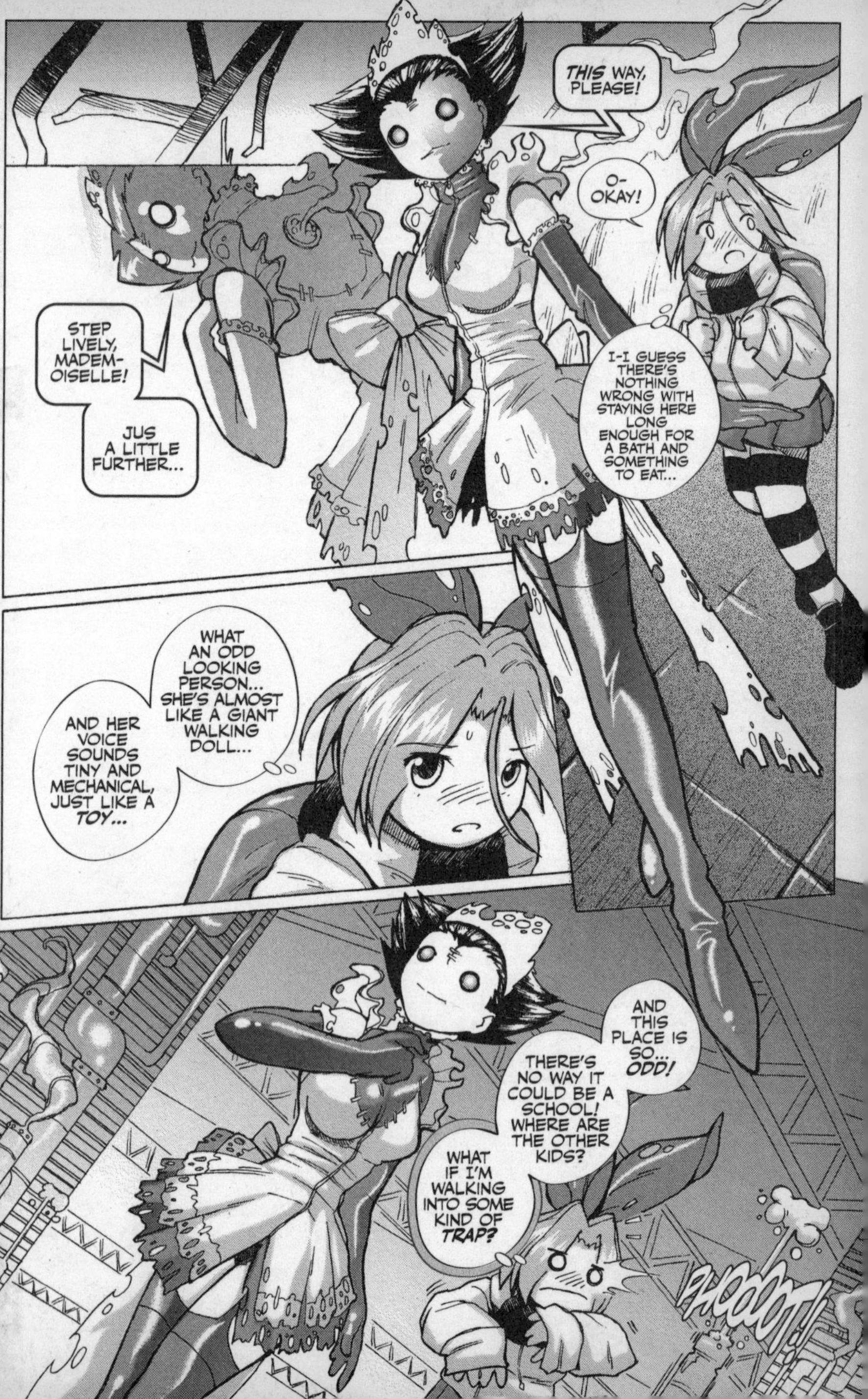
THIS WAY, PLEASE!
O-OKAY!
STEP LIVELY, MADEMOISELLE!
JUS A LITTLE FURTHER...
I-I GUESS THERE'S NOTHING WRONG WITH STAYING HERE LONG ENOUGH FOR A BATH AND SOMETHING TO EAT...
WHAT AN ODD LOOKING PERSON... SHE'S ALMOST LIKE A GIANT WALKING DOLL...
AND HER VOICE SOUNDS TINY AND MECHANICAL, JUST LIKE A TOY...
AND THIS PLACE IS SO... ODD!
THERE'S NO WAY IT COULD BE A SCHOOL! WHERE ARE THE OTHER KIDS?
WHAT IF I'M WALKING INTO SOME KIND OF TRAP?
PHOOOT!!

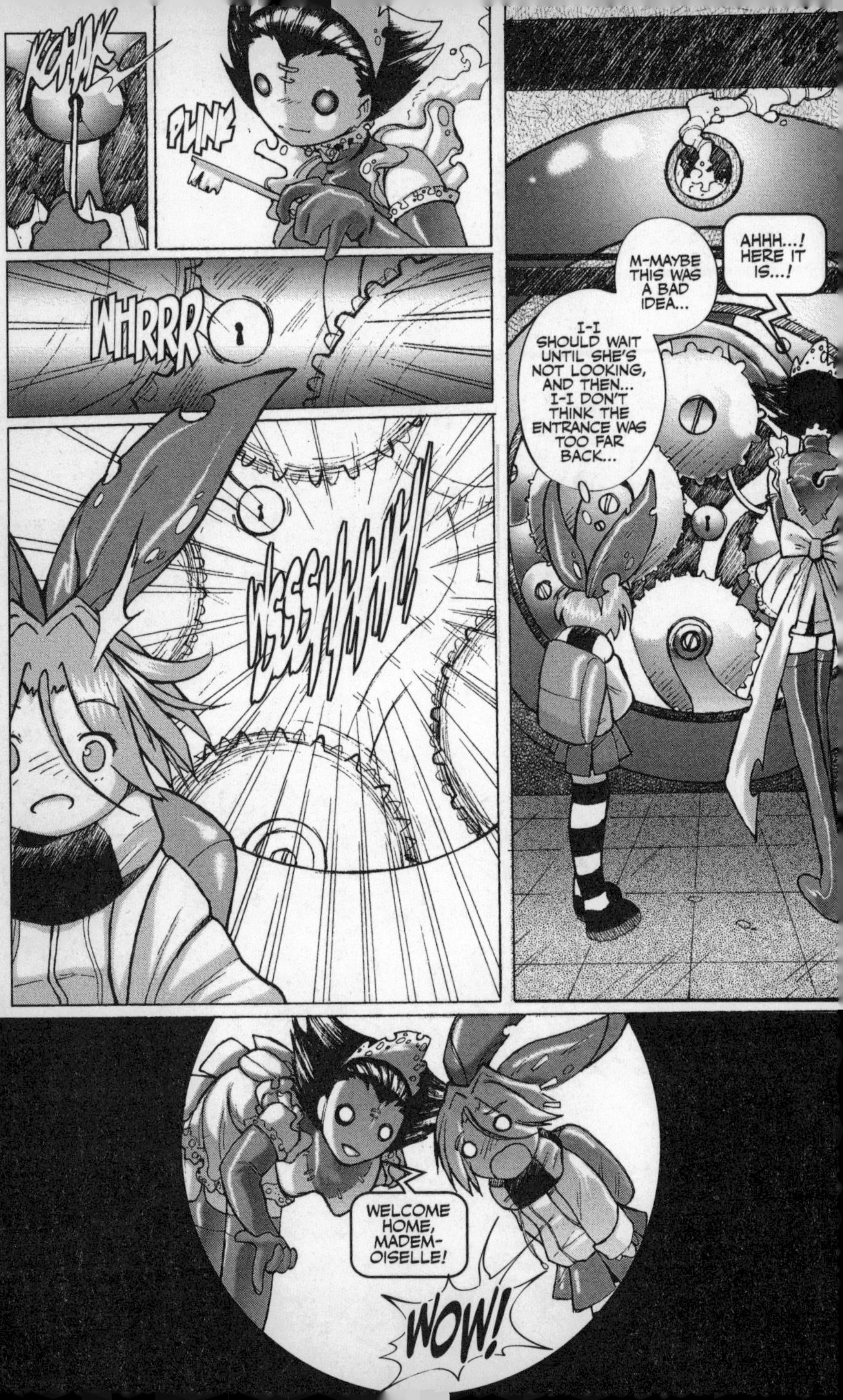
AHHH...! HERE IT IS...!
M-MAYBE THIS WAS A BAD IDEA...
I-I SHOULD WAIT UNTIL SHE'S NOT LOOKING, AND THEN... I-I DON'T THINK THE ENTRANCE WAS TOO FAR BACK...
PLINK
KCHAK
WHRRR
WSSSHHHH!
WELCOME HOME, MADEM-OISELLE!
WOW!

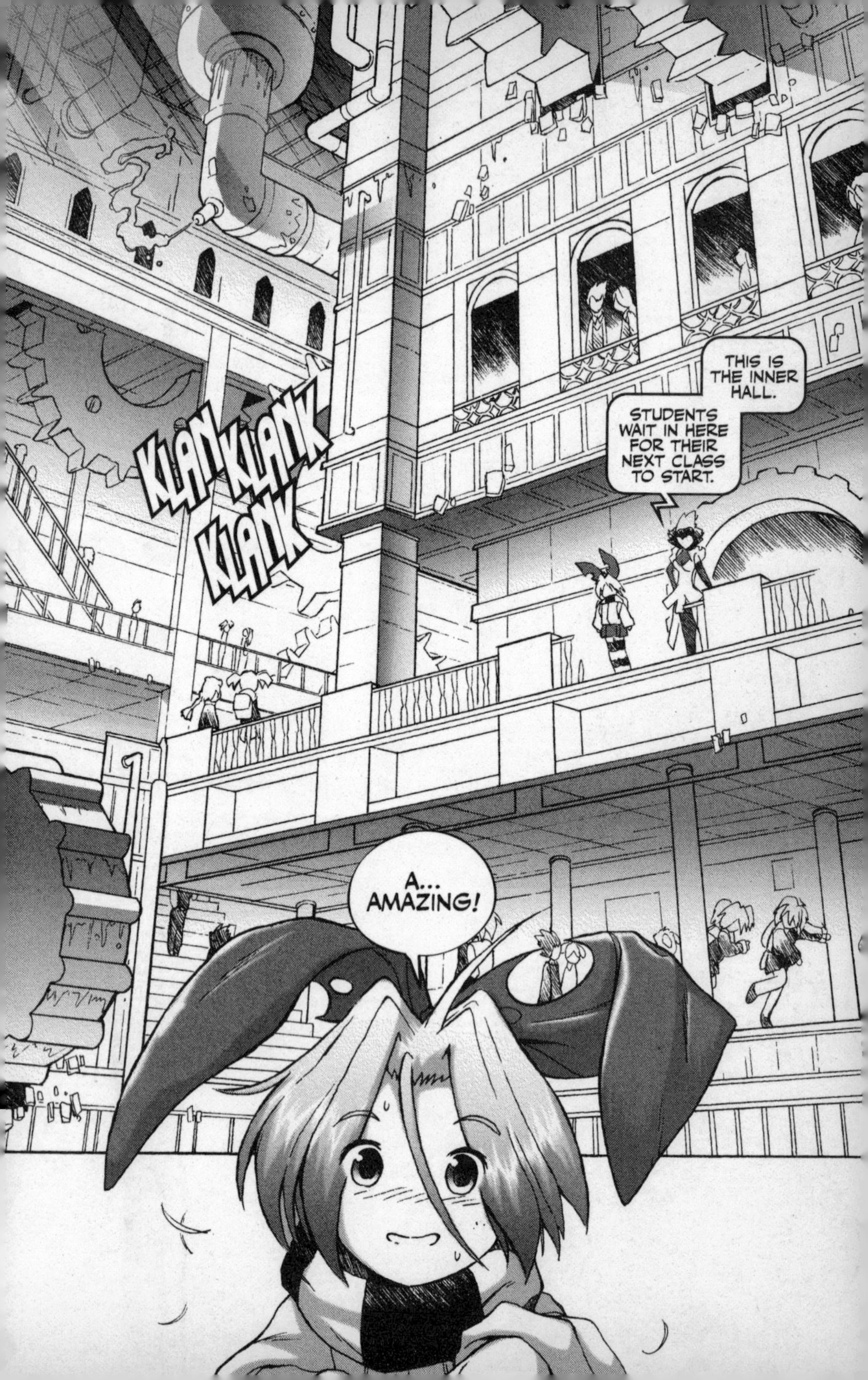
THIS IS THE INNER HALL.
STUDENTS WAIT IN HERE FOR THEIR NEXT CLASS TO START.
KLANKLANK KLANK
A... AMAZING!

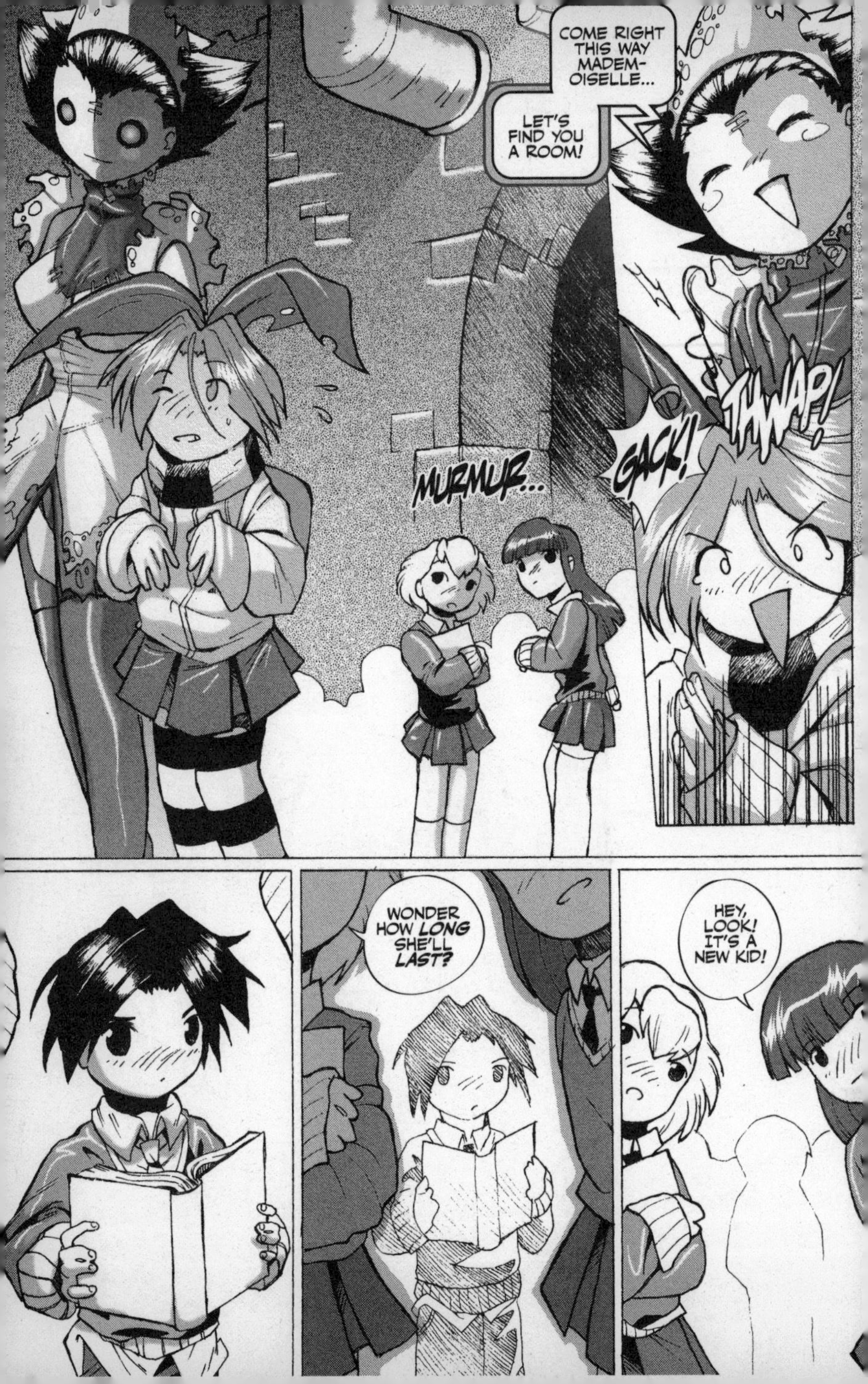
COME RIGHT THIS WAY MADEMOISELLE...
LET'S FIND YOU A ROOM!
THWAP!
GACK!
MURMUR...
HEY, LOOK! IT'S A NEW KID!
WONDER HOW LONG SHE'LL LAST?

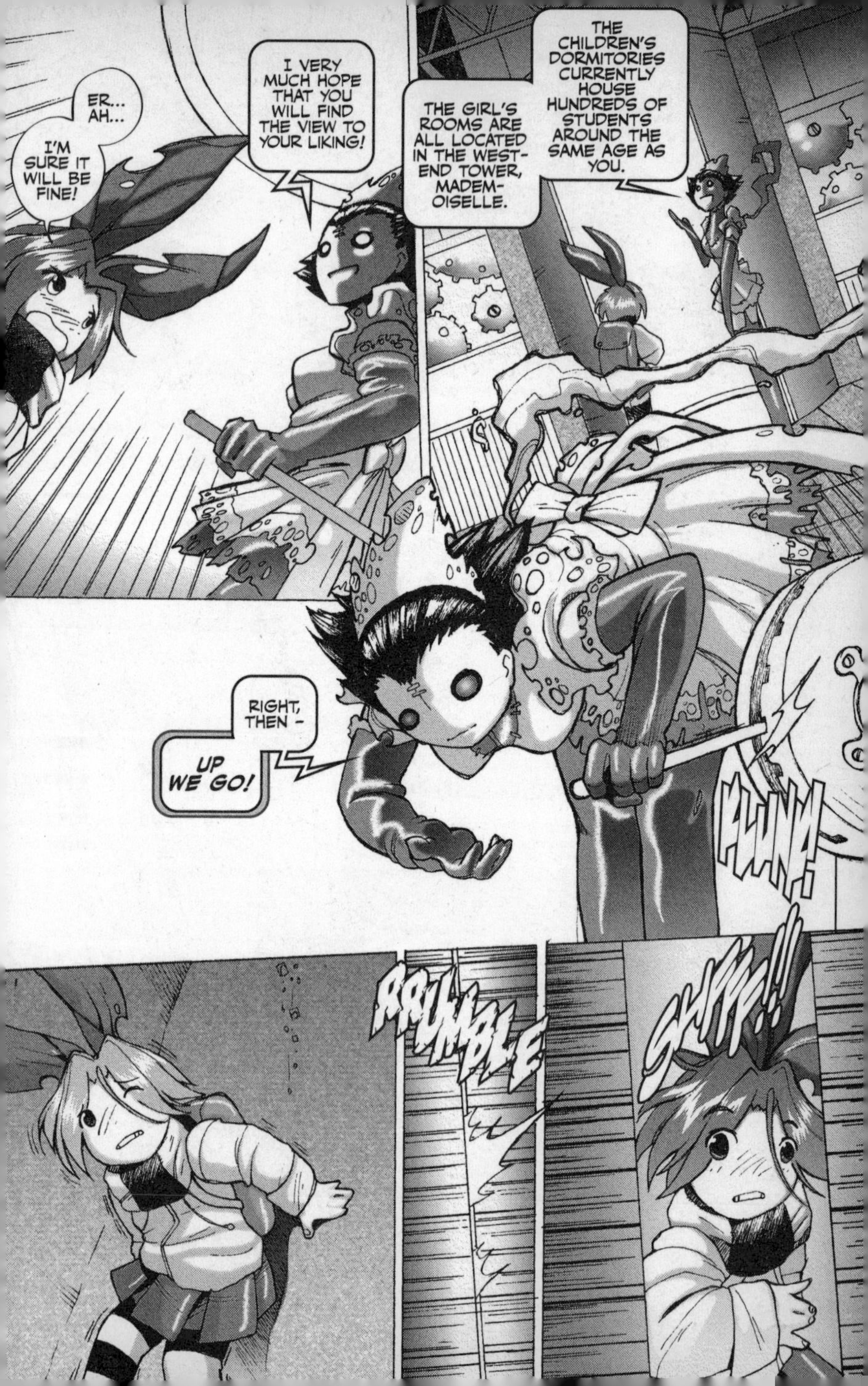
THE CHILDREN'S DORMITORIES CURRENTLY HOUSE HUNDREDS OF STUDENTS AROUND THE SAME AGE AS YOU.
THE GIRL'S ROOMS ARE ALL LOCATED IN THE WEST-END TOWER, MADEM-OISELLE.
I VERY MUCH HOPE THAT YOU WILL FIND THE VIEW TO YOUR LIKING!
ER... AH...
I'M SURE IT WILL BE FINE!
RIGHT, THEN -
UP WE GO!
KLUNK!
RRUMBLE

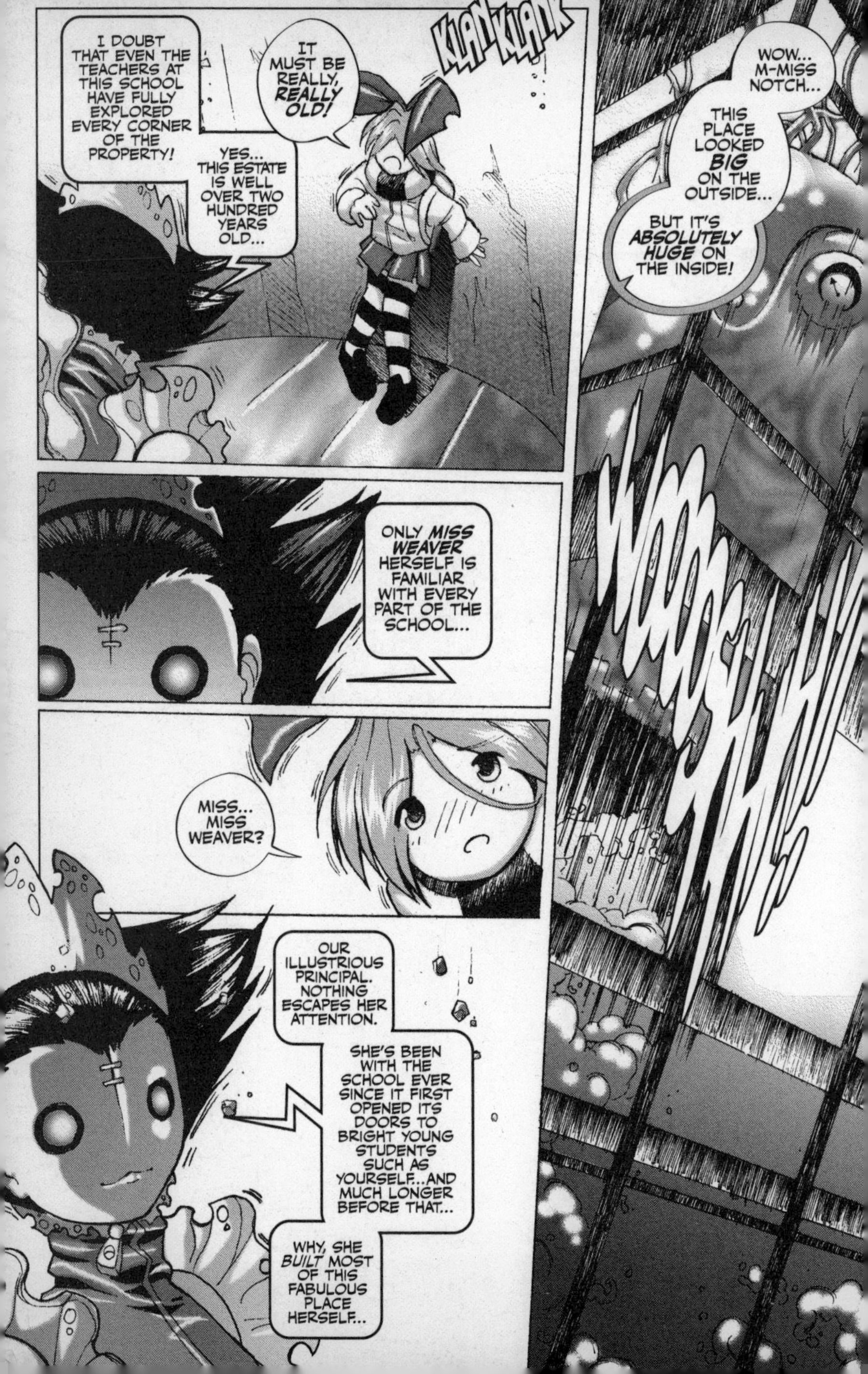
WOW... M-MISS NOTCH...
THIS PLACE LOOKED BIG ON THE OUTSIDE...
BUT IT'S ABSOLUTELY HUGE ON THE INSIDE!
KLANK KLANK
IT MUST BE REALLY, REALLY OLD!
I DOUBT THAT EVEN THE TEACHERS AT THIS SCHOOL HAVE FULLY EXPLORED EVERY CORNER OF THE PROPERTY!
YES... THIS ESTATE IS WELL OVER TWO HUNDRED YEARS OLD...
ONLY MISS WEAVER HERSELF IS FAMILIAR WITH EVERY PART OF THE SCHOOL...
MISS... MISS WEAVER?
OUR ILLUSTRIOUS PRINCIPAL. NOTHING ESCAPES HER ATTENTION.
SHE'S BEEN WITH THE SCHOOL EVER SINCE IT FIRST OPENED ITS DOORS TO BRIGHT YOUNG STUDENTS SUCH AS YOURSELF...AND MUCH LONGER BEFORE THAT...
WHY, SHE BUILT MOST OF THIS FABULOUS PLACE HERSELF...

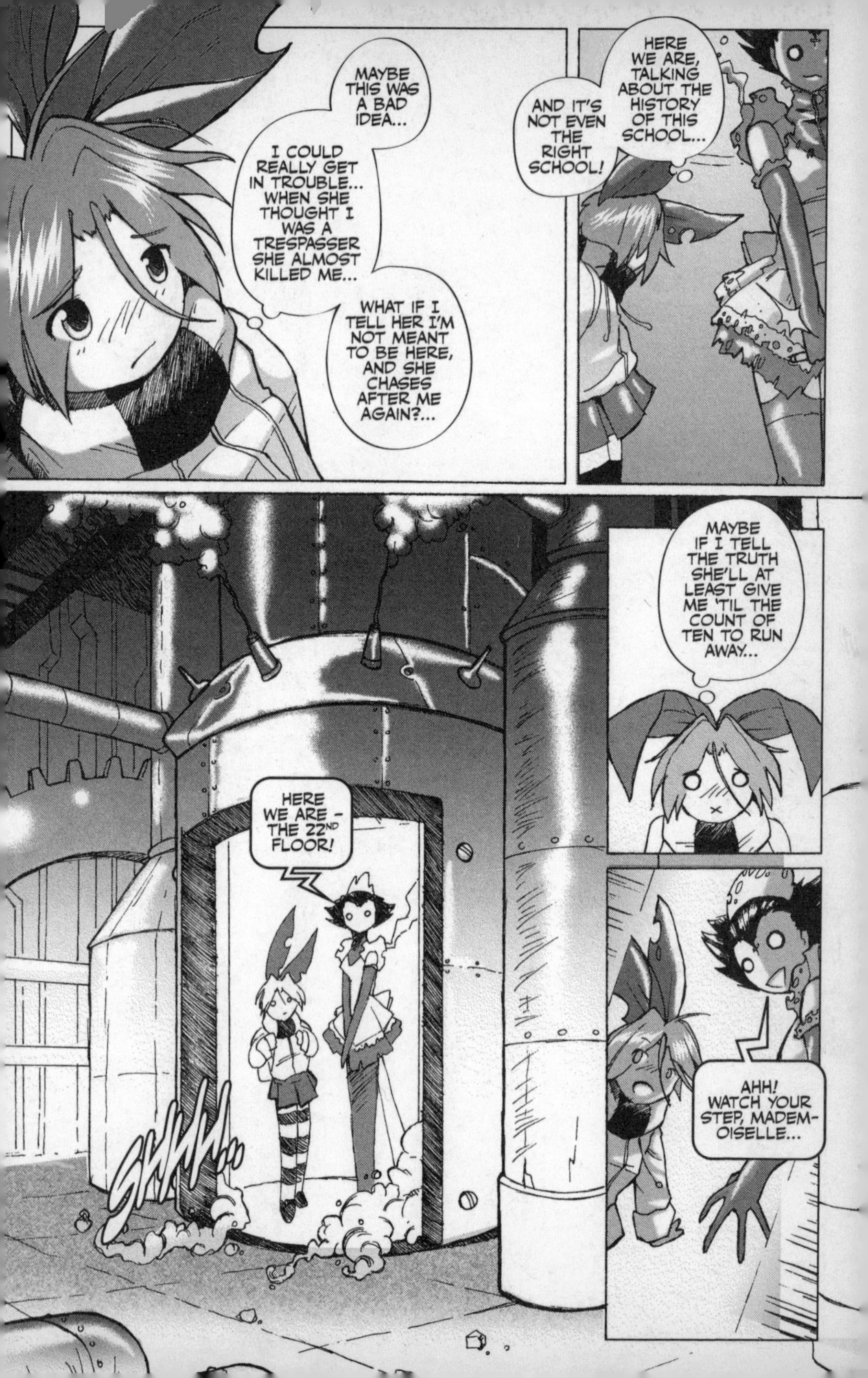
HERE WE ARE, TALKING ABOUT THE HISTORY OF THIS SCHOOL...
AND IT'S NOT EVEN THE RIGHT SCHOOL!
MAYBE THIS WAS A BAD IDEA...
I COULD REALLY GET IN TROUBLE... WHEN SHE THOUGHT I WAS A TRESPASSER SHE ALMOST KILLED ME...
WHAT IF I TELL HER I'M NOT MEANT TO BE HERE, AND SHE CHASES AFTER ME AGAIN?...
MAYBE IF I TELL THE TRUTH SHE'LL AT LEAST GIVE ME 'TIL THE COUNT OF TEN TO RUN AWAY...
AHH! WATCH YOUR STEP, MADEMOISELLE...
HERE WE ARE - THE 22ND FLOOR!
SHHH...

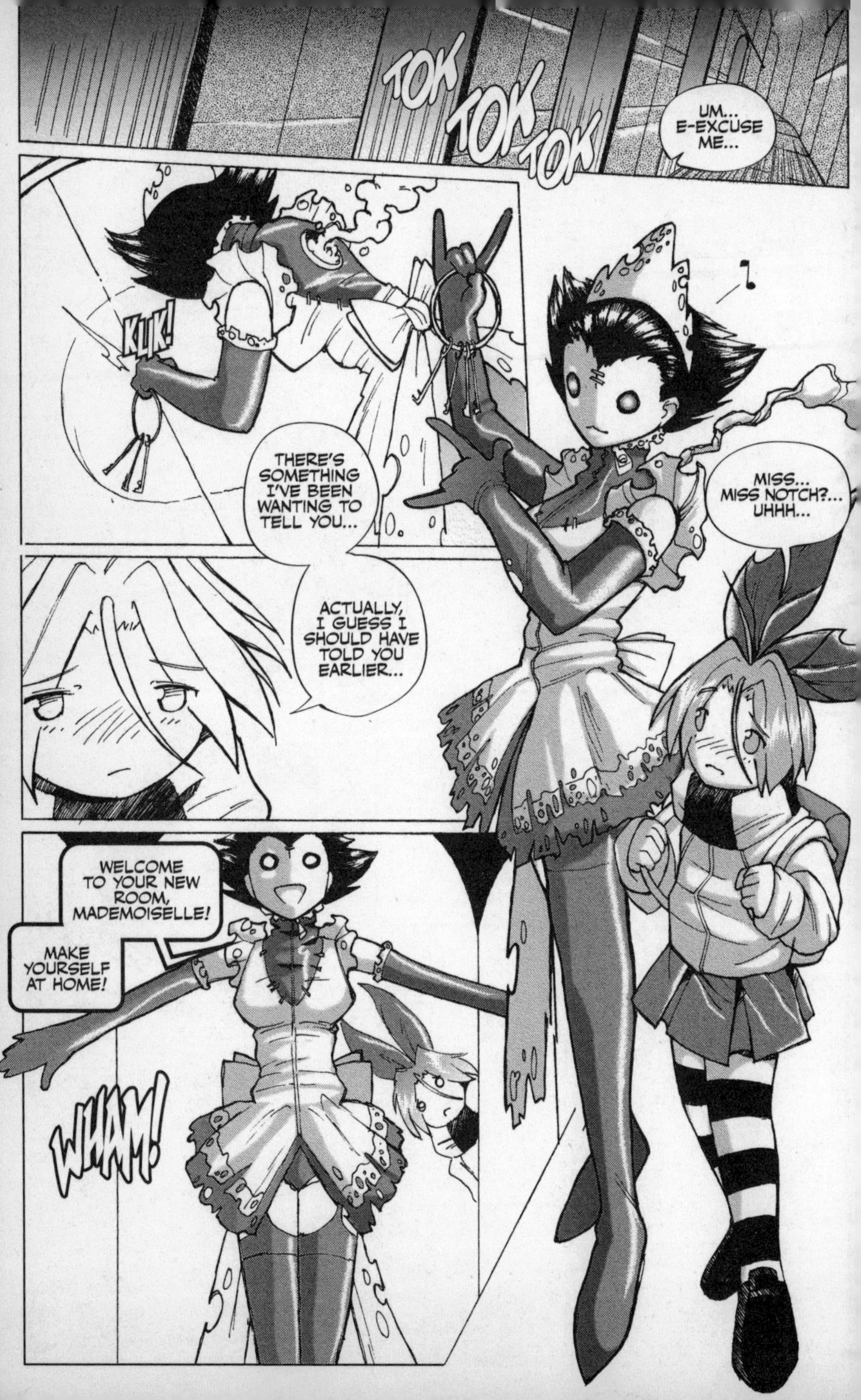
TOK TOK TOK
UM... E-EXCUSE ME...
KLIK!
THERE'S SOMETHING I'VE BEEN WANTING TO TELL YOU...
MISS... MISS NOTCH?... UHHH...
ACTUALLY, I GUESS I SHOULD HAVE TOLD YOU EARLIER...
WELCOME TO YOUR NEW ROOM, MADEMOISELLE!
MAKE YOURSELF AT HOME!
WHAM!

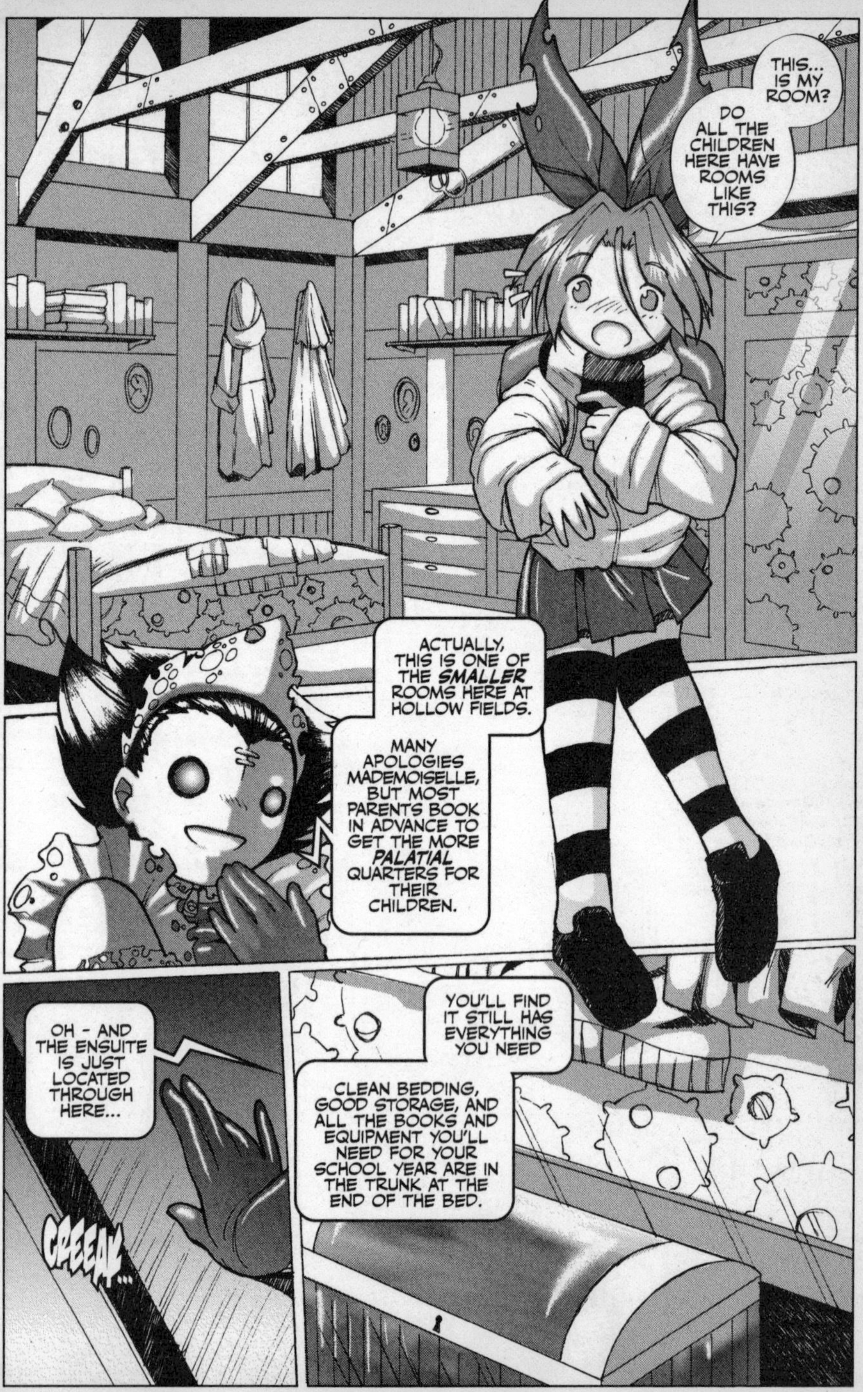
THIS... IS MY ROOM?
DO ALL THE CHILDREN HERE HAVE ROOMS LIKE THIS?
ACTUALLY, THIS IS ONE OF THE SMALLER ROOMS HERE AT HOLLOW FIELDS.
MANY APOLOGIES MADEMOISELLE, BUT MOST PARENTS BOOK IN ADVANCE TO GET THE MORE PALATIAL QUARTERS FOR THEIR CHILDREN.
YOU'LL FIND IT STILL HAS EVERYTHING YOU NEED
CLEAN BEDDING, GOOD STORAGE, AND ALL THE BOOKS AND EQUIPMENT YOU'LL NEED FOR YOUR SCHOOL YEAR ARE IN THE TRUNK AT THE END OF THE BED.
OH - AND THE ENSUITE IS JUST LOCATED THROUGH HERE...
CREEAK...

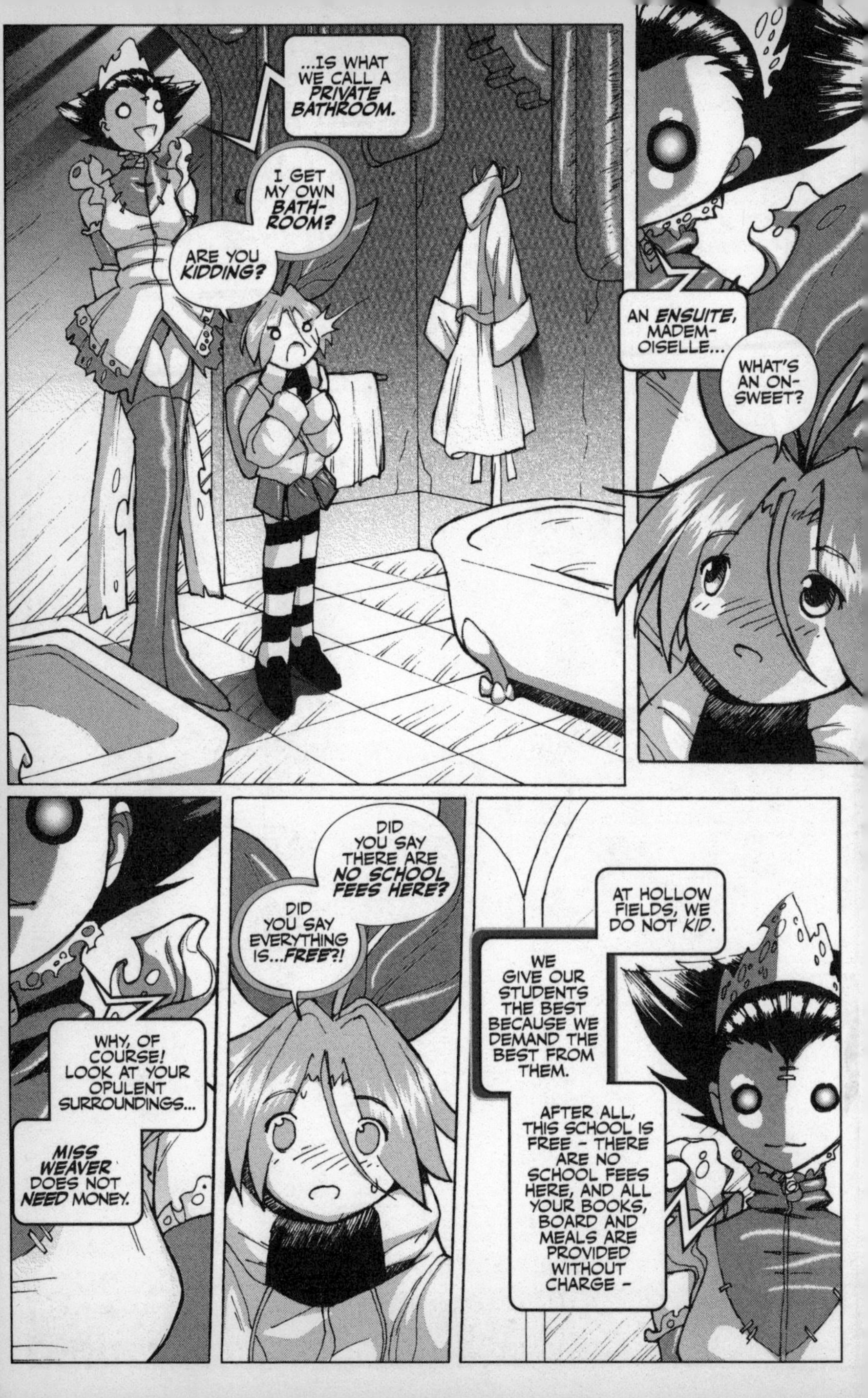
AN ENSUITE, MADEMOISELLE...
WHAT'S AN ON-SWEET?
...IS WHAT WE CALL A PRIVATE BATHROOM.
I GET MY OWN BATHROOM?
ARE YOU KIDDING?
AT HOLLOW FIELDS, WE DO NOT KID.
WE GIVE OUR STUDENTS THE BEST BECAUSE WE DEMAND THE BEST FROM THEM.
AFTER ALL, THIS SCHOOL IS FREE - THERE ARE NO SCHOOL FEES HERE, AND ALL YOUR BOOKS, BOARD AND MEALS ARE PROVIDED WITHOUT CHARGE -
DID YOU SAY THERE ARE NO SCHOOL FEES HERE?
DID YOU SAY EVERYTHING IS...FREE?!
WHY, OF COURSE! LOOK AT YOUR OPULENT SURROUNDINGS...
MISS WEAVER DOES NOT NEED MONEY.

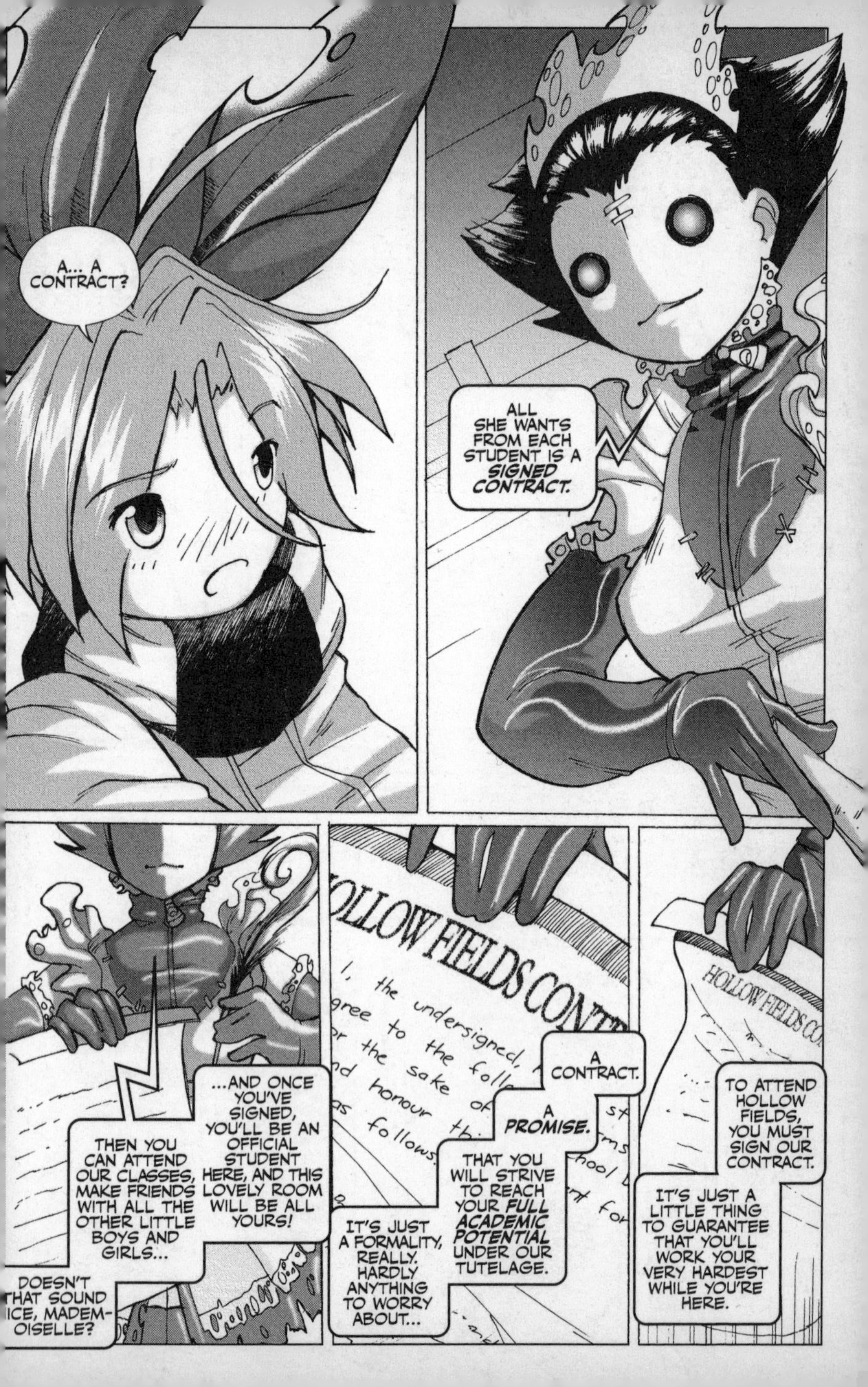
ALL SHE WANTS FROM EACH STUDENT IS A *SIGNED CONTRACT.*
A... A CONTRACT?
TO ATTEND HOLLOW FIELDS, YOU MUST SIGN OUR CONTRACT.
IT'S JUST A LITTLE THING TO GUARANTEE THAT YOU'LL WORK YOUR VERY HARDEST WHILE YOU'RE HERE.
A CONTRACT.
A *PROMISE.*
THAT YOU WILL STRIVE TO REACH YOUR *FULL ACADEMIC POTENTIAL* UNDER OUR TUTELAGE.
IT'S JUST A FORMALITY, REALLY. HARDLY ANYTHING TO WORRY ABOUT...
...AND ONCE YOU'VE SIGNED, YOU'LL BE AN OFFICIAL STUDENT HERE, AND THIS LOVELY ROOM WILL BE ALL YOURS!
THEN YOU CAN ATTEND OUR CLASSES, MAKE FRIENDS WITH ALL THE OTHER LITTLE BOYS AND GIRLS...
DOESN'T THAT SOUND ICE, MADEM-OISELLE?

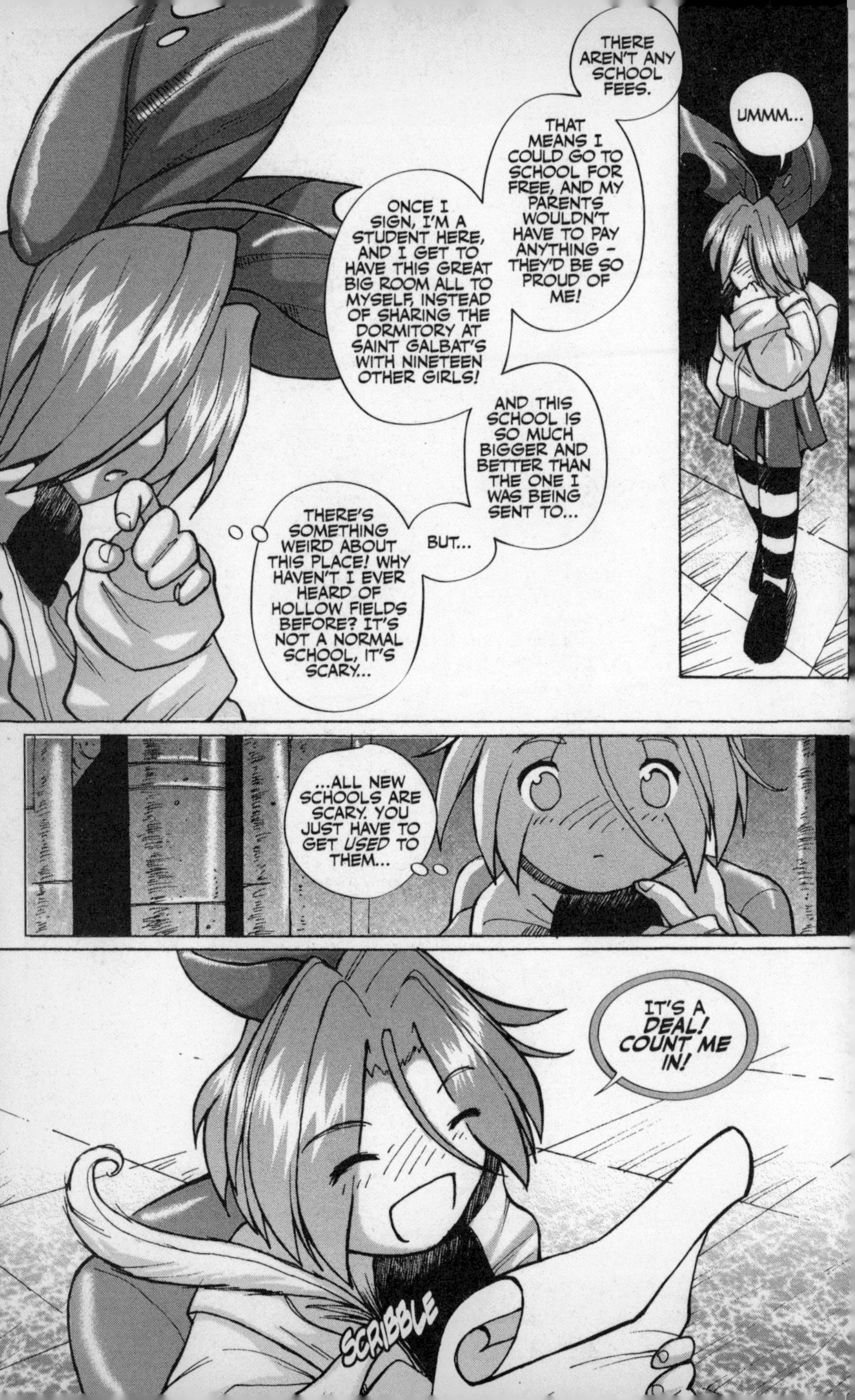
UMMM...
THERE AREN'T ANY SCHOOL FEES.
THAT MEANS I COULD GO TO SCHOOL FOR FREE, AND MY PARENTS WOULDN'T HAVE TO PAY ANYTHING - THEY'D BE SO PROUD OF ME!
ONCE I SIGN, I'M A STUDENT HERE, AND I GET TO HAVE THIS GREAT BIG ROOM ALL TO MYSELF, INSTEAD OF SHARING THE DORMITORY AT SAINT GALBAT'S WITH NINETEEN OTHER GIRLS!
AND THIS SCHOOL IS SO MUCH BIGGER AND BETTER THAN THE ONE I WAS BEING SENT TO...
BUT...
THERE'S SOMETHING WEIRD ABOUT THIS PLACE! WHY HAVEN'T I EVER HEARD OF HOLLOW FIELDS BEFORE? IT'S NOT A NORMAL SCHOOL, IT'S SCARY...
...ALL NEW SCHOOLS ARE SCARY. YOU JUST HAVE TO GET *USED* TO THEM...
IT'S A *DEAL!* COUNT ME IN!
SCRIBBLE

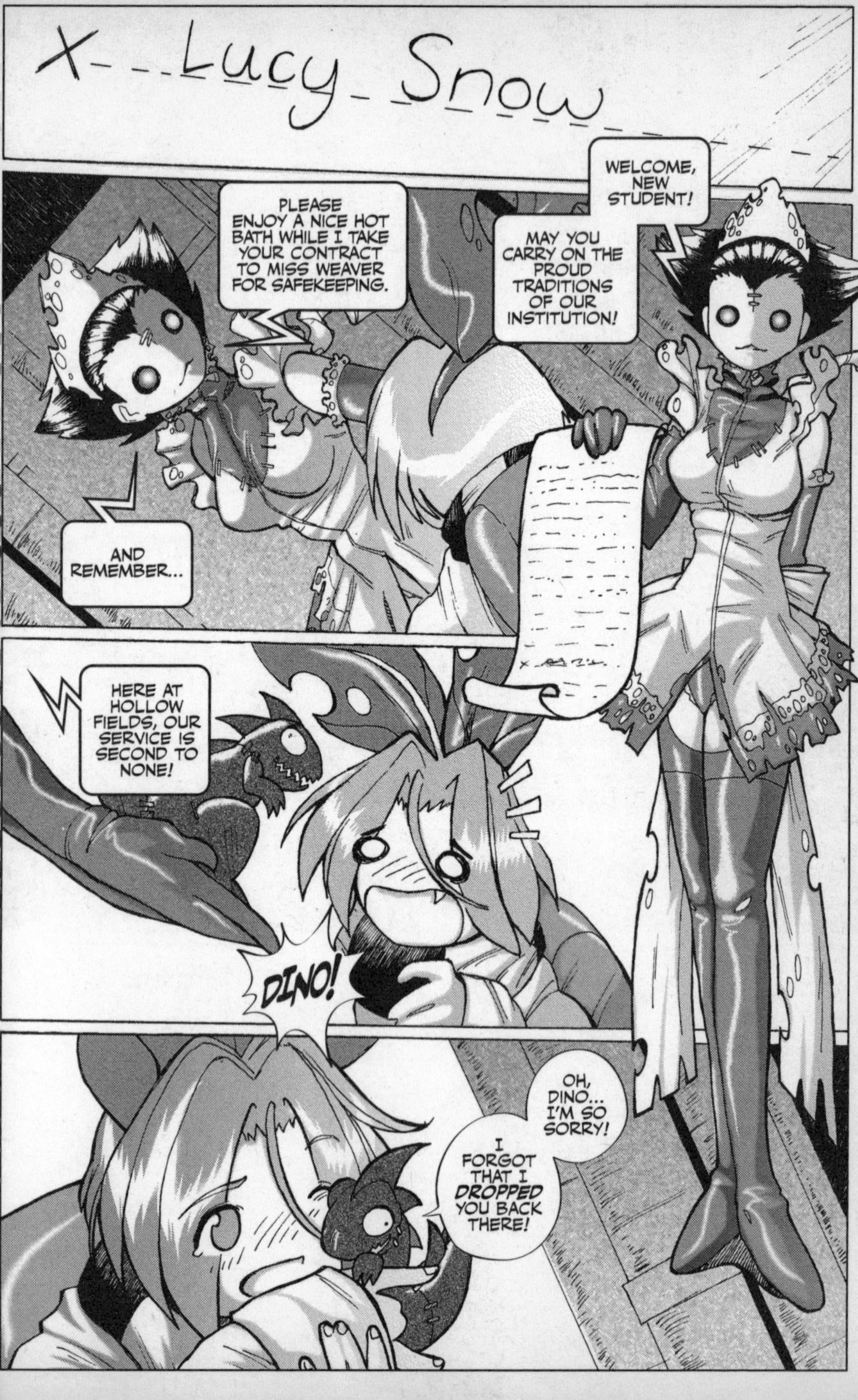
X Lucy Snow
WELCOME, NEW STUDENT!
MAY YOU CARRY ON THE PROUD TRADITIONS OF OUR INSTITUTION!
PLEASE ENJOY A NICE HOT BATH WHILE I TAKE YOUR CONTRACT TO MISS WEAVER FOR SAFEKEEPING.
AND REMEMBER...
HERE AT HOLLOW FIELDS, OUR SERVICE IS SECOND TO NONE!
DINO!
OH, DINO... I'M SO SORRY!
I FORGOT THAT I *DROPPED* YOU BACK THERE!

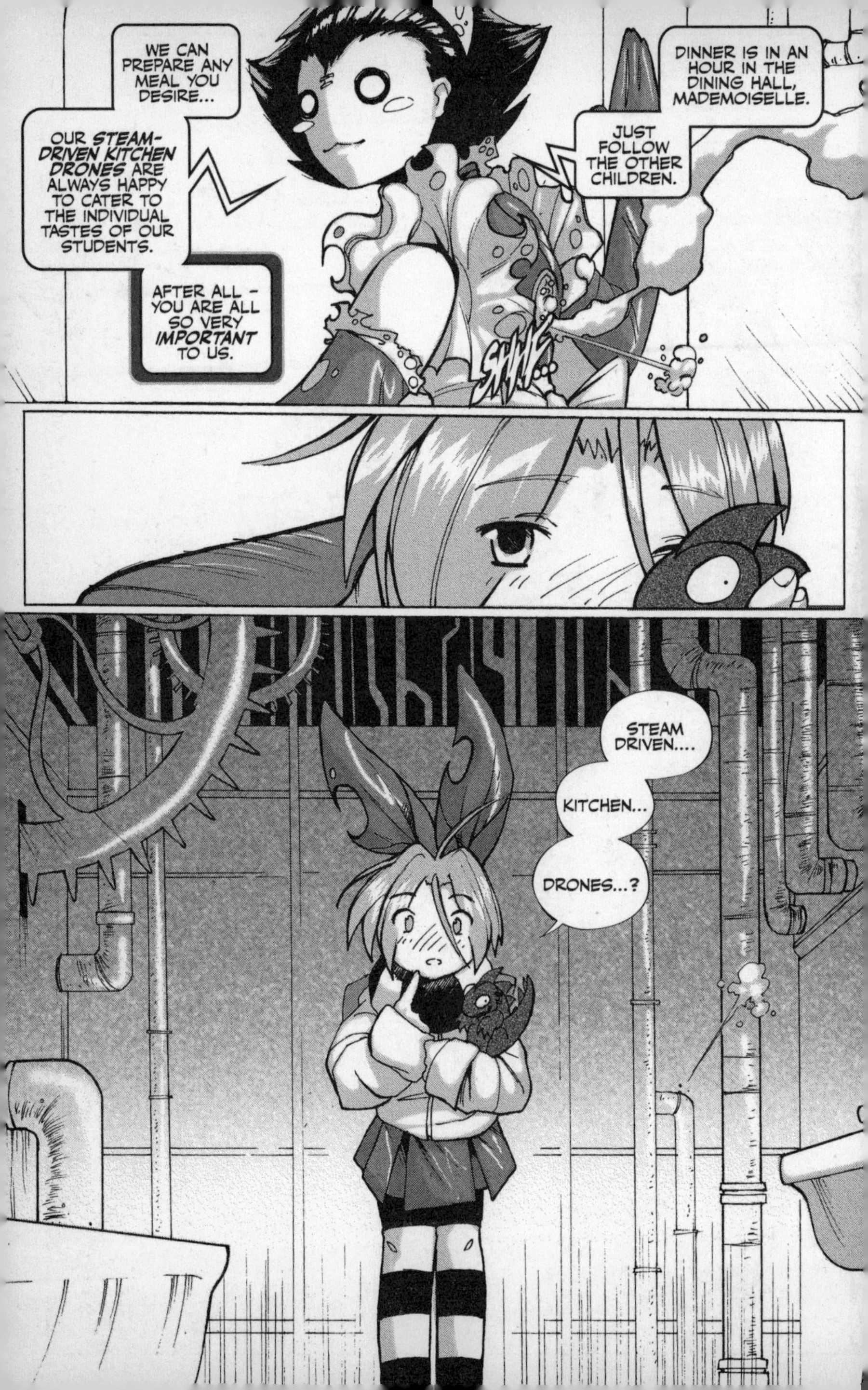
DINNER IS IN AN HOUR IN THE DINING HALL, MADEMOISELLE.
JUST FOLLOW THE OTHER CHILDREN.
WE CAN PREPARE ANY MEAL YOU DESIRE...
OUR *STEAM-DRIVEN KITCHEN DRONES* ARE ALWAYS HAPPY TO CATER TO THE INDIVIDUAL TASTES OF OUR STUDENTS.
AFTER ALL - YOU ARE ALL SO VERY *IMPORTANT* TO US.
STEAM DRIVEN....
KITCHEN...
DRONES...?

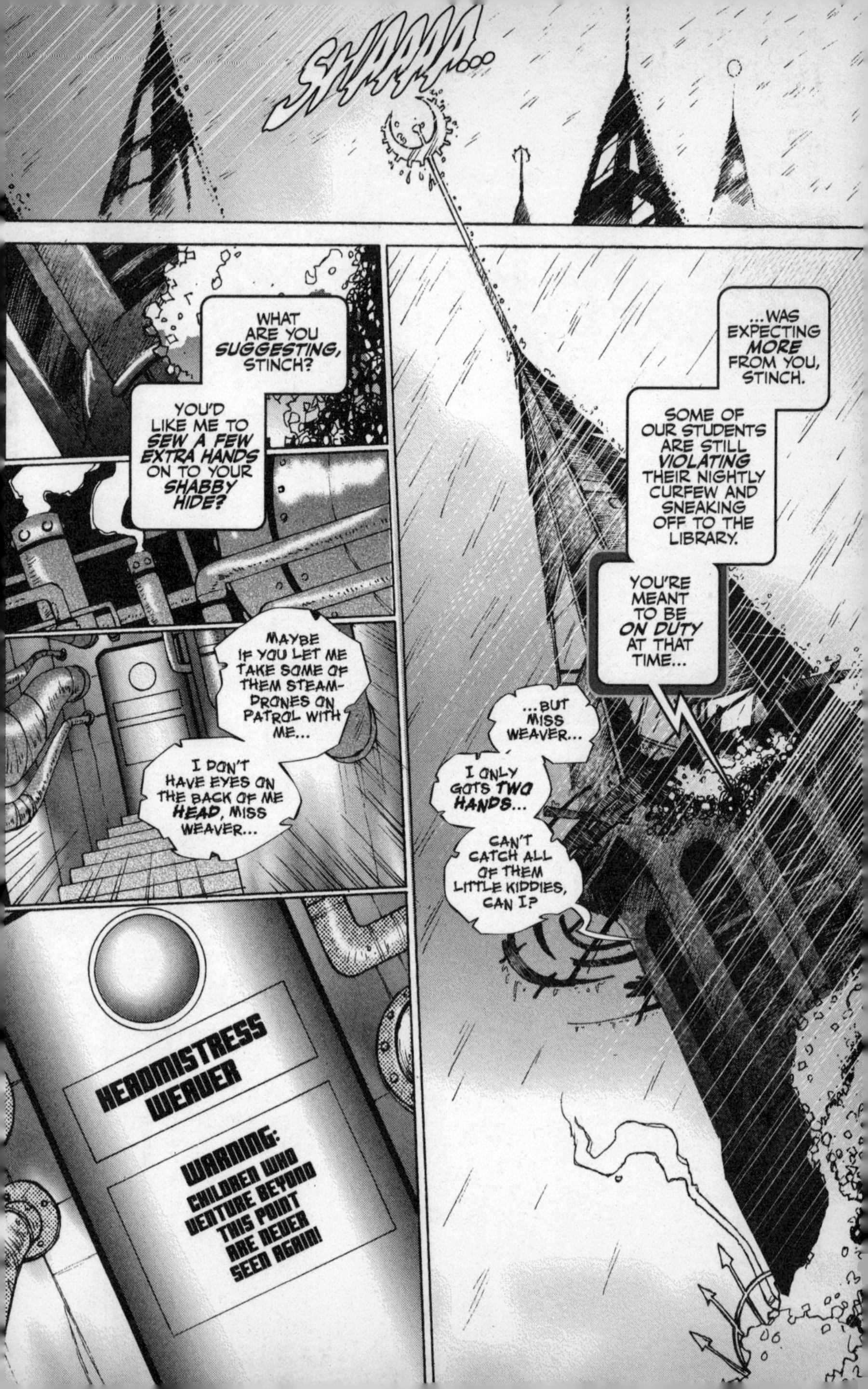
SHAAAA...
...WAS EXPECTING MORE FROM YOU, STINCH.
SOME OF OUR STUDENTS ARE STILL VIOLATING THEIR NIGHTLY CURFEW AND SNEAKING OFF TO THE LIBRARY.
YOU'RE MEANT TO BE ON DUTY AT THAT TIME...
...BUT MISS WEAVER...
I ONLY GOTS TWO HANDS...
CAN'T CATCH ALL OF THEM LITTLE KIDDIES, CAN I?
WHAT ARE YOU SUGGESTING, STINCH?
YOU'D LIKE ME TO SEW A FEW EXTRA HANDS ON TO YOUR SHABBY HIDE?
MAYBE IF YOU LET ME TAKE SOME OF THEM STEAM-DRONES ON PATROL WITH ME...
I DON'T HAVE EYES ON THE BACK OF ME HEAD, MISS WEAVER...
HEADMISTRESS WEAVER
WARNING: CHILDREN WHO VENTURE BEYOND THIS POINT ARE NEVER SEEN AGAIN!

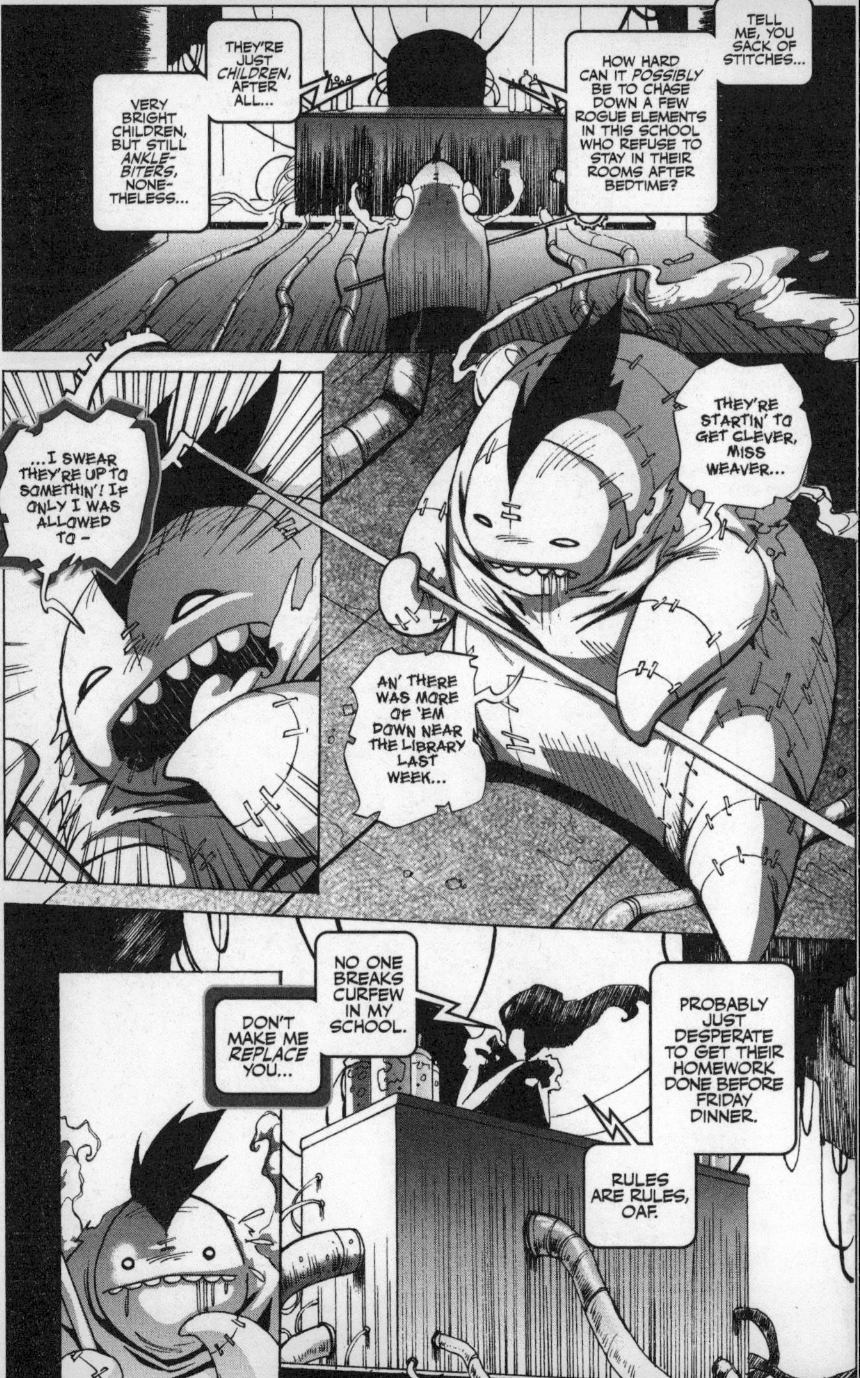
TELL ME, YOU SACK OF STITCHES...
HOW HARD CAN IT *POSSIBLY* BE TO CHASE DOWN A FEW ROGUE ELEMENTS IN THIS SCHOOL WHO REFUSE TO STAY IN THEIR ROOMS AFTER BEDTIME?
THEY'RE JUST *CHILDREN,* AFTER ALL...
VERY BRIGHT CHILDREN, BUT STILL *ANKLE-BITERS,* NONE-THELESS...
THEY'RE STARTIN' TO GET CLEVER, MISS WEAVER...
AN' THERE WAS MORE OF 'EM DOWN NEAR THE LIBRARY LAST WEEK...
...I SWEAR THEY'RE UP TO SOMETHIN'! IF ONLY I WAS ALLOWED TO -
PROBABLY JUST DESPERATE TO GET THEIR HOMEWORK DONE BEFORE FRIDAY DINNER.
RULES ARE RULES, OAF.
NO ONE BREAKS CURFEW IN MY SCHOOL.
DON'T MAKE ME *REPLACE* YOU...

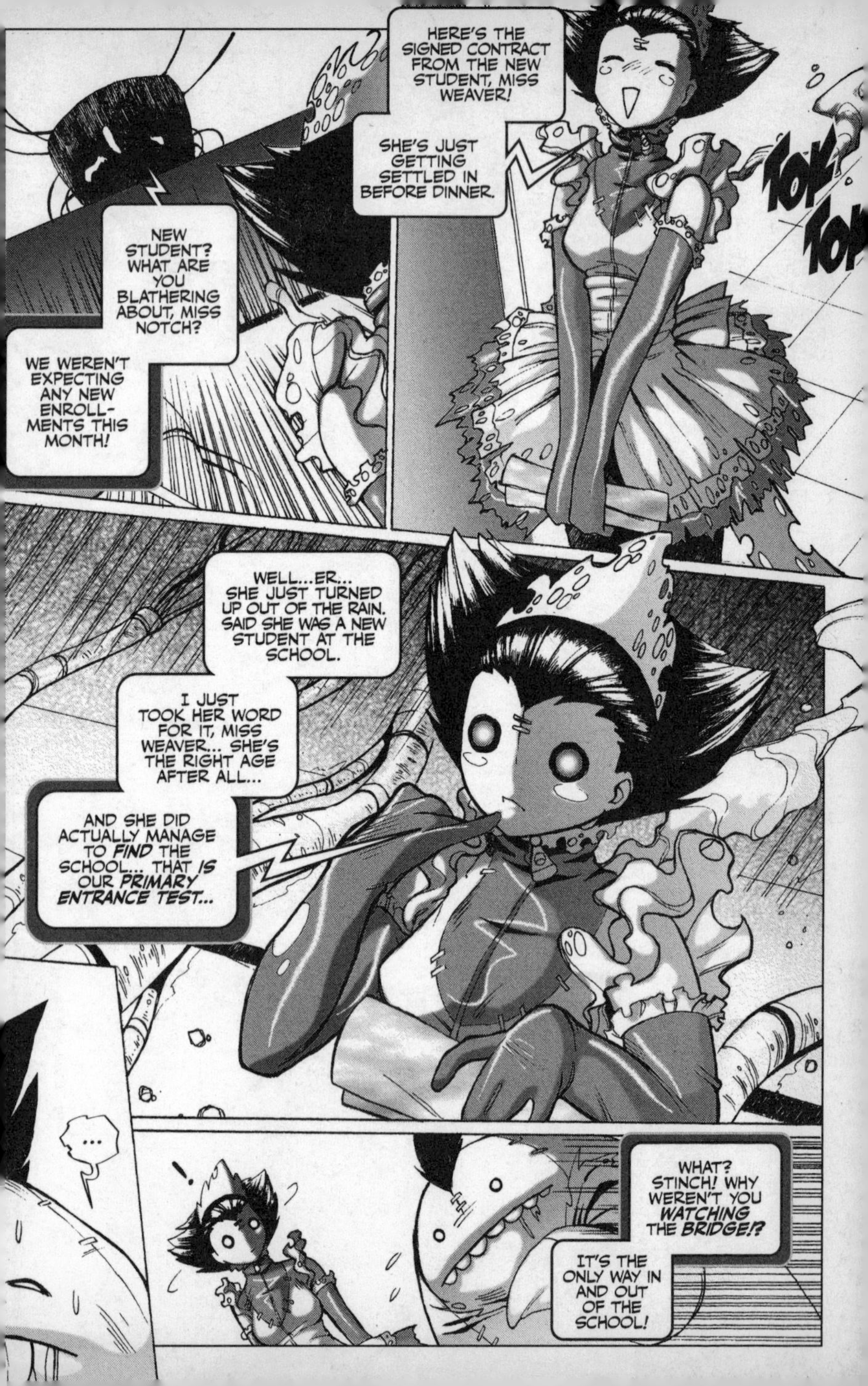
TOK TOK
HERE'S THE SIGNED CONTRACT FROM THE NEW STUDENT, MISS WEAVER!
SHE'S JUST GETTING SETTLED IN BEFORE DINNER.
NEW STUDENT? WHAT ARE YOU BLATHERING ABOUT, MISS NOTCH?
WE WEREN'T EXPECTING ANY NEW ENROLL-MENTS THIS MONTH!
WELL...ER... SHE JUST TURNED UP OUT OF THE RAIN. SAID SHE WAS A NEW STUDENT AT THE SCHOOL.
I JUST TOOK HER WORD FOR IT, MISS WEAVER... SHE'S THE RIGHT AGE AFTER ALL...
AND SHE DID ACTUALLY MANAGE TO *FIND* THE SCHOOL... THAT *IS* OUR *PRIMARY ENTRANCE TEST*...
WHAT? STINCH! WHY WEREN'T YOU *WATCHING* THE *BRIDGE!?*
IT'S THE ONLY WAY IN AND OUT OF THE SCHOOL!
!
...

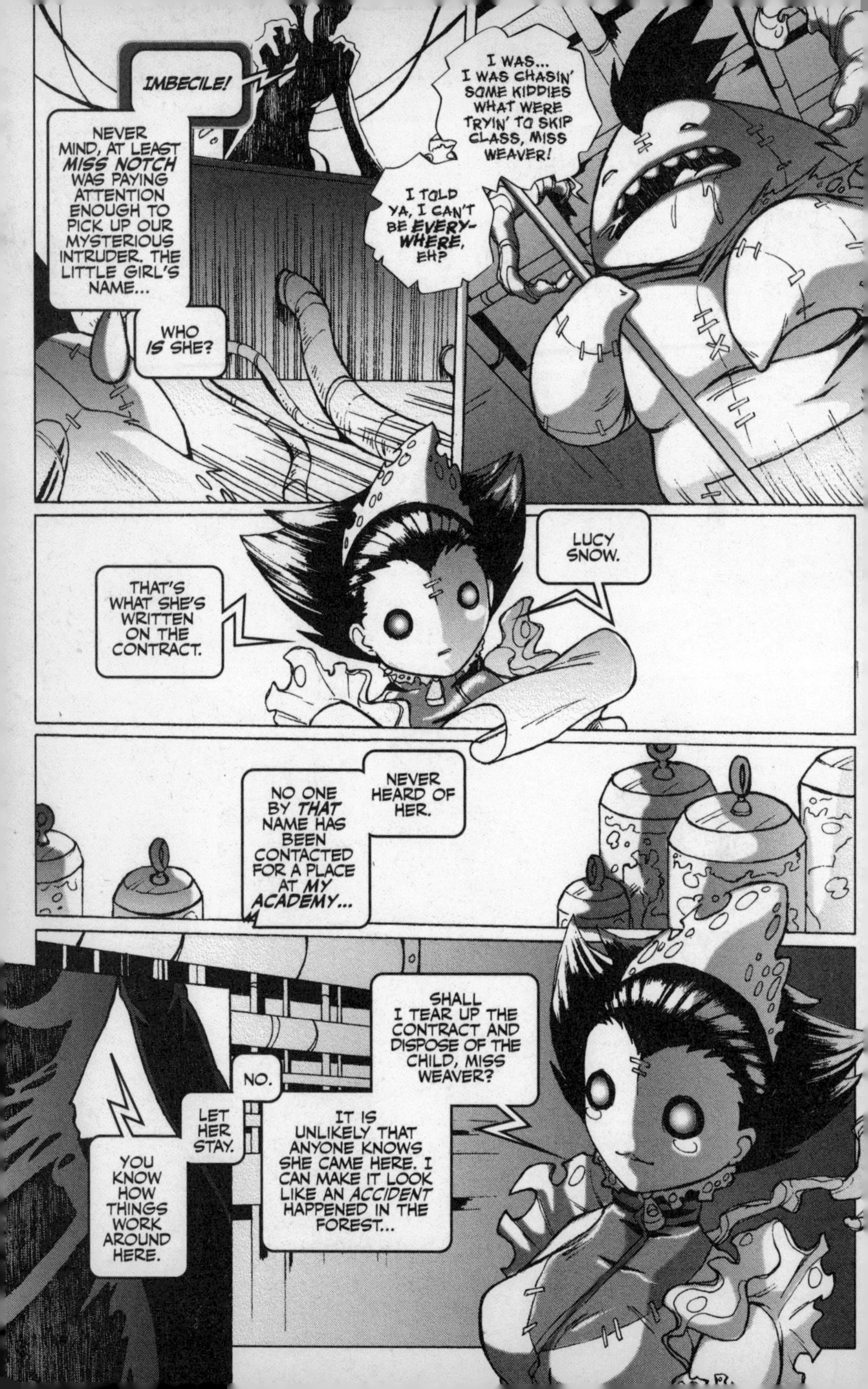
IMBECILE!
I WAS... I WAS CHASIN' SOME KIDDIES WHAT WERE TRYIN' TO SKIP CLASS, MISS WEAVER!
I TOLD YA, I CAN'T BE EVERYWHERE, EH?
NEVER MIND, AT LEAST MISS NOTCH WAS PAYING ATTENTION ENOUGH TO PICK UP OUR MYSTERIOUS INTRUDER. THE LITTLE GIRL'S NAME...
WHO IS SHE?
LUCY SNOW.
THAT'S WHAT SHE'S WRITTEN ON THE CONTRACT.
NEVER HEARD OF HER.
NO ONE BY THAT NAME HAS BEEN CONTACTED FOR A PLACE AT MY ACADEMY...
SHALL I TEAR UP THE CONTRACT AND DISPOSE OF THE CHILD, MISS WEAVER?
IT IS UNLIKELY THAT ANYONE KNOWS SHE CAME HERE. I CAN MAKE IT LOOK LIKE AN ACCIDENT HAPPENED IN THE FOREST...
NO.
LET HER STAY.
YOU KNOW HOW THINGS WORK AROUND HERE.

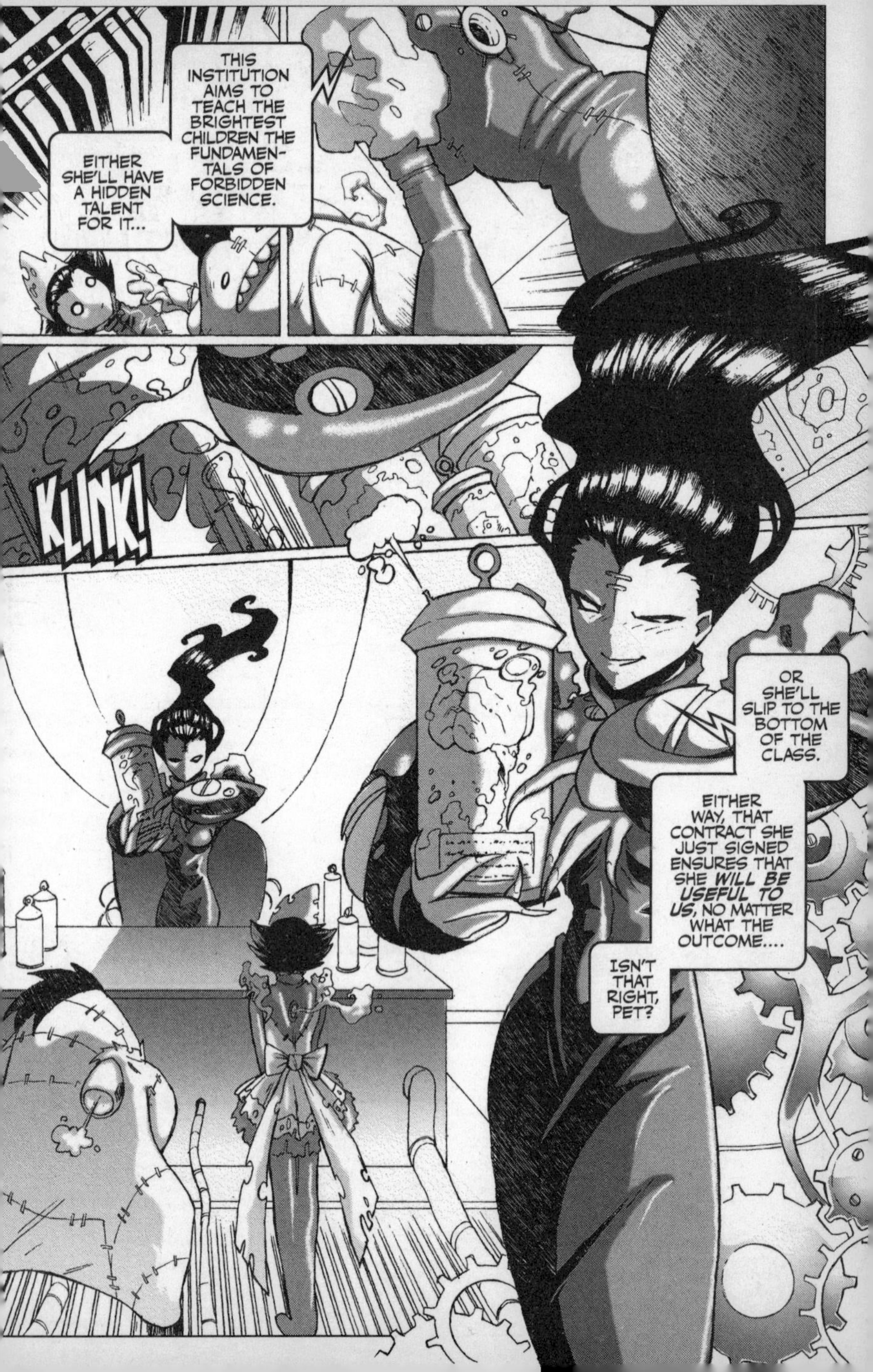
THIS INSTITUTION AIMS TO TEACH THE BRIGHTEST CHILDREN THE FUNDAMEN-TALS OF FORBIDDEN SCIENCE.
EITHER SHE'LL HAVE A HIDDEN TALENT FOR IT...
KLINK!
OR SHE'LL SLIP TO THE BOTTOM OF THE CLASS.
EITHER WAY, THAT CONTRACT SHE JUST SIGNED ENSURES THAT SHE *WILL BE USEFUL TO US,* NO MATTER WHAT THE OUTCOME....
ISN'T THAT RIGHT, PET?

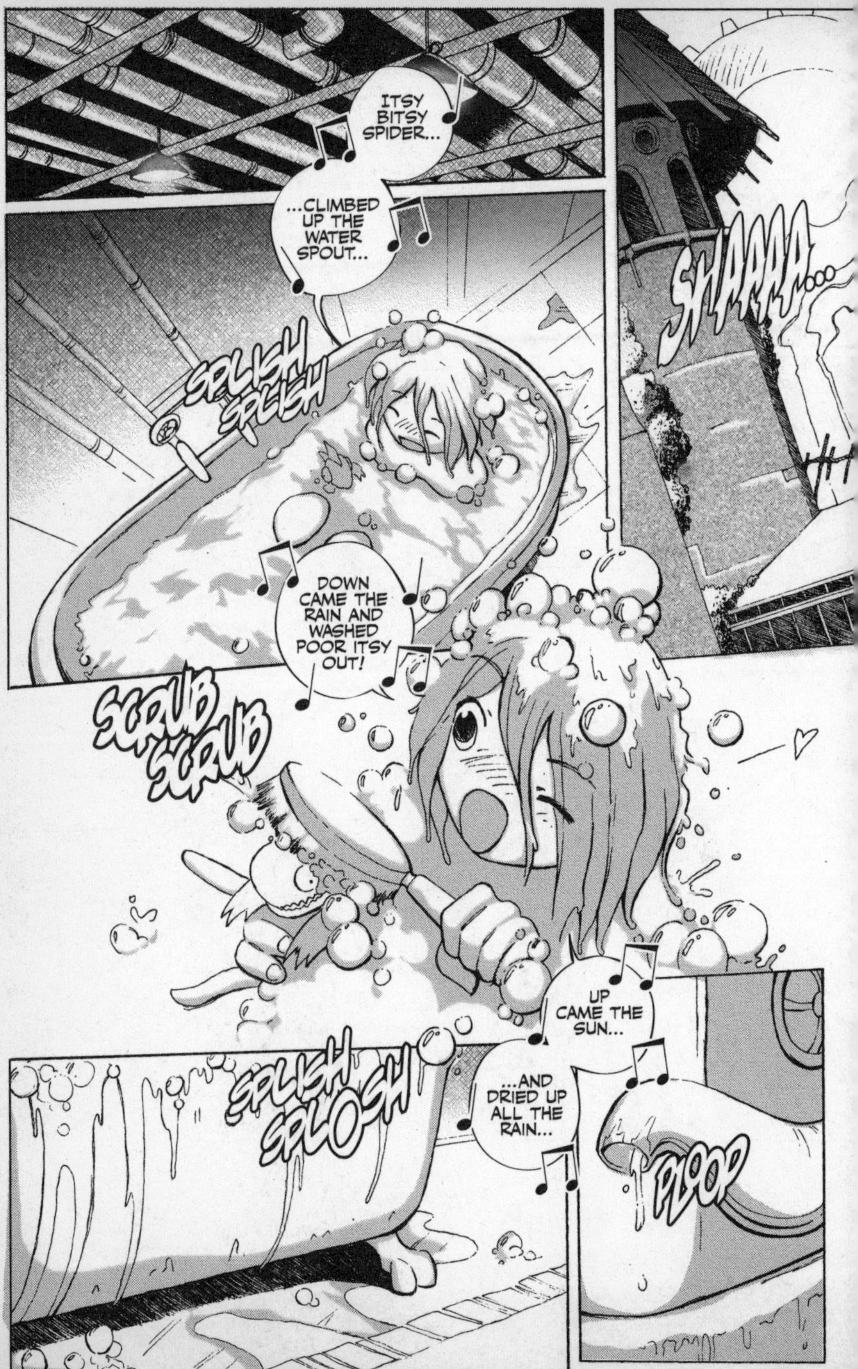
SHAAAA...
ITSY BITSY SPIDER...
...CLIMBED UP THE WATER SPOUT...
SPLISH SPLISH
DOWN CAME THE RAIN AND WASHED POOR ITSY OUT!
SCRUB SCRUB
UP CAME THE SUN...
...AND DRIED UP ALL THE RAIN...
PLOOP
SPLISH SPLOSH

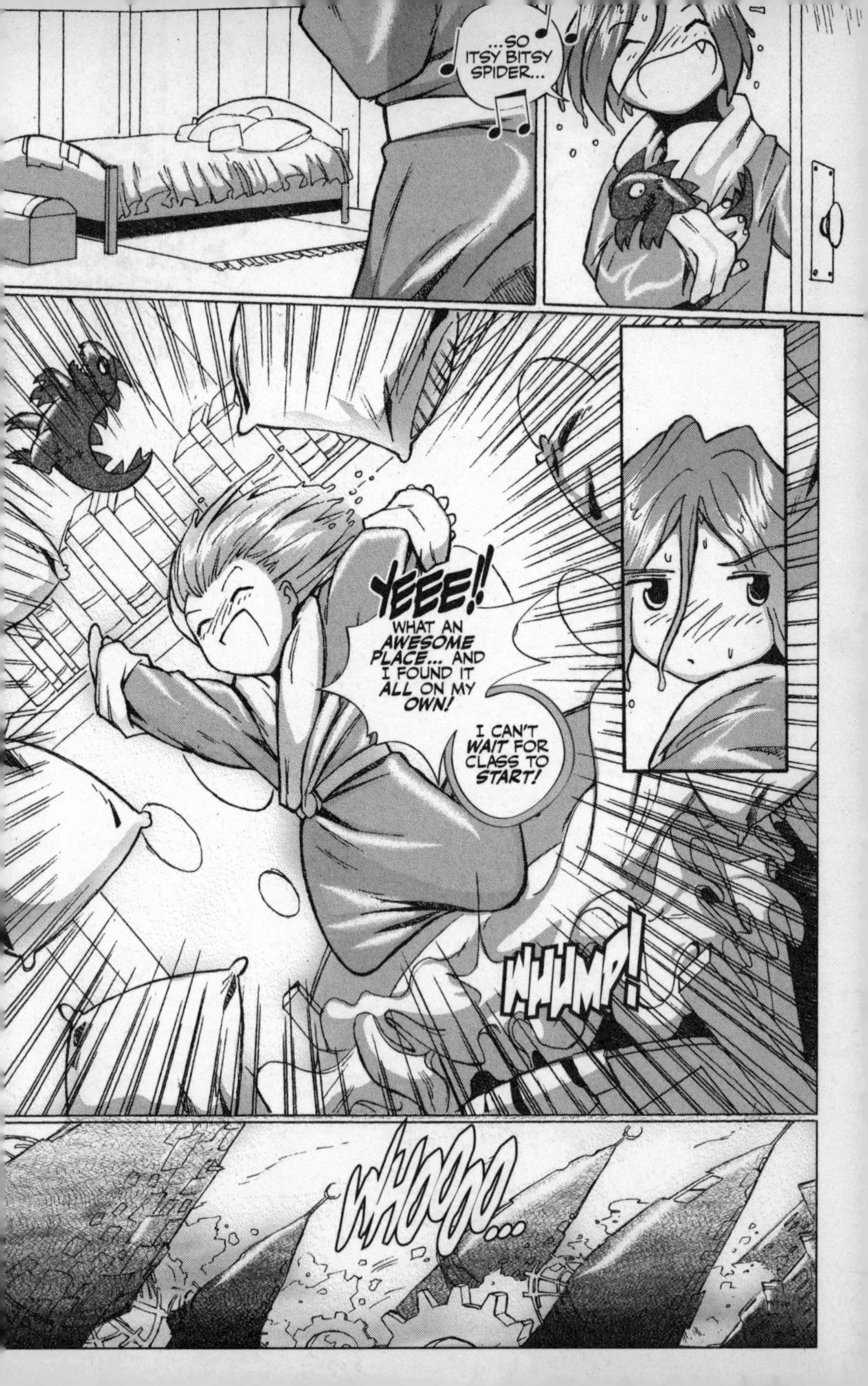
...SO ITSY BITSY SPIDER...
YEEE!! WHAT AN AWESOME PLACE... AND I FOUND IT ALL ON MY OWN!
I CAN'T WAIT FOR CLASS TO START!
WHUMP!
WHOOOO...

CHAPTER TWO
DINNER AND A SHOW

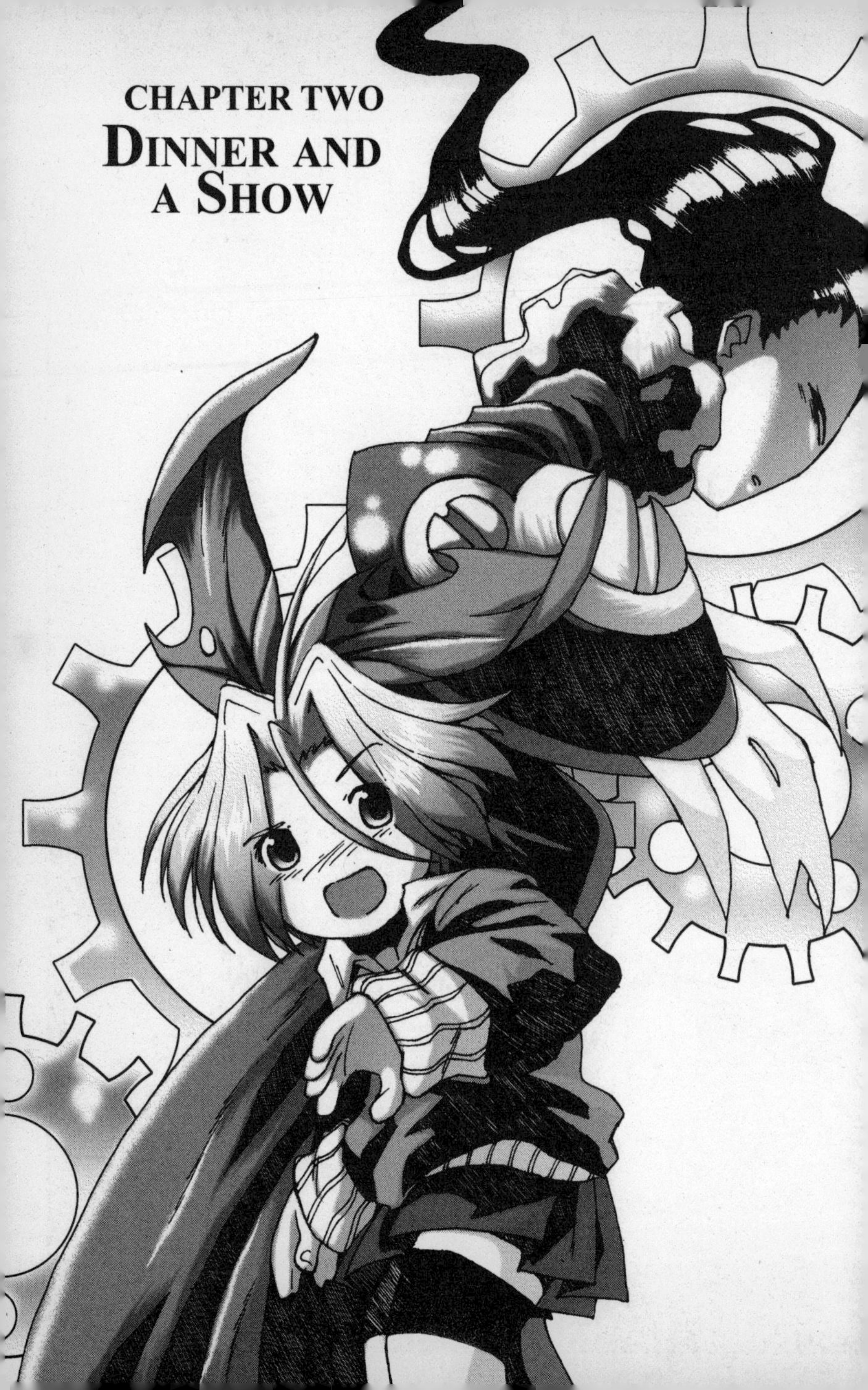

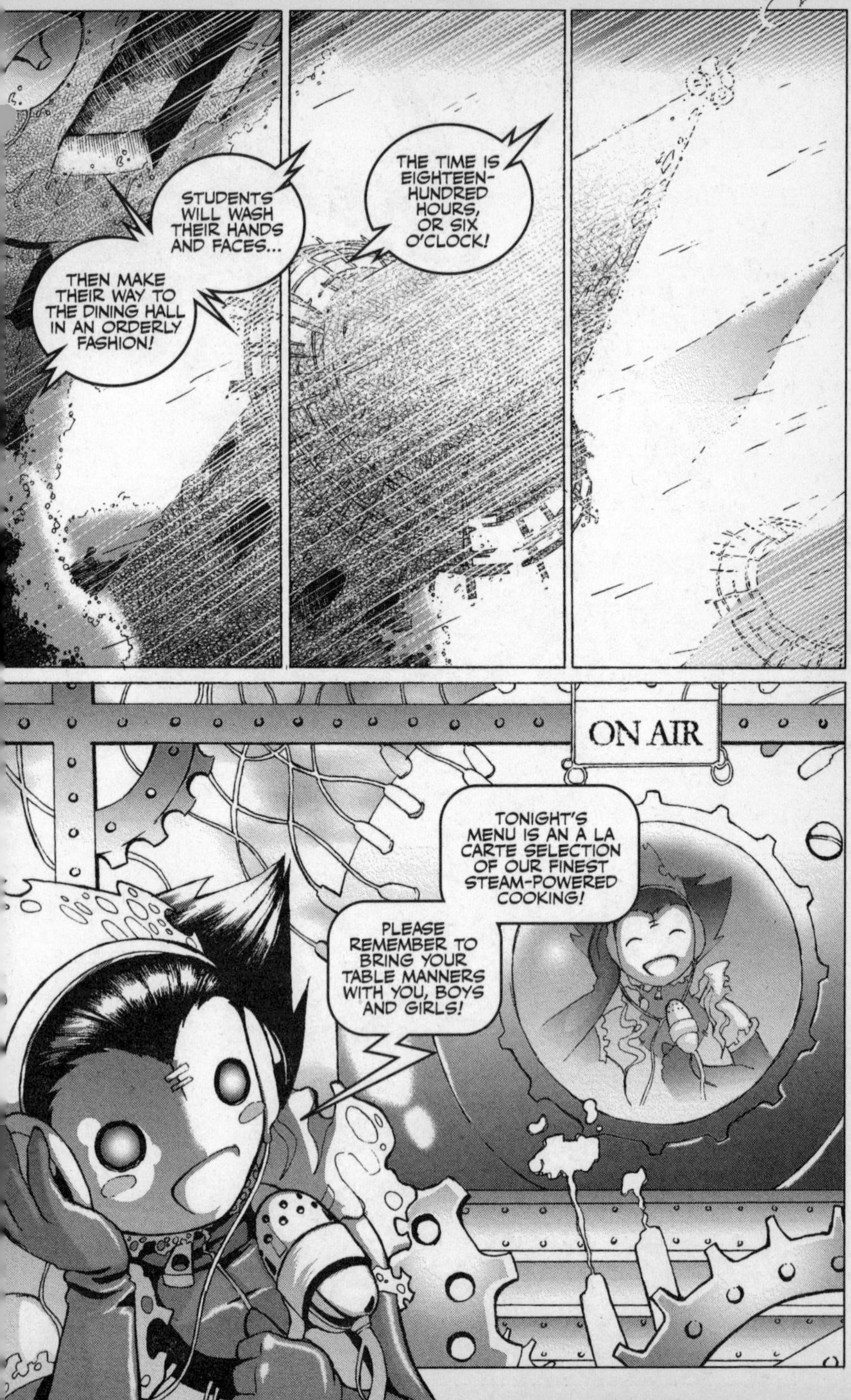
THE TIME IS EIGHTEEN-HUNDRED HOURS, OR SIX O'CLOCK!
STUDENTS WILL WASH THEIR HANDS AND FACES...
THEN MAKE THEIR WAY TO THE DINING HALL IN AN ORDERLY FASHION!
ON AIR
TONIGHT'S MENU IS AN A LA CARTE SELECTION OF OUR FINEST STEAM-POWERED COOKING!
PLEASE REMEMBER TO BRING YOUR TABLE MANNERS WITH YOU, BOYS AND GIRLS!

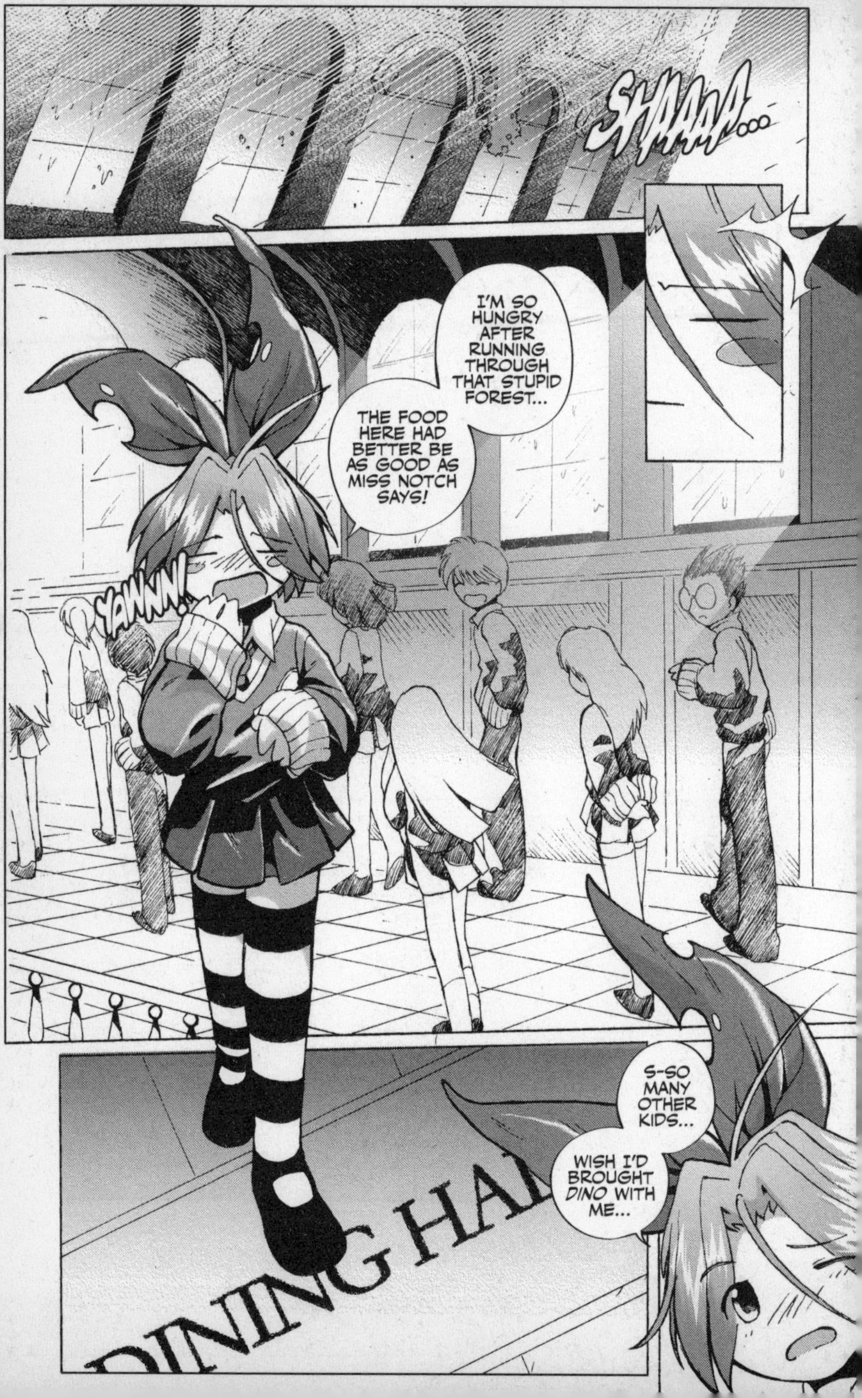
SHAAAA...
I'M SO HUNGRY AFTER RUNNING THROUGH THAT STUPID FOREST...
THE FOOD HERE HAD BETTER BE AS GOOD AS MISS NOTCH SAYS!
YAWNN!
S-SO MANY OTHER KIDS...
WISH I'D BROUGHT *DINO* WITH ME...
DINING HAL

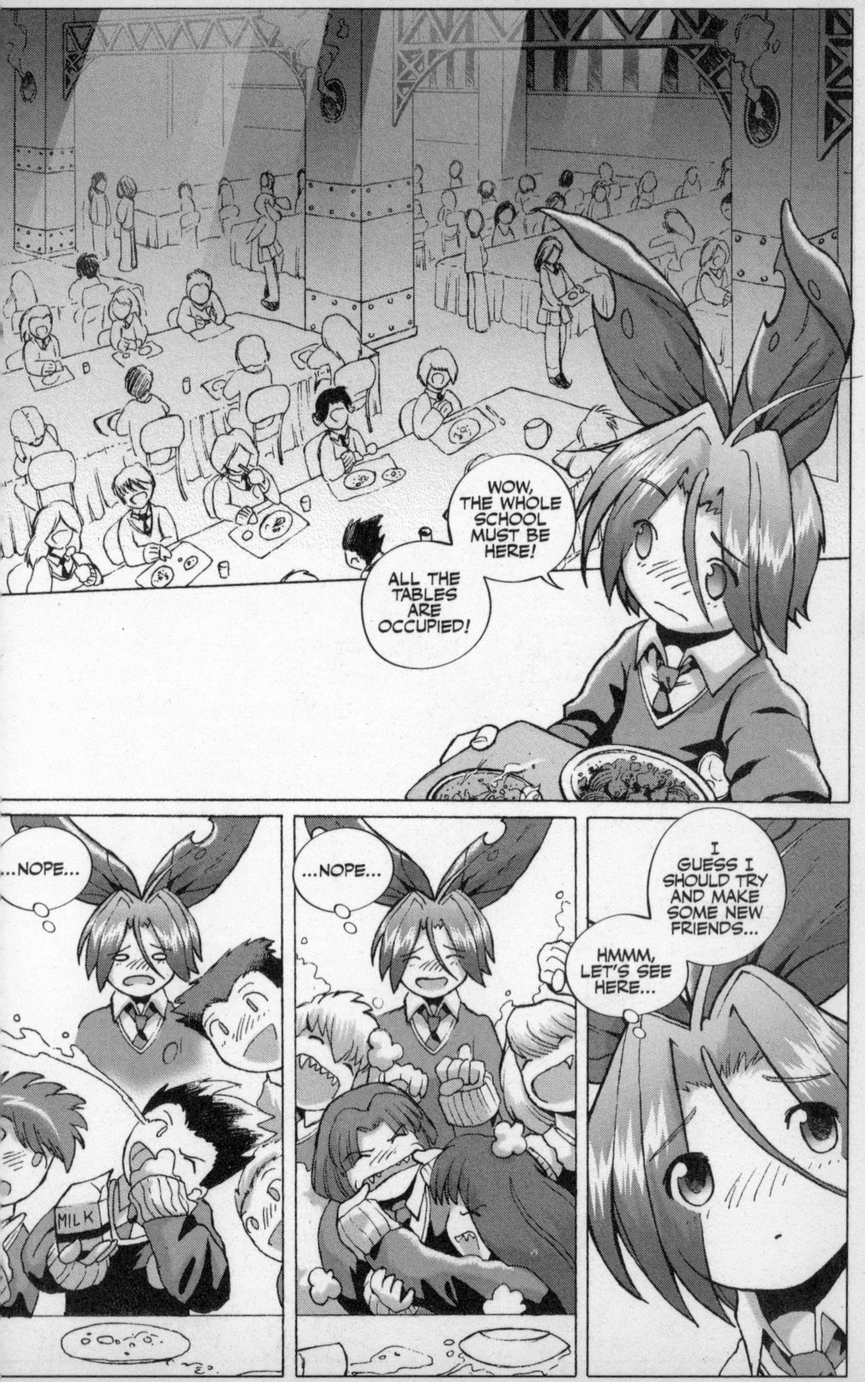
WOW, THE WHOLE SCHOOL MUST BE HERE!
ALL THE TABLES ARE OCCUPIED!
I GUESS I SHOULD TRY AND MAKE SOME NEW FRIENDS...
HMMM, LET'S SEE HERE...
...NOPE...
...NOPE...
MILK

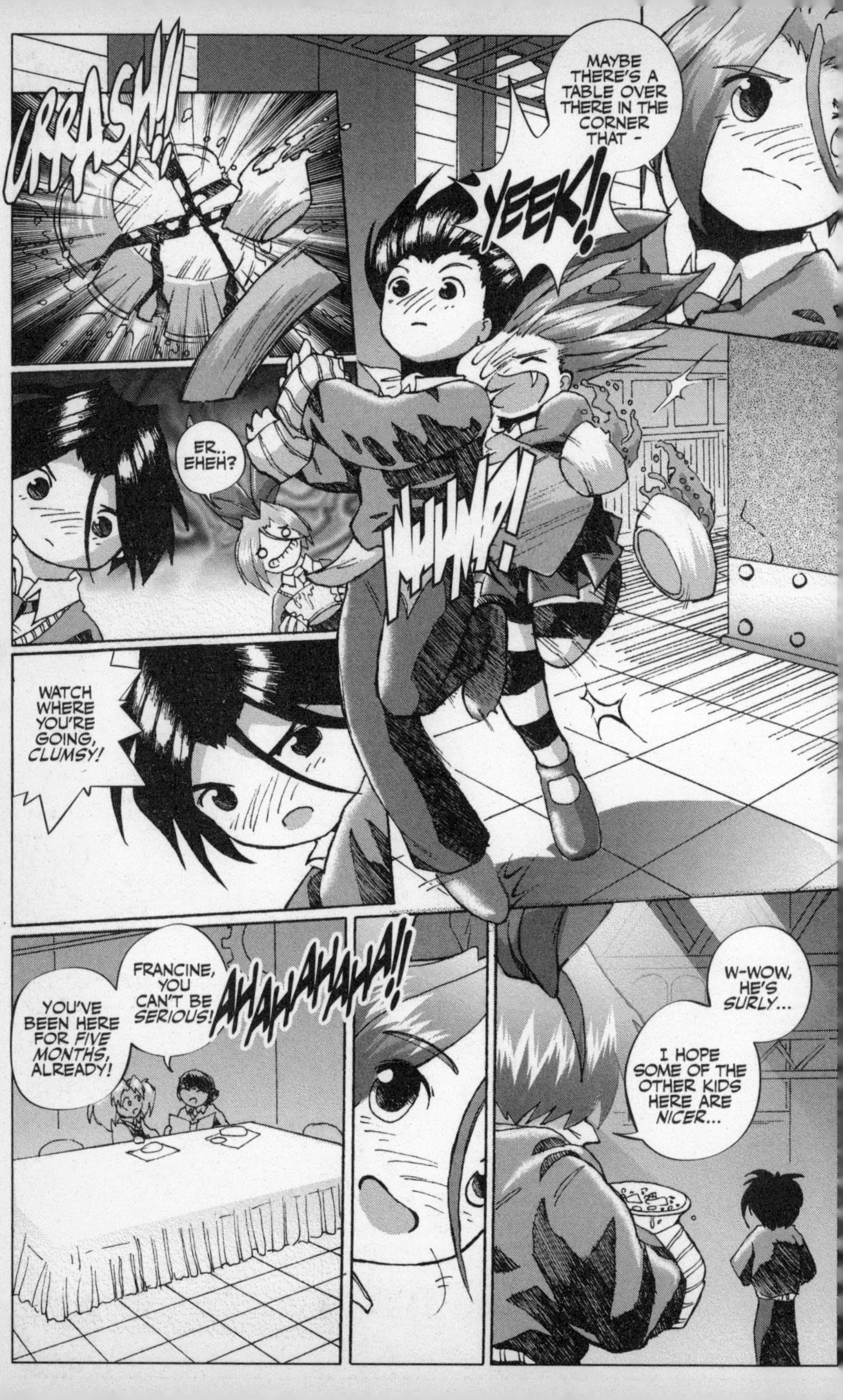
MAYBE THERE'S A TABLE OVER THERE IN THE CORNER THAT -
YEEK!!
CRASH!!
WHUMP!
ER.. EHEH?
WATCH WHERE YOU'RE GOING, *CLUMSY!*
W-WOW, HE'S *SURLY...*
I HOPE SOME OF THE OTHER KIDS HERE ARE *NICER...*
FRANCINE, YOU CAN'T BE *SERIOUS!*
AHAHAHAHA!!
YOU'VE BEEN HERE FOR *FIVE MONTHS,* ALREADY!

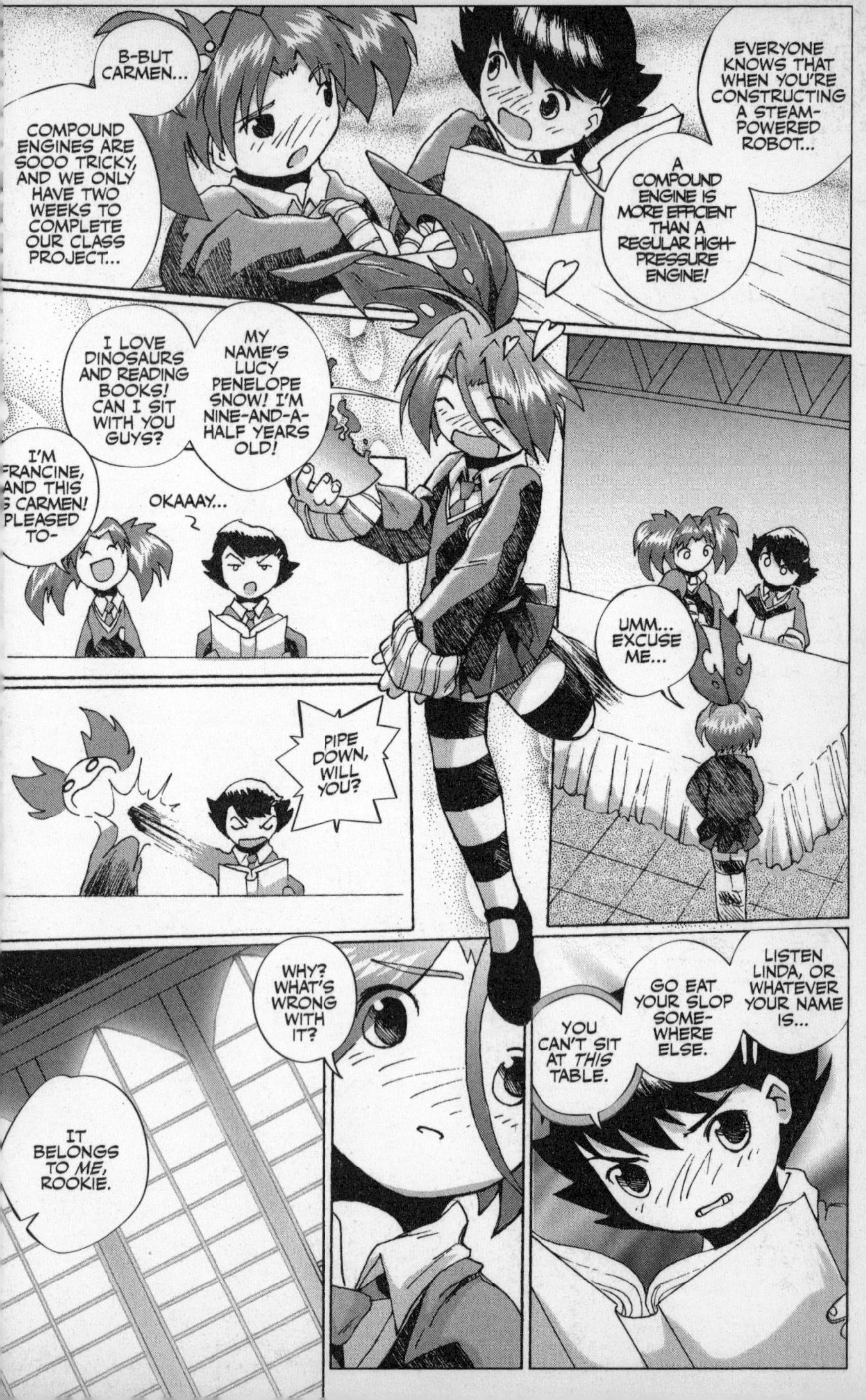
EVERYONE KNOWS THAT WHEN YOU'RE CONSTRUCTING A STEAM-POWERED ROBOT...
A COMPOUND ENGINE IS MORE EFFICIENT THAN A REGULAR HIGH-PRESSURE ENGINE!
B-BUT CARMEN...
COMPOUND ENGINES ARE SOOO TRICKY, AND WE ONLY HAVE TWO WEEKS TO COMPLETE OUR CLASS PROJECT...
UMM... EXCUSE ME...
MY NAME'S LUCY PENELOPE SNOW! I'M NINE-AND-A-HALF YEARS OLD!
I LOVE DINOSAURS AND READING BOOKS! CAN I SIT WITH YOU GUYS?
I'M FRANCINE, AND THIS IS CARMEN! PLEASED TO-
OKAAAY...
PIPE DOWN, WILL YOU?
LISTEN LINDA, OR WHATEVER YOUR NAME IS...
GO EAT YOUR SLOP SOME-WHERE ELSE.
YOU CAN'T SIT AT *THIS* TABLE.
WHY? WHAT'S WRONG WITH IT?
IT BELONGS TO *ME*, ROOKIE.

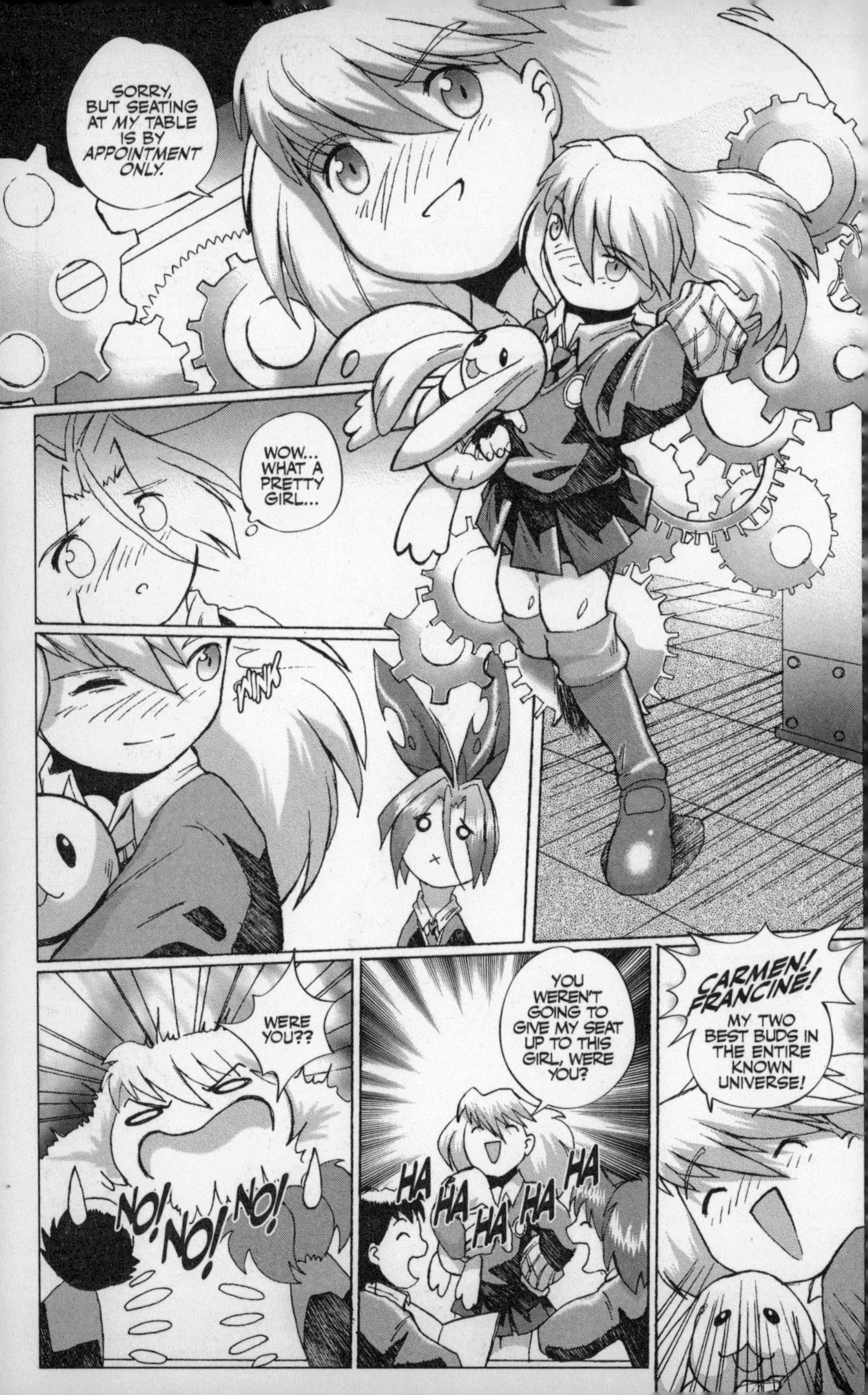
SORRY, BUT SEATING AT MY TABLE IS BY APPOINTMENT ONLY.
WOW... WHAT A PRETTY GIRL...
WINK
CARMEN! FRANCINE!
MY TWO BEST BUDS IN THE ENTIRE KNOWN UNIVERSE!
YOU WEREN'T GOING TO GIVE MY SEAT UP TO THIS GIRL, WERE YOU?
HA HA HA HA HA HA
WERE YOU??
NO! NO! NO!

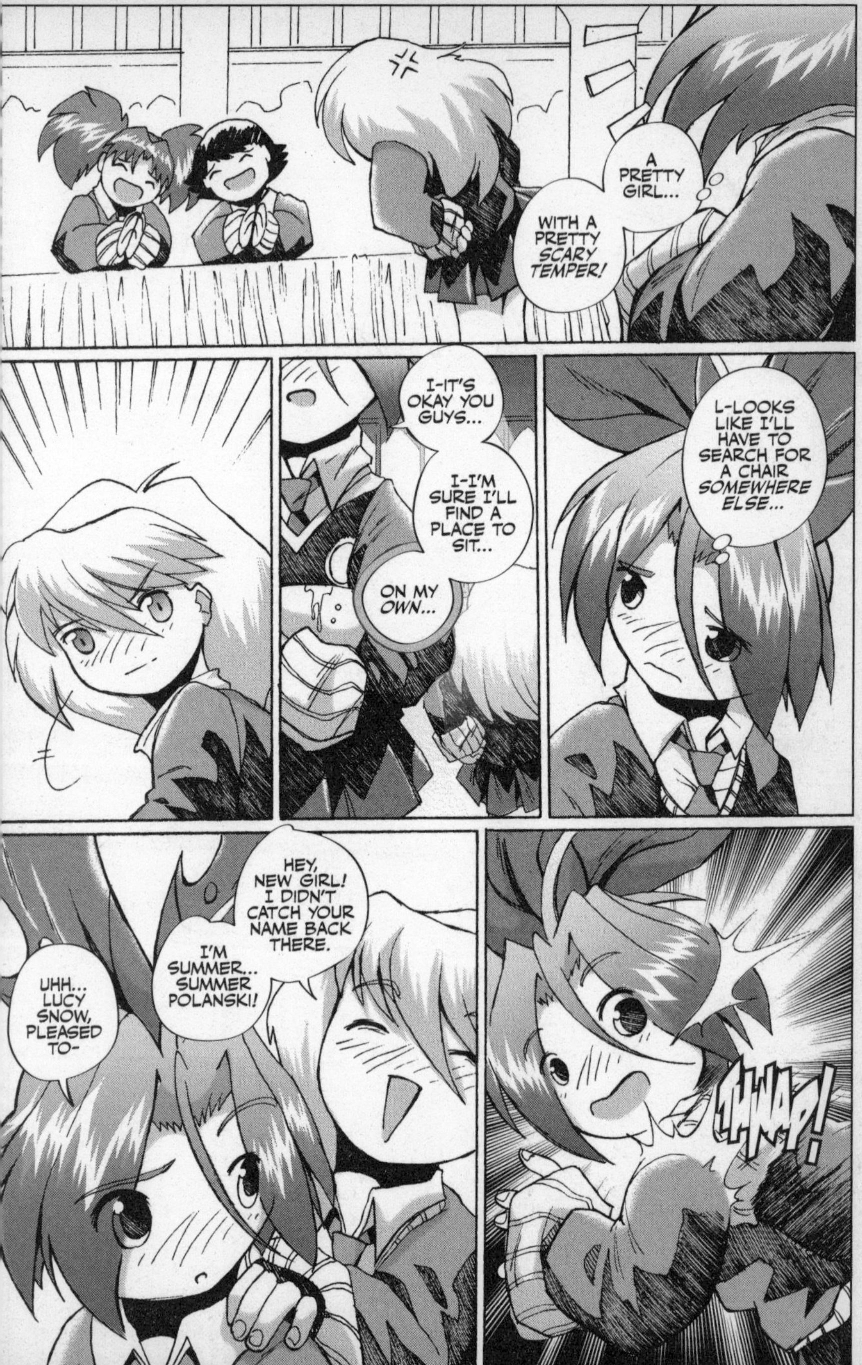
A PRETTY GIRL...
WITH A PRETTY SCARY TEMPER!
I-IT'S OKAY YOU GUYS...
I-I'M SURE I'LL FIND A PLACE TO SIT...
ON MY OWN...
L-LOOKS LIKE I'LL HAVE TO SEARCH FOR A CHAIR SOMEWHERE ELSE...
HEY, NEW GIRL! I DIDN'T CATCH YOUR NAME BACK THERE.
I'M SUMMER... SUMMER POLANSKI!
UHH... LUCY SNOW, PLEASED TO-
THWAP!

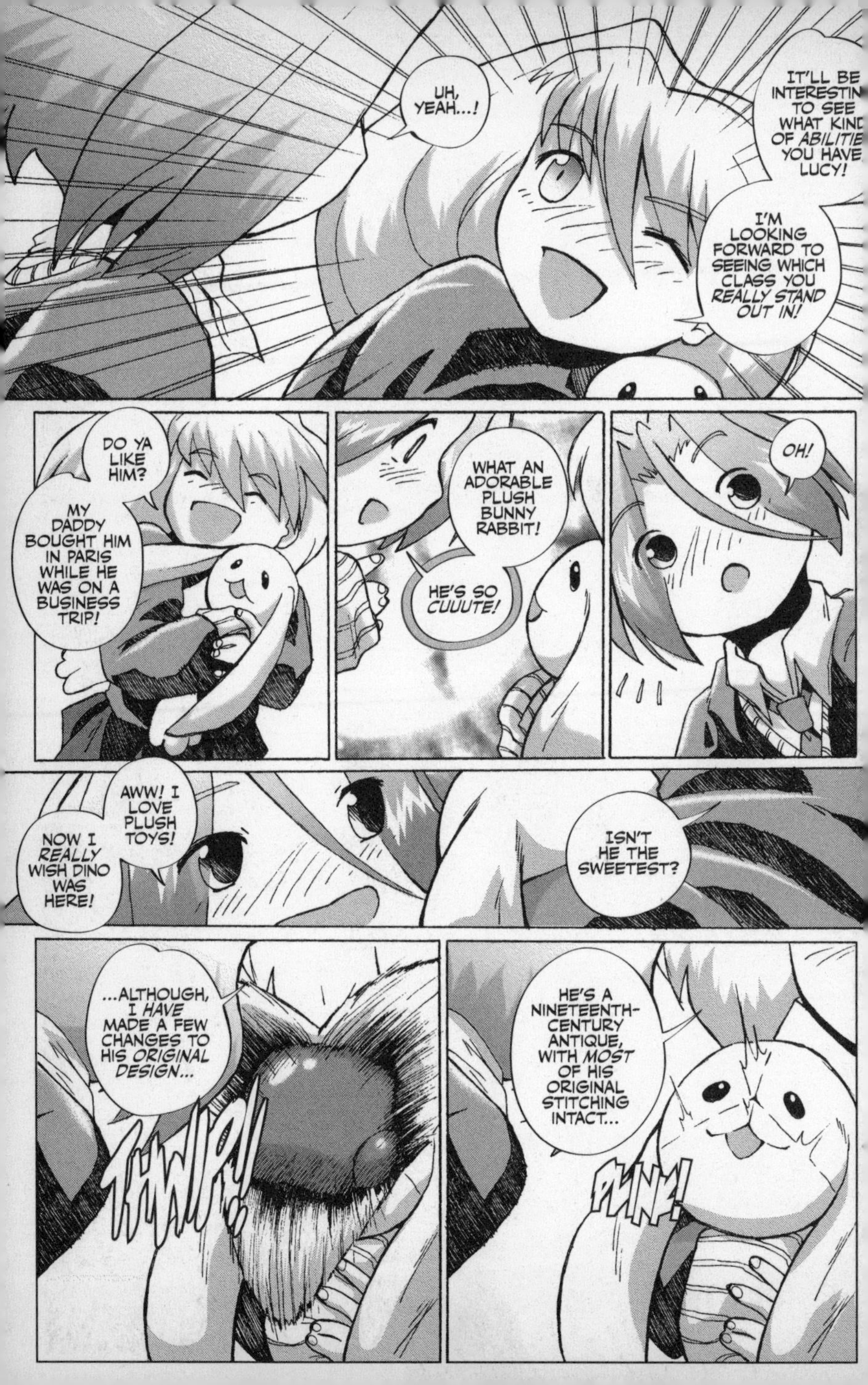
IT'LL BE INTERESTIN TO SEE WHAT KIND OF *ABILITIE* YOU HAVE LUCY!
I'M LOOKING FORWARD TO SEEING WHICH CLASS YOU *REALLY STAND OUT IN!*
UH, YEAH...!
OH!
WHAT AN ADORABLE PLUSH BUNNY RABBIT!
HE'S SO *CUUUTE!*
DO YA LIKE HIM?
MY DADDY BOUGHT HIM IN PARIS WHILE HE WAS ON A BUSINESS TRIP!
ISN'T HE THE SWEETEST?
AWW! I LOVE PLUSH TOYS!
NOW I *REALLY* WISH DINO WAS HERE!
HE'S A NINETEENTH-CENTURY ANTIQUE, WITH *MOST* OF HIS ORIGINAL STITCHING INTACT...
PLINK!
...ALTHOUGH, I *HAVE* MADE A FEW CHANGES TO HIS *ORIGINAL DESIGN*...

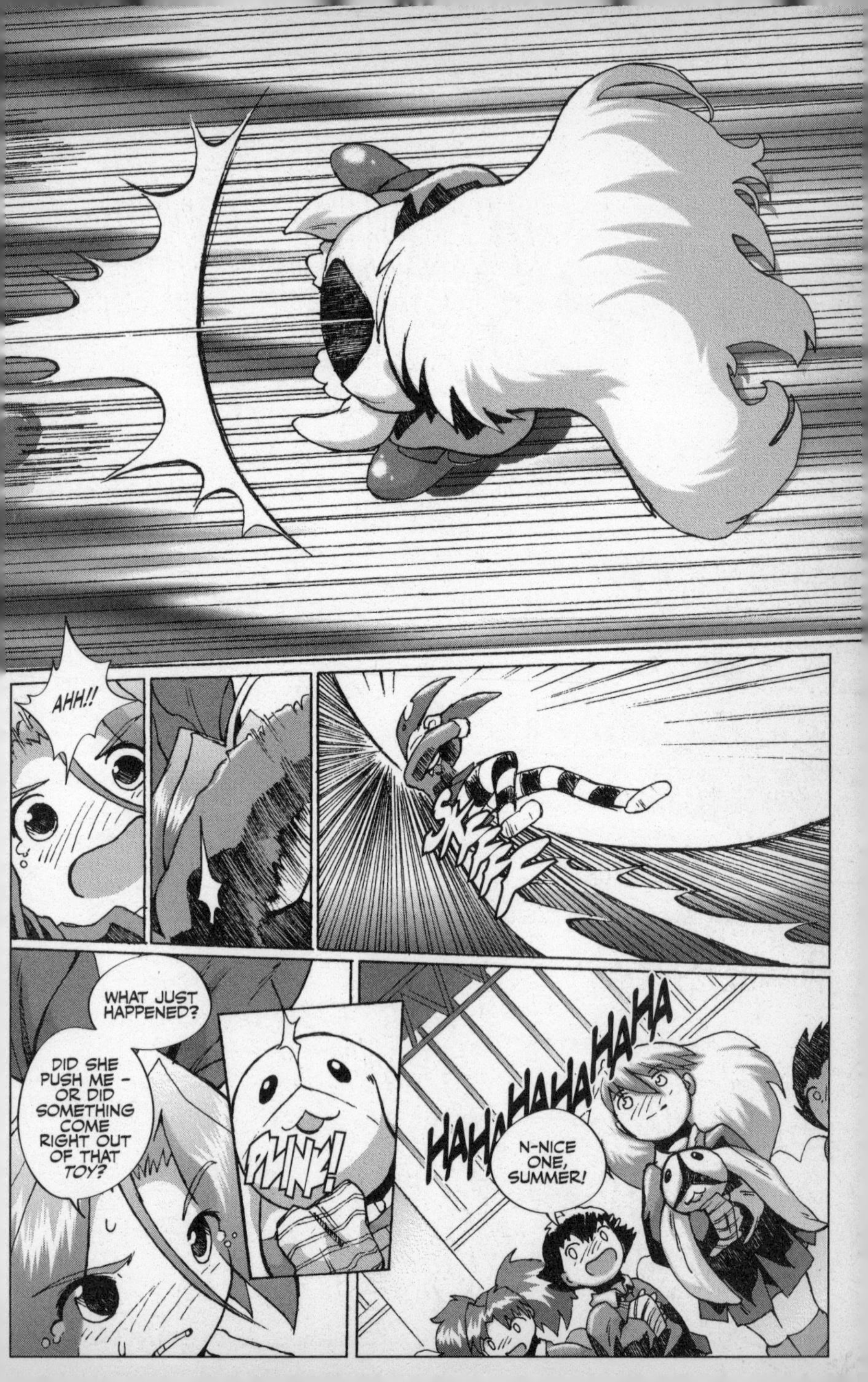
AHH!!
HAHAHAHAHAHA
N-NICE ONE, SUMMER!
PLINK!
WHAT JUST HAPPENED?
DID SHE PUSH ME - OR DID SOMETHING COME RIGHT OUT OF THAT TOY?

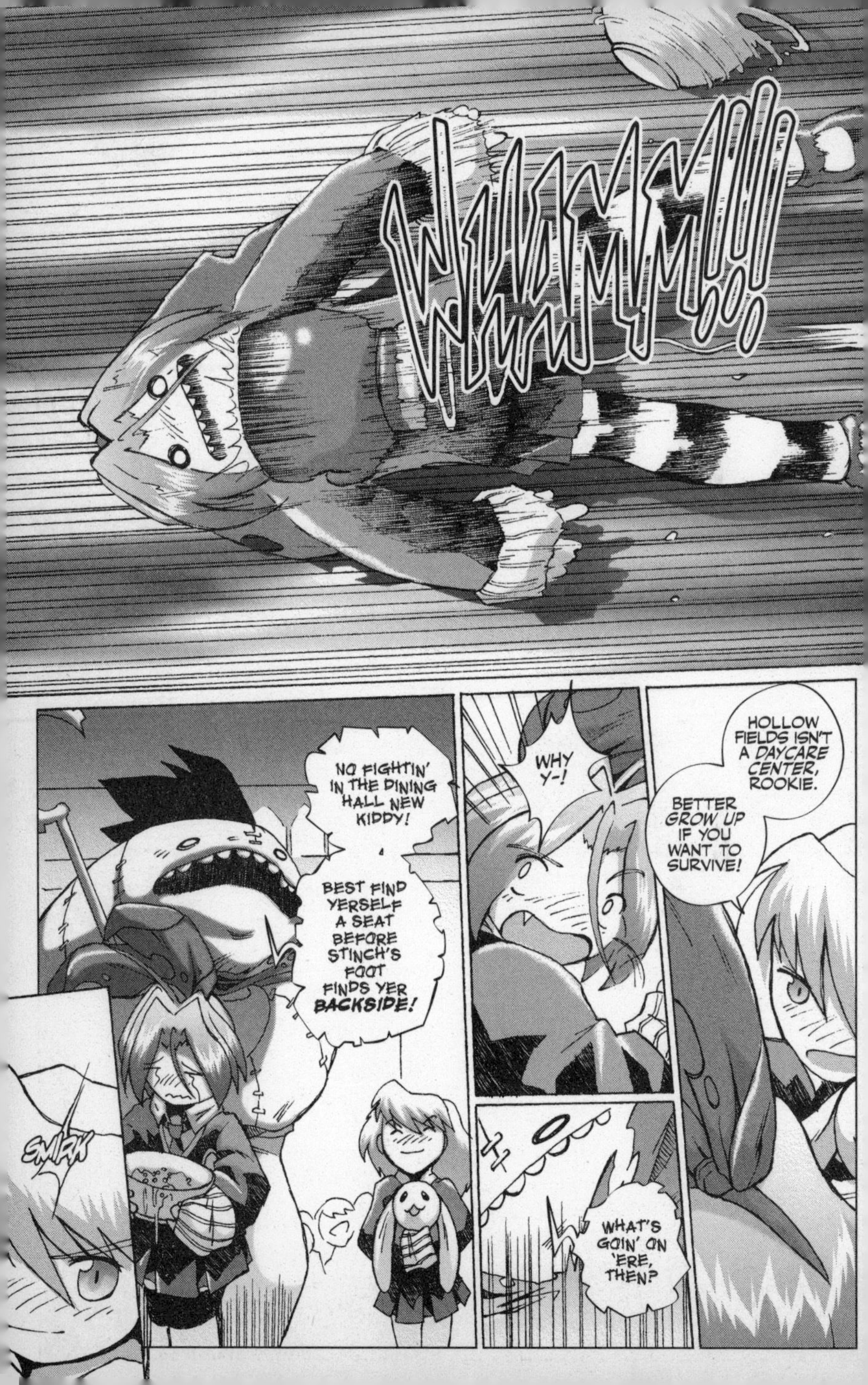
WHAMM!!
HOLLOW FIELDS ISN'T A *DAYCARE CENTER*, ROOKIE.
BETTER *GROW UP* IF YOU WANT TO SURVIVE!
WHY Y-!
WHAT'S GOIN' ON 'ERE, THEN?
NO FIGHTIN' IN THE DINING HALL NEW KIDDY!
BEST FIND YERSELF A SEAT BEFORE STINCH'S FOOT FINDS YER **BACKSIDE!**
SMIRK

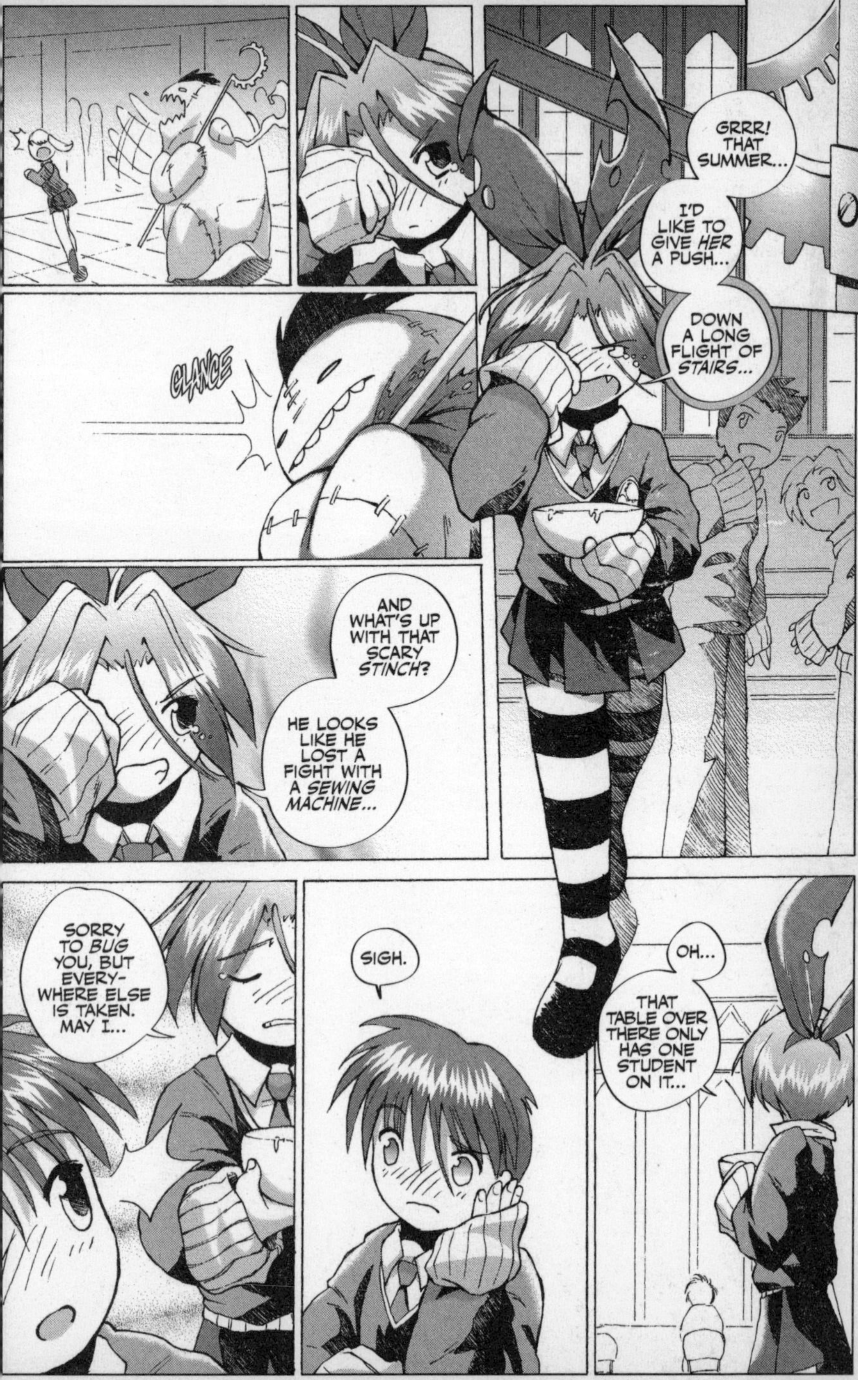
GRRR! THAT SUMMER...
I'D LIKE TO GIVE *HER* A PUSH...
DOWN A LONG FLIGHT OF *STAIRS*...
GLANCE
AND WHAT'S UP WITH THAT SCARY *STINCH*?
HE LOOKS LIKE HE LOST A FIGHT WITH A *SEWING MACHINE*...
OH...
THAT TABLE OVER THERE ONLY HAS ONE STUDENT ON IT...
SIGH.
SORRY TO *BUG* YOU, BUT EVERY-WHERE ELSE IS TAKEN. MAY I...

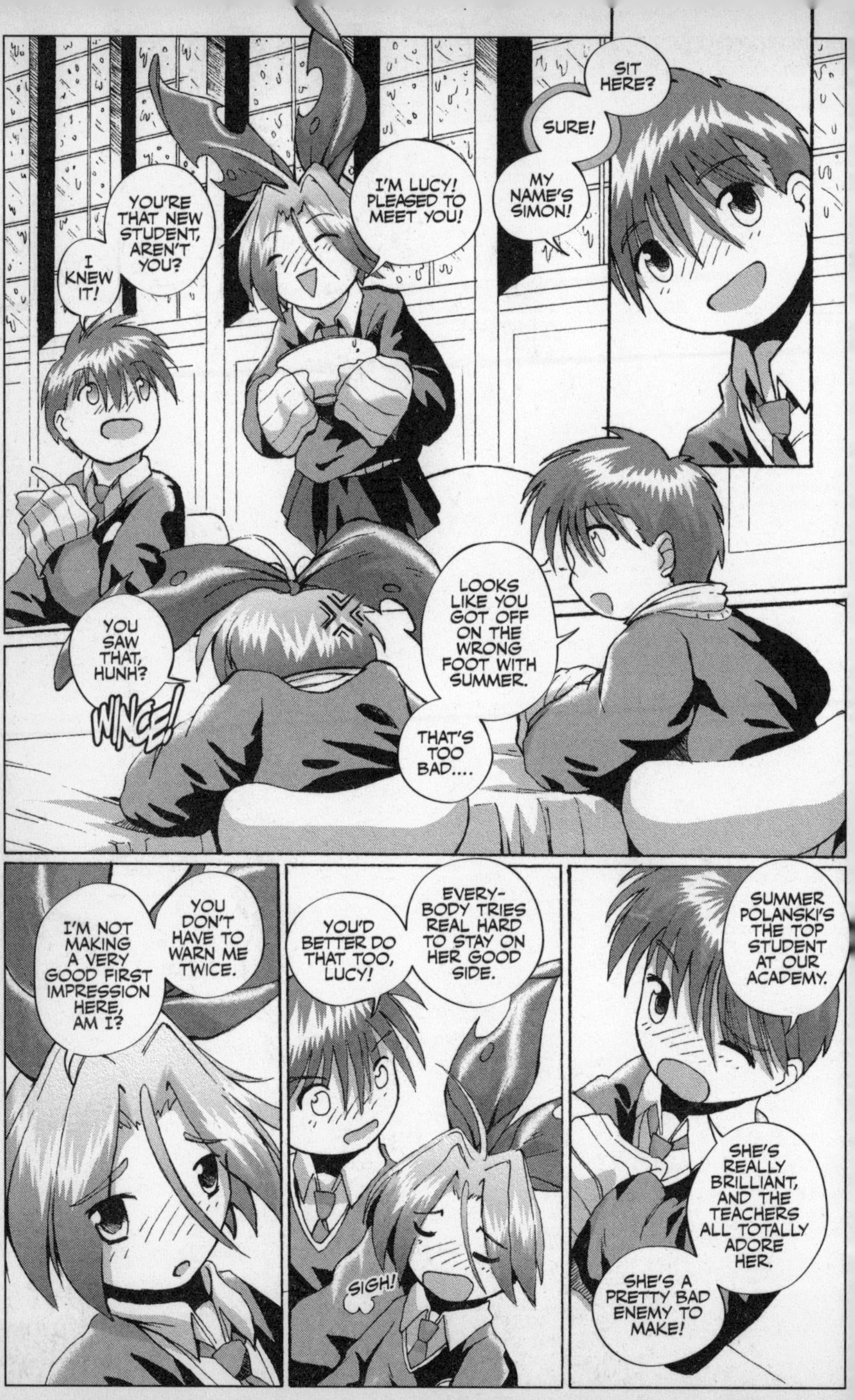
SIT HERE?
SURE!
MY NAME'S SIMON!
I'M LUCY! PLEASED TO MEET YOU!
YOU'RE THAT NEW STUDENT, AREN'T YOU?
I KNEW IT!
LOOKS LIKE YOU GOT OFF ON THE WRONG FOOT WITH SUMMER.
THAT'S TOO BAD....
YOU SAW THAT, HUNH?
WINCE!
SUMMER POLANSKI'S THE TOP STUDENT AT OUR ACADEMY.
SHE'S REALLY BRILLIANT, AND THE TEACHERS ALL TOTALLY ADORE HER.
SHE'S A PRETTY BAD ENEMY TO MAKE!
EVERY-BODY TRIES REAL HARD TO STAY ON HER GOOD SIDE.
YOU'D BETTER DO THAT TOO, LUCY!
SIGH!
YOU DON'T HAVE TO WARN ME TWICE.
I'M NOT MAKING A VERY GOOD FIRST IMPRESSION HERE, AM I?

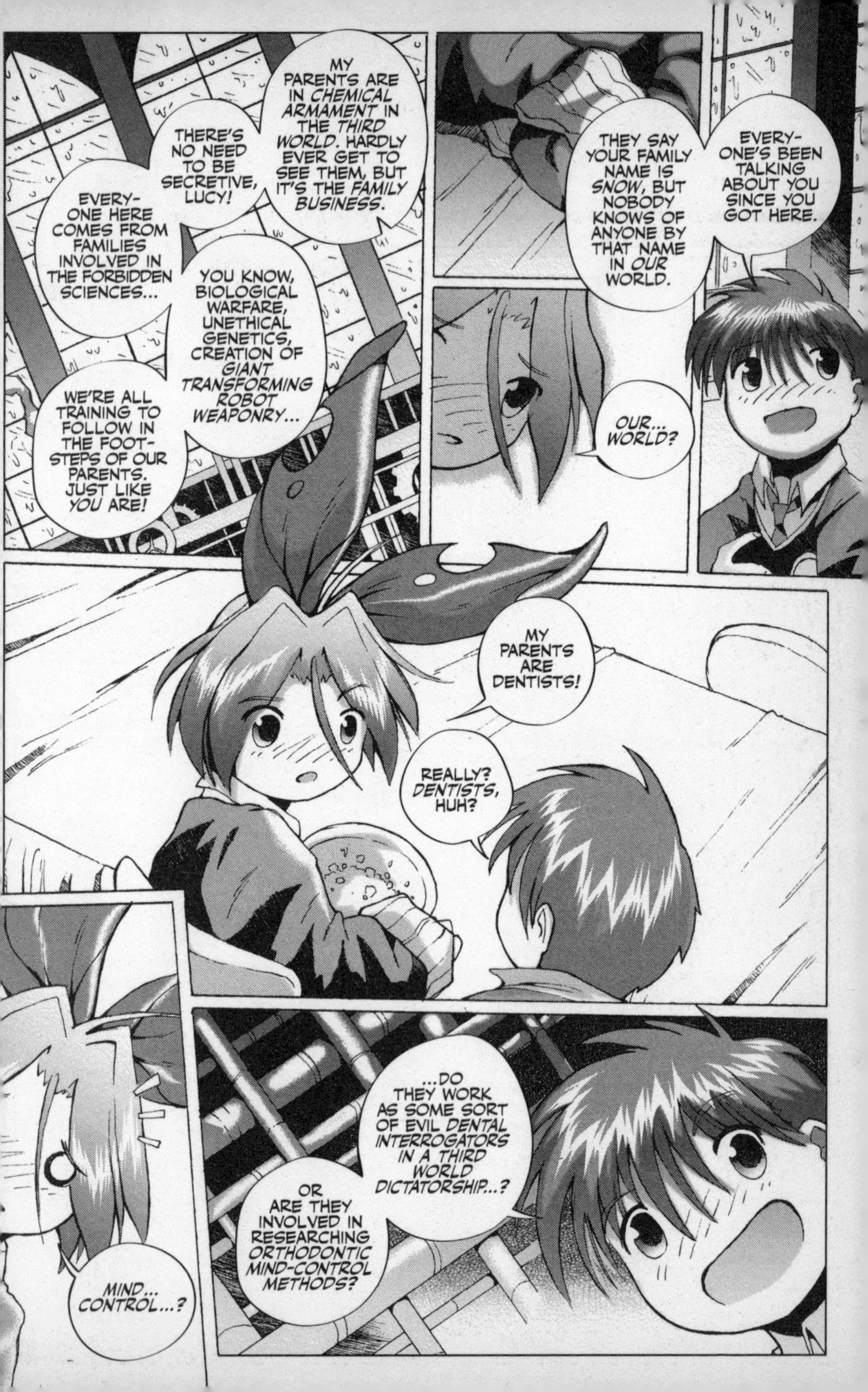
EVERY-ONE'S BEEN TALKING ABOUT YOU SINCE YOU GOT HERE.
THEY SAY YOUR FAMILY NAME IS *SNOW*, BUT NOBODY KNOWS OF ANYONE BY THAT NAME IN *OUR* WORLD.
OUR... WORLD?
MY PARENTS ARE IN *CHEMICAL ARMAMENT* IN THE *THIRD WORLD*. HARDLY EVER GET TO SEE THEM, BUT IT'S THE *FAMILY BUSINESS*.
THERE'S NO NEED TO BE SECRETIVE, LUCY!
EVERY-ONE HERE COMES FROM FAMILIES INVOLVED IN THE FORBIDDEN SCIENCES...
YOU KNOW, BIOLOGICAL WARFARE, UNETHICAL GENETICS, CREATION OF *GIANT TRANSFORMING ROBOT WEAPONRY*...
WE'RE ALL TRAINING TO FOLLOW IN THE FOOT-STEPS OF OUR PARENTS. JUST LIKE *YOU* ARE!
MY PARENTS ARE DENTISTS!
REALLY? *DENTISTS*, HUH?
...DO THEY WORK AS SOME SORT OF EVIL *DENTAL INTERROGATORS* IN A *THIRD WORLD* DICTATORSHIP...?
OR ARE THEY INVOLVED IN RESEARCHING *ORTHODONTIC MIND-CONTROL* METHODS?
MIND... CONTROL...?

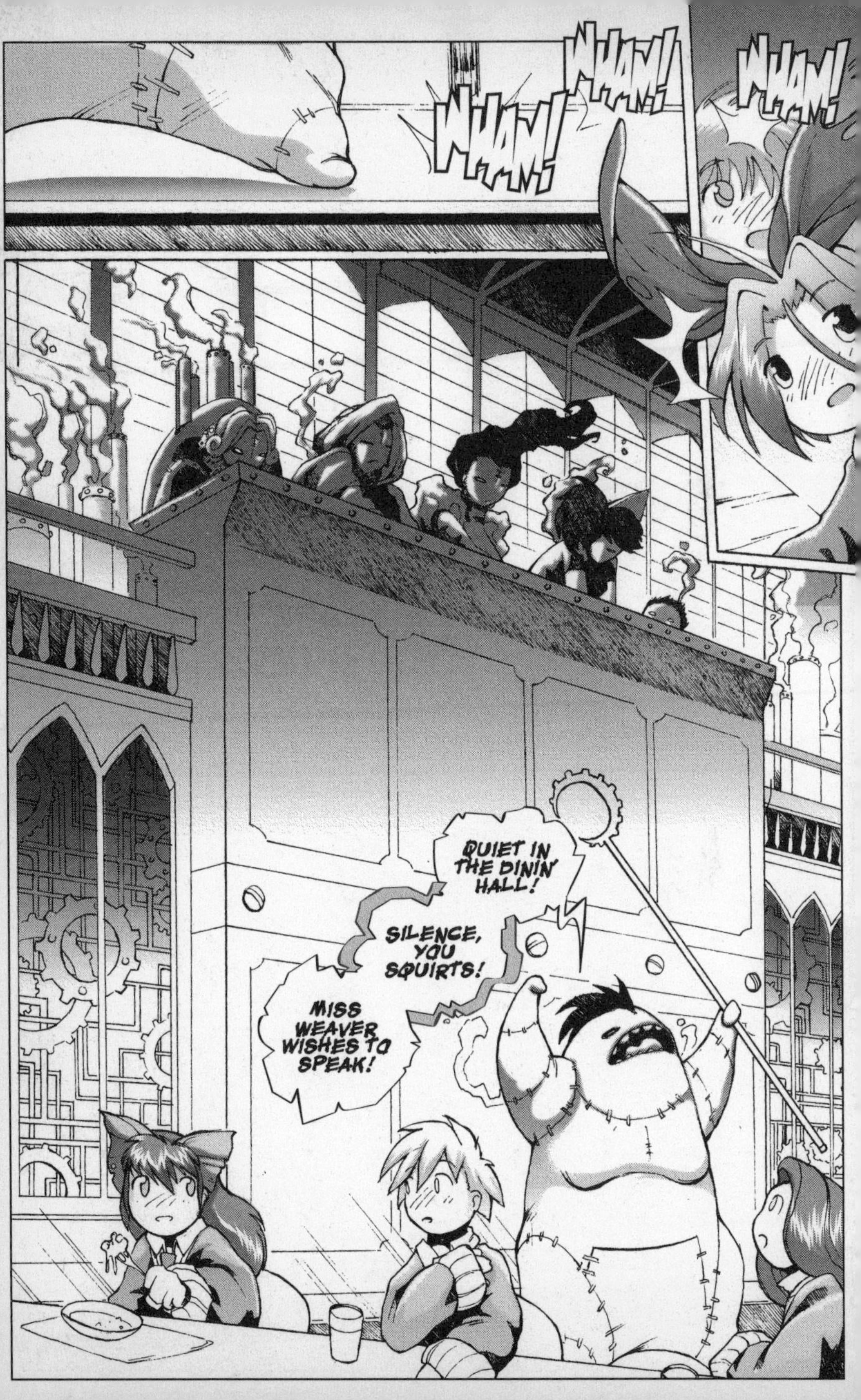
WHAM!
WHAM!
WHAM!
QUIET IN THE DININ' HALL!
SILENCE, YOU SQUIRTS!
MISS WEAVER WISHES TO SPEAK!

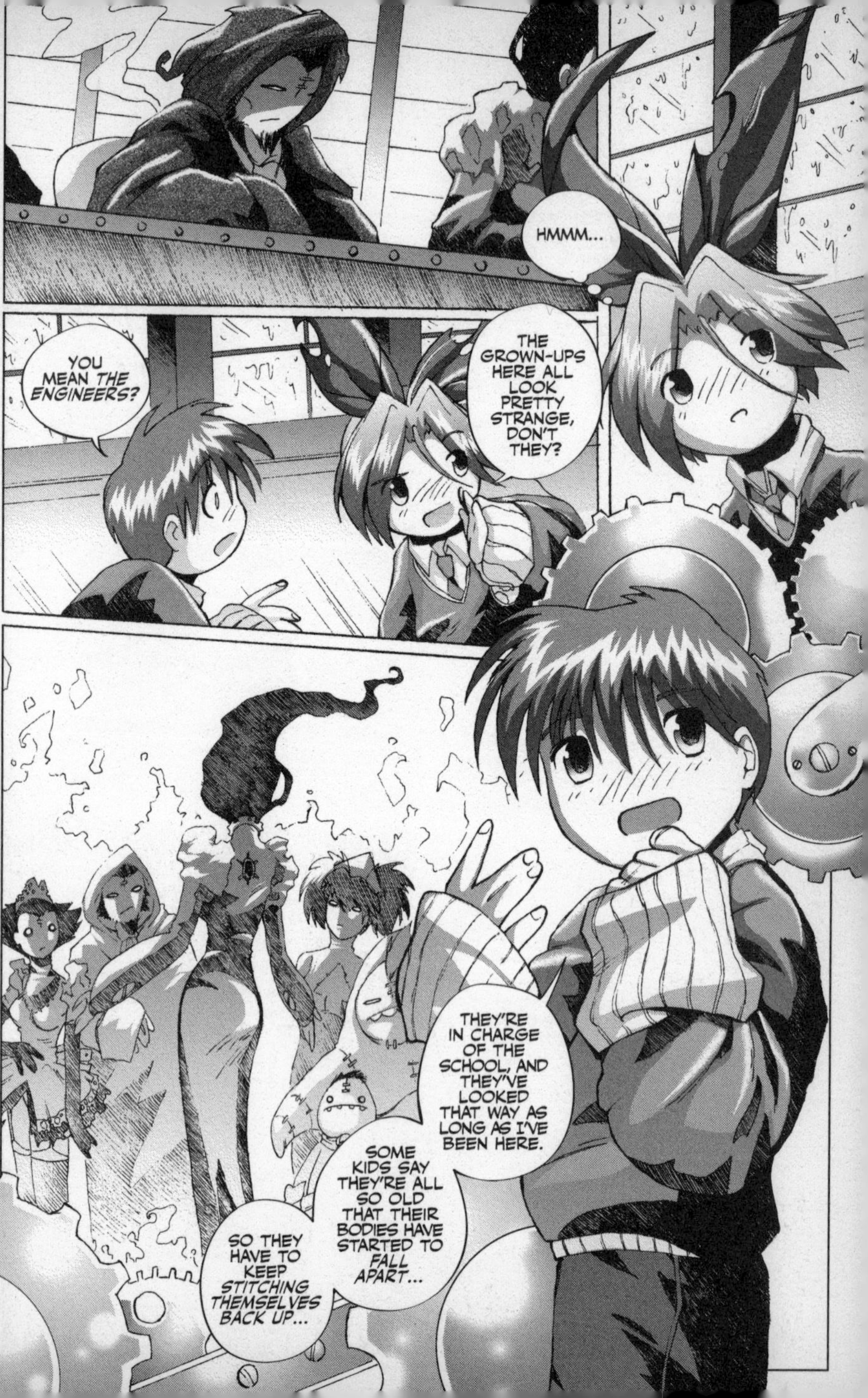
HMMM...
THE GROWN-UPS HERE ALL LOOK PRETTY STRANGE, DON'T THEY?
YOU MEAN *THE ENGINEERS?*
THEY'RE IN CHARGE OF THE SCHOOL, AND THEY'VE LOOKED THAT WAY AS LONG AS I'VE BEEN HERE.
SOME KIDS SAY THEY'RE ALL SO OLD THAT THEIR BODIES HAVE STARTED TO *FALL APART*...
SO THEY HAVE TO KEEP *STITCHING THEMSELVES* BACK UP...

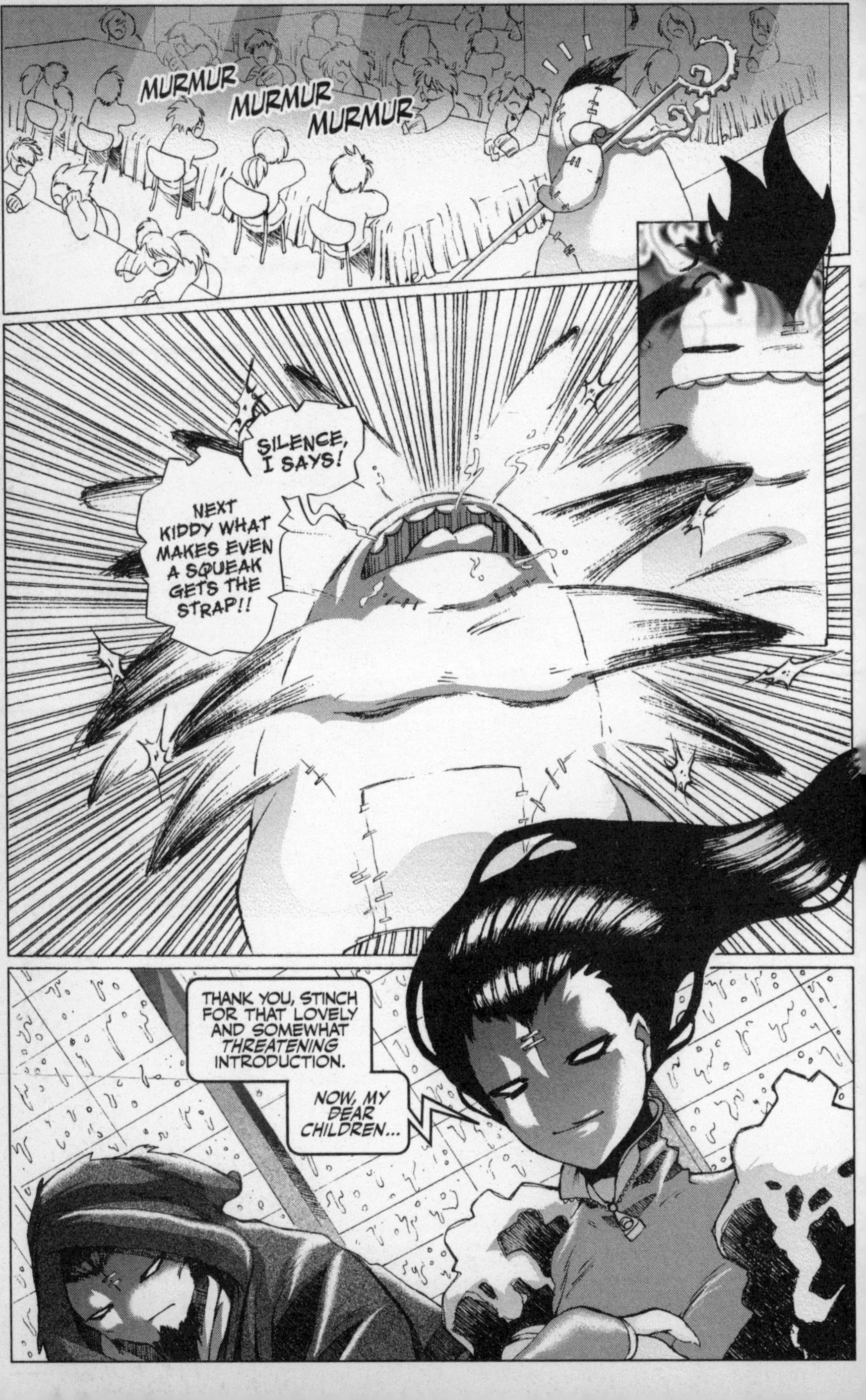
MURMUR MURMUR MURMUR
SILENCE, I SAYS!
NEXT KIDDY WHAT MAKES EVEN A SQUEAK GETS THE STRAP!!
THANK YOU, STINCH FOR THAT LOVELY AND SOMEWHAT *THREATENING* INTRODUCTION.
NOW, MY DEAR CHILDREN...

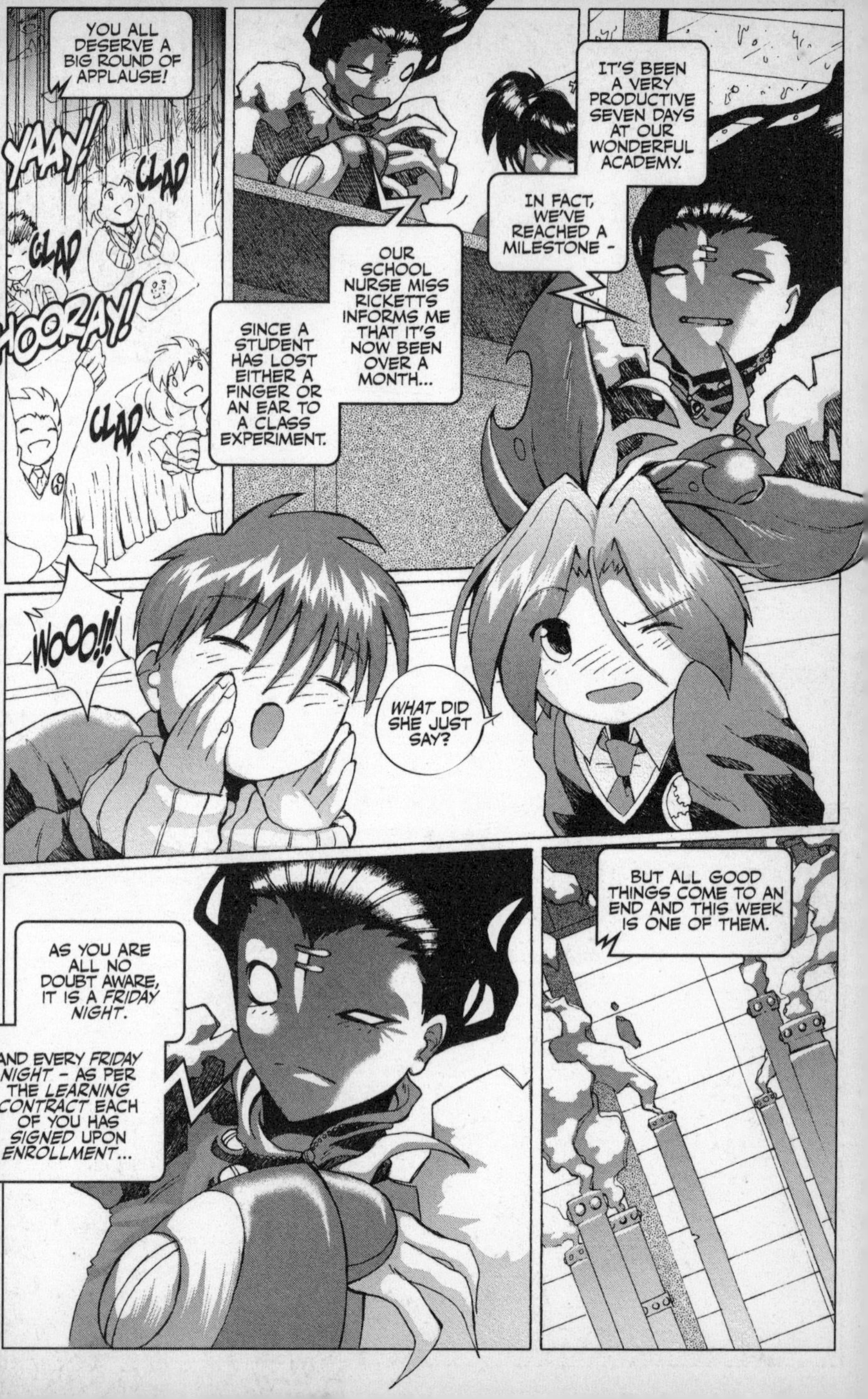
IT'S BEEN A VERY PRODUCTIVE SEVEN DAYS AT OUR WONDERFUL ACADEMY.
IN FACT, WE'VE REACHED A MILESTONE -
OUR SCHOOL NURSE MISS RICKETTS INFORMS ME THAT IT'S NOW BEEN OVER A MONTH...
SINCE A STUDENT HAS LOST EITHER A FINGER OR AN EAR TO A CLASS EXPERIMENT.
YOU ALL DESERVE A BIG ROUND OF APPLAUSE!
YAAY!
CLAP
CLAP
HOORAY!
CLAP
WOOO!!!
WHAT DID SHE JUST SAY?
BUT ALL GOOD THINGS COME TO AN END AND THIS WEEK IS ONE OF THEM.
AS YOU ARE ALL NO DOUBT AWARE, IT IS A *FRIDAY NIGHT*.
AND EVERY *FRIDAY NIGHT* - AS PER THE *LEARNING CONTRACT* EACH OF YOU HAS *SIGNED* UPON *ENROLLMENT*...

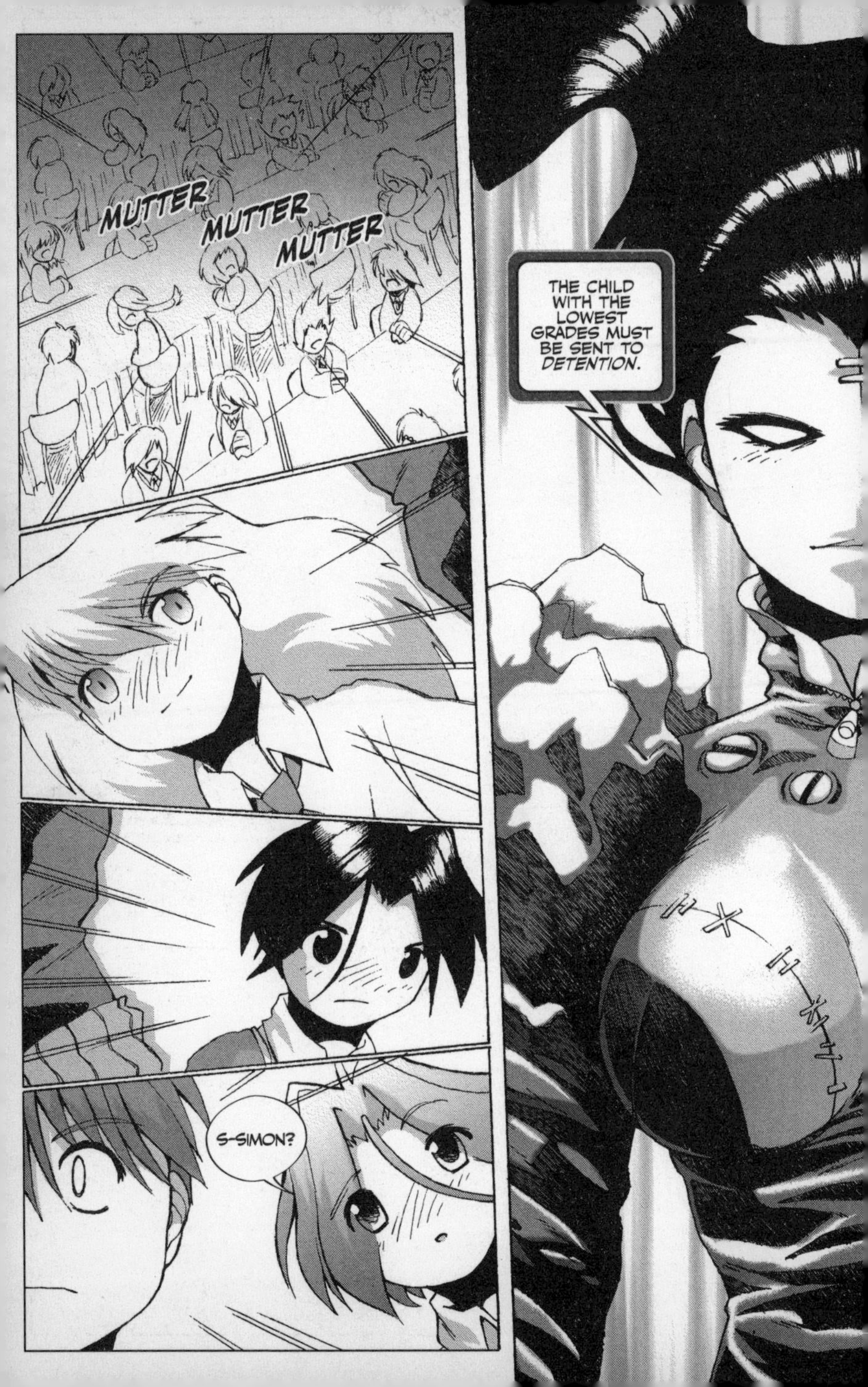
THE CHILD WITH THE LOWEST GRADES MUST BE SENT TO DETENTION.
MUTTER
MUTTER
MUTTER
S-SIMON?

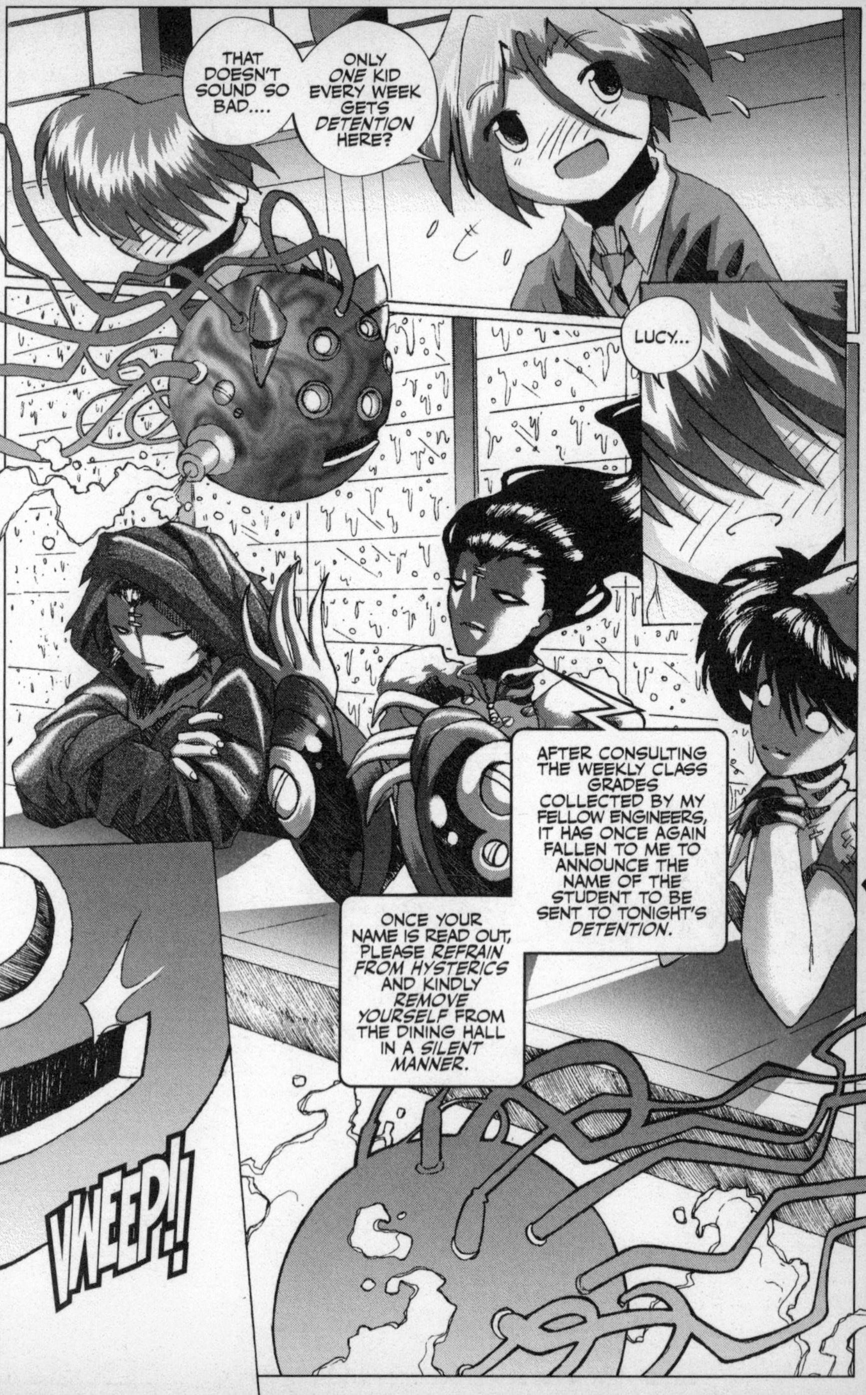
ONLY *ONE KID* EVERY WEEK GETS *DETENTION* HERE?
THAT DOESN'T SOUND SO BAD....
LUCY...
AFTER CONSULTING THE WEEKLY CLASS GRADES COLLECTED BY MY FELLOW ENGINEERS, IT HAS ONCE AGAIN FALLEN TO ME TO ANNOUNCE THE NAME OF THE STUDENT TO BE SENT TO TONIGHT'S *DETENTION*.
ONCE YOUR NAME IS READ OUT, PLEASE *REFRAIN FROM HYSTERICS* AND KINDLY *REMOVE YOURSELF* FROM THE DINING HALL IN A *SILENT MANNER*.
VWEEP!!

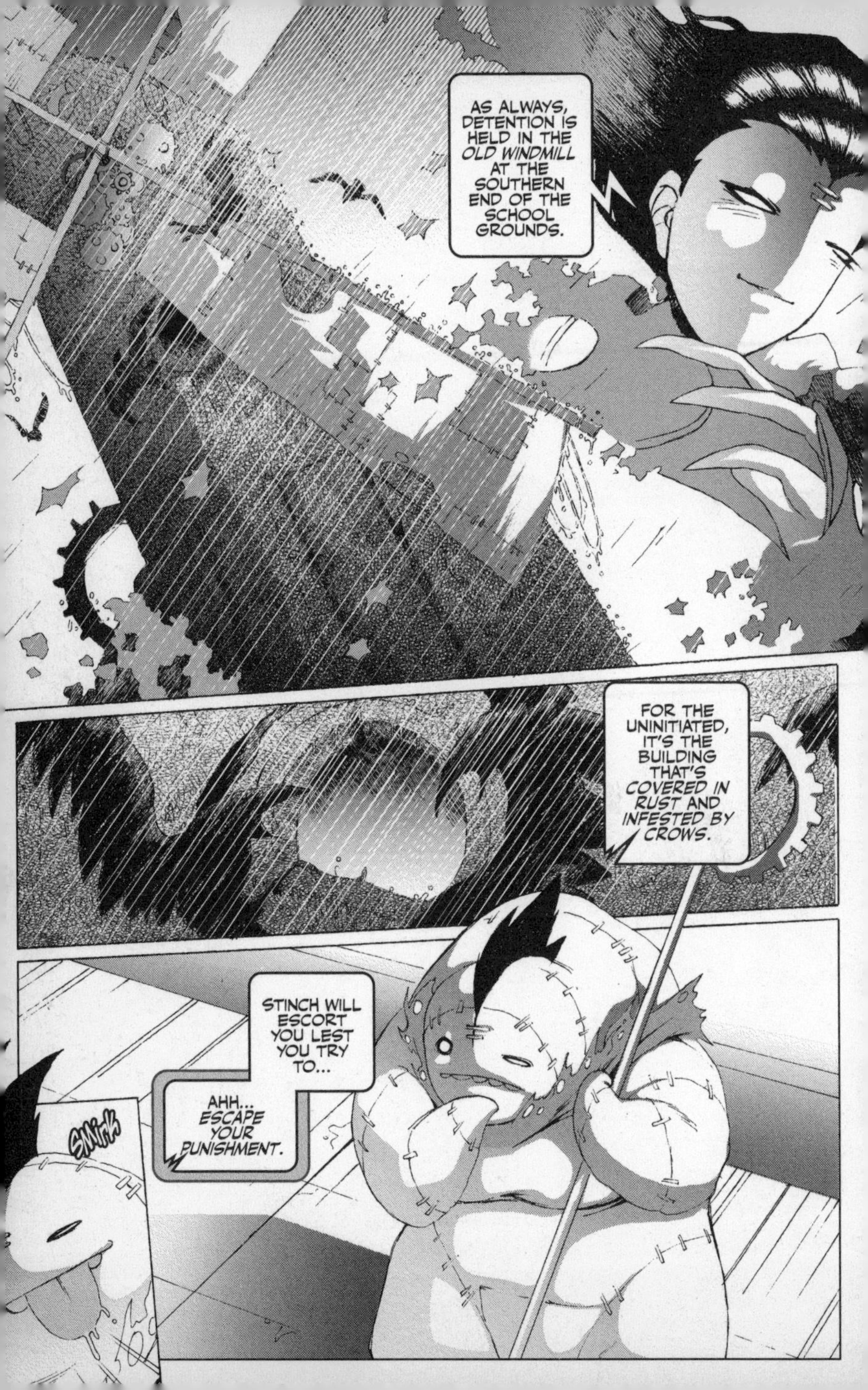
AS ALWAYS, DETENTION IS HELD IN THE *OLD WINDMILL* AT THE SOUTHERN END OF THE SCHOOL GROUNDS.
FOR THE UNINITIATED, IT'S THE BUILDING THAT'S *COVERED IN RUST AND INFESTED BY CROWS.*
STINCH WILL ESCORT YOU LEST YOU TRY TO...
AHH... *ESCAPE YOUR PUNISHMENT.*
SNIRK

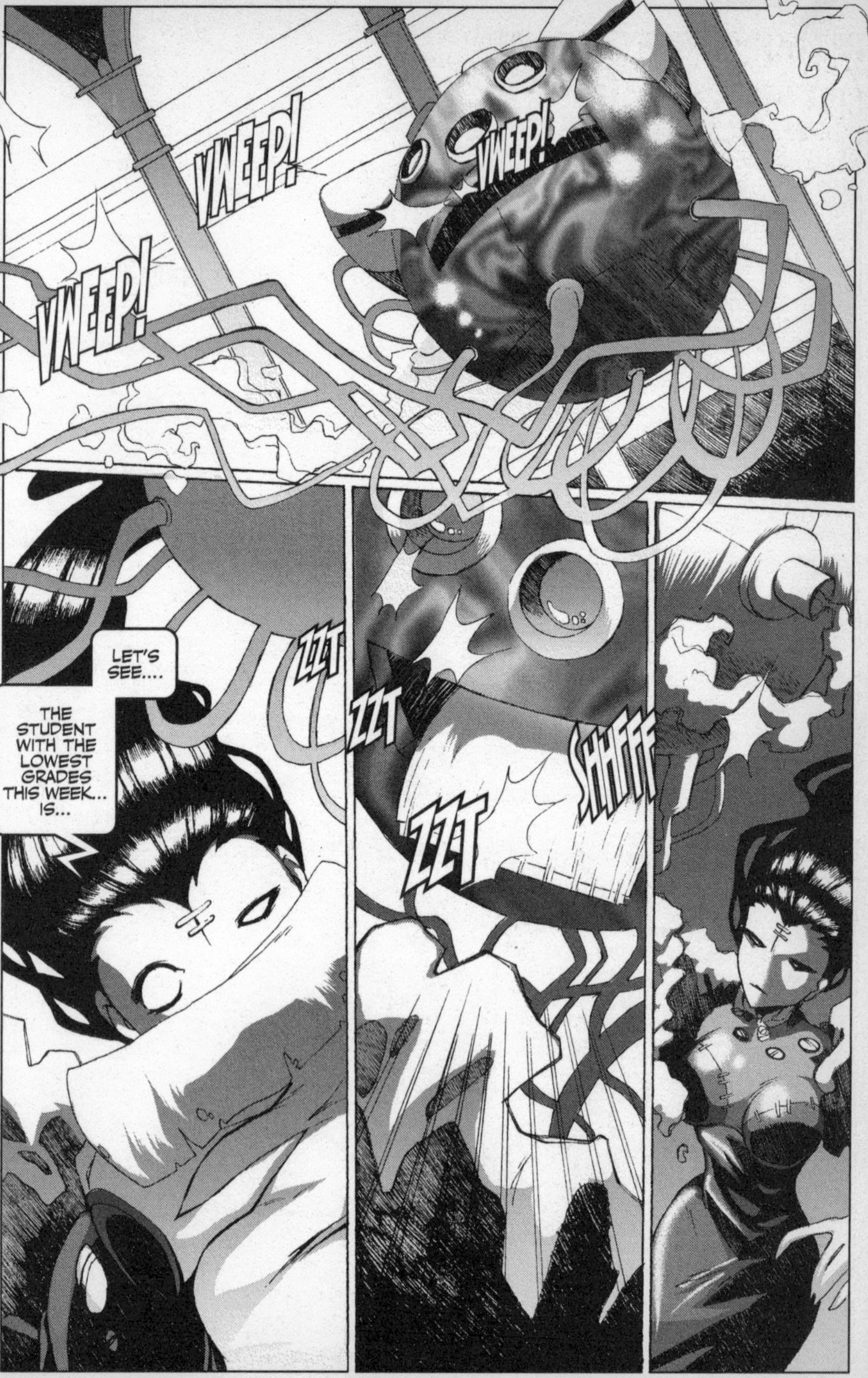
VWEEP!
VWEEP!
VWEEP!
SHHFFF
ZZT
ZZT
ZZT
LET'S SEE....
THE STUDENT WITH THE LOWEST GRADES THIS WEEK... IS...

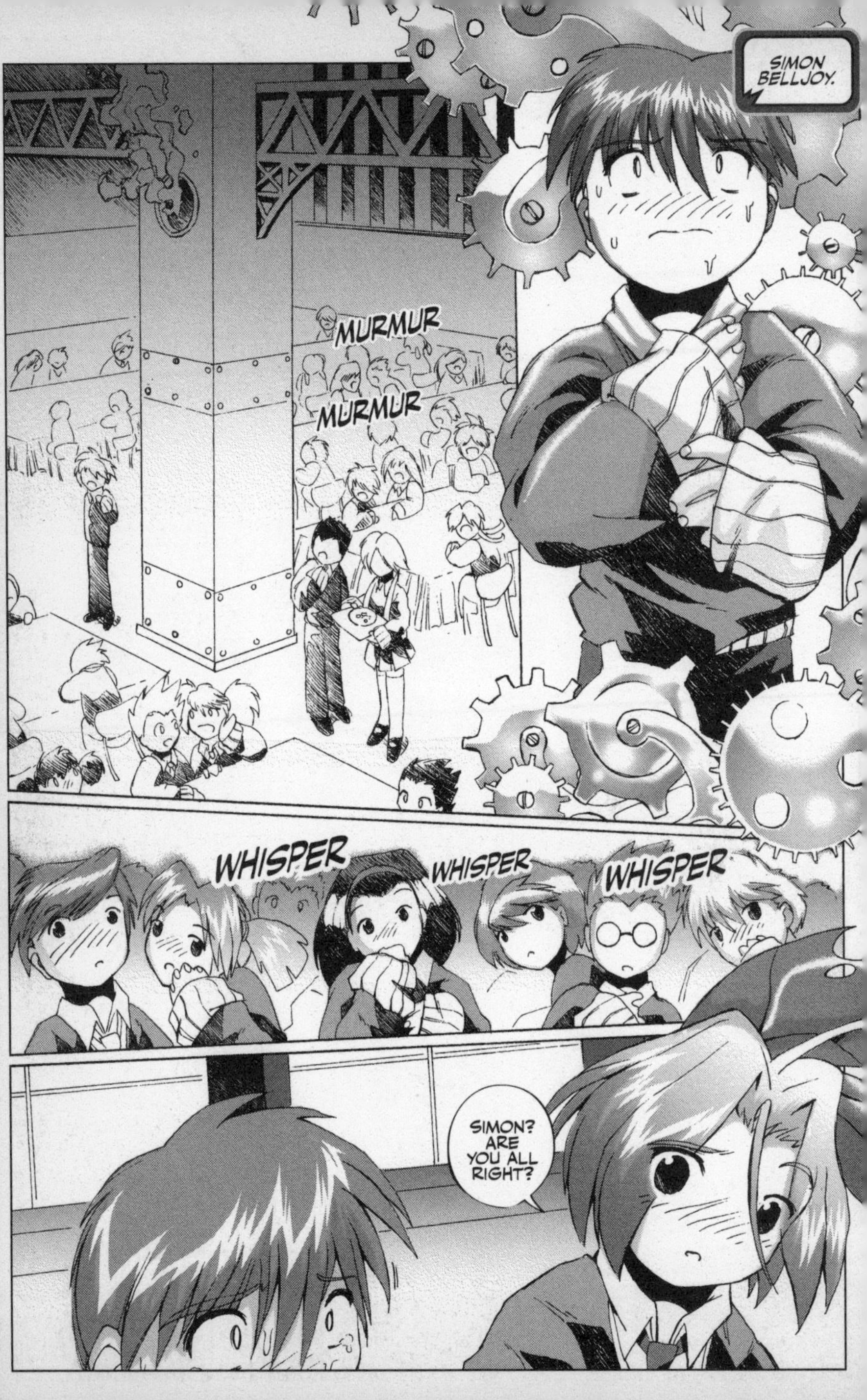
SIMON BELLJOY.
MURMUR
MURMUR
WHISPER
WHISPER
WHISPER
SIMON? ARE YOU ALL RIGHT?

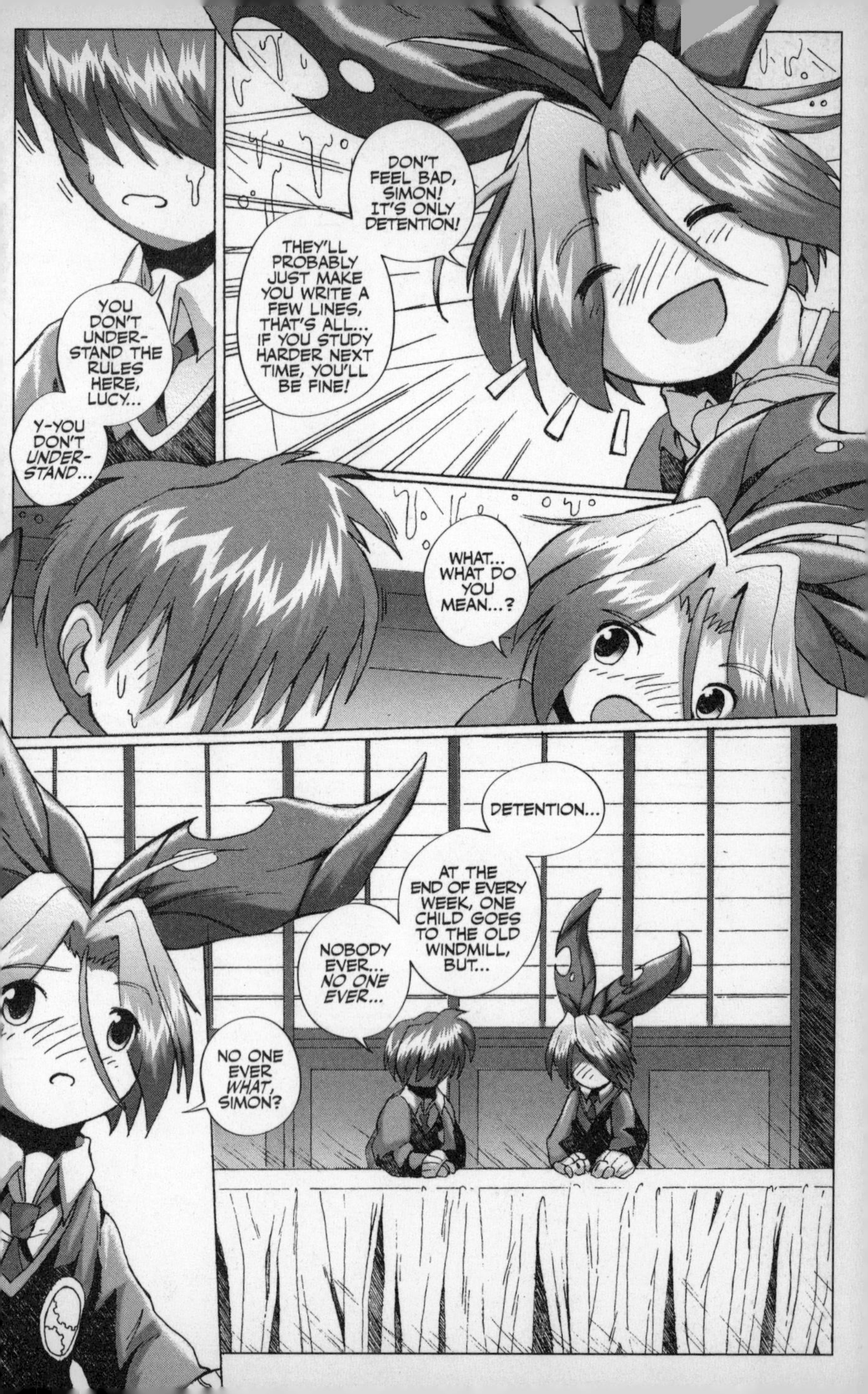
DON'T FEEL BAD, SIMON! IT'S ONLY DETENTION!
THEY'LL PROBABLY JUST MAKE YOU WRITE A FEW LINES, THAT'S ALL... IF YOU STUDY HARDER NEXT TIME, YOU'LL BE FINE!
YOU DON'T UNDER-STAND THE RULES HERE, LUCY...
Y-YOU DON'T *UNDER-STAND*...
WHAT... WHAT DO YOU MEAN...?
DETENTION...
AT THE END OF EVERY WEEK, ONE CHILD GOES TO THE OLD WINDMILL, BUT...
NOBODY EVER... *NO ONE EVER*...
NO ONE EVER *WHAT*, SIMON?

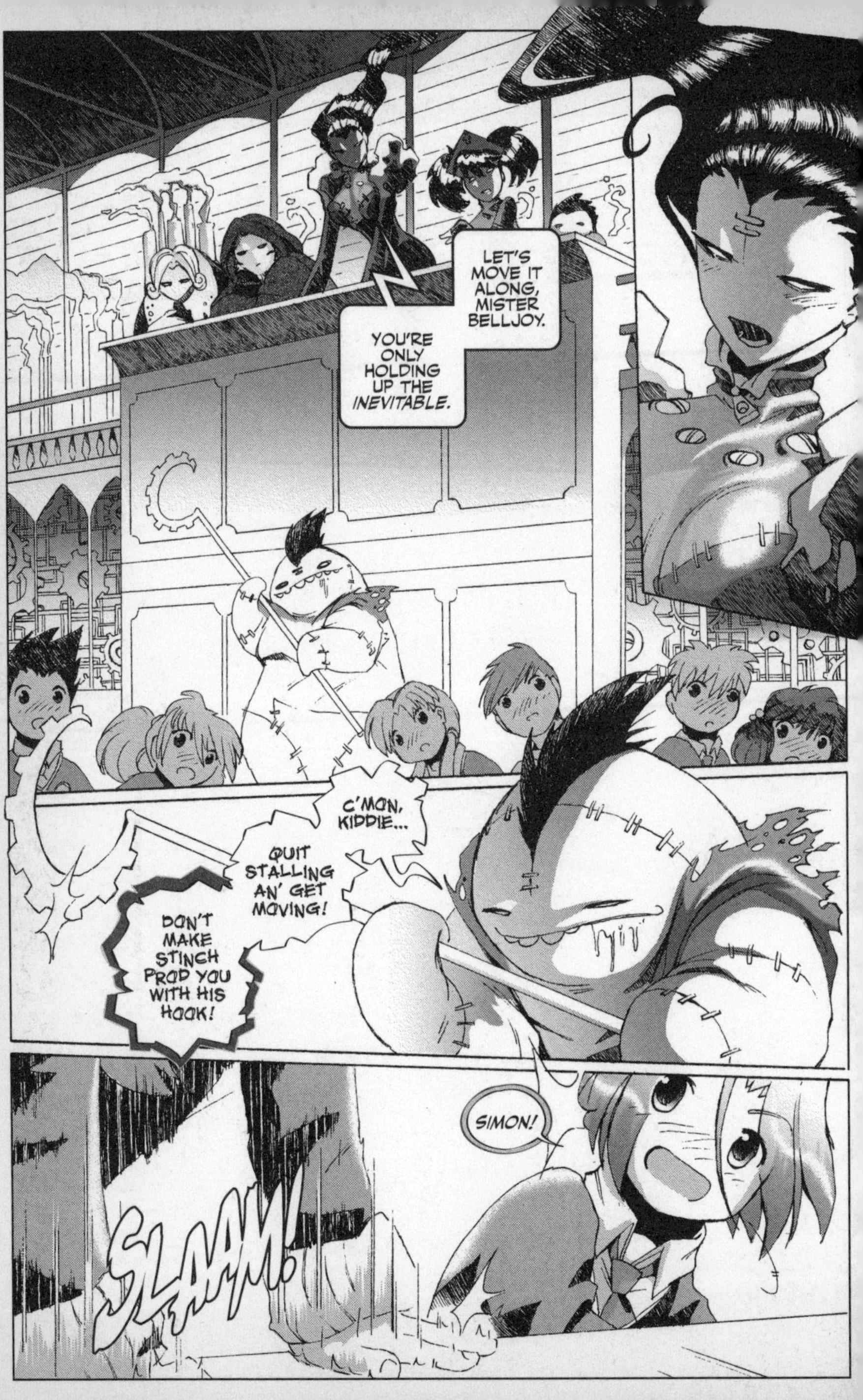
LET'S MOVE IT ALONG, MISTER BELLJOY.
YOU'RE ONLY HOLDING UP THE *INEVITABLE.*
C'MON, KIDDIE...
QUIT STALLING AN' GET MOVING!
DON'T MAKE STINCH PROD YOU WITH HIS HOOK!
SIMON!
SLAAM!

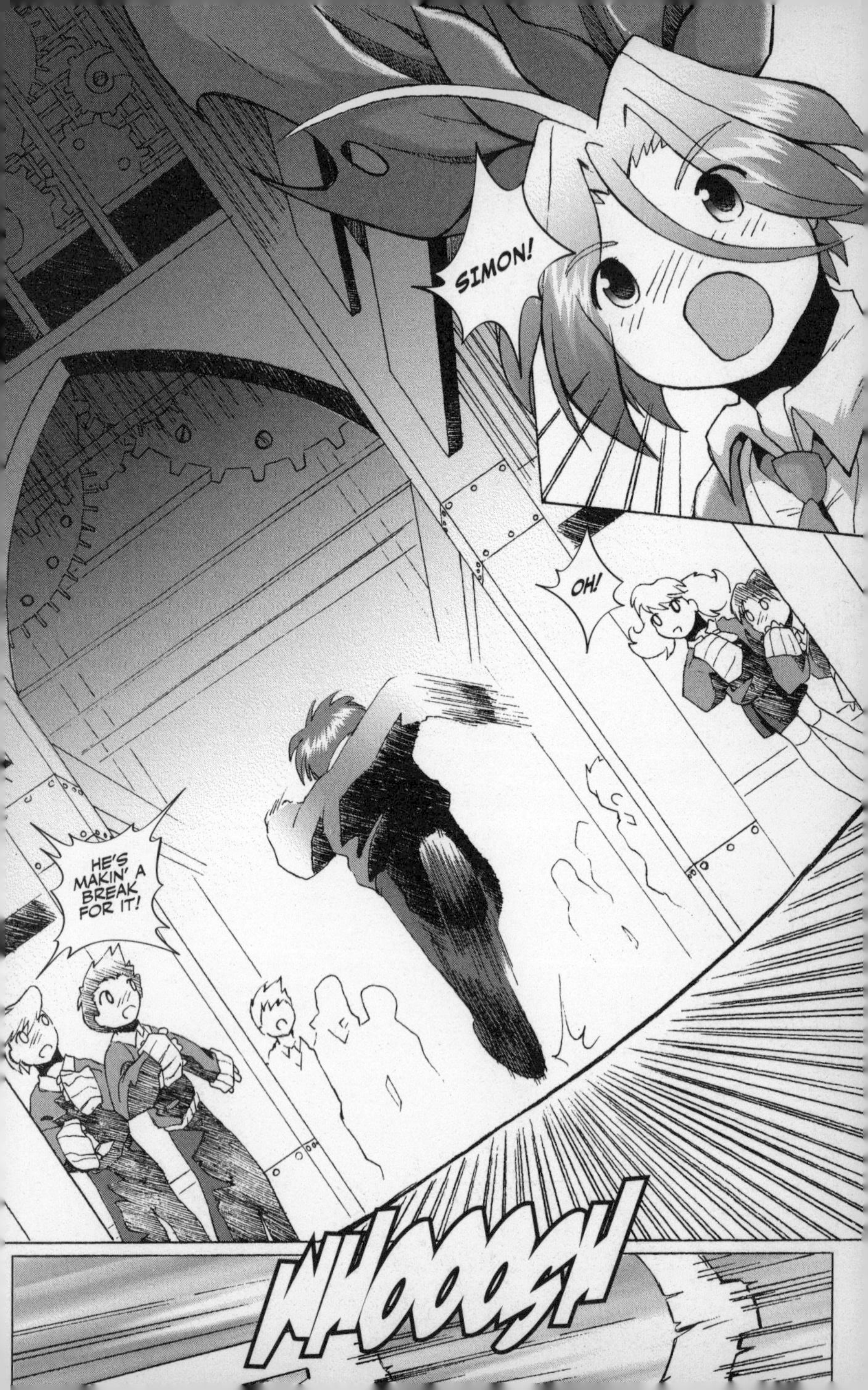
SIMON!
OH!
HE'S MAKIN' A BREAK FOR IT!
WHOOOSH

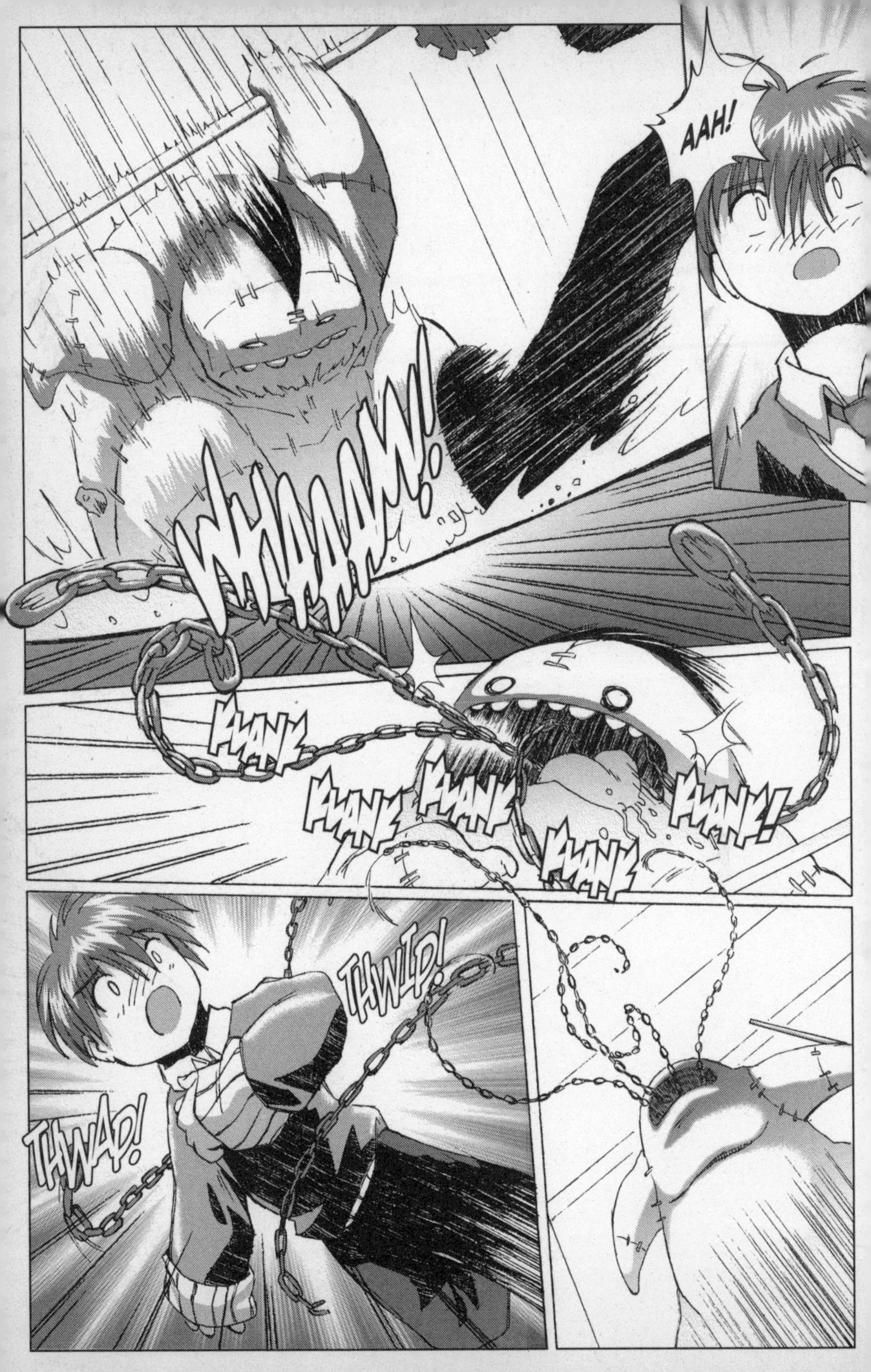
AAH!
WHAAAM!
KLANK!
KLANK
KLANK
KLANK
KLANK!
THWIP!
THWAP!

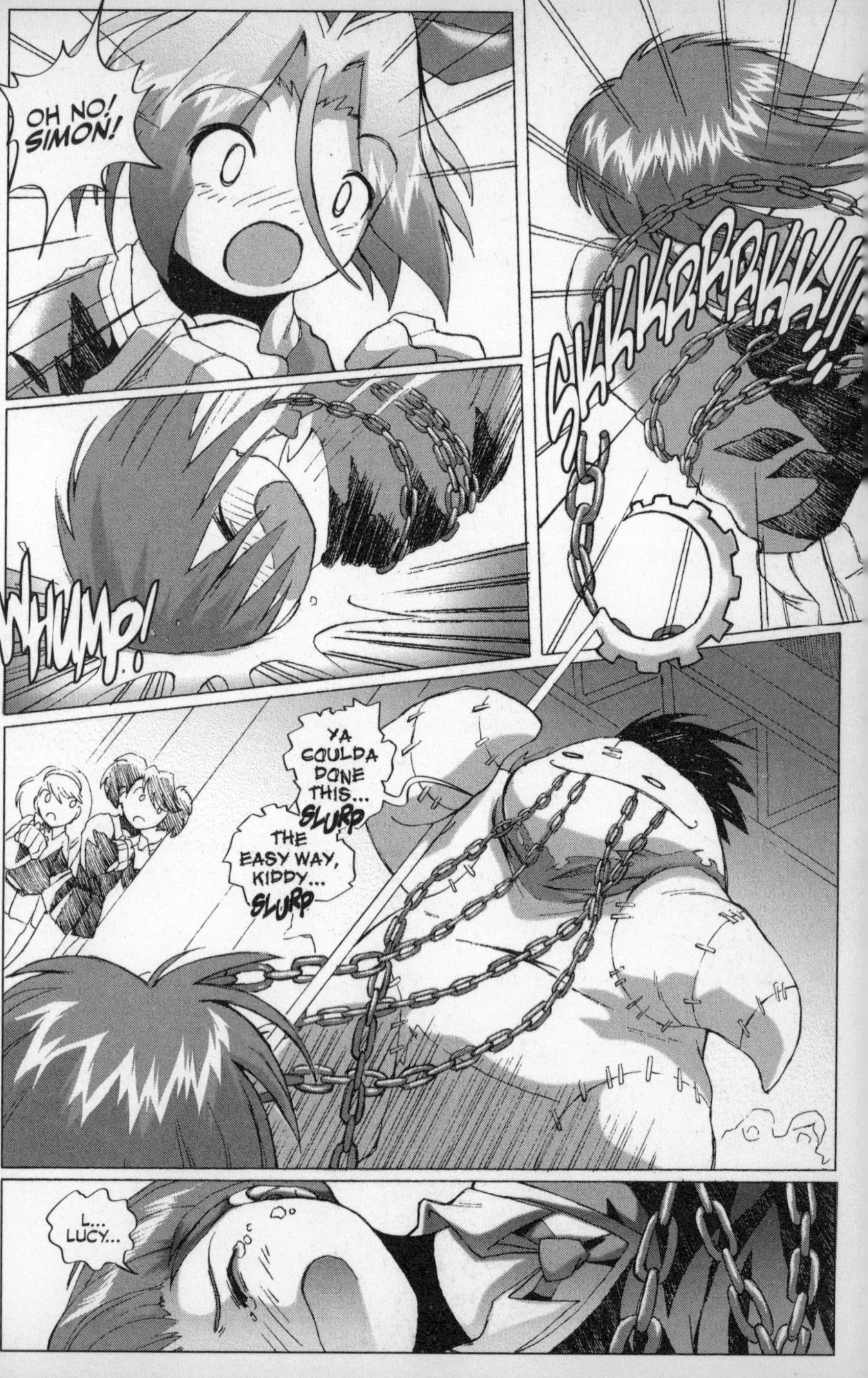
SKKKRRRKK!!
OH NO! SIMON!
WHUMP!
YA COULDA DONE THIS... SLURP
THE EASY WAY, KIDDY... SLURP
L... LUCY...

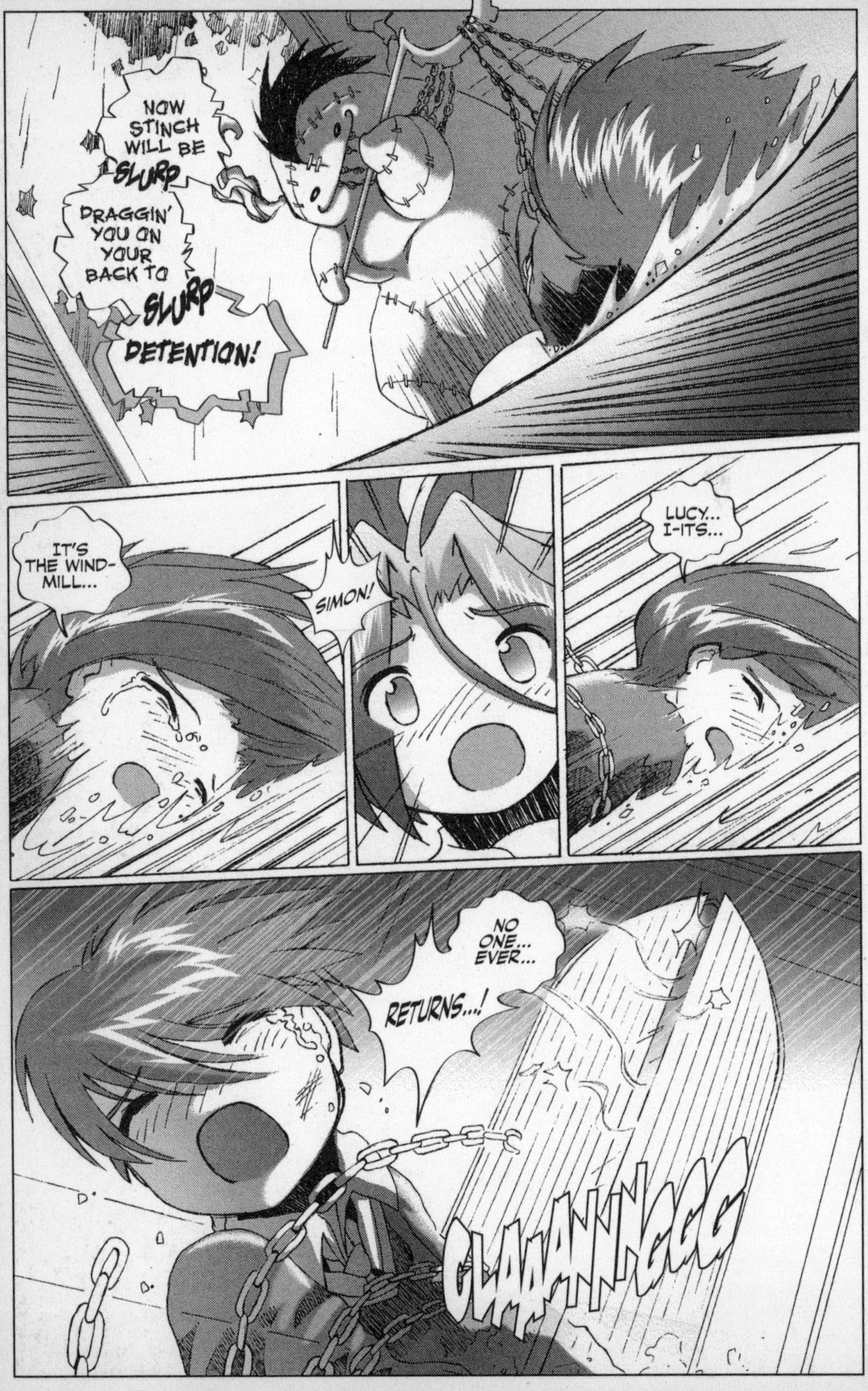
NOW STINCH WILL BE SLURP
DRAGGIN' YOU ON YOUR BACK TO SLURP DETENTION!
IT'S THE WIND-MILL...
SIMON!
LUCY... I-ITS...
NO ONE... EVER...
RETURNS...!
CLAAANNGGG

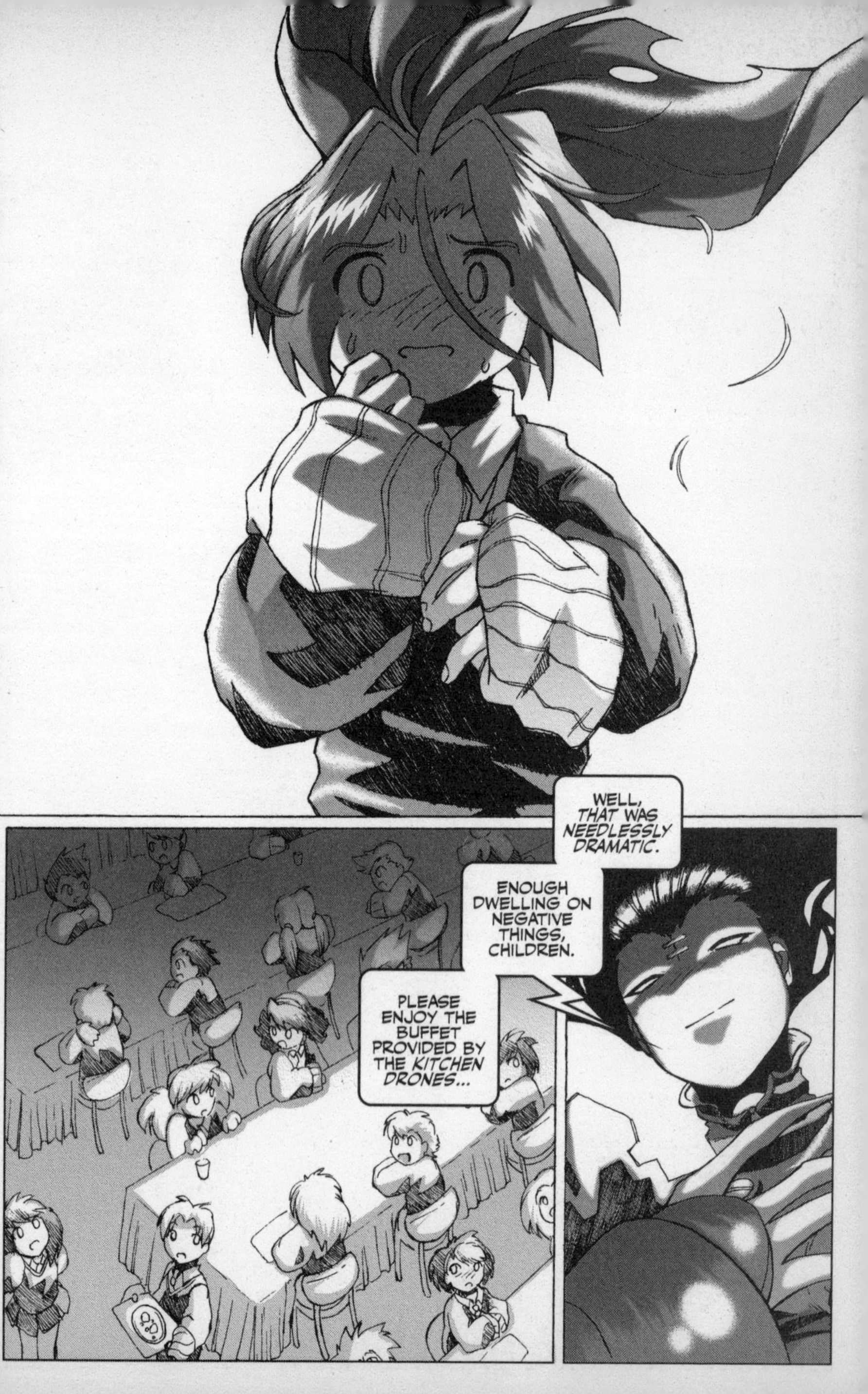
WELL, THAT WAS NEEDLESSLY DRAMATIC.
ENOUGH DWELLING ON NEGATIVE THINGS, CHILDREN.
PLEASE ENJOY THE BUFFET PROVIDED BY THE KITCHEN DRONES...

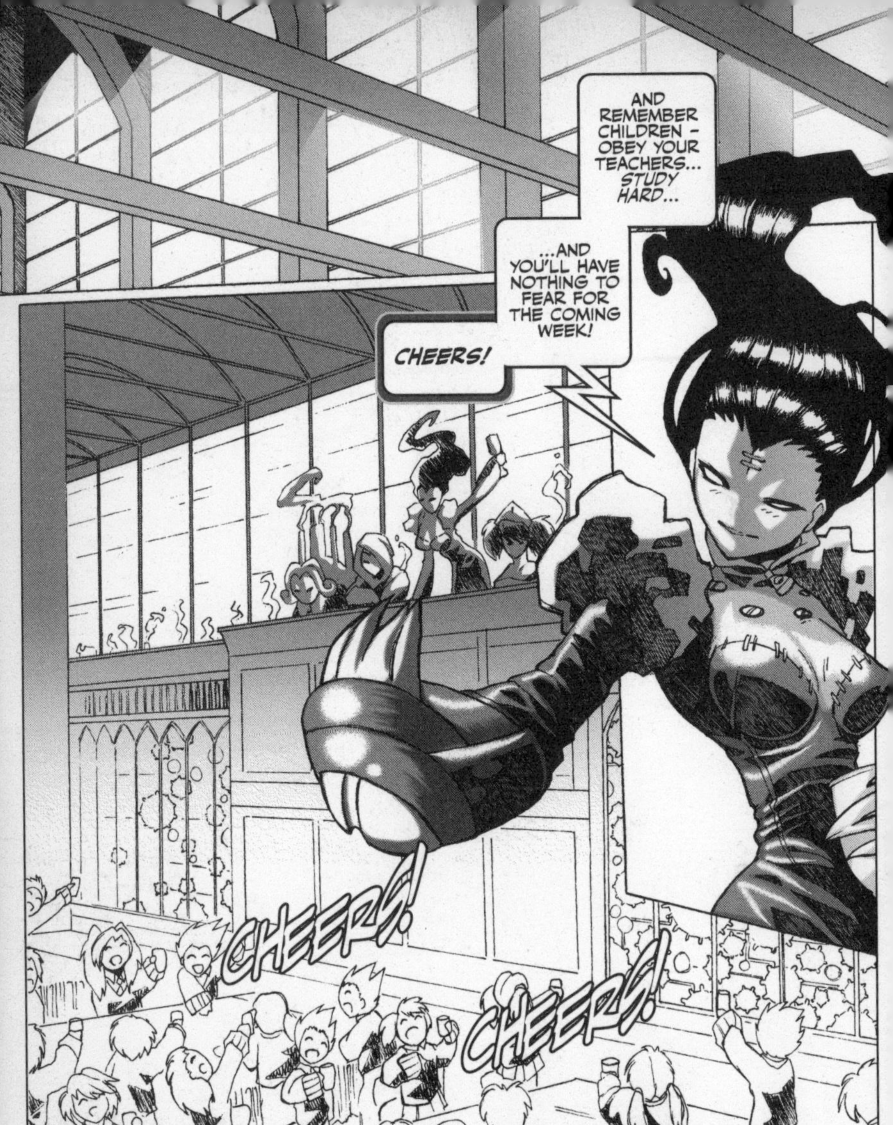
AND REMEMBER CHILDREN - OBEY YOUR TEACHERS... STUDY HARD...
...AND YOU'LL HAVE NOTHING TO FEAR FOR THE COMING WEEK!
CHEERS!
CHEERS!
CHEERS!
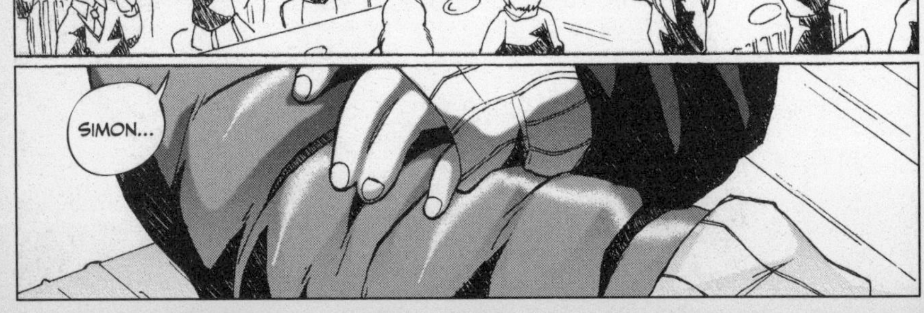
SIMON...

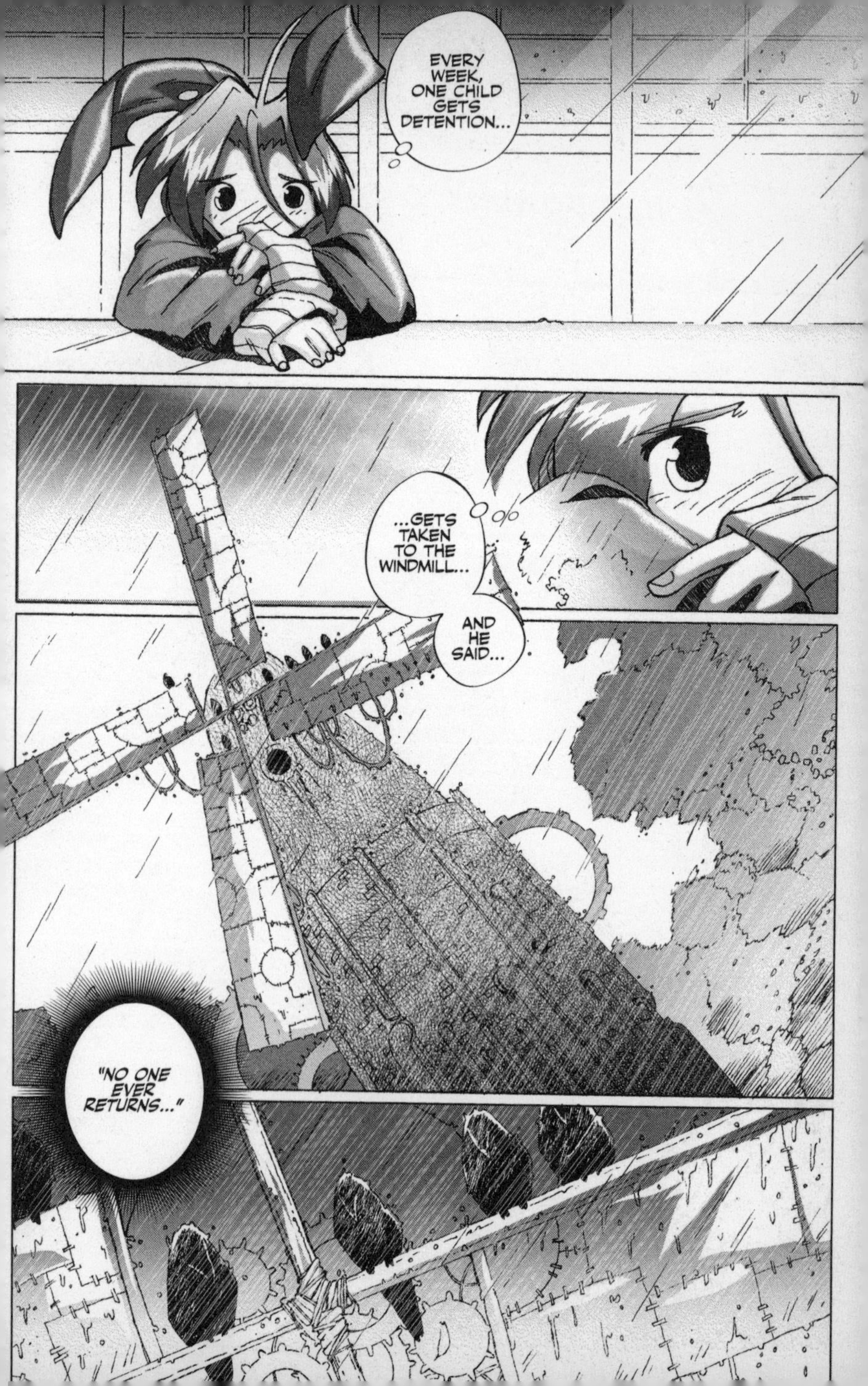
EVERY WEEK, ONE CHILD GETS DETENTION...
...GETS TAKEN TO THE WINDMILL...
AND HE SAID...
"NO ONE EVER RETURNS..."

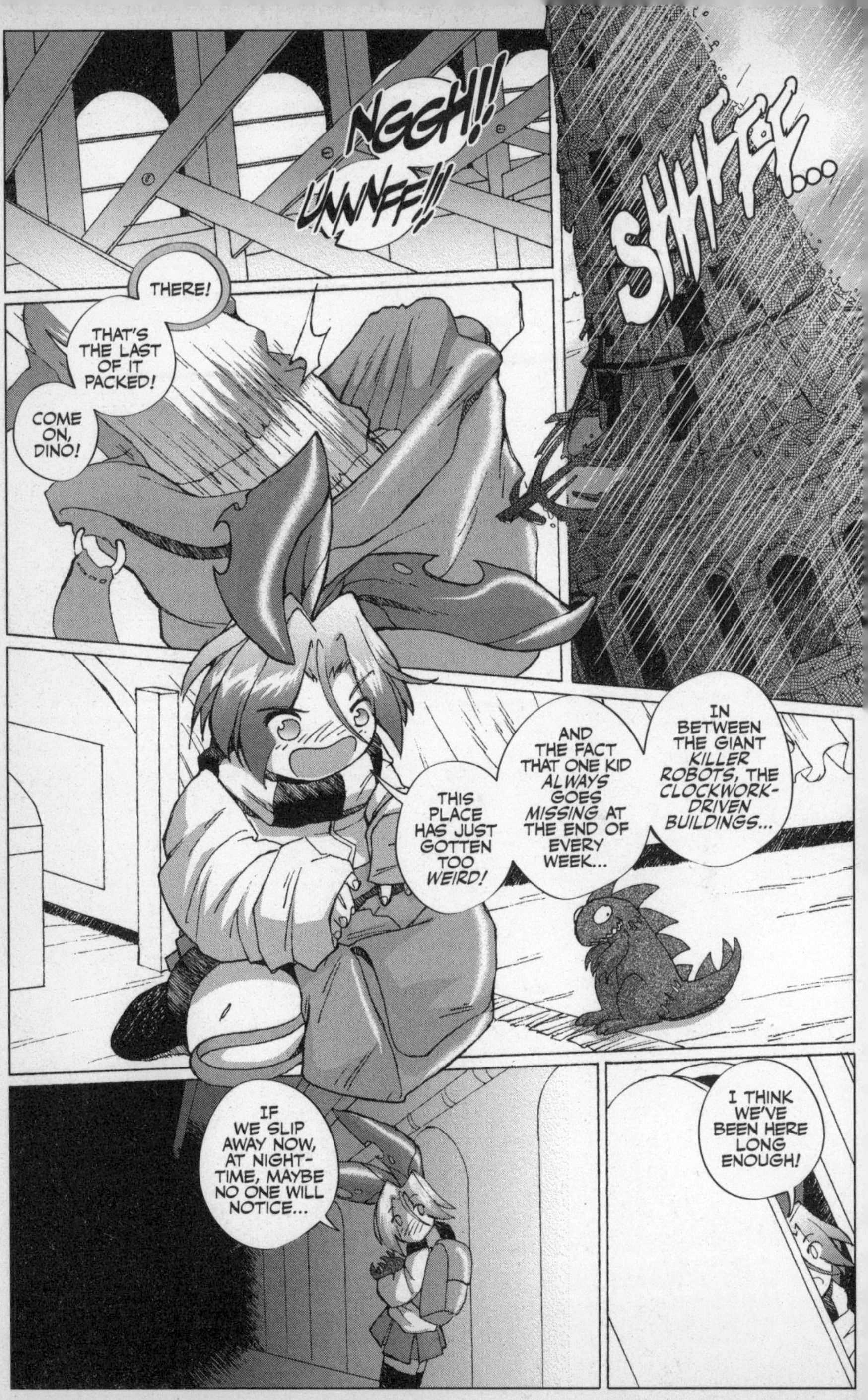
SHUFFF...
NGGH!! UNNFF!!
THERE!
THAT'S THE LAST OF IT PACKED!
COME ON, DINO!
IN BETWEEN THE GIANT *KILLER* ROBOTS, THE CLOCKWORK-DRIVEN BUILDINGS...
AND THE FACT THAT ONE KID *ALWAYS* GOES *MISSING* AT THE END OF EVERY WEEK...
THIS PLACE HAS JUST GOTTEN TOO *WEIRD!*
I THINK WE'VE BEEN HERE LONG ENOUGH!
IF WE SLIP AWAY NOW, AT NIGHT-TIME, MAYBE NO ONE WILL NOTICE...

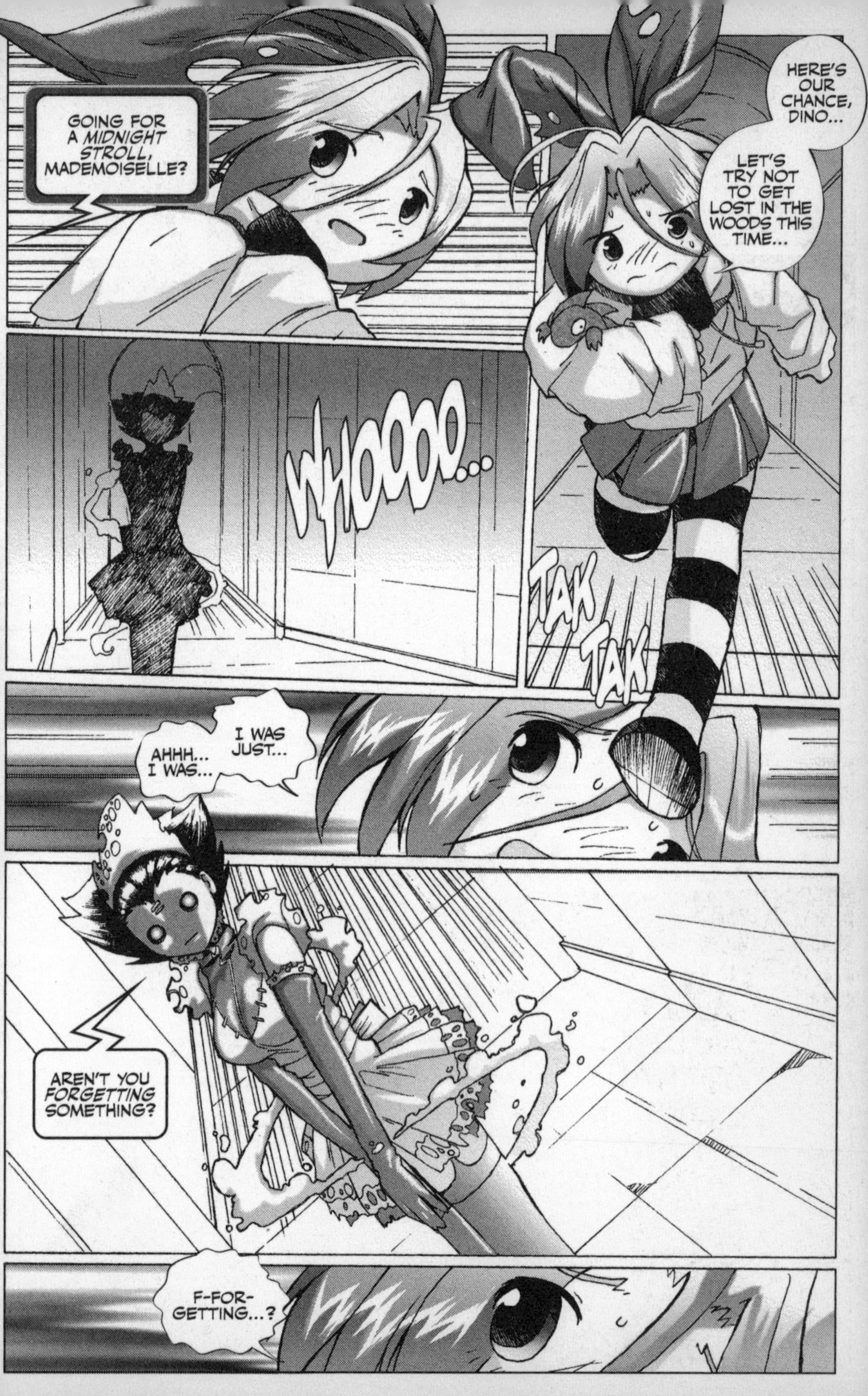
HERE'S OUR CHANCE, DINO...
LET'S TRY NOT TO GET LOST IN THE WOODS THIS TIME...
GOING FOR A *MIDNIGHT STROLL,* MADEMOISELLE?
TAK TAK
WHOOOO...
AHHH... I WAS...
I WAS JUST...
AREN'T YOU *FORGETTING* SOMETHING?
F-FOR-GETTING...?

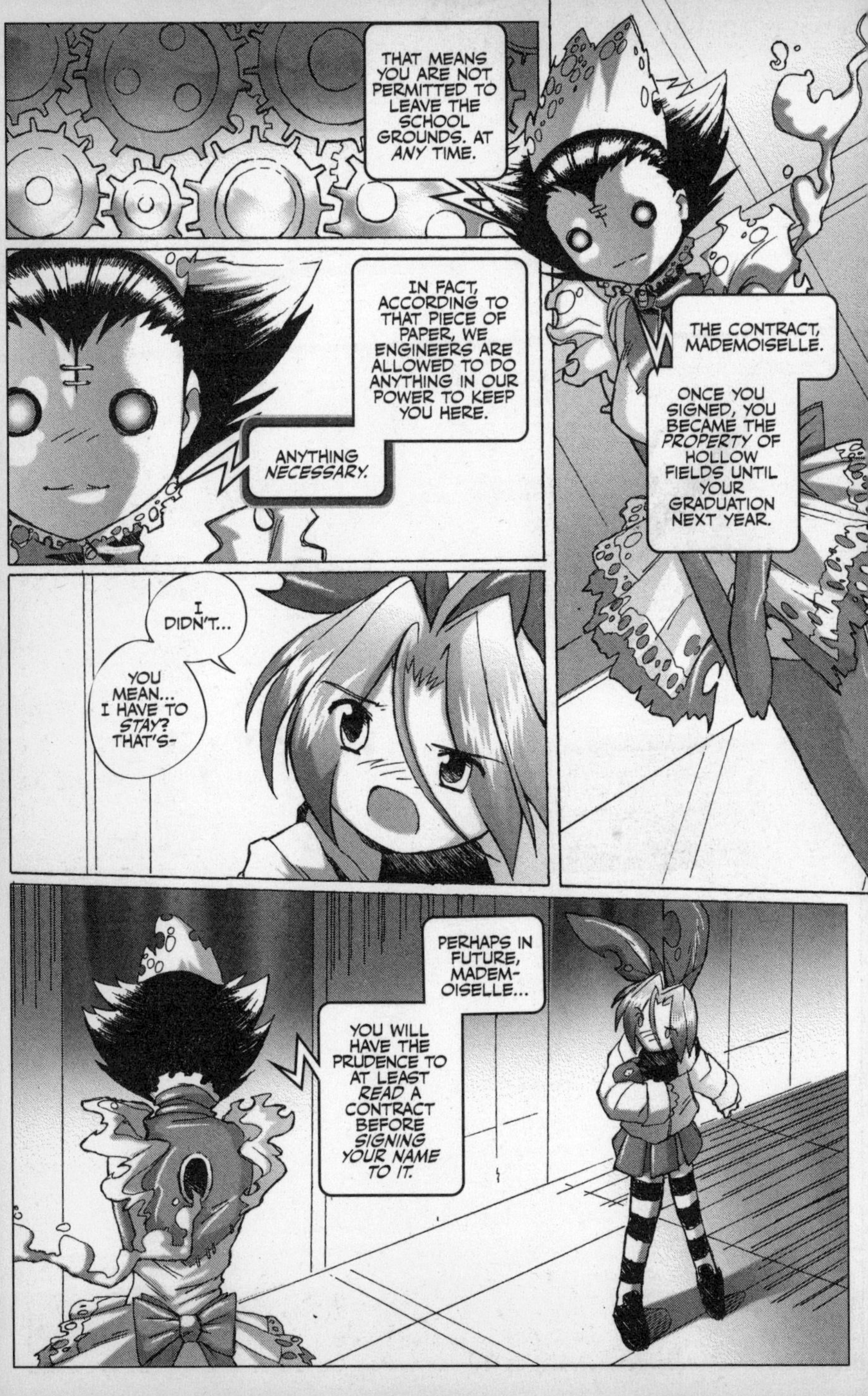
THE CONTRACT, MADEMOISELLE.
ONCE YOU SIGNED, YOU BECAME THE *PROPERTY* OF HOLLOW FIELDS UNTIL YOUR GRADUATION NEXT YEAR.
THAT MEANS YOU ARE NOT PERMITTED TO LEAVE THE SCHOOL GROUNDS. AT *ANY* TIME.
IN FACT, ACCORDING TO THAT PIECE OF PAPER, WE ENGINEERS ARE ALLOWED TO DO ANYTHING IN OUR POWER TO KEEP YOU HERE.
ANYTHING *NECESSARY.*
I DIDN'T...
YOU MEAN... I HAVE TO *STAY?* THAT'S-
PERHAPS IN FUTURE, MADEM-OISELLE...
YOU WILL HAVE THE PRUDENCE TO AT LEAST *READ* A CONTRACT BEFORE *SIGNING* *YOUR NAME* TO IT.

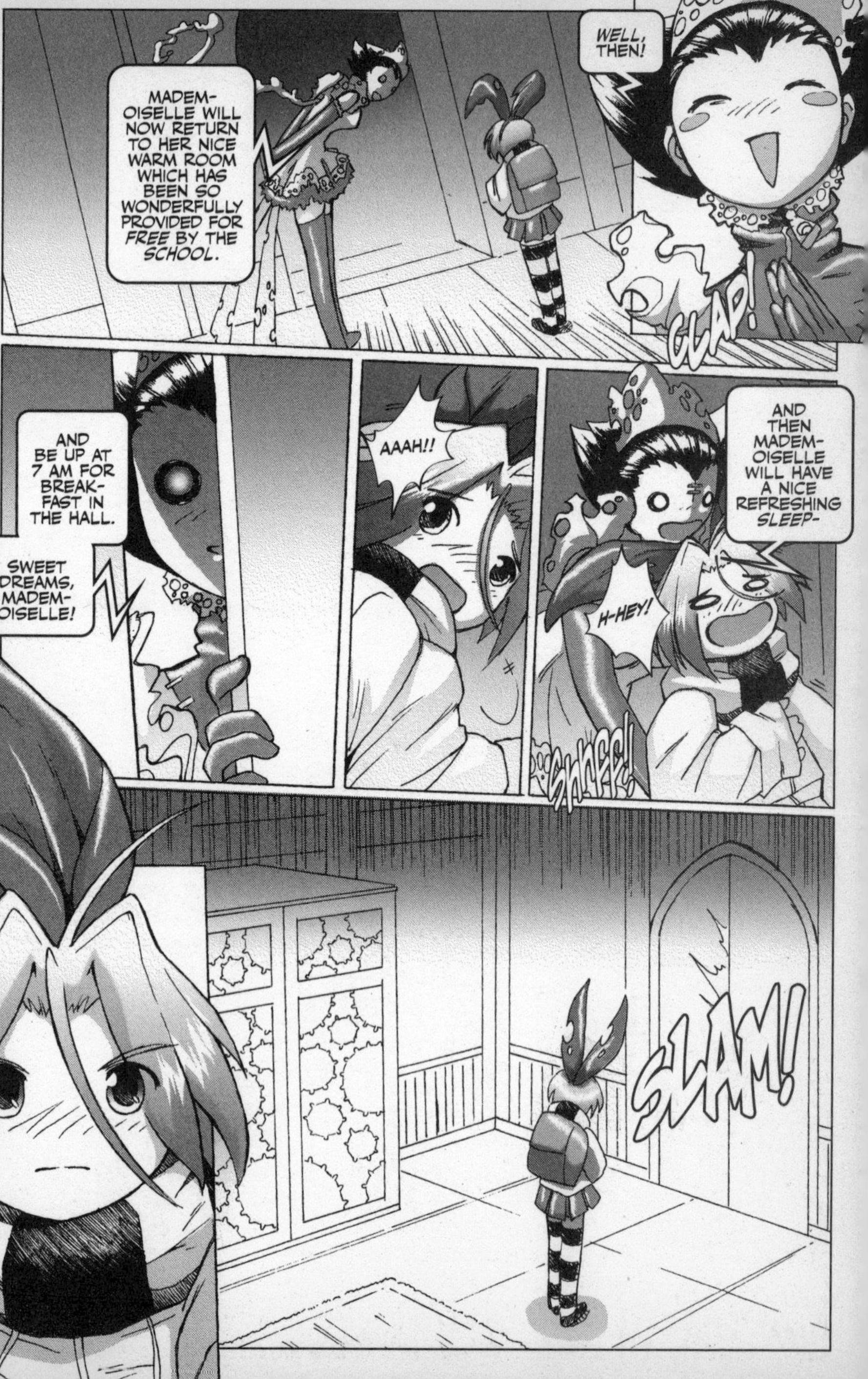
WELL, THEN!
CLAP!
MADEMOISELLE WILL NOW RETURN TO HER NICE WARM ROOM WHICH HAS BEEN SO WONDERFULLY PROVIDED FOR *FREE* BY THE *SCHOOL*.
AND THEN MADEMOISELLE WILL HAVE A NICE REFRESHING *SLEEP*-
H-HEY!
AAAH!!
AND BE UP AT 7 AM FOR BREAKFAST IN THE HALL.
SWEET DREAMS, MADEMOISELLE!
SLAM!

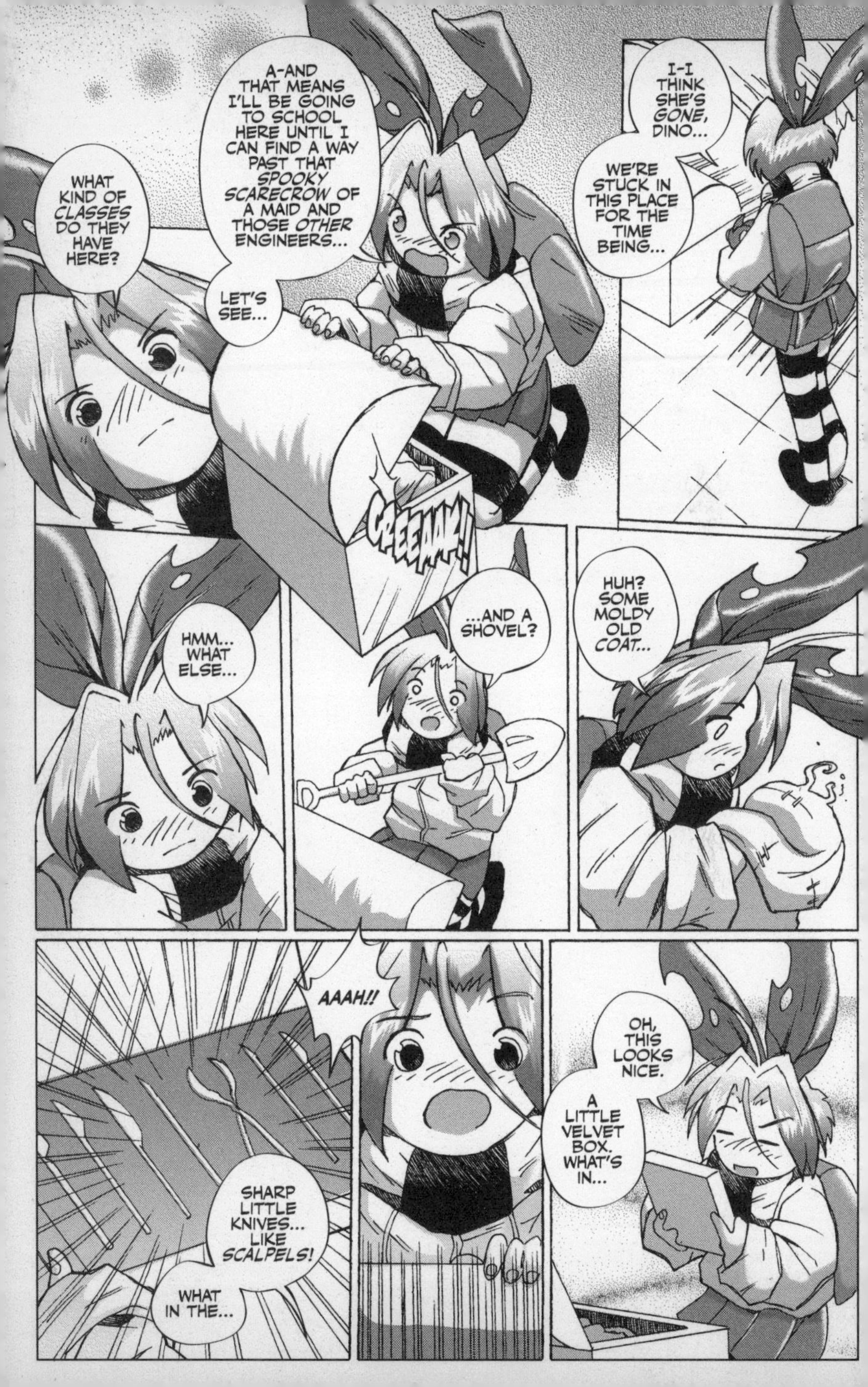
I-I THINK SHE'S GONE, DINO...
WE'RE STUCK IN THIS PLACE FOR THE TIME BEING...
A-AND THAT MEANS I'LL BE GOING TO SCHOOL HERE UNTIL I CAN FIND A WAY PAST THAT SPOOKY SCARECROW OF A MAID AND THOSE OTHER ENGINEERS...
LET'S SEE...
WHAT KIND OF CLASSES DO THEY HAVE HERE?
CREEAAK!!
HUH? SOME MOLDY OLD COAT...
...AND A SHOVEL?
HMM... WHAT ELSE...
OH, THIS LOOKS NICE.
A LITTLE VELVET BOX. WHAT'S IN...
AAAH!!
SHARP LITTLE KNIVES... LIKE SCALPELS!
WHAT IN THE...

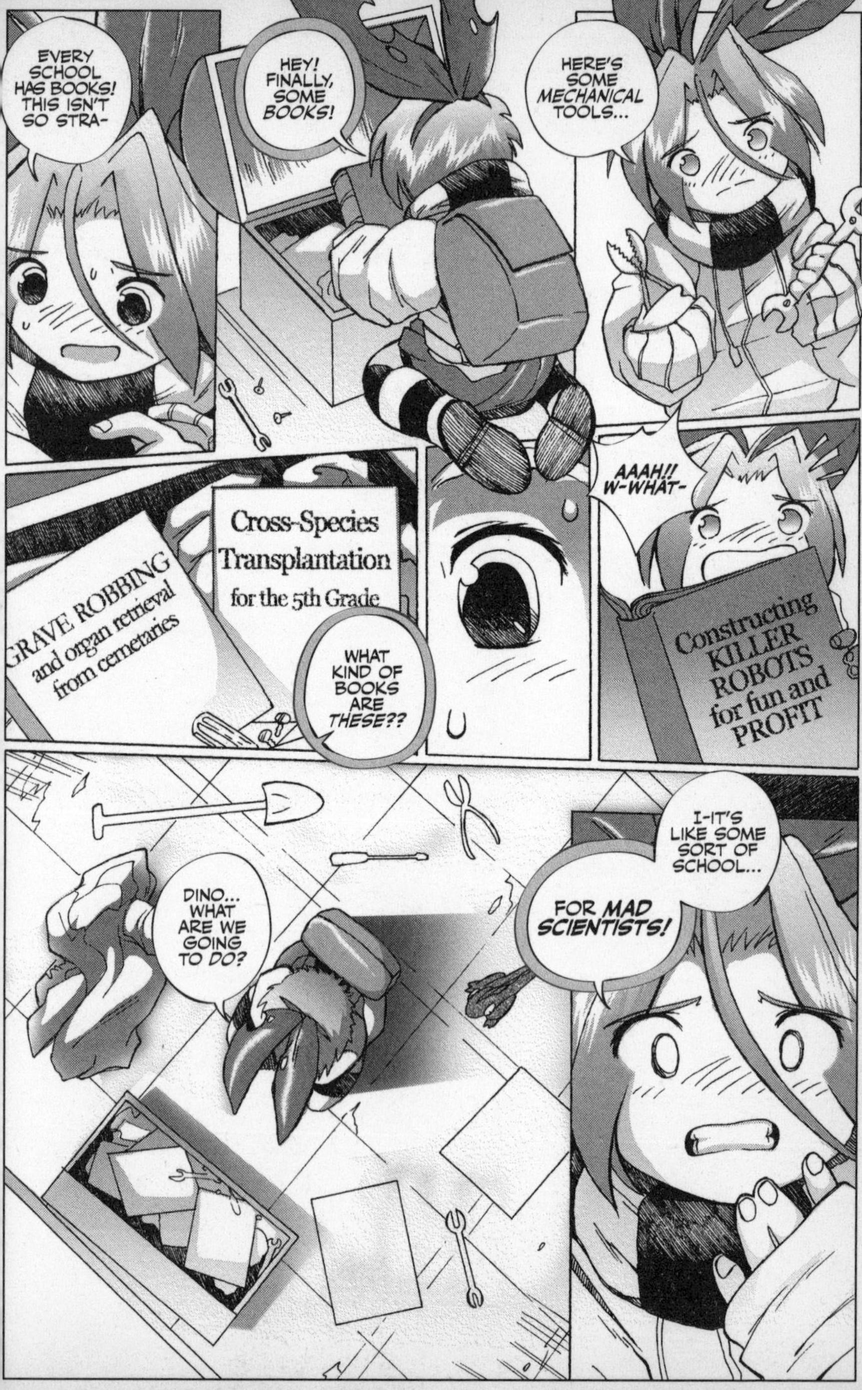
HERE'S SOME MECHANICAL TOOLS...
HEY! FINALLY, SOME BOOKS!
EVERY SCHOOL HAS BOOKS! THIS ISN'T SO STRA-
AAAH!! W-WHAT-
Constructing KILLER ROBOTS for fun and PROFIT
WHAT KIND OF BOOKS ARE THESE??
Cross-Species Transplantation for the 5th Grade
GRAVE ROBBING and organ retrieval from cemetaries
I-IT'S LIKE SOME SORT OF SCHOOL...
FOR MAD SCIENTISTS!
DINO... WHAT ARE WE GOING TO DO?

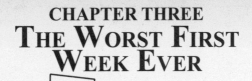

CHAPTER THREE
THE WORST FIRST WEEK EVER

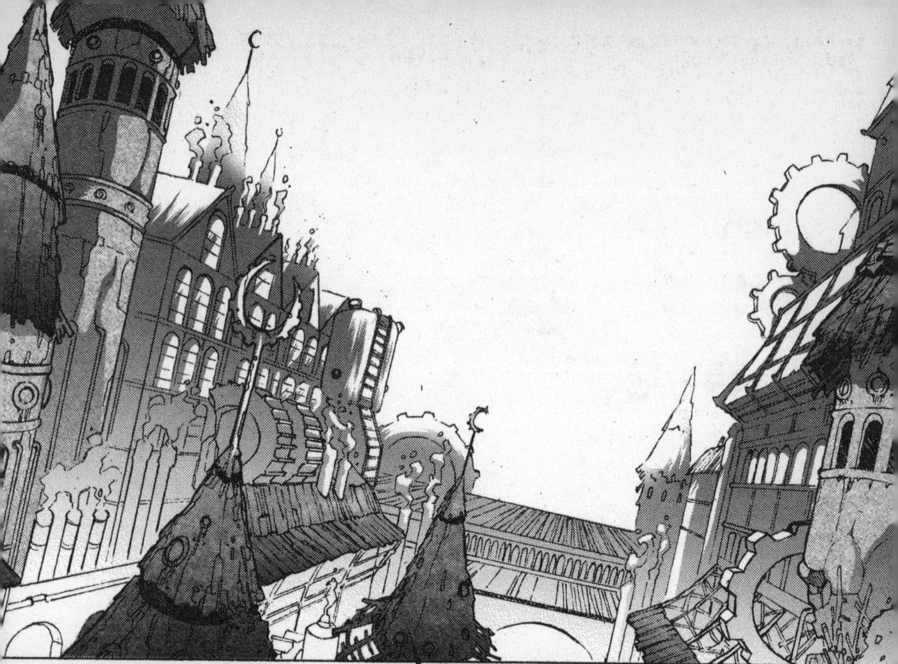

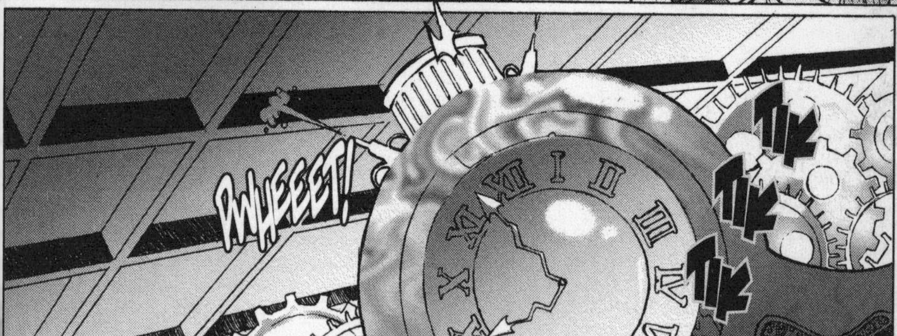
TIK
TIK
TIK
PWHEEET!

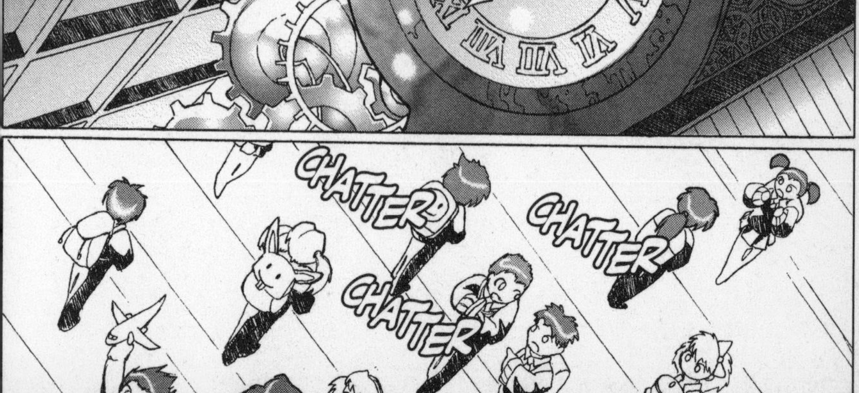
CHATTER
CHATTER
CHATTER

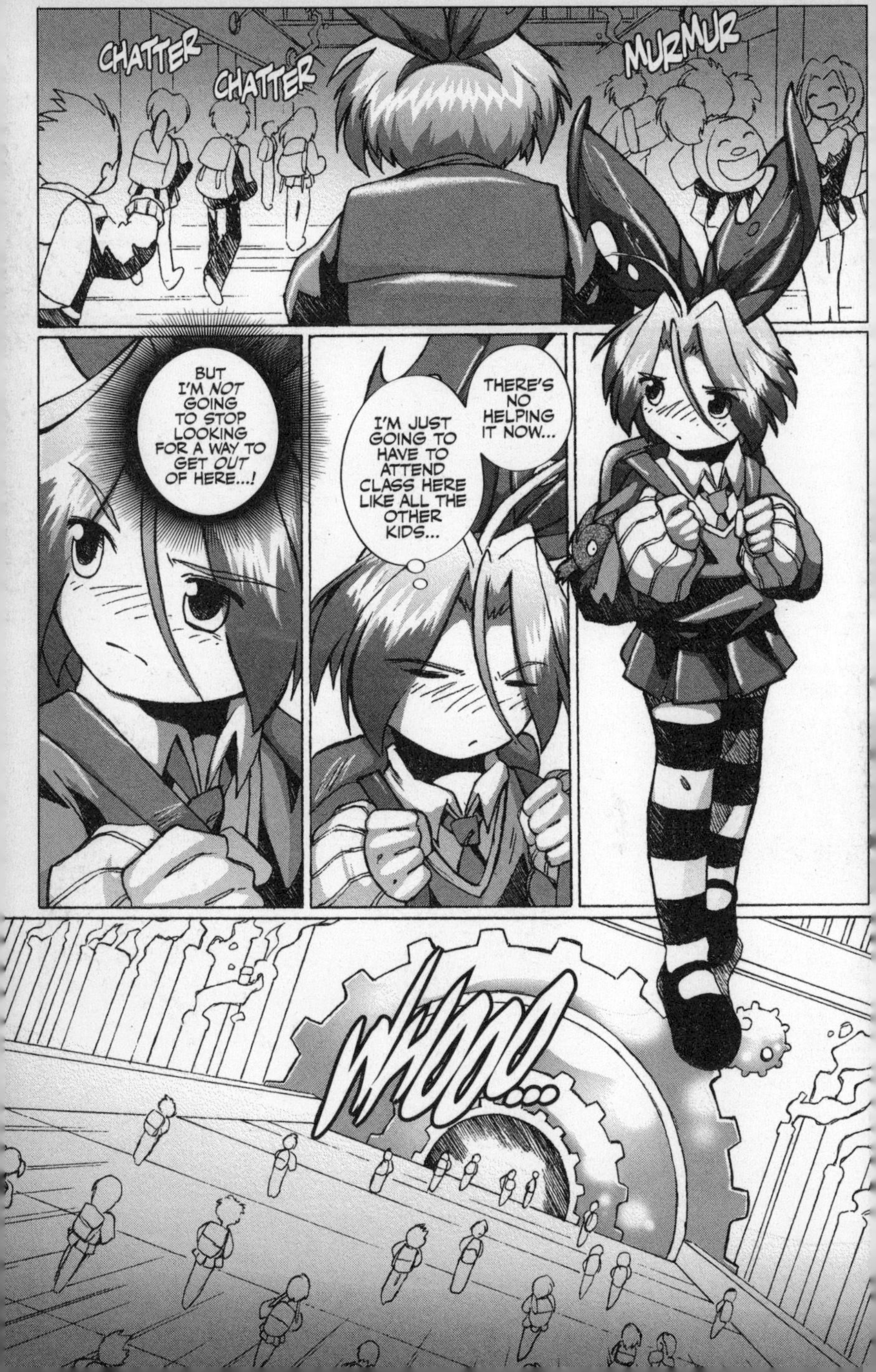
MURMUR
CHATTER
CHATTER
THERE'S NO HELPING IT NOW...
I'M JUST GOING TO HAVE TO ATTEND CLASS HERE LIKE ALL THE OTHER KIDS...
BUT I'M *NOT* GOING TO STOP LOOKING FOR A WAY TO GET *OUT* OF HERE...!
WHOO...

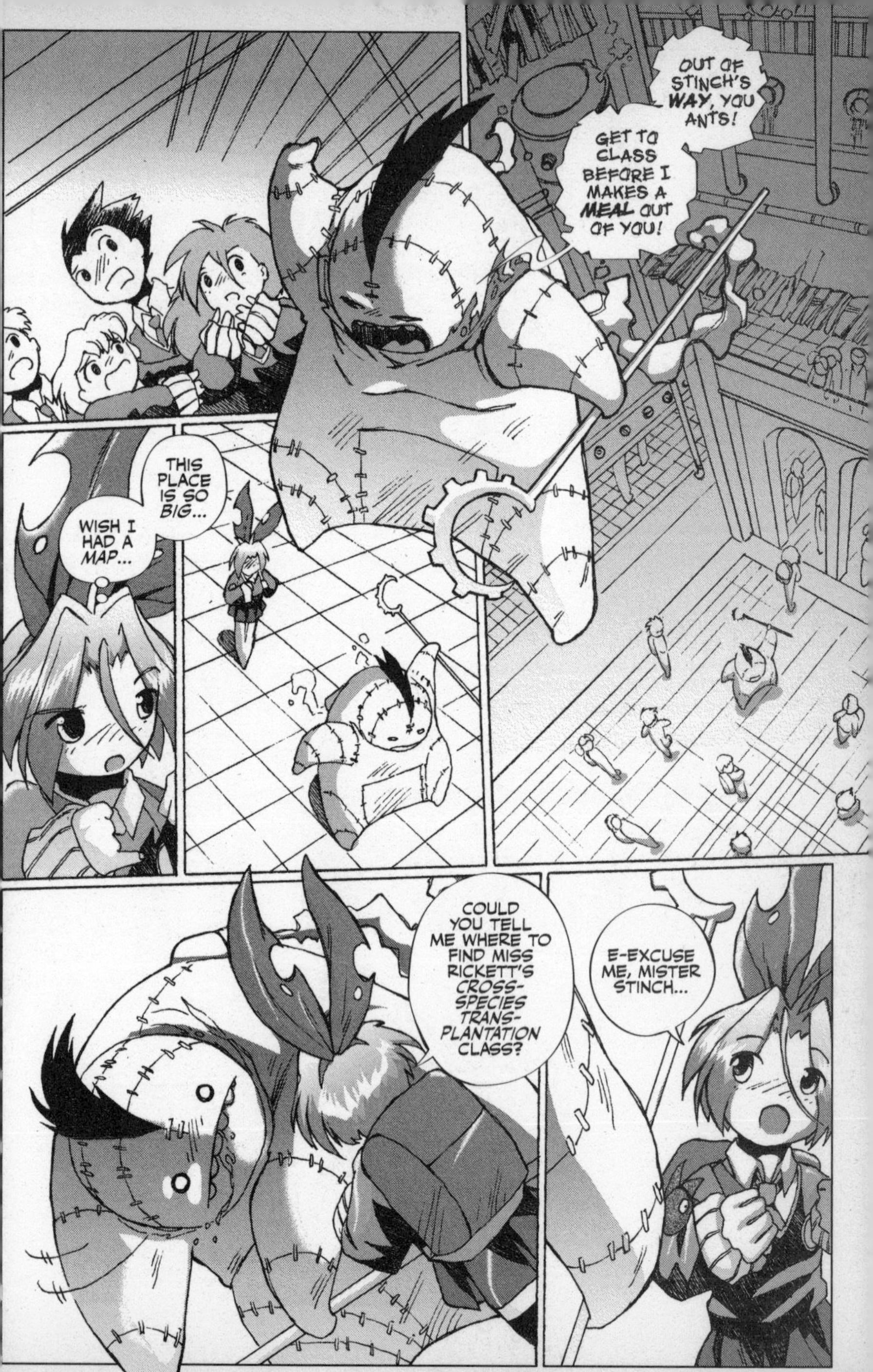
OUT OF STINCH'S **WAY**, YOU ANTS!
GET TO CLASS BEFORE I MAKES A **MEAL** OUT OF YOU!
THIS PLACE IS SO *BIG*...
WISH I HAD A *MAP*...
E-EXCUSE ME, MISTER STINCH...
COULD YOU TELL ME WHERE TO FIND MISS RICKETT'S *CROSS-SPECIES TRANS-PLANTATION* CLASS?

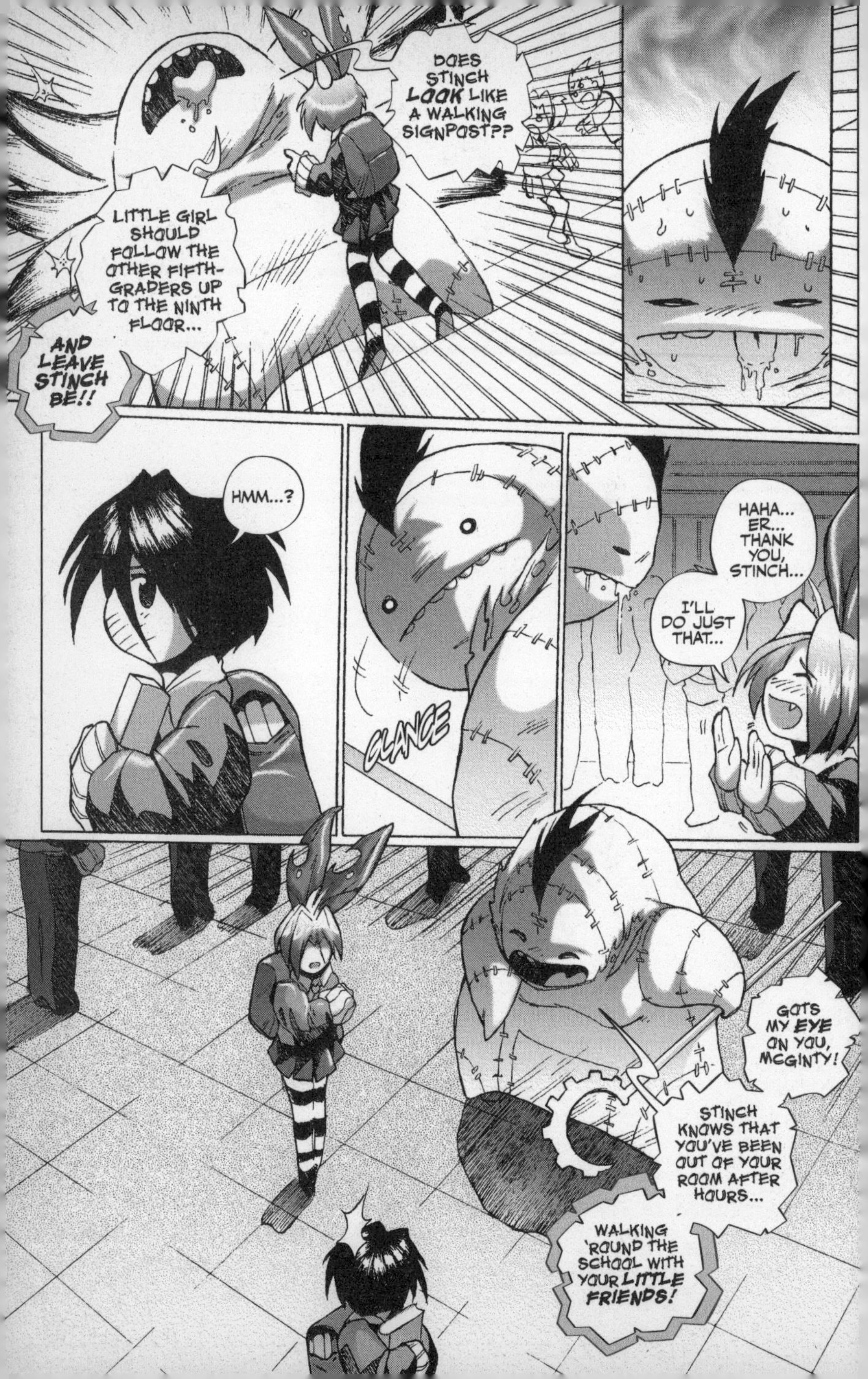
DOES STINCH LOOK LIKE A WALKING SIGNPOST??
LITTLE GIRL SHOULD FOLLOW THE OTHER FIFTH-GRADERS UP TO THE NINTH FLOOR...
AND LEAVE STINCH BE!!
HMM...?
GLANCE
HAHA... ER... THANK YOU, STINCH...
I'LL DO JUST THAT...
GOTS MY EYE ON YOU, MCGINTY!
STINCH KNOWS THAT YOU'VE BEEN OUT OF YOUR ROOM AFTER HOURS...
WALKING 'ROUND THE SCHOOL WITH YOUR LITTLE FRIENDS!

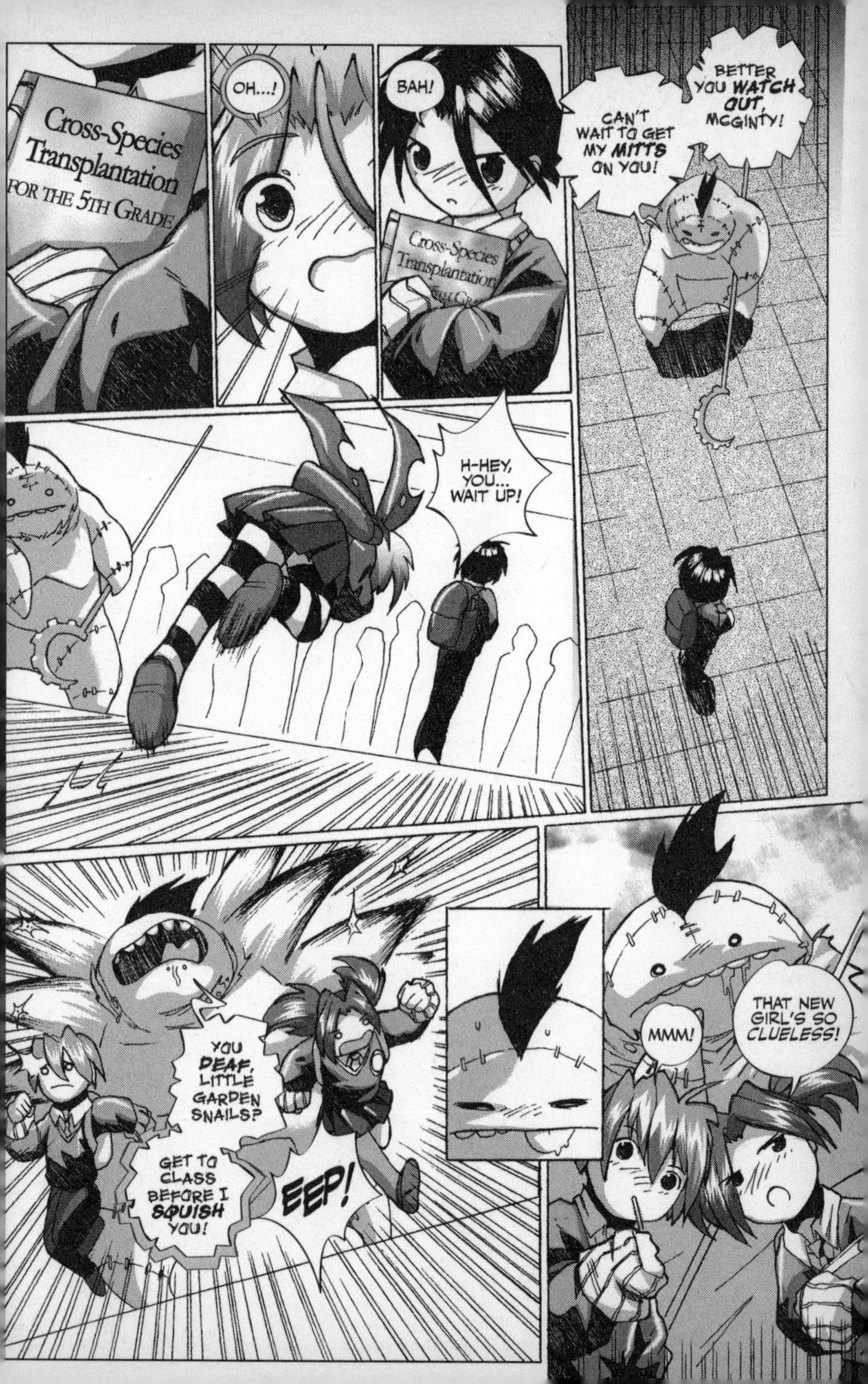
Cross-Species Transplantation FOR THE 5TH GRADE
OH...!
BAH!
Cross-Species Transplantation
H-HEY, YOU... WAIT UP!
BETTER YOU WATCH OUT, MCGINTY!
CAN'T WAIT TO GET MY MITTS ON YOU!
YOU DEAF, LITTLE GARDEN SNAILS?
GET TO CLASS BEFORE I SQUISH YOU!
EEP!
MMM!
THAT NEW GIRL'S SO CLUELESS!

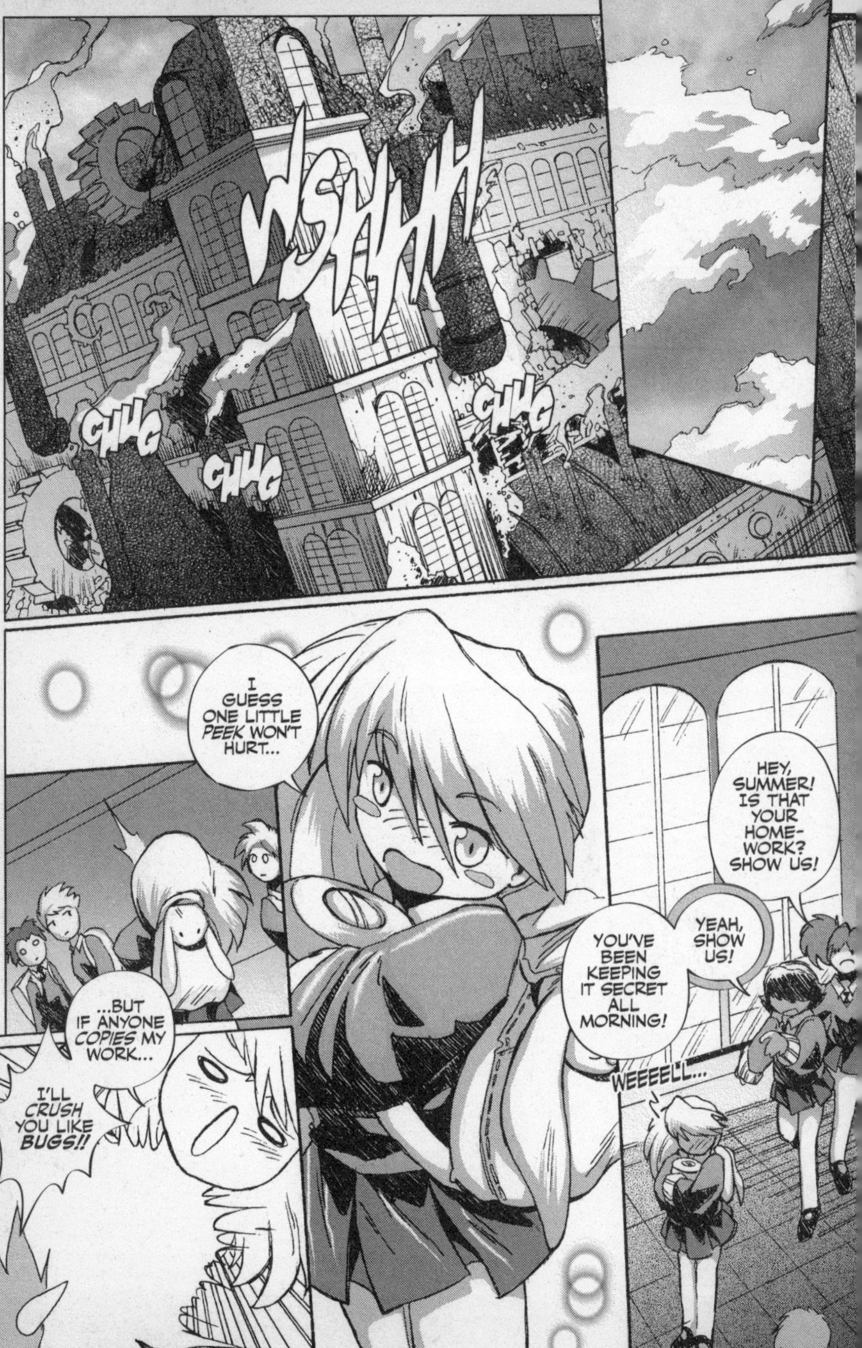
WSHAAH
CHUG
CHUG
CHUG
HEY, SUMMER! IS THAT YOUR HOME-WORK? SHOW US!
YEAH, SHOW US!
YOU'VE BEEN KEEPING IT SECRET ALL MORNING!
WEEEELL...
I GUESS ONE LITTLE PEEK WON'T HURT...
...BUT IF ANYONE COPIES MY WORK...
I'LL CRUSH YOU LIKE BUGS!!

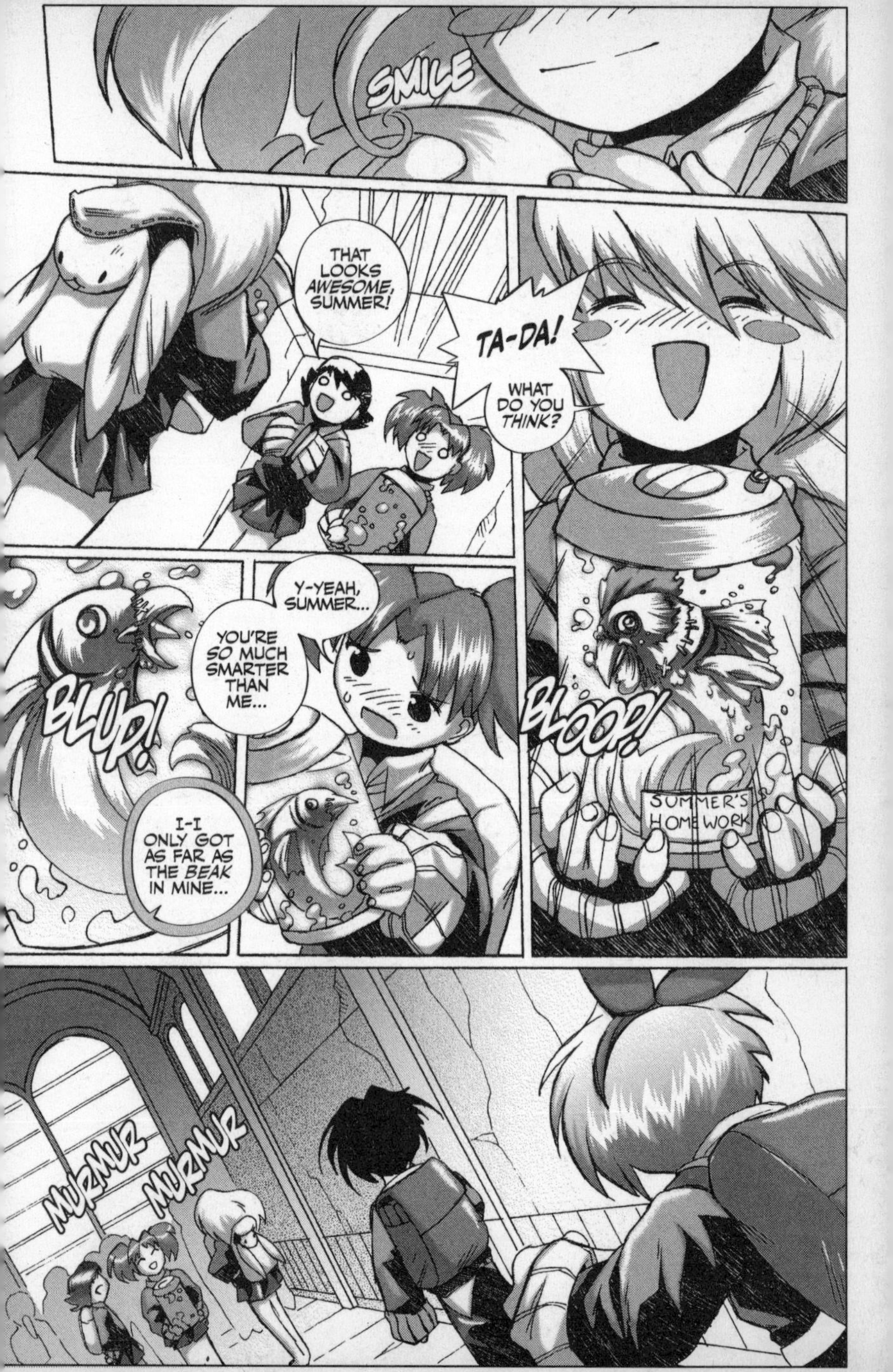
SMILE
TA-DA!
WHAT DO YOU THINK?
THAT LOOKS *AWESOME*, SUMMER!
BLOOP!
SUMMER'S HOMEWORK
Y-YEAH, SUMMER...
YOU'RE SO MUCH SMARTER THAN ME...
BLUP!
I-I ONLY GOT AS FAR AS THE *BEAK* IN MINE...
MURMUR
MURMUR

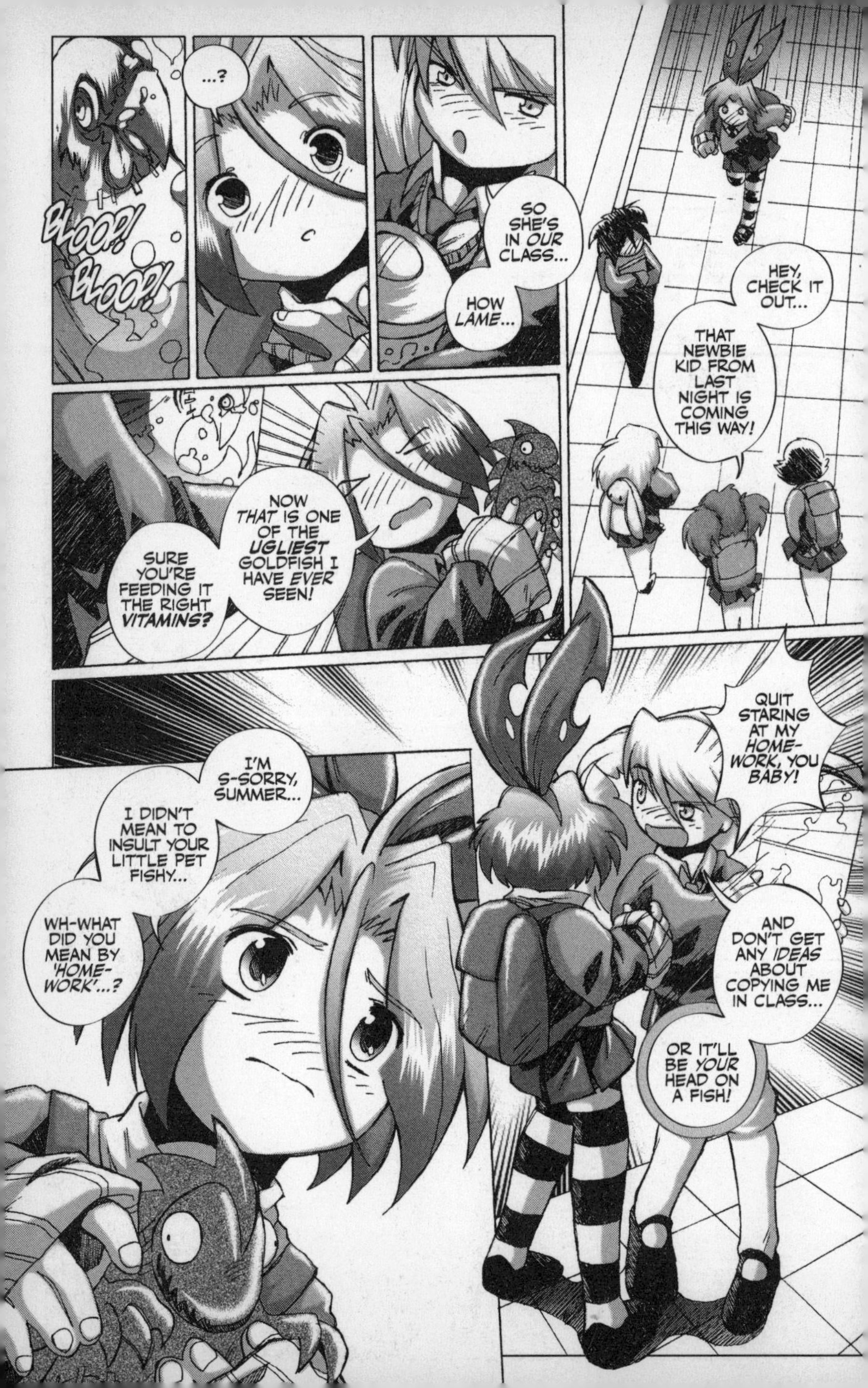
HEY, CHECK IT OUT...
THAT NEWBIE KID FROM LAST NIGHT IS COMING THIS WAY!
SO SHE'S IN *OUR* CLASS...
HOW *LAME*...
...?
BLOOP! BLOOP!
NOW *THAT* IS ONE OF THE ***UGLIEST*** GOLDFISH I HAVE *EVER* SEEN!
SURE YOU'RE FEEDING IT THE RIGHT ***VITAMINS?***
QUIT STARING AT MY *HOME-WORK*, YOU *BABY!*
AND DON'T GET ANY *IDEAS* ABOUT COPYING ME IN CLASS...
OR IT'LL BE *YOUR* HEAD ON A FISH!
I'M S-SORRY, SUMMER...
I DIDN'T MEAN TO INSULT YOUR LITTLE PET FISHY...
WH-WHAT DID YOU MEAN BY *'HOME-WORK'*...?

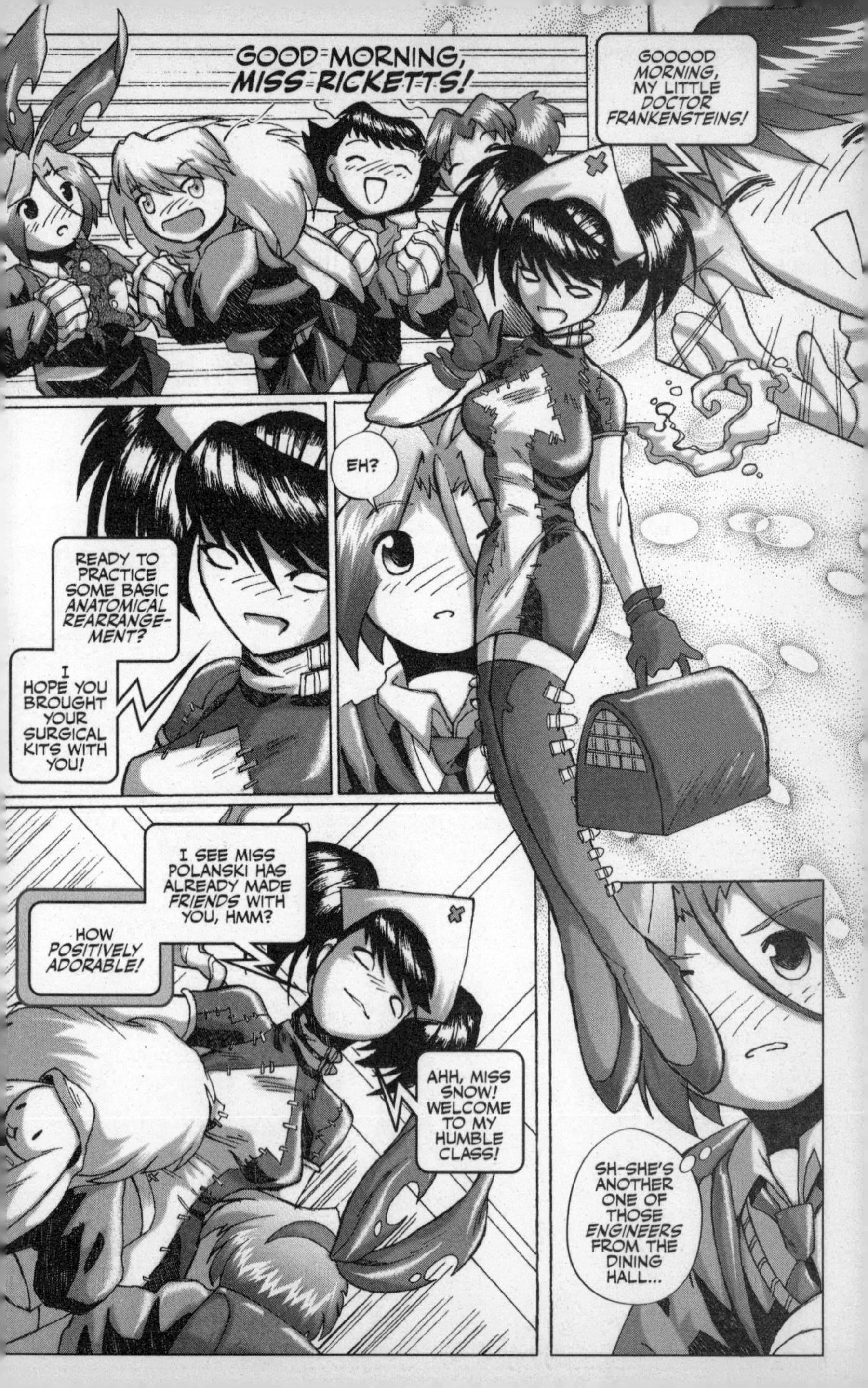
GOOD MORNING, MISS RICKETTS!
GOOOOD MORNING, MY LITTLE DOCTOR FRANKENSTEINS!
READY TO PRACTICE SOME BASIC ANATOMICAL REARRANGE-MENT?
I HOPE YOU BROUGHT YOUR SURGICAL KITS WITH YOU!
EH?
I SEE MISS POLANSKI HAS ALREADY MADE FRIENDS WITH YOU, HMM?
HOW POSITIVELY ADORABLE!
AHH, MISS SNOW! WELCOME TO MY HUMBLE CLASS!
SH-SHE'S ANOTHER ONE OF THOSE ENGINEERS FROM THE DINING HALL...

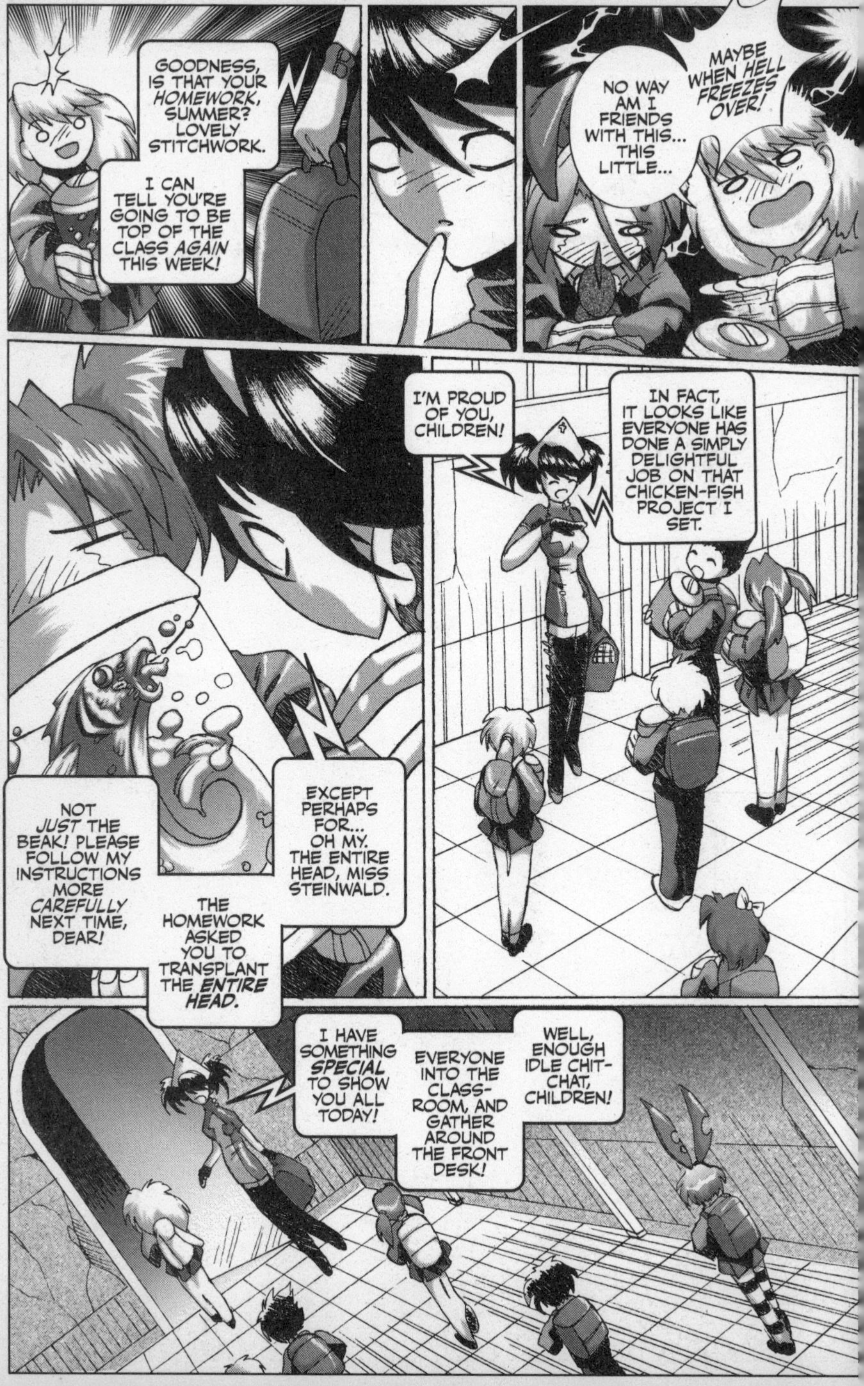
NO WAY AM I FRIENDS WITH THIS... THIS LITTLE...
MAYBE WHEN *HELL FREEZES OVER!*
GOODNESS, IS THAT YOUR *HOMEWORK*, SUMMER? LOVELY STITCHWORK.
I CAN TELL YOU'RE GOING TO BE TOP OF THE CLASS *AGAIN* THIS WEEK!
I'M PROUD OF YOU, CHILDREN!
IN FACT, IT LOOKS LIKE EVERYONE HAS DONE A SIMPLY DELIGHTFUL JOB ON THAT CHICKEN-FISH PROJECT I SET.
EXCEPT PERHAPS FOR... OH MY. THE ENTIRE HEAD, MISS STEINWALD.
NOT *JUST* THE BEAK! PLEASE FOLLOW MY INSTRUCTIONS MORE *CAREFULLY* NEXT TIME, DEAR!
THE HOMEWORK ASKED YOU TO TRANSPLANT THE *ENTIRE HEAD*.
WELL, ENOUGH IDLE CHIT-CHAT, CHILDREN!
EVERYONE INTO THE CLASS-ROOM, AND GATHER AROUND THE FRONT DESK!
I HAVE SOMETHING *SPECIAL* TO SHOW YOU ALL TODAY!

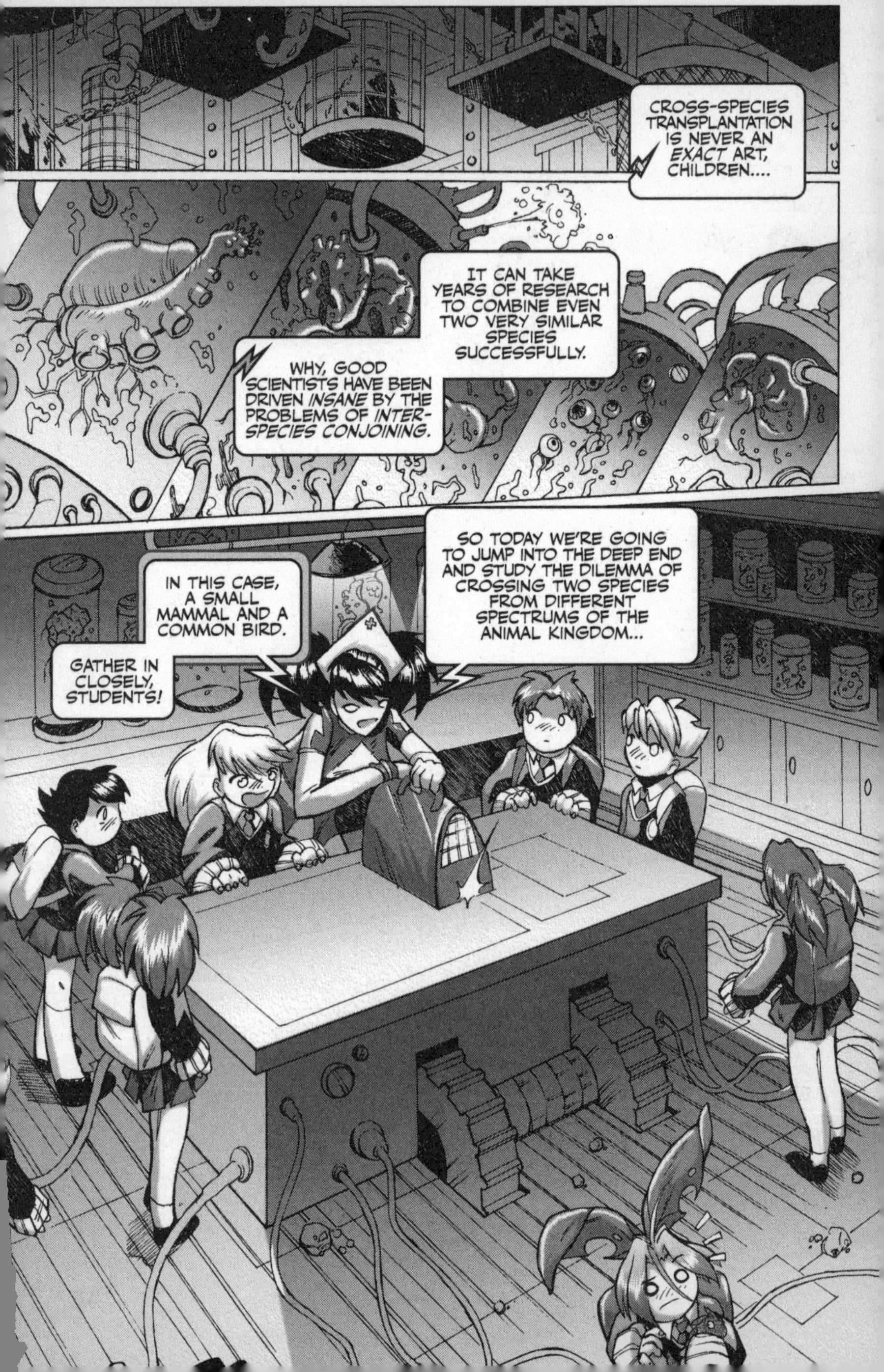
CROSS-SPECIES TRANSPLANTATION IS NEVER AN *EXACT* ART, CHILDREN....
IT CAN TAKE YEARS OF RESEARCH TO COMBINE EVEN TWO VERY SIMILAR SPECIES SUCCESSFULLY.
WHY, GOOD SCIENTISTS HAVE BEEN DRIVEN *INSANE* BY THE PROBLEMS OF *INTER-SPECIES CONJOINING.*
SO TODAY WE'RE GOING TO JUMP INTO THE DEEP END AND STUDY THE DILEMMA OF CROSSING TWO SPECIES FROM DIFFERENT SPECTRUMS OF THE ANIMAL KINGDOM...
IN THIS CASE, A SMALL MAMMAL AND A COMMON BIRD.
GATHER IN CLOSELY, STUDENTS!

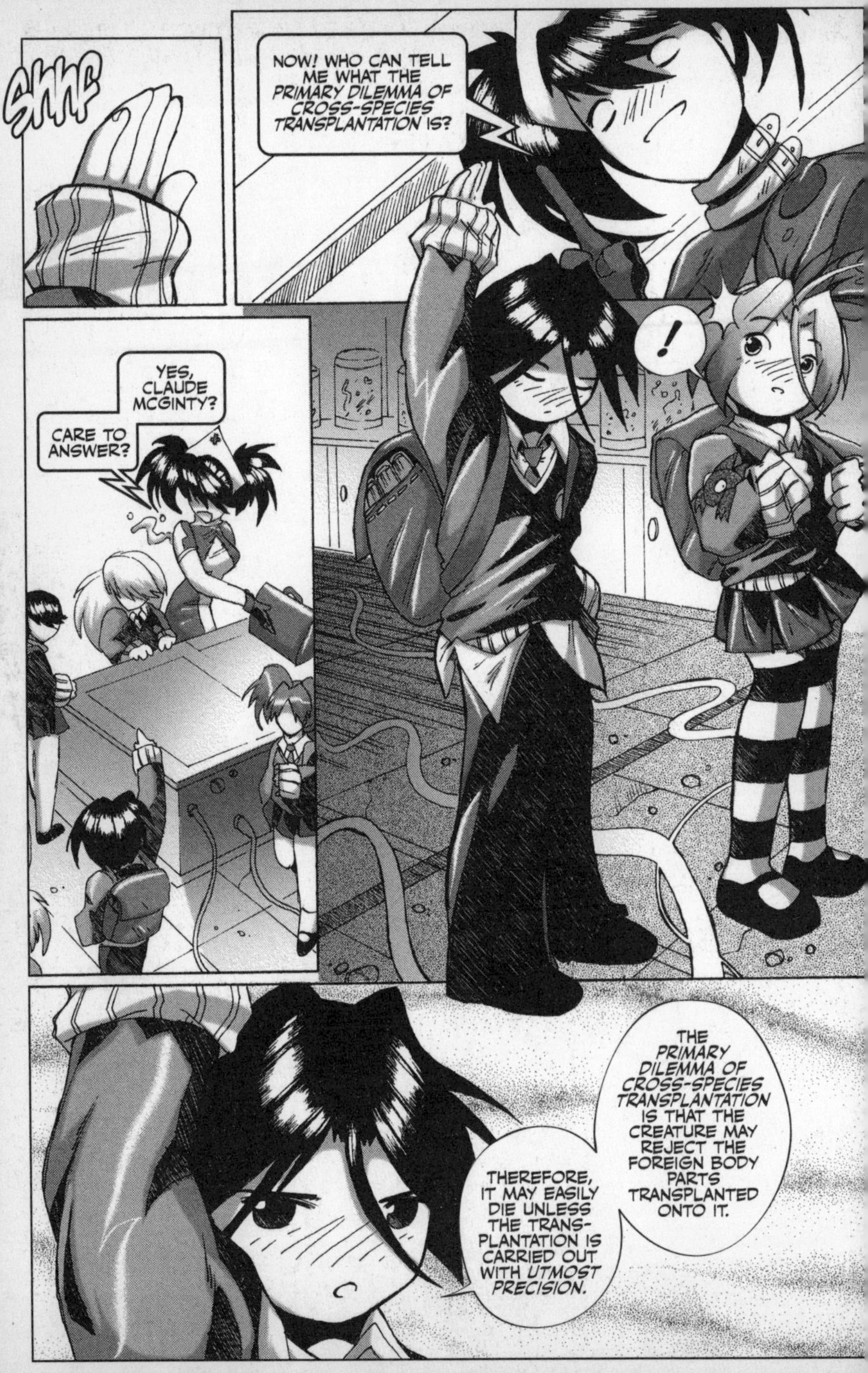
NOW! WHO CAN TELL ME WHAT THE *PRIMARY DILEMMA OF CROSS-SPECIES TRANSPLANTATION* IS?
SHHF
!
YES, CLAUDE MCGINTY?
CARE TO ANSWER?
THE *PRIMARY DILEMMA OF CROSS-SPECIES TRANSPLANTATION* IS THAT THE CREATURE MAY REJECT THE FOREIGN BODY PARTS TRANSPLANTED ONTO IT.
THEREFORE, IT MAY EASILY DIE UNLESS THE TRANS-PLANTATION IS CARRIED OUT WITH *UTMOST PRECISION.*

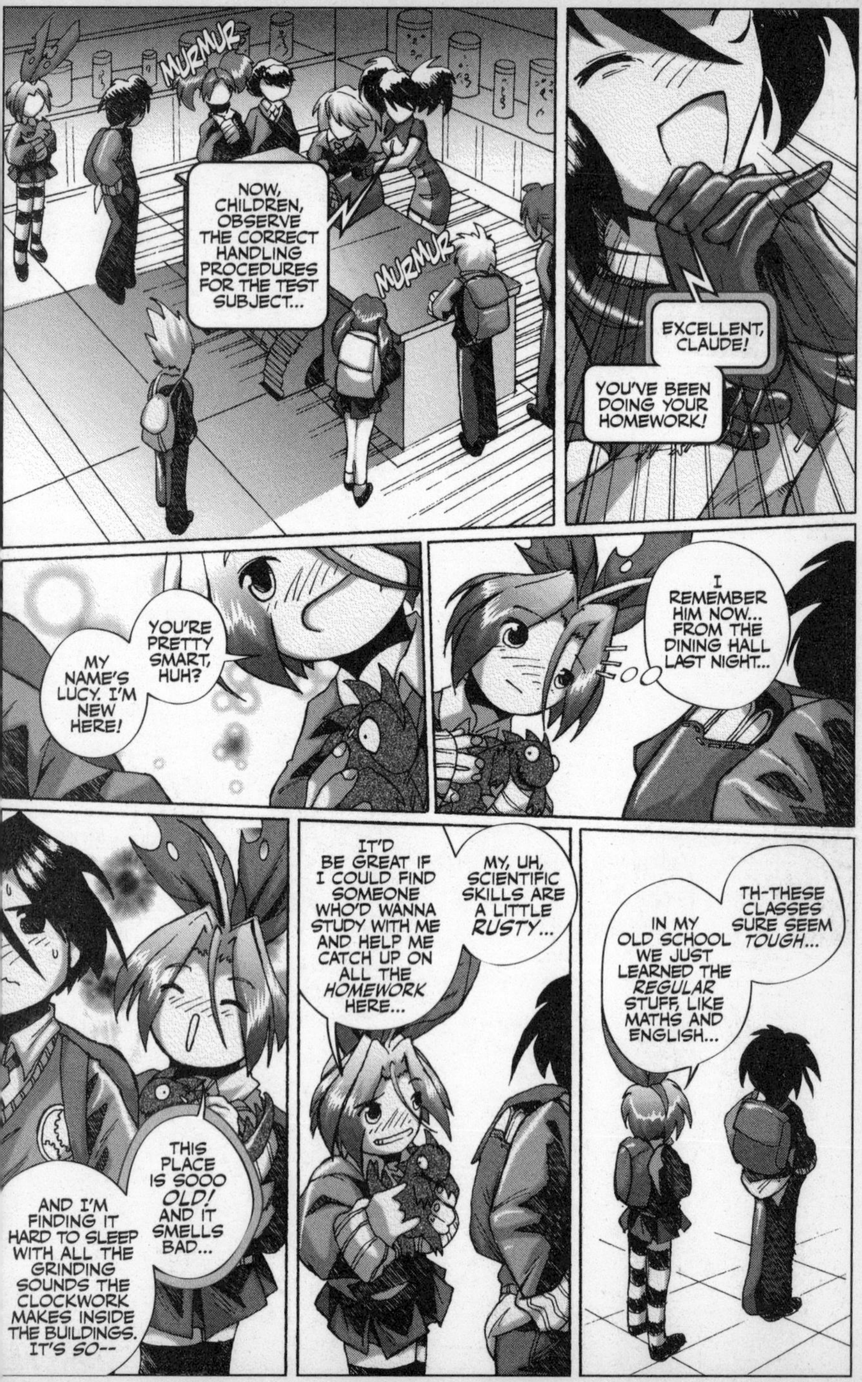
EXCELLENT, CLAUDE!
YOU'VE BEEN DOING YOUR HOMEWORK!
MURMUR
NOW, CHILDREN, OBSERVE THE CORRECT HANDLING PROCEDURES FOR THE TEST SUBJECT...
MURMUR
I REMEMBER HIM NOW... FROM THE DINING HALL LAST NIGHT...
YOU'RE PRETTY SMART, HUH?
MY NAME'S LUCY. I'M NEW HERE!
TH-THESE CLASSES SURE SEEM *TOUGH*...
IN MY OLD SCHOOL WE JUST LEARNED THE *REGULAR* STUFF, LIKE MATHS AND ENGLISH...
MY, UH, SCIENTIFIC SKILLS ARE A LITTLE *RUSTY*...
IT'D BE GREAT IF I COULD FIND SOMEONE WHO'D WANNA STUDY WITH ME AND HELP ME CATCH UP ON ALL THE *HOMEWORK* HERE...
THIS PLACE IS SOOO *OLD!* AND IT SMELLS BAD...
AND I'M FINDING IT HARD TO SLEEP WITH ALL THE GRINDING SOUNDS THE CLOCKWORK MAKES INSIDE THE BUILDINGS. IT'S *SO*--

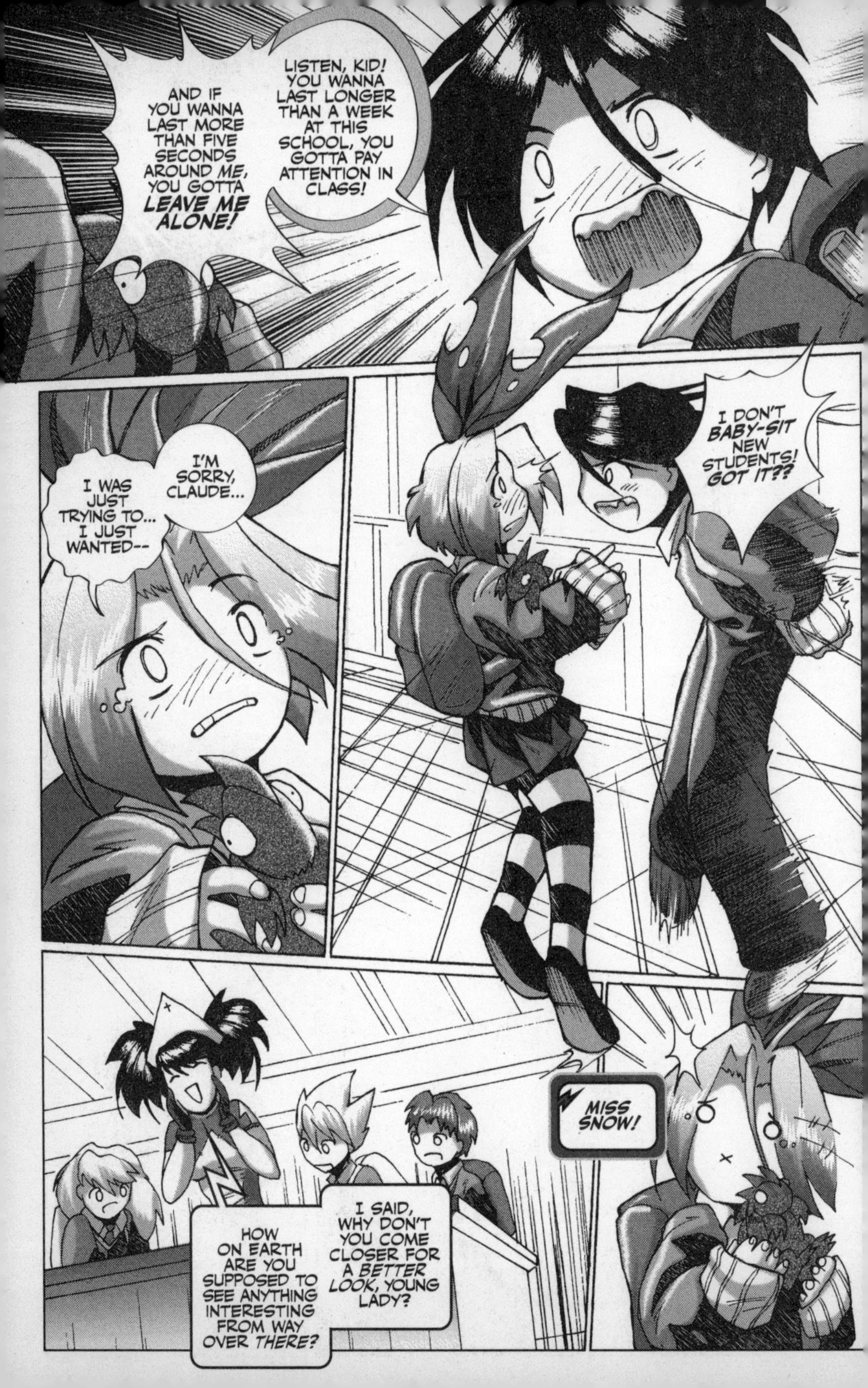
LISTEN, KID! YOU WANNA LAST LONGER THAN A WEEK AT THIS SCHOOL, YOU GOTTA PAY ATTENTION IN CLASS!
AND IF YOU WANNA LAST MORE THAN FIVE SECONDS AROUND *ME*, YOU GOTTA ***LEAVE ME ALONE!***
I DON'T *BABY-SIT* NEW STUDENTS! *GOT IT??*
I'M SORRY, CLAUDE...
I WAS JUST TRYING TO... I JUST WANTED--
MISS SNOW!
I SAID, WHY DON'T YOU COME CLOSER FOR A *BETTER LOOK*, YOUNG LADY?
HOW ON EARTH ARE YOU SUPPOSED TO SEE ANYTHING INTERESTING FROM WAY OVER *THERE*?

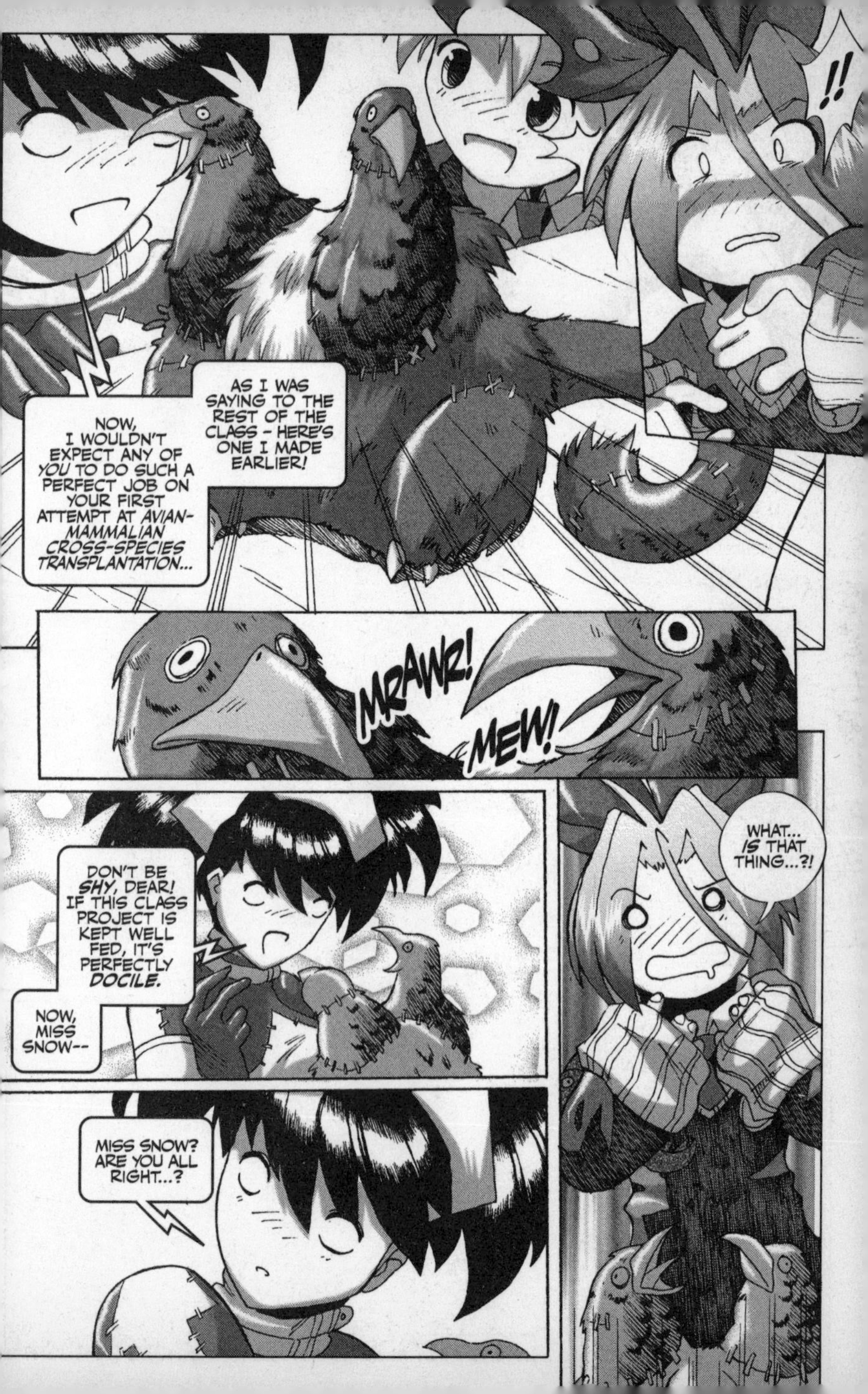
!!
AS I WAS SAYING TO THE REST OF THE CLASS - HERE'S ONE I MADE EARLIER!
NOW, I WOULDN'T EXPECT ANY OF *YOU* TO DO SUCH A PERFECT JOB ON YOUR FIRST ATTEMPT AT *AVIAN-MAMMALIAN CROSS-SPECIES TRANSPLANTATION...*
MRAWR!
MEW!
WHAT... *IS* THAT THING...?!
DON'T BE ***SHY***, DEAR! IF THIS CLASS PROJECT IS KEPT WELL FED, IT'S PERFECTLY ***DOCILE.***
NOW, MISS SNOW--
MISS SNOW? ARE YOU ALL RIGHT...?

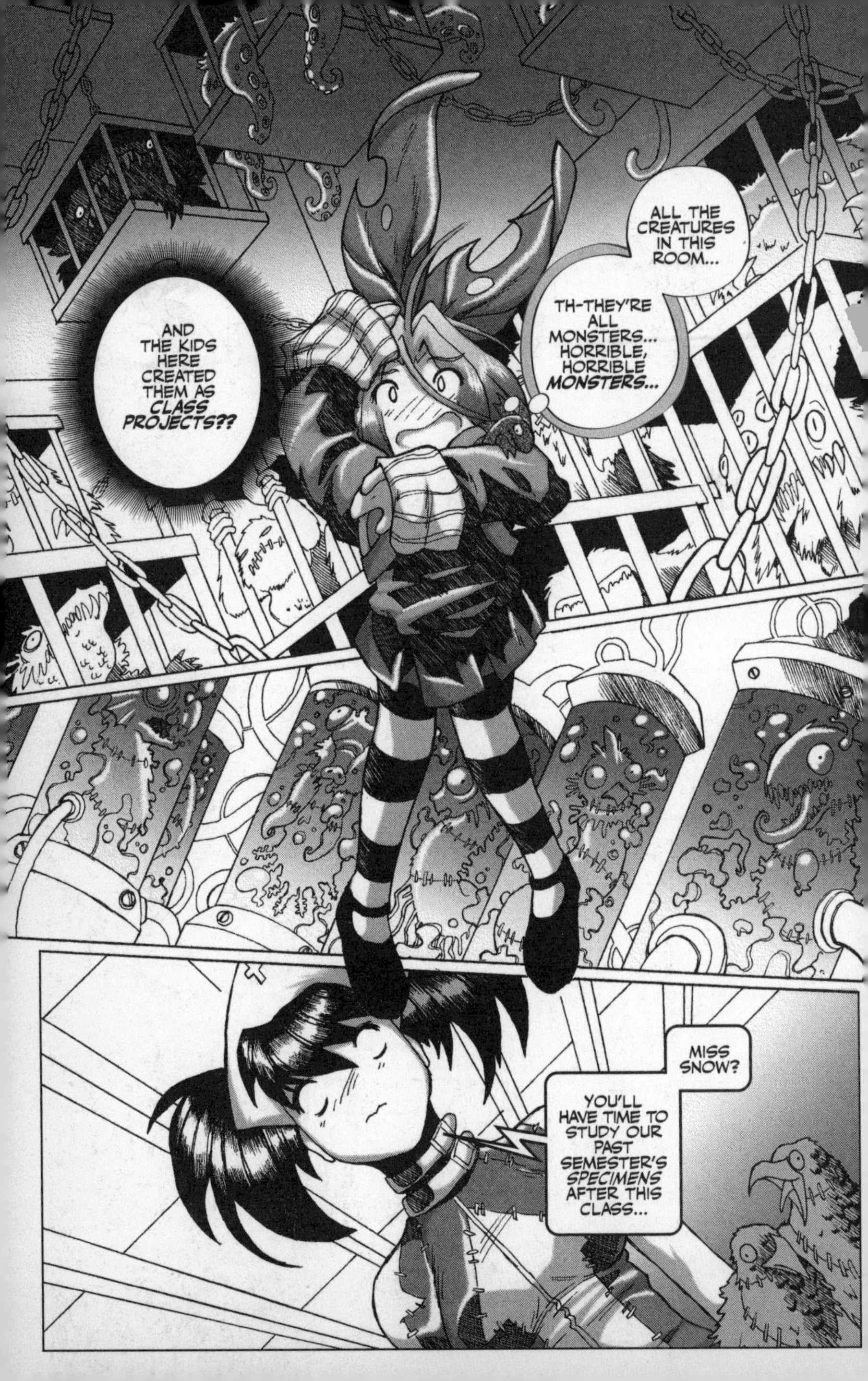
ALL THE CREATURES IN THIS ROOM...
TH-THEY'RE ALL MONSTERS... HORRIBLE, HORRIBLE *MONSTERS*...
AND THE KIDS HERE CREATED THEM AS *CLASS PROJECTS??*
MISS SNOW?
YOU'LL HAVE TIME TO STUDY OUR PAST SEMESTER'S *SPECIMENS* AFTER THIS CLASS...

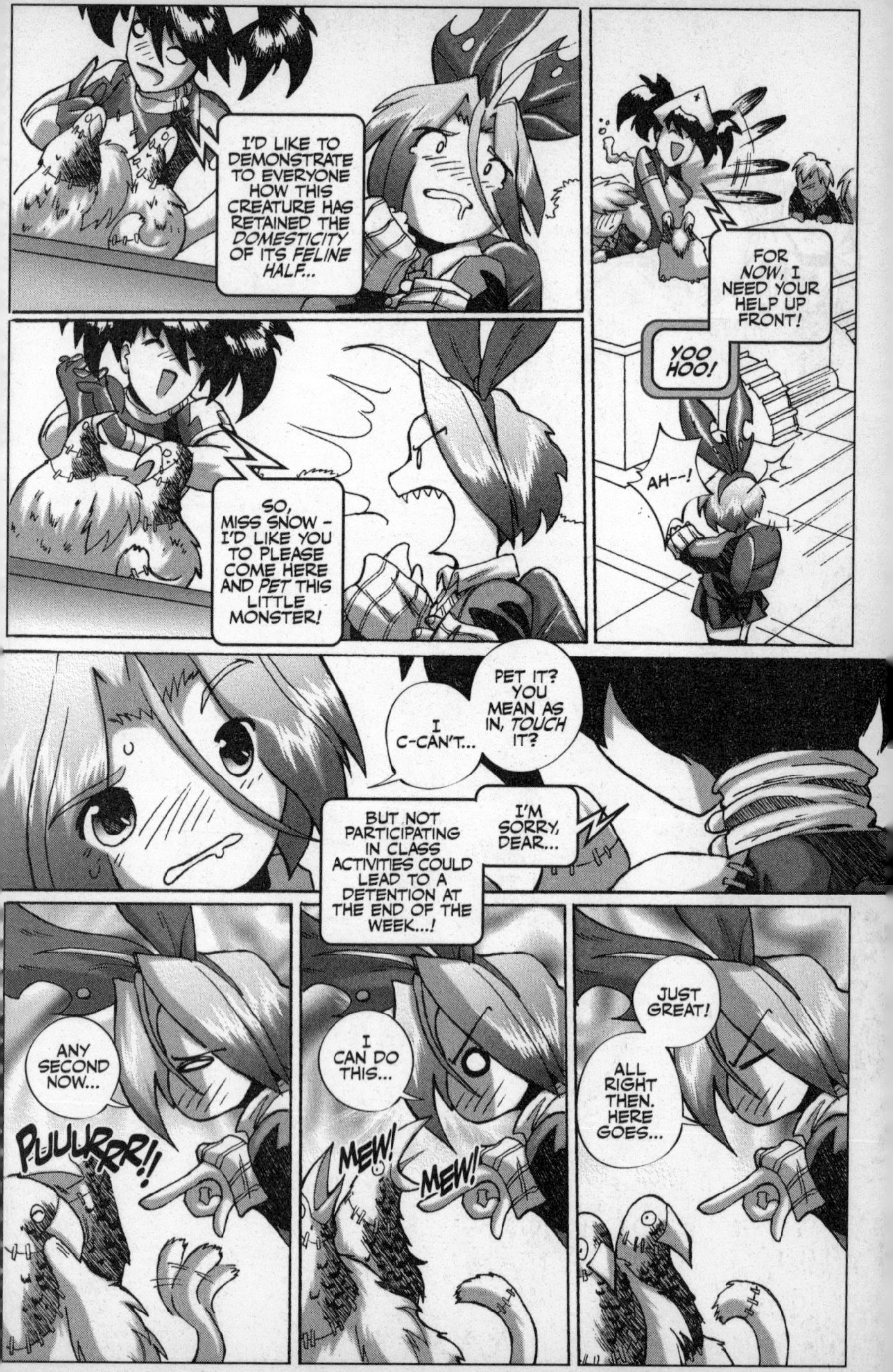
I'D LIKE TO DEMONSTRATE TO EVERYONE HOW THIS CREATURE HAS RETAINED THE *DOMESTICITY* OF ITS *FELINE* HALF...
FOR *NOW*, I NEED YOUR HELP UP FRONT!
YOO HOO!
AH--!
SO, MISS SNOW - I'D LIKE YOU TO PLEASE COME HERE AND *PET* THIS LITTLE MONSTER!
PET IT? YOU MEAN AS IN, *TOUCH* IT?
I C-CAN'T...
I'M SORRY, DEAR...
BUT NOT PARTICIPATING IN CLASS ACTIVITIES COULD LEAD TO A DETENTION AT THE END OF THE WEEK...!
ANY SECOND NOW...
PUUURRR!!
I CAN DO THIS...
MEW!
MEW!
JUST GREAT!
ALL RIGHT THEN. HERE GOES...

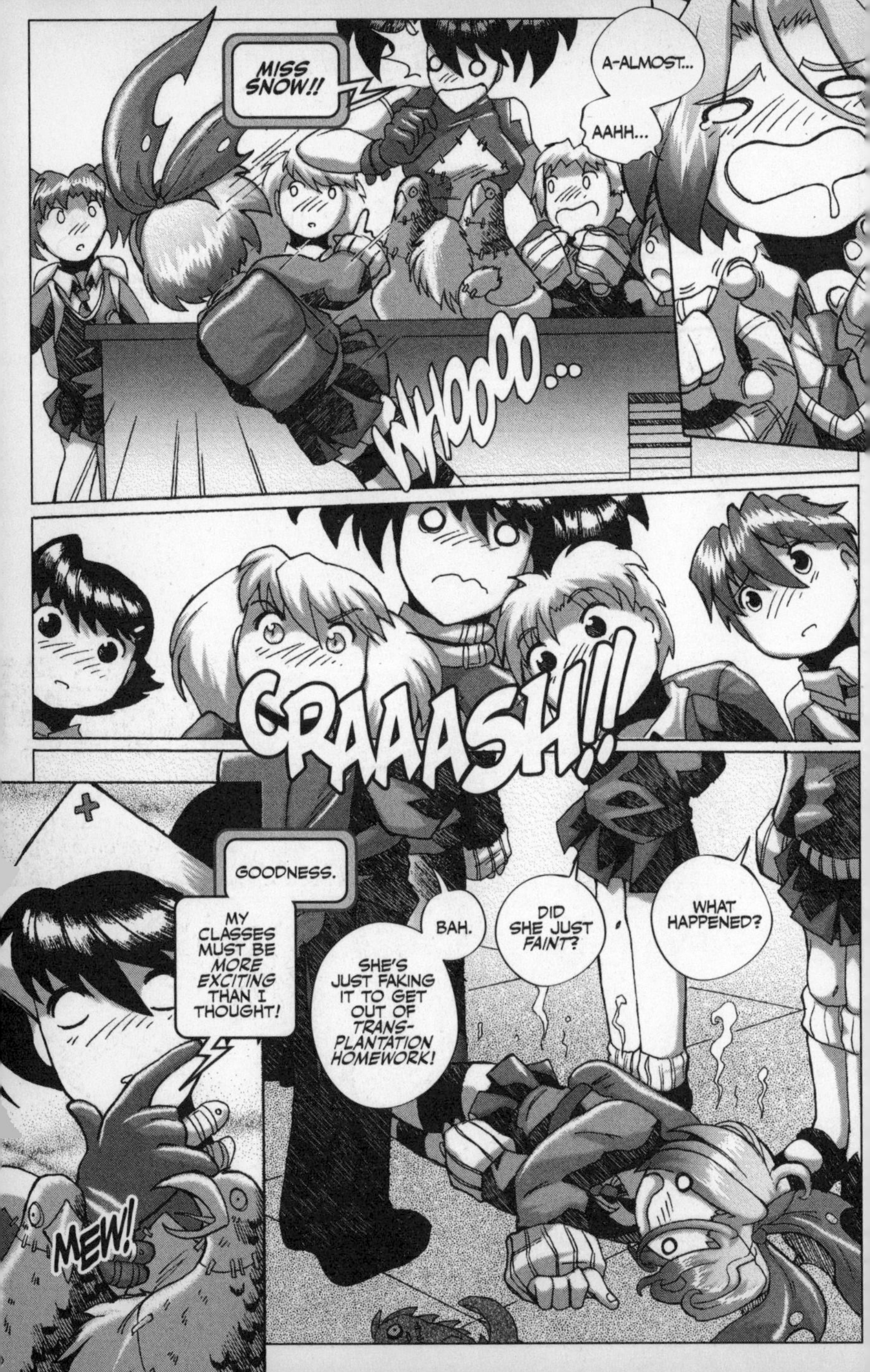
A-ALMOST...
AAHH...
MISS SNOW!!
WHOOOO...
CRAAASH!!
WHAT HAPPENED?
DID SHE JUST FAINT?
BAH.
SHE'S JUST FAKING IT TO GET OUT OF TRANS-PLANTATION HOMEWORK!
GOODNESS.
MY CLASSES MUST BE MORE EXCITING THAN I THOUGHT!
MEW!

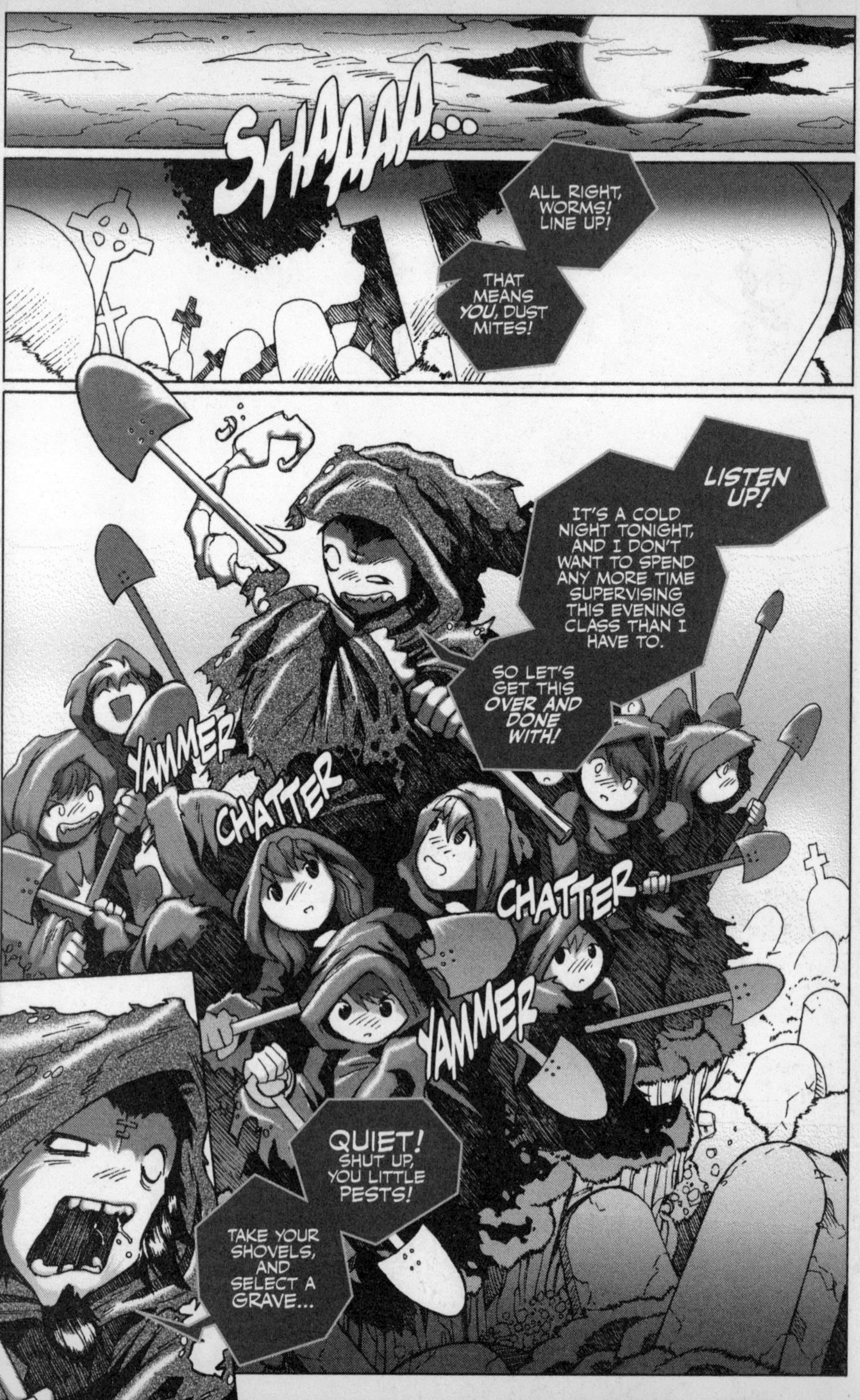
SHAAAA...
ALL RIGHT, WORMS! LINE UP!
THAT MEANS YOU, DUST MITES!
LISTEN UP!
IT'S A COLD NIGHT TONIGHT, AND I DON'T WANT TO SPEND ANY MORE TIME SUPERVISING THIS EVENING CLASS THAN I HAVE TO.
SO LET'S GET THIS OVER AND DONE WITH!
YAMMER
CHATTER
CHATTER
YAMMER
QUIET! SHUT UP, YOU LITTLE PESTS!
TAKE YOUR SHOVELS, AND SELECT A GRAVE...

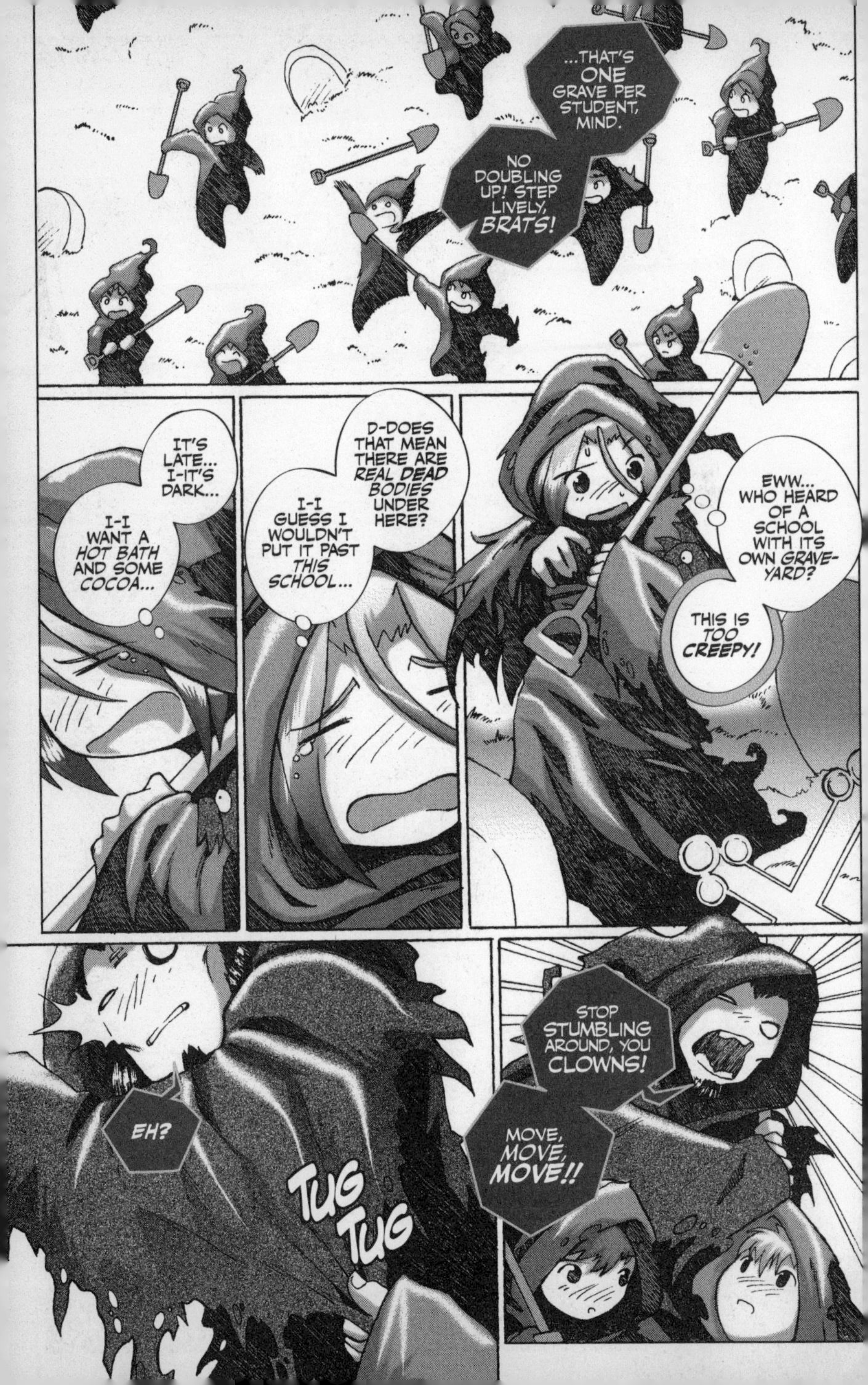
...THAT'S ONE GRAVE PER STUDENT, MIND.
NO DOUBLING UP! STEP LIVELY, BRATS!
EWW... WHO HEARD OF A SCHOOL WITH ITS OWN GRAVE-YARD?
THIS IS TOO CREEPY!
D-DOES THAT MEAN THERE ARE REAL DEAD BODIES UNDER HERE?
I-I GUESS I WOULDN'T PUT IT PAST THIS SCHOOL...
IT'S LATE... I-IT'S DARK...
I-I WANT A HOT BATH AND SOME COCOA...
STOP STUMBLING AROUND, YOU CLOWNS!
MOVE, MOVE, MOVE!!
EH?
TUG TUG

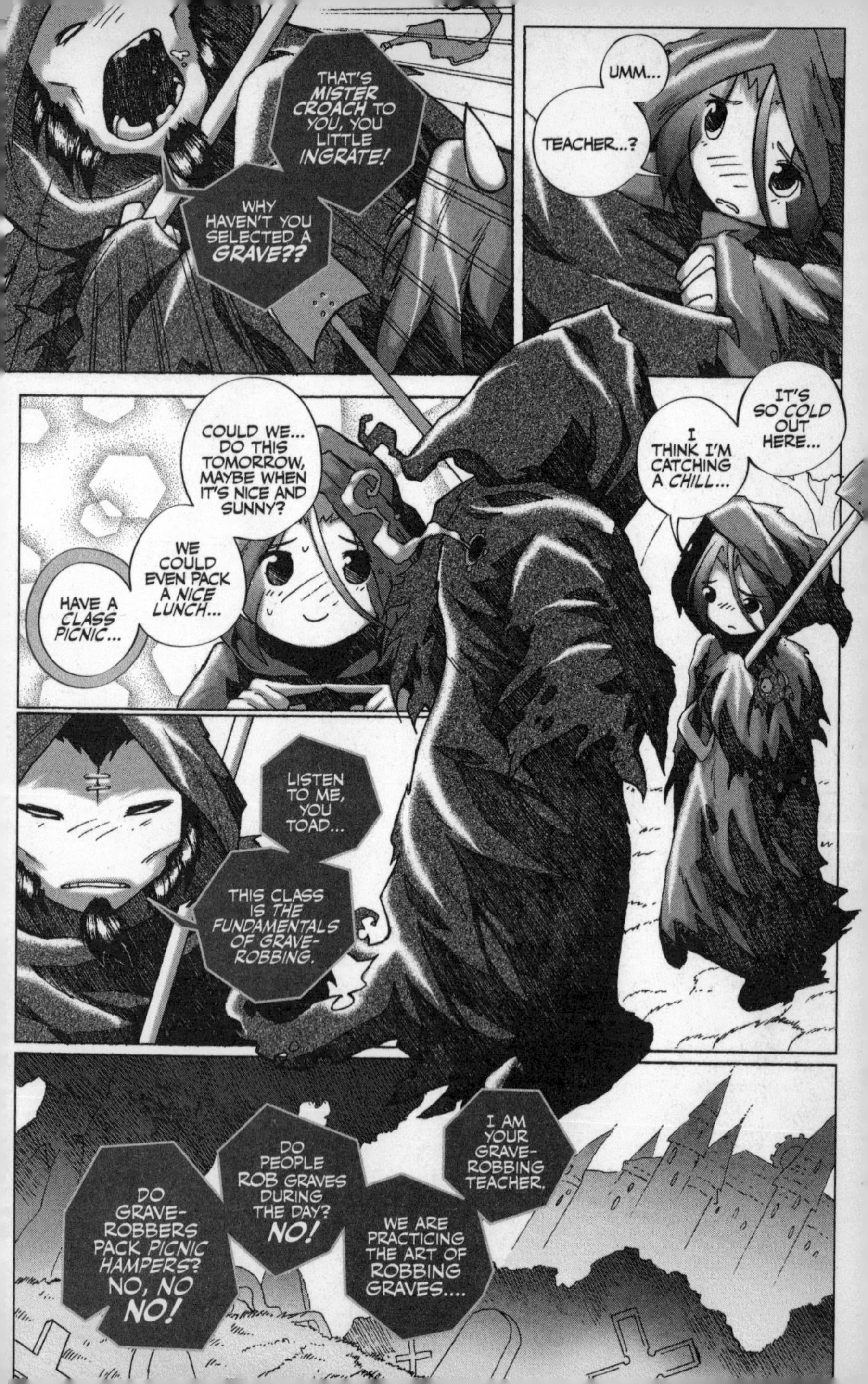
UMM...
TEACHER...?
THAT'S MISTER CROACH TO YOU, YOU LITTLE INGRATE!
WHY HAVEN'T YOU SELECTED A GRAVE??
IT'S SO COLD OUT HERE...
I THINK I'M CATCHING A CHILL...
COULD WE... DO THIS TOMORROW, MAYBE WHEN IT'S NICE AND SUNNY?
WE COULD EVEN PACK A NICE LUNCH...
HAVE A CLASS PICNIC...
LISTEN TO ME, YOU TOAD...
THIS CLASS IS THE FUNDAMENTALS OF GRAVE-ROBBING.
I AM YOUR GRAVE-ROBBING TEACHER.
WE ARE PRACTICING THE ART OF ROBBING GRAVES....
DO PEOPLE ROB GRAVES DURING THE DAY? NO!
DO GRAVE-ROBBERS PACK PICNIC HAMPERS? NO, NO NO!

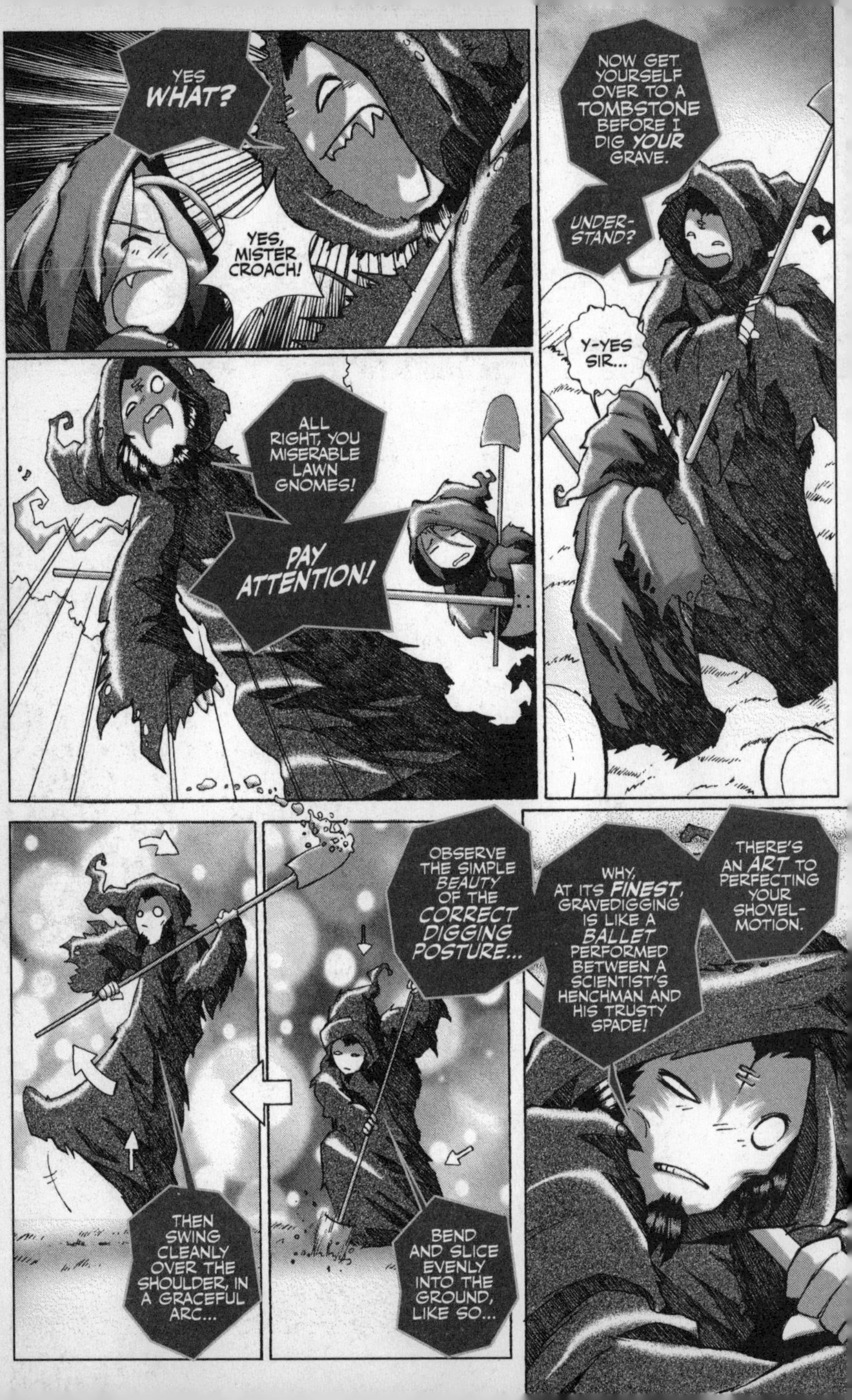
YES WHAT?
YES, MISTER CROACH!
NOW GET YOURSELF OVER TO A TOMBSTONE BEFORE I DIG YOUR GRAVE.
UNDER-STAND?
Y-YES SIR...
ALL RIGHT, YOU MISERABLE LAWN GNOMES!
PAY ATTENTION!
THERE'S AN ART TO PERFECTING YOUR SHOVEL-MOTION.
WHY, AT ITS FINEST, GRAVEDIGGING IS LIKE A BALLET PERFORMED BETWEEN A SCIENTIST'S HENCHMAN AND HIS TRUSTY SPADE!
OBSERVE THE SIMPLE BEAUTY OF THE CORRECT DIGGING POSTURE...
BEND AND SLICE EVENLY INTO THE GROUND, LIKE SO...
THEN SWING CLEANLY OVER THE SHOULDER, IN A GRACEFUL ARC...

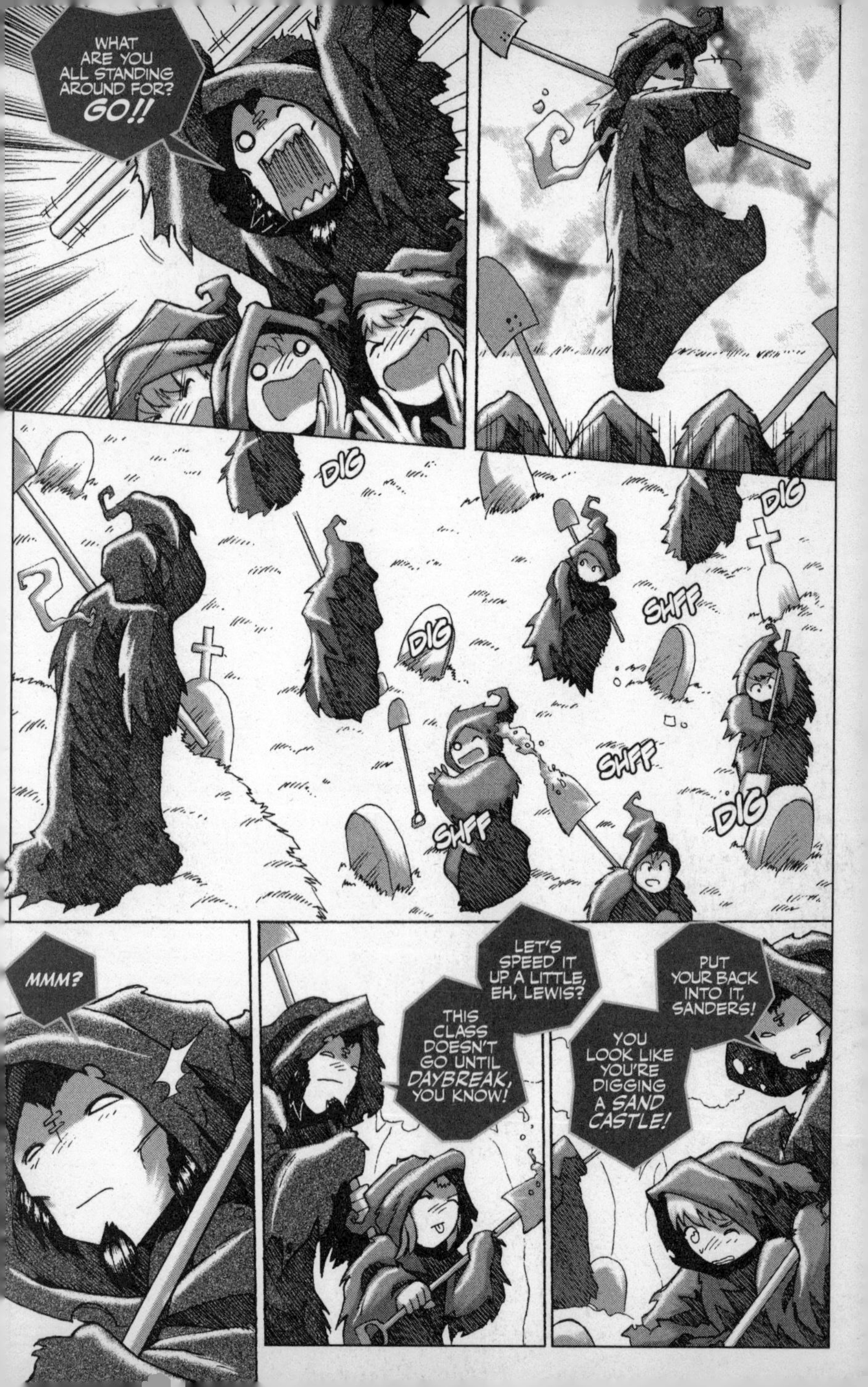
WHAT ARE YOU ALL STANDING AROUND FOR? GO!!
DIG
DIG
DIG
SHFF
SHFF
SHFF
DIG
MMM?
LET'S SPEED IT UP A LITTLE, EH, LEWIS?
THIS CLASS DOESN'T GO UNTIL DAYBREAK, YOU KNOW!
PUT YOUR BACK INTO IT, SANDERS!
YOU LOOK LIKE YOU'RE DIGGING A SAND CASTLE!

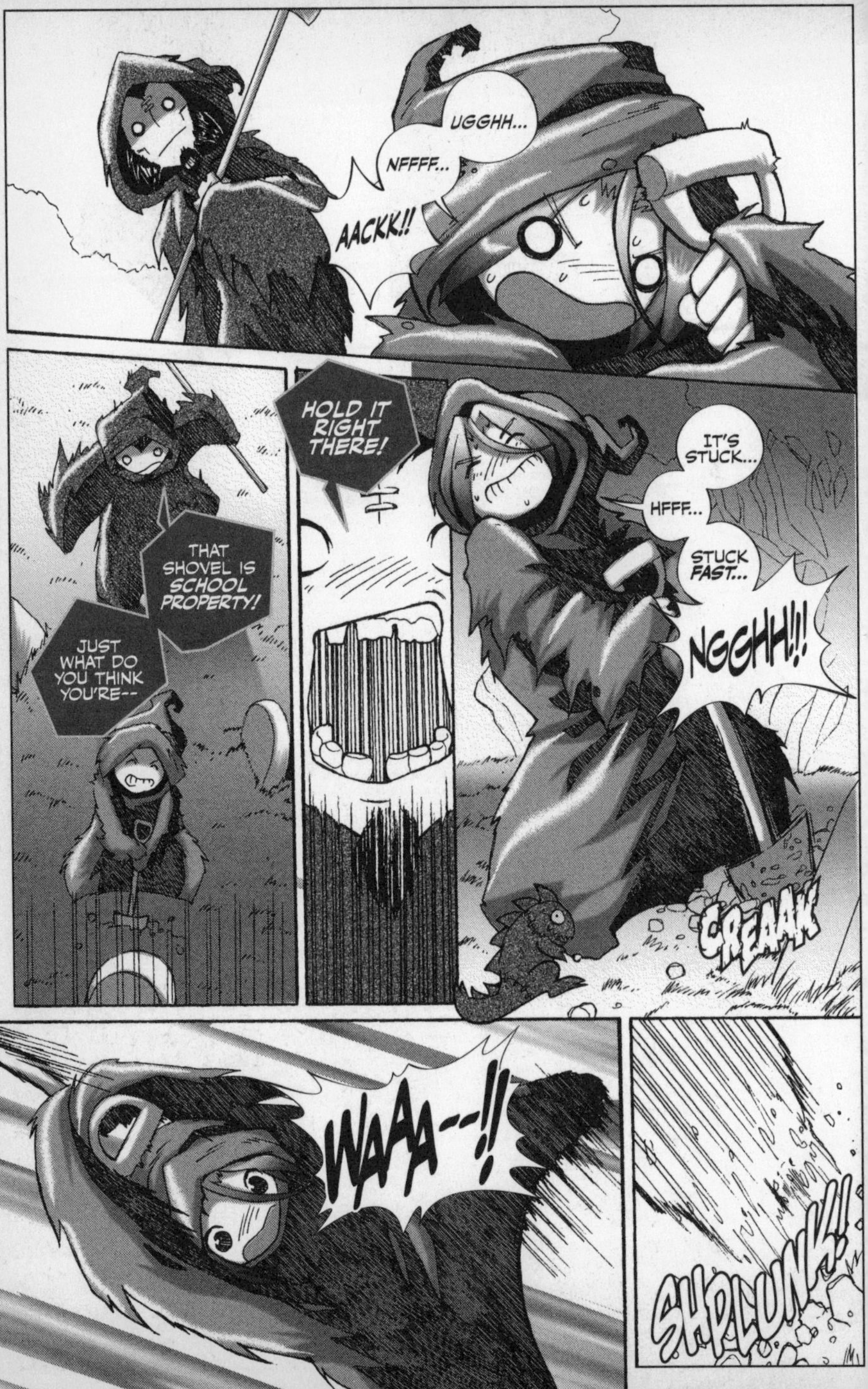
UGGHH...
NFFFF...
AACKK!!
IT'S STUCK...
HFFF...
STUCK FAST...
NGGHH!!!
CREAAK
HOLD IT RIGHT THERE!
THAT SHOVEL IS SCHOOL PROPERTY!
JUST WHAT DO YOU THINK YOU'RE--
SHPLUNK!
WAAA--!!

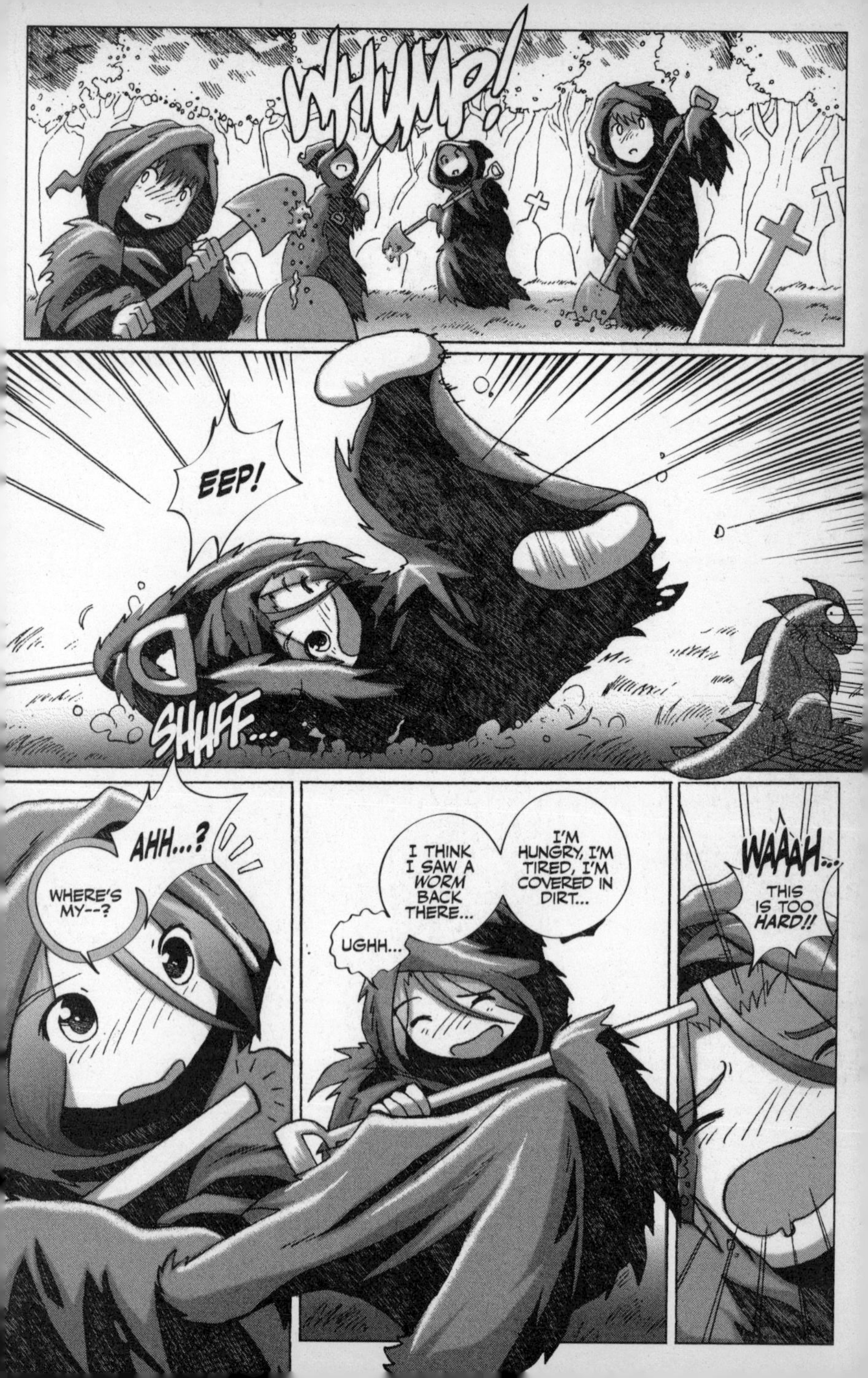
WHUMP!
EEP!
SHUFF...
WAAAH...
THIS IS TOO HARD!!
I'M HUNGRY, I'M TIRED, I'M COVERED IN DIRT...
I THINK I SAW A WORM BACK THERE...
UGHH...
AHH...?
WHERE'S MY--?

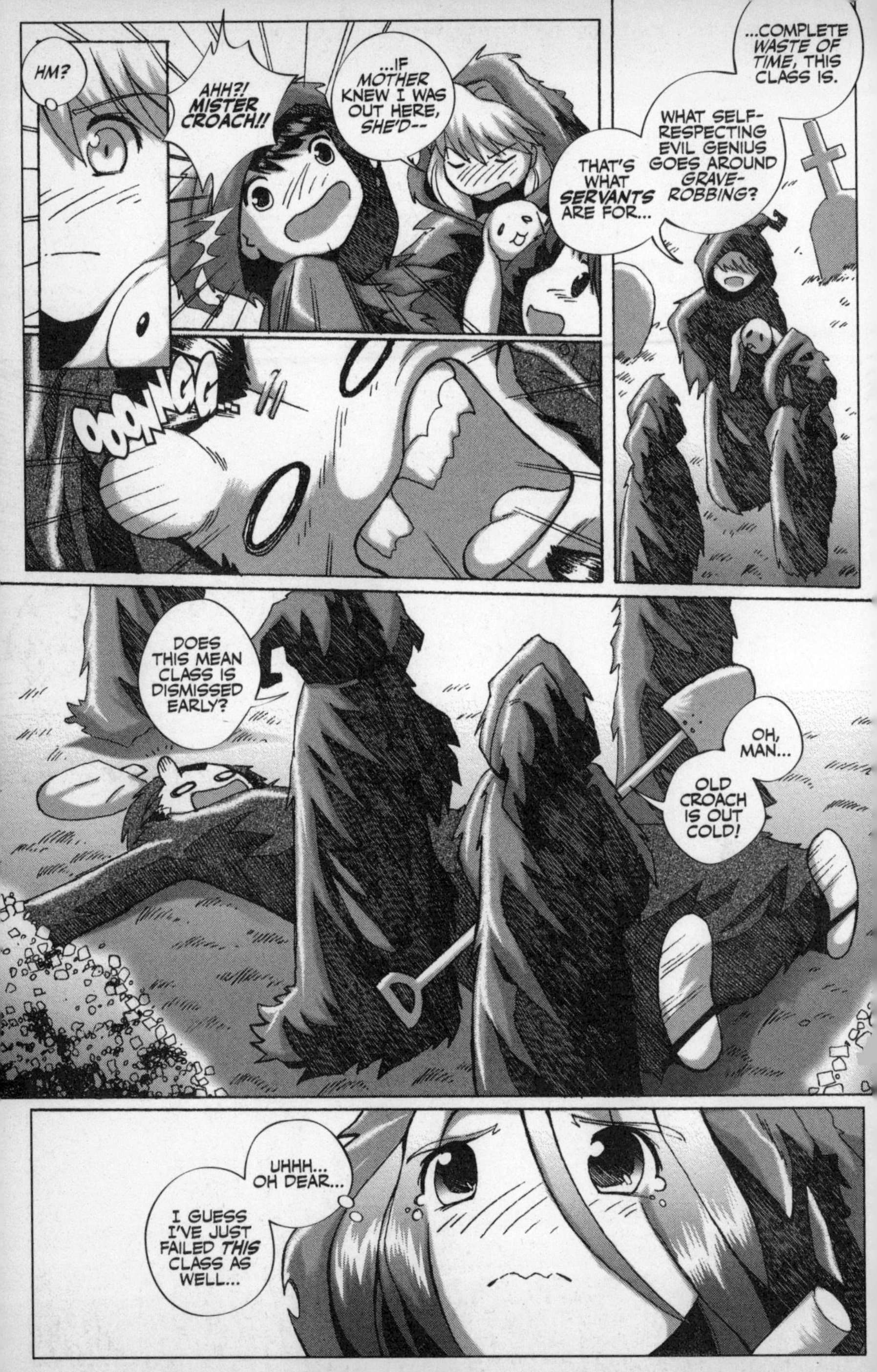
...COMPLETE WASTE OF TIME, THIS CLASS IS.
WHAT SELF-RESPECTING EVIL GENIUS GOES AROUND GRAVE-ROBBING?
THAT'S WHAT SERVANTS ARE FOR...
...IF MOTHER KNEW I WAS OUT HERE, SHE'D--
AHH?! MISTER CROACH!!
HM?
OOONNGG
OH, MAN... OLD CROACH IS OUT COLD!
DOES THIS MEAN CLASS IS DISMISSED EARLY?
UHHH... OH DEAR...
I GUESS I'VE JUST FAILED THIS CLASS AS WELL...

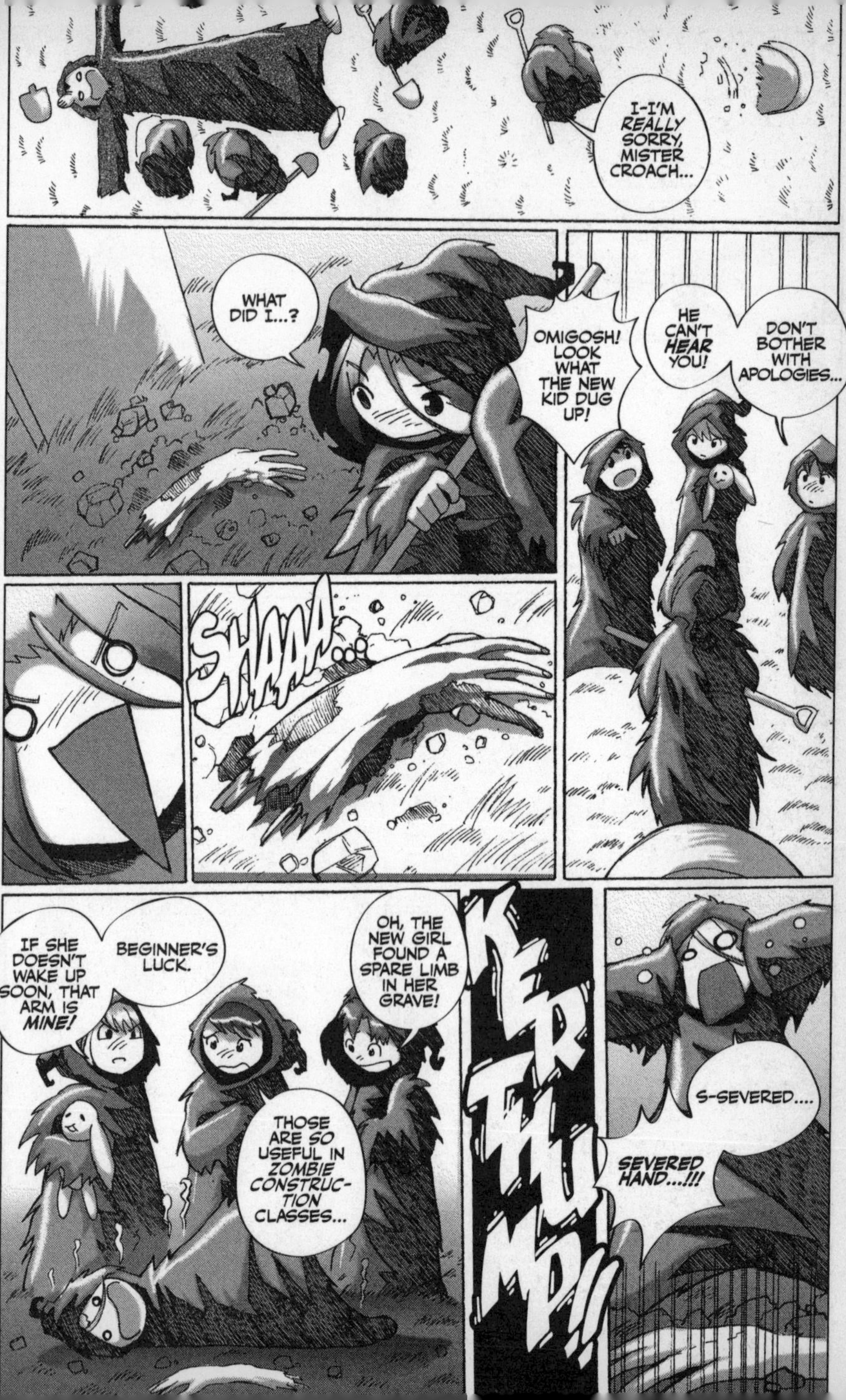
I-I'M REALLY SORRY, MISTER CROACH...
DON'T BOTHER WITH APOLOGIES...
HE CAN'T HEAR YOU!
OMIGOSH! LOOK WHAT THE NEW KID DUG UP!
WHAT DID I...?
SHAAA...
S-SEVERED....
SEVERED HAND...!!!
KERTHUMP!!
OH, THE NEW GIRL FOUND A SPARE LIMB IN HER GRAVE!
THOSE ARE SO USEFUL IN ZOMBIE CONSTRUCTION CLASSES...
BEGINNER'S LUCK.
IF SHE DOESN'T WAKE UP SOON, THAT ARM IS MINE!

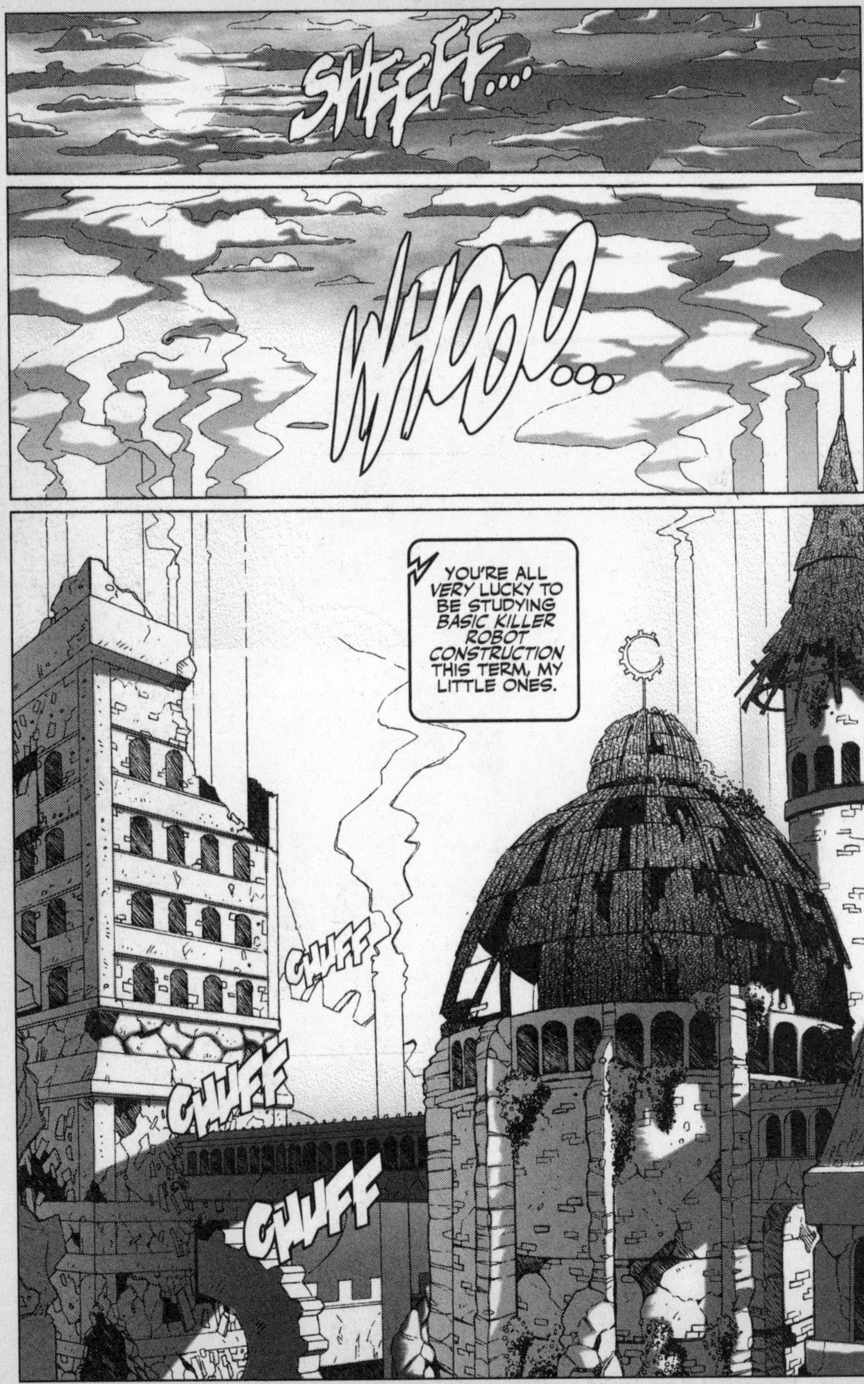
SHFFF...
WHOOO...
YOU'RE ALL VERY LUCKY TO BE STUDYING BASIC KILLER ROBOT CONSTRUCTION THIS TERM, MY LITTLE ONES.
CHUFF
CHUFF
CHUFF

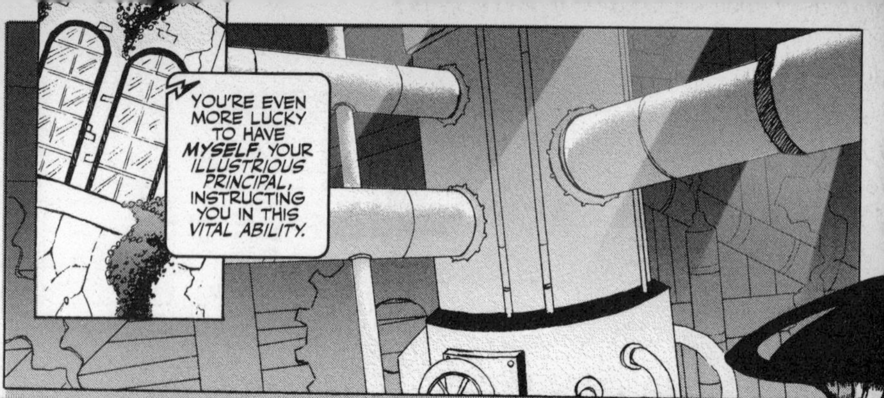
YOU'RE EVEN MORE LUCKY TO HAVE MYSELF, YOUR ILLUSTRIOUS PRINCIPAL, INSTRUCTING YOU IN THIS VITAL ABILITY.

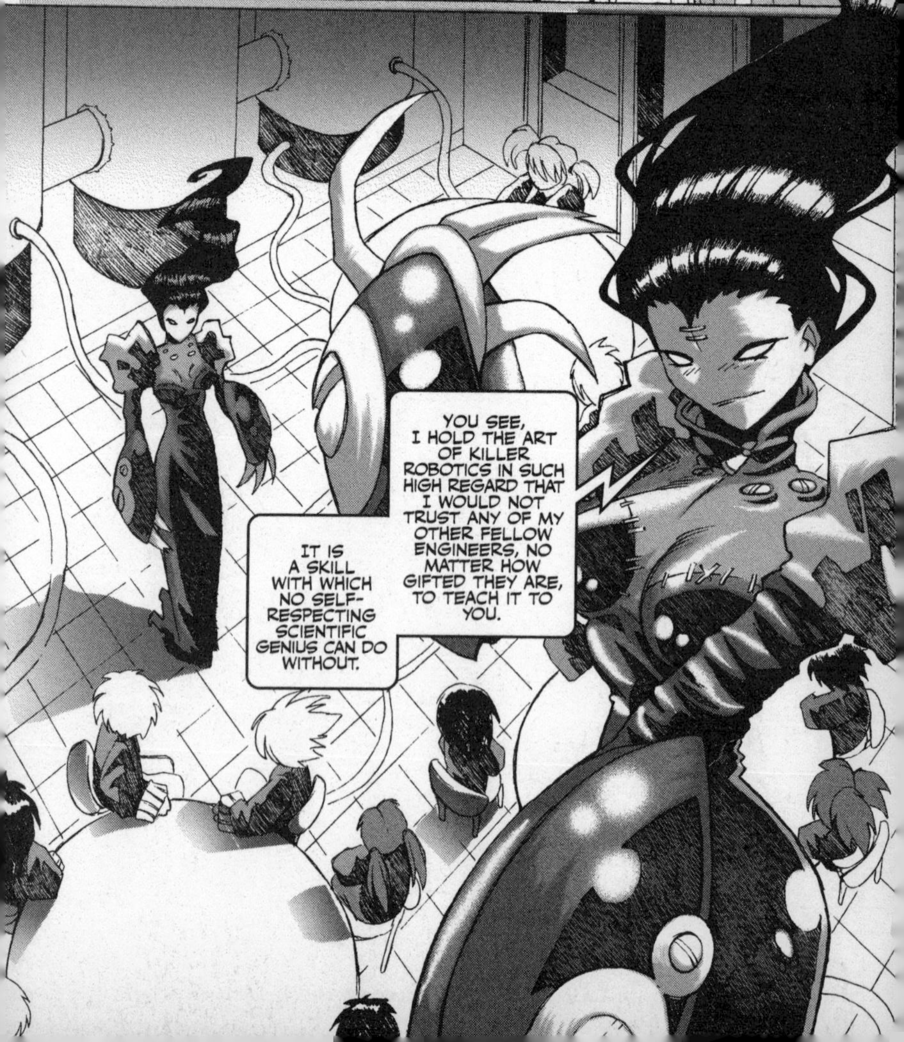
YOU SEE, I HOLD THE ART OF KILLER ROBOTICS IN SUCH HIGH REGARD THAT I WOULD NOT TRUST ANY OF MY OTHER FELLOW ENGINEERS, NO MATTER HOW GIFTED THEY ARE, TO TEACH IT TO YOU.
IT IS A SKILL WITH WHICH NO SELF-RESPECTING SCIENTIFIC GENIUS CAN DO WITHOUT.

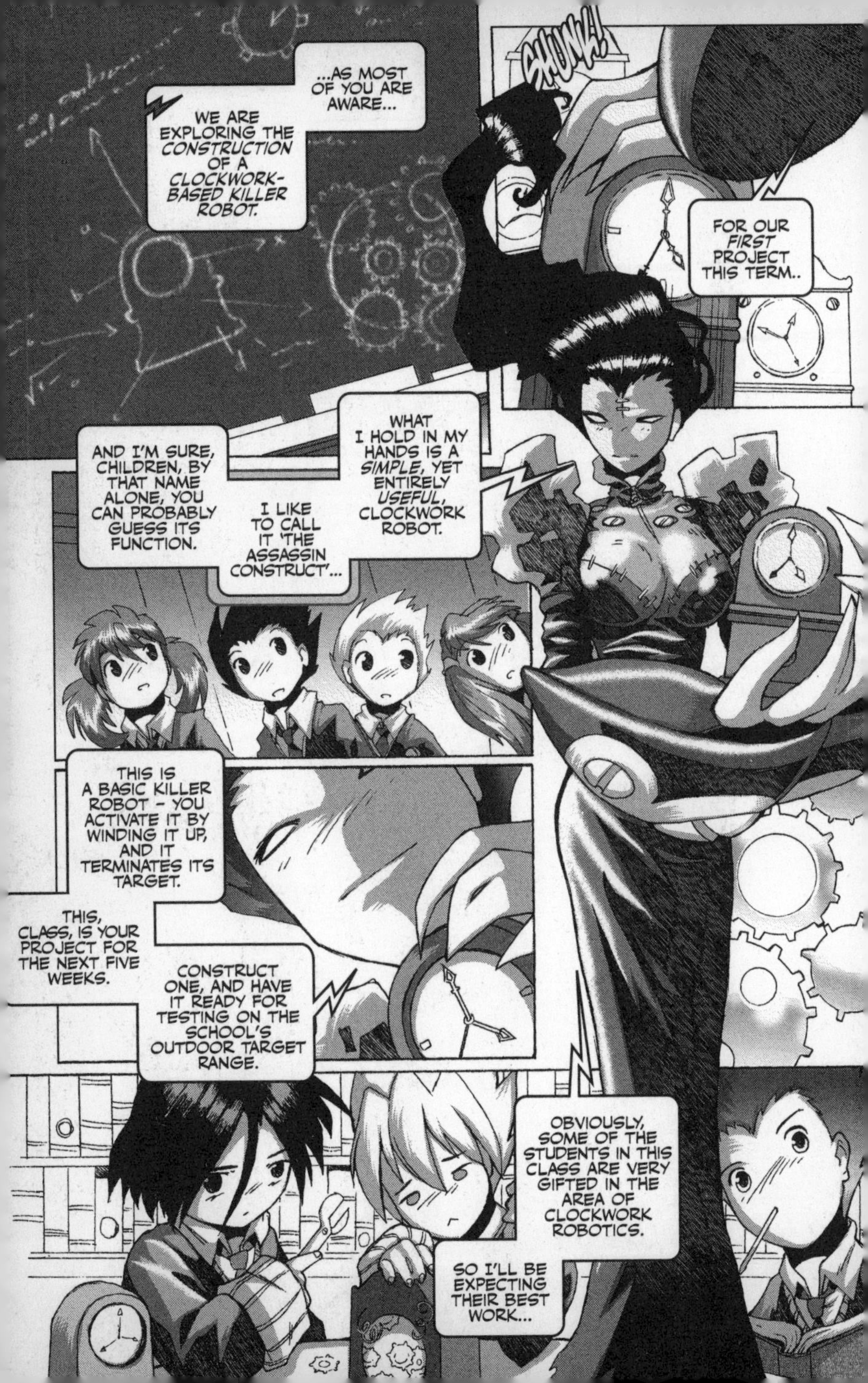
SHUNK!
...AS MOST OF YOU ARE AWARE...
WE ARE EXPLORING THE *CONSTRUCTION* OF A *CLOCKWORK-BASED KILLER ROBOT.*
FOR OUR *FIRST* PROJECT THIS TERM..
WHAT I HOLD IN MY HANDS IS A *SIMPLE*, YET ENTIRELY *USEFUL*, CLOCKWORK ROBOT.
I LIKE TO CALL IT 'THE ASSASSIN CONSTRUCT'...
AND I'M SURE, CHILDREN, BY THAT NAME ALONE, YOU CAN PROBABLY GUESS ITS FUNCTION.
THIS IS A BASIC KILLER ROBOT - YOU ACTIVATE IT BY WINDING IT UP, AND IT TERMINATES ITS TARGET.
THIS, CLASS, IS YOUR PROJECT FOR THE NEXT FIVE WEEKS.
CONSTRUCT ONE, AND HAVE IT READY FOR TESTING ON THE SCHOOL'S OUTDOOR TARGET RANGE.
OBVIOUSLY, SOME OF THE STUDENTS IN THIS CLASS ARE VERY GIFTED IN THE AREA OF CLOCKWORK ROBOTICS.
SO I'LL BE EXPECTING THEIR BEST WORK...

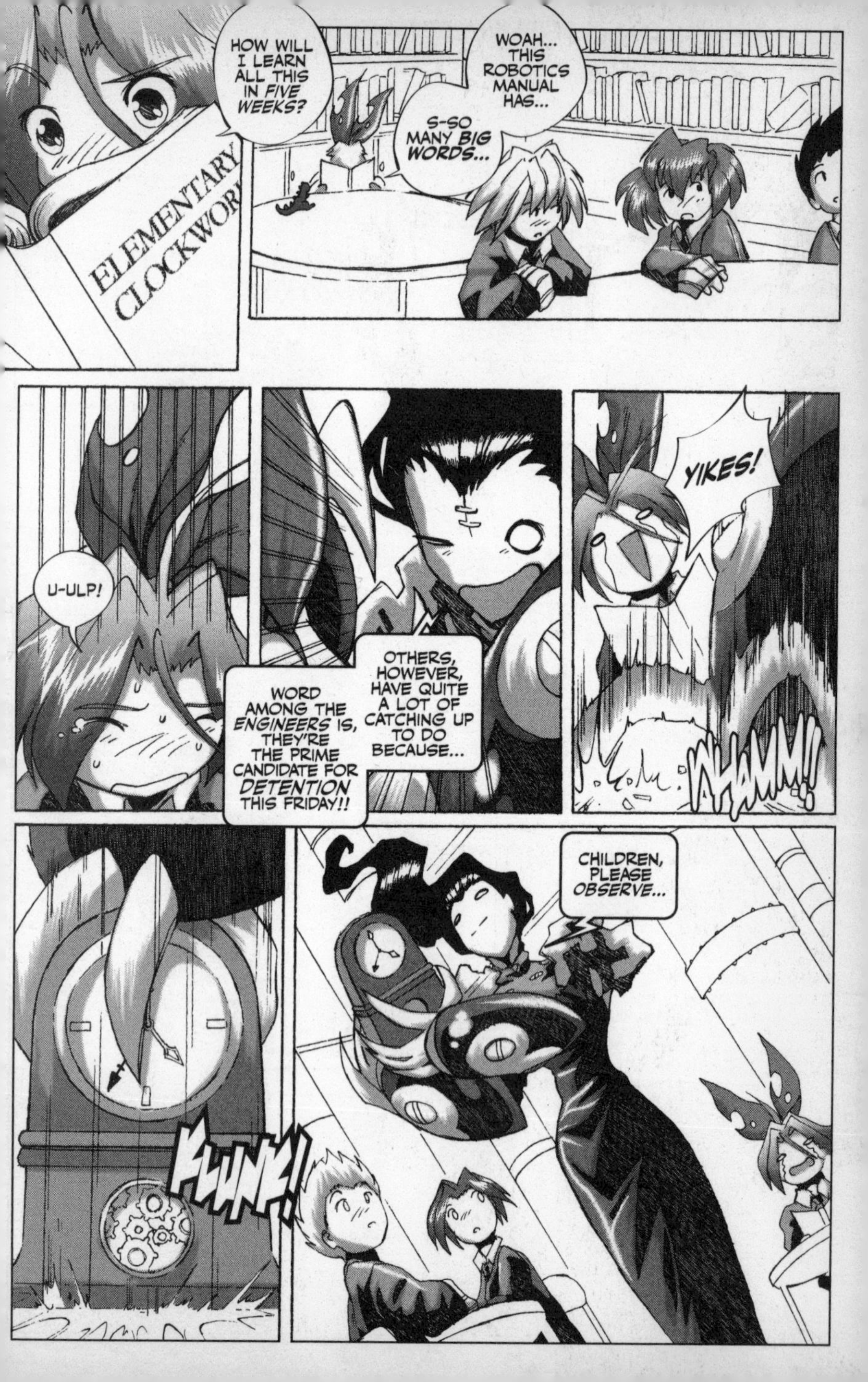
WOAH... THIS ROBOTICS MANUAL HAS...
S-SO MANY BIG WORDS...
HOW WILL I LEARN ALL THIS IN FIVE WEEKS?
ELEMENTARY CLOCKWORK
YIKES!
WHAMM!!
OTHERS, HOWEVER, HAVE QUITE A LOT OF CATCHING UP TO DO BECAUSE...
WORD AMONG THE ENGINEERS IS, THEY'RE THE PRIME CANDIDATE FOR DETENTION THIS FRIDAY!!
U-ULP!
CHILDREN, PLEASE OBSERVE...
KLUNK!

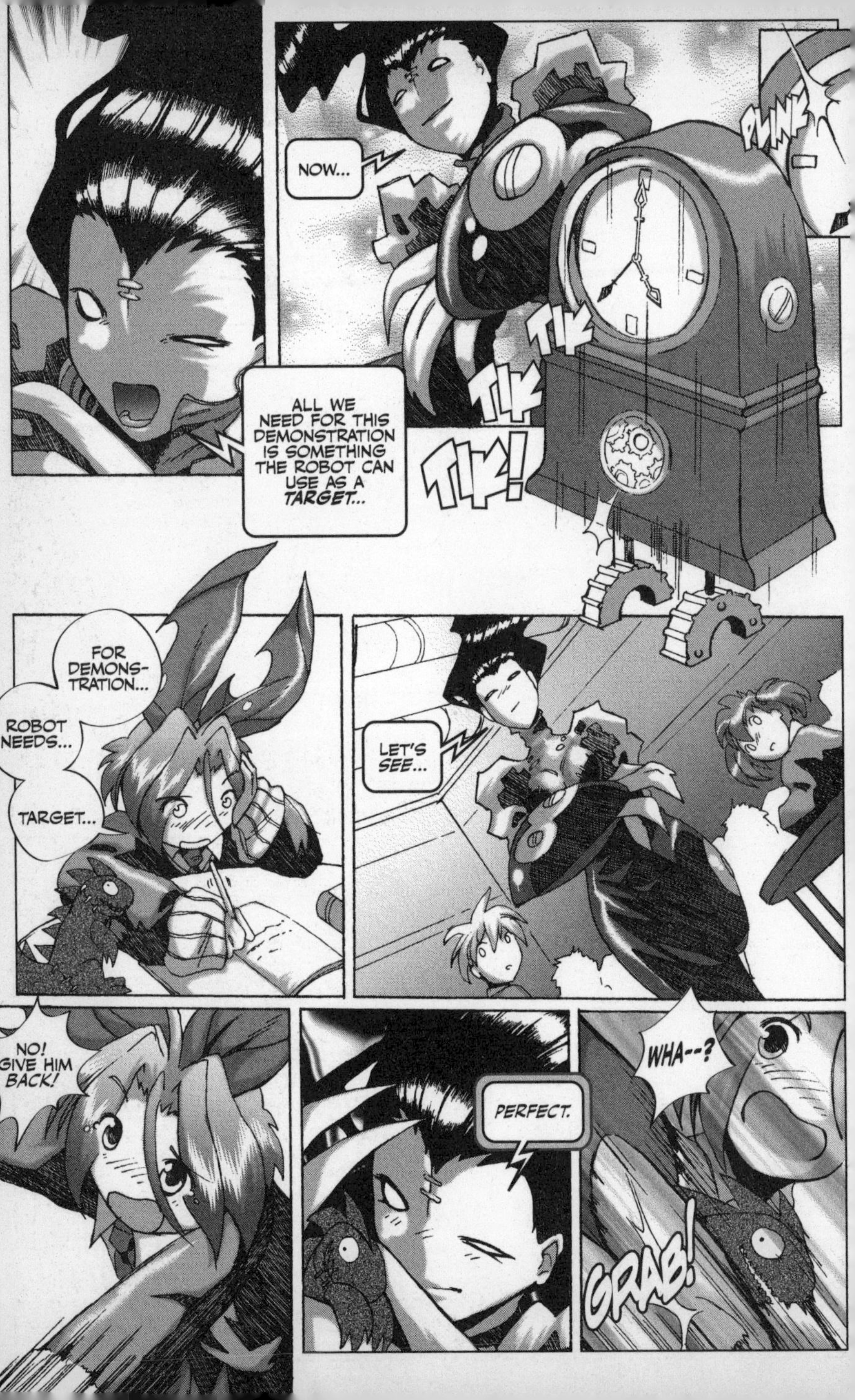
PLINK
NOW...
TIK
TIK
TIK!
ALL WE NEED FOR THIS DEMONSTRATION IS SOMETHING THE ROBOT CAN USE AS A *TARGET*...
LET'S SEE...
FOR DEMONSTRATION...
ROBOT NEEDS...
TARGET...
WHA--?
GRAB!
PERFECT.
NO! GIVE HIM BACK!

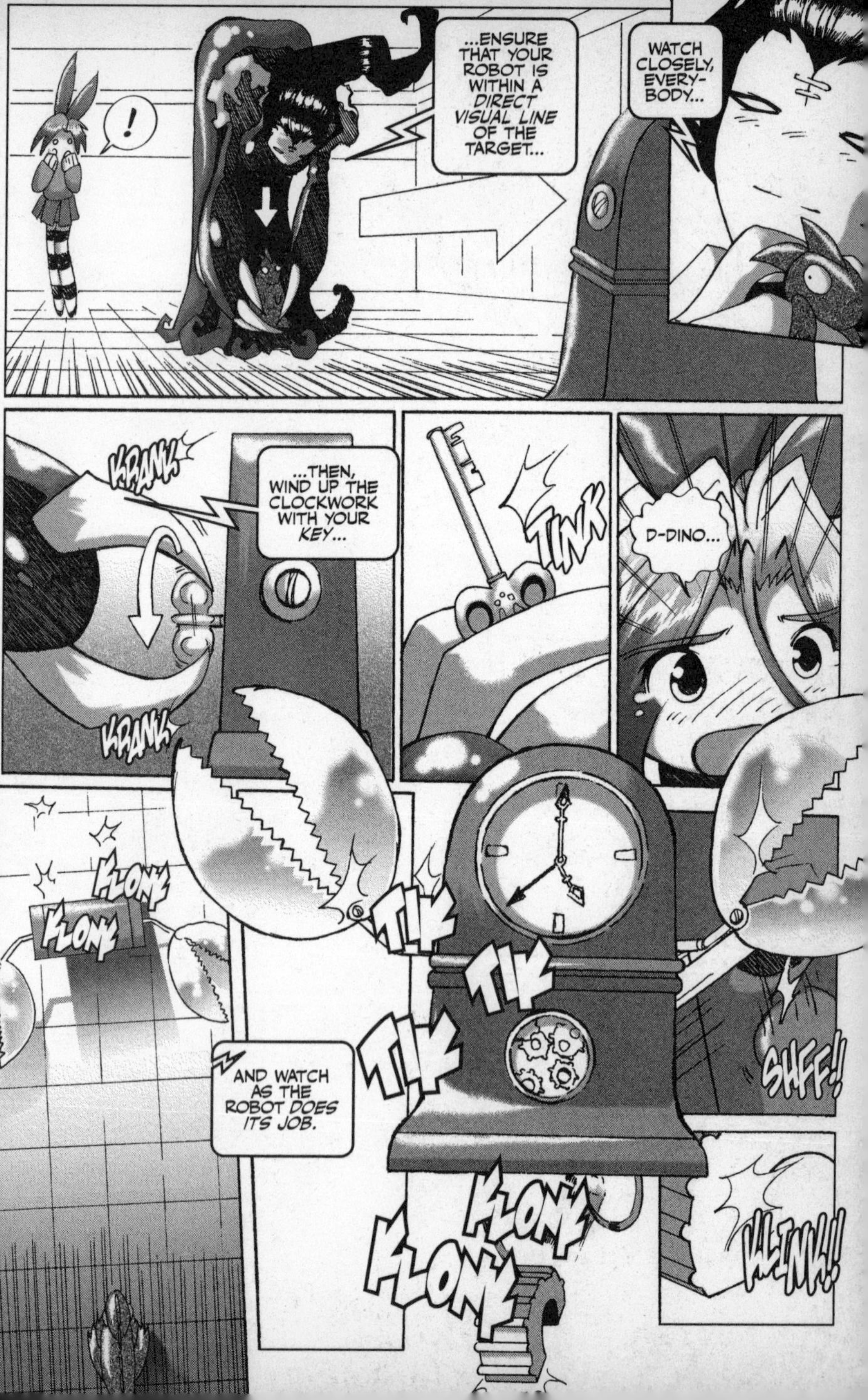
WATCH CLOSELY, EVERYBODY...
...ENSURE THAT YOUR ROBOT IS WITHIN A *DIRECT VISUAL LINE* OF THE TARGET...
!
D-DINO...
TINK
...THEN, WIND UP THE CLOCKWORK WITH YOUR *KEY*...
KRANK
KRANK
SHFF!!
KLINK!!
TIK
TIK
TIK
KLONK
KLONK
AND WATCH AS THE ROBOT *DOES ITS JOB*.
KLONK
KLONK

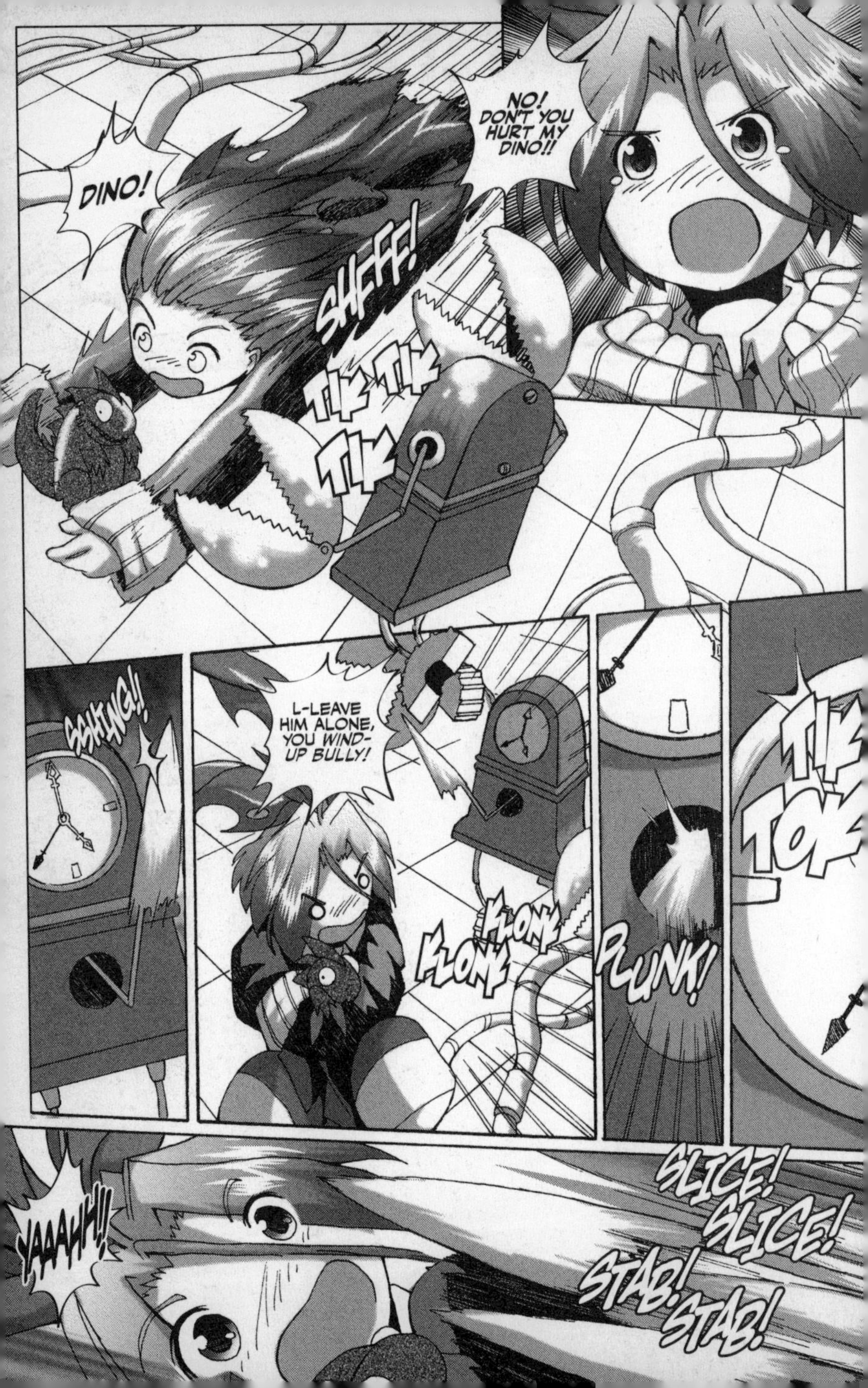
NO! DON'T YOU HURT MY DINO!!
DINO!
SHFFF!
TIK TIK TIK
TIK TOK
PLUNK!
L-LEAVE HIM ALONE, YOU WIND-UP BULLY!
KLONK KLONK
SSHING!!
SLICE! SLICE!
STAB! STAB!
YAAAHH!!

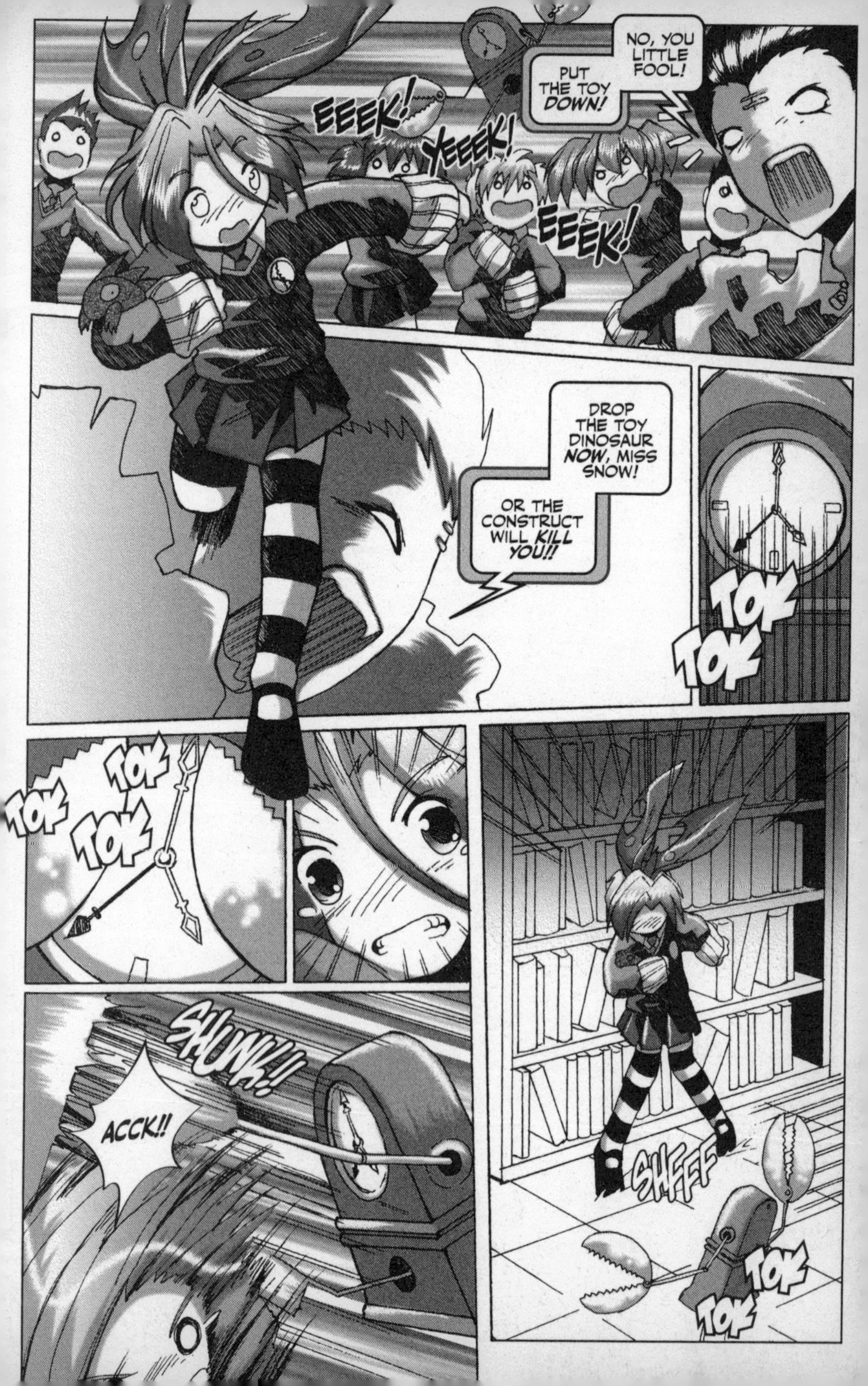
EEEK!
YEEEK!
EEEK!
NO, YOU LITTLE FOOL!
PUT THE TOY DOWN!
DROP THE TOY DINOSAUR NOW, MISS SNOW!
OR THE CONSTRUCT WILL KILL YOU!!
TOK TOK
TOK TOK TOK
SHFFF
TOK TOK
SHUNK!!
ACCK!!

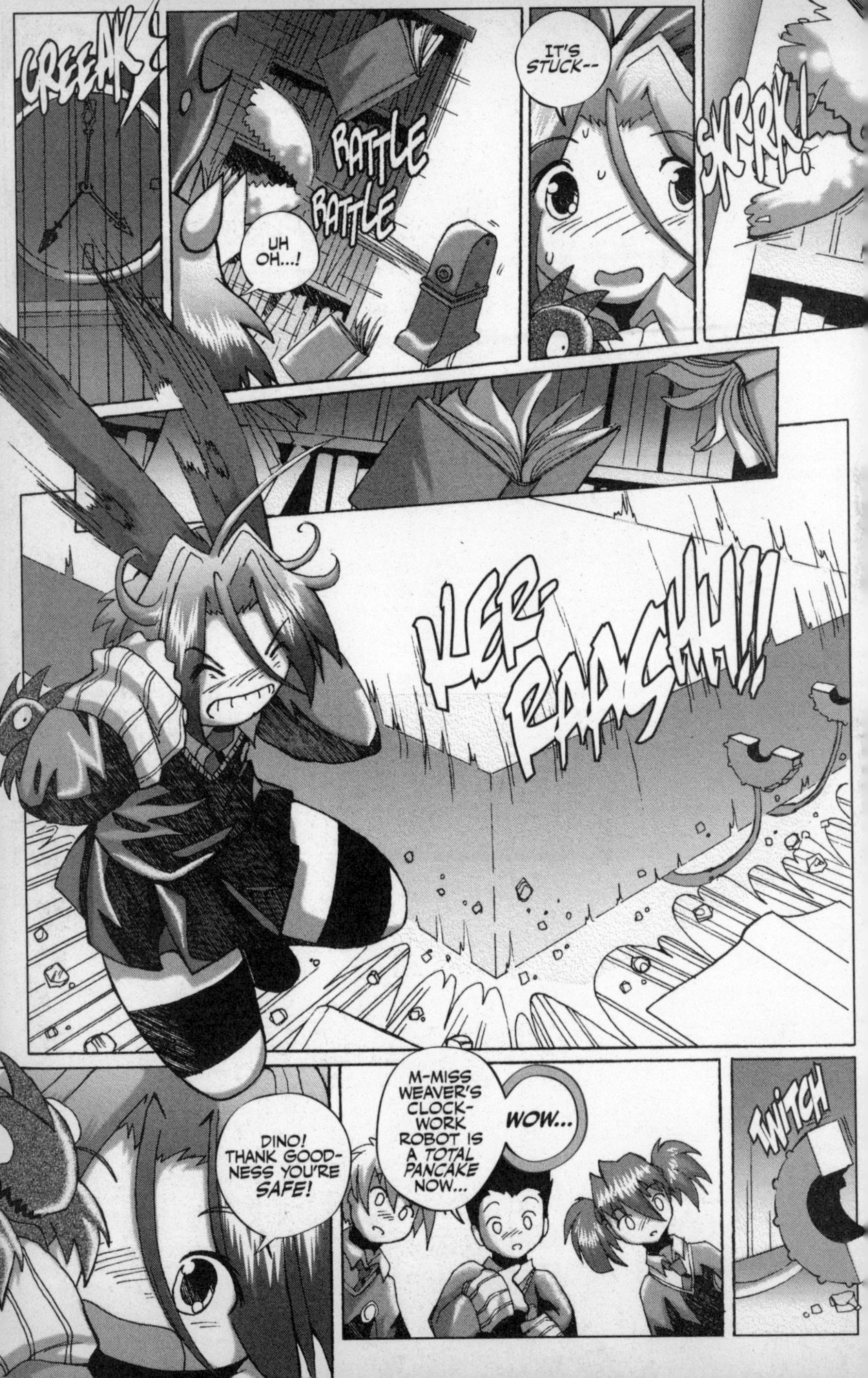
SKRRK!
IT'S STUCK--
RATTLE
RATTLE
UH OH...!
CREEAK!
KER-RAASH!!
TWITCH
WOW...
M-MISS WEAVER'S CLOCK-WORK ROBOT IS A *TOTAL* PANCAKE NOW...
DINO! THANK GOOD-NESS YOU'RE *SAFE!*

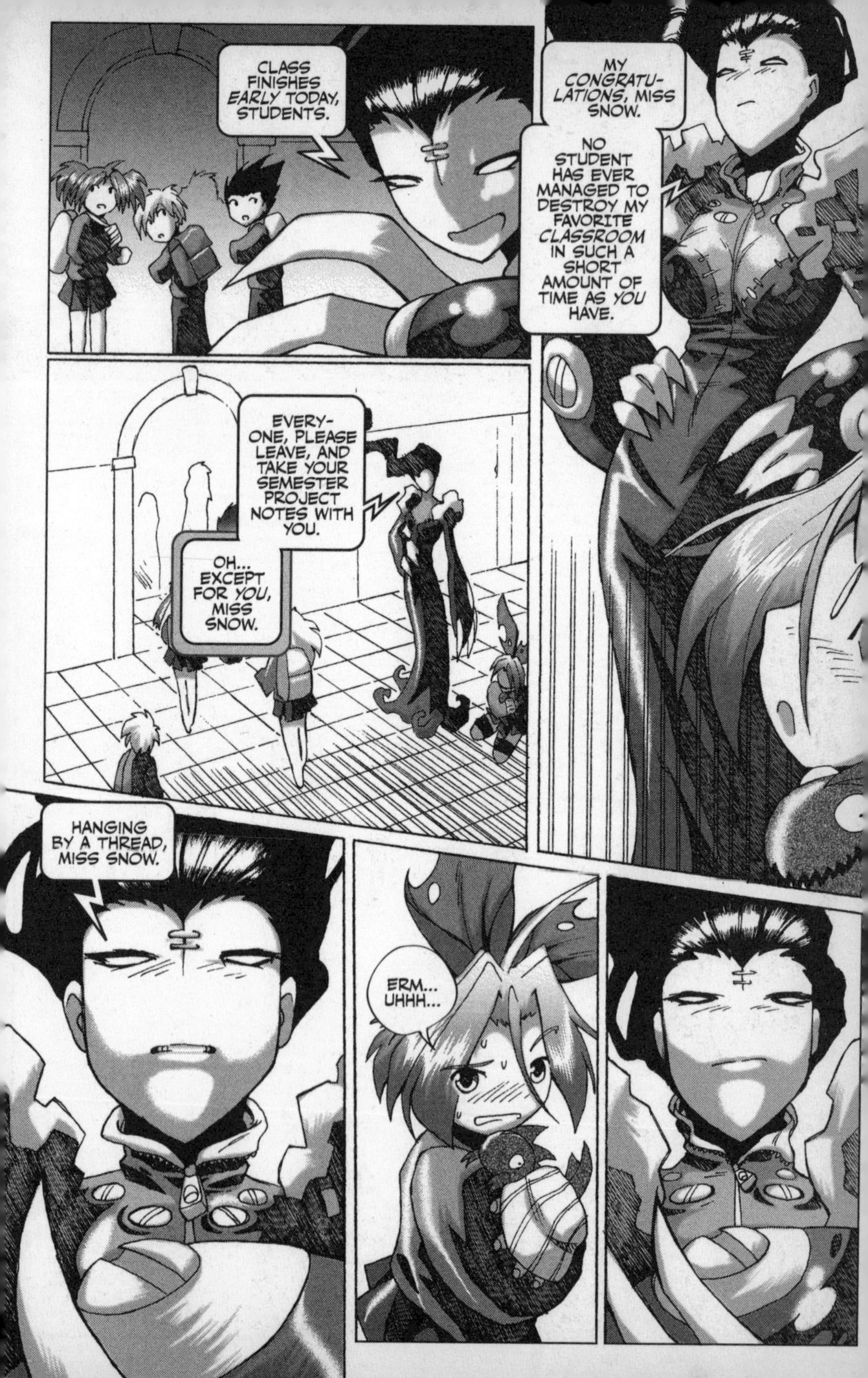
CLASS FINISHES EARLY TODAY, STUDENTS.
EVERYONE, PLEASE LEAVE, AND TAKE YOUR SEMESTER PROJECT NOTES WITH YOU.
OH... EXCEPT FOR YOU, MISS SNOW.
MY CONGRATULATIONS, MISS SNOW.
NO STUDENT HAS EVER MANAGED TO DESTROY MY FAVORITE CLASSROOM IN SUCH A SHORT AMOUNT OF TIME AS YOU HAVE.
HANGING BY A THREAD, MISS SNOW.
ERM... UHHH...

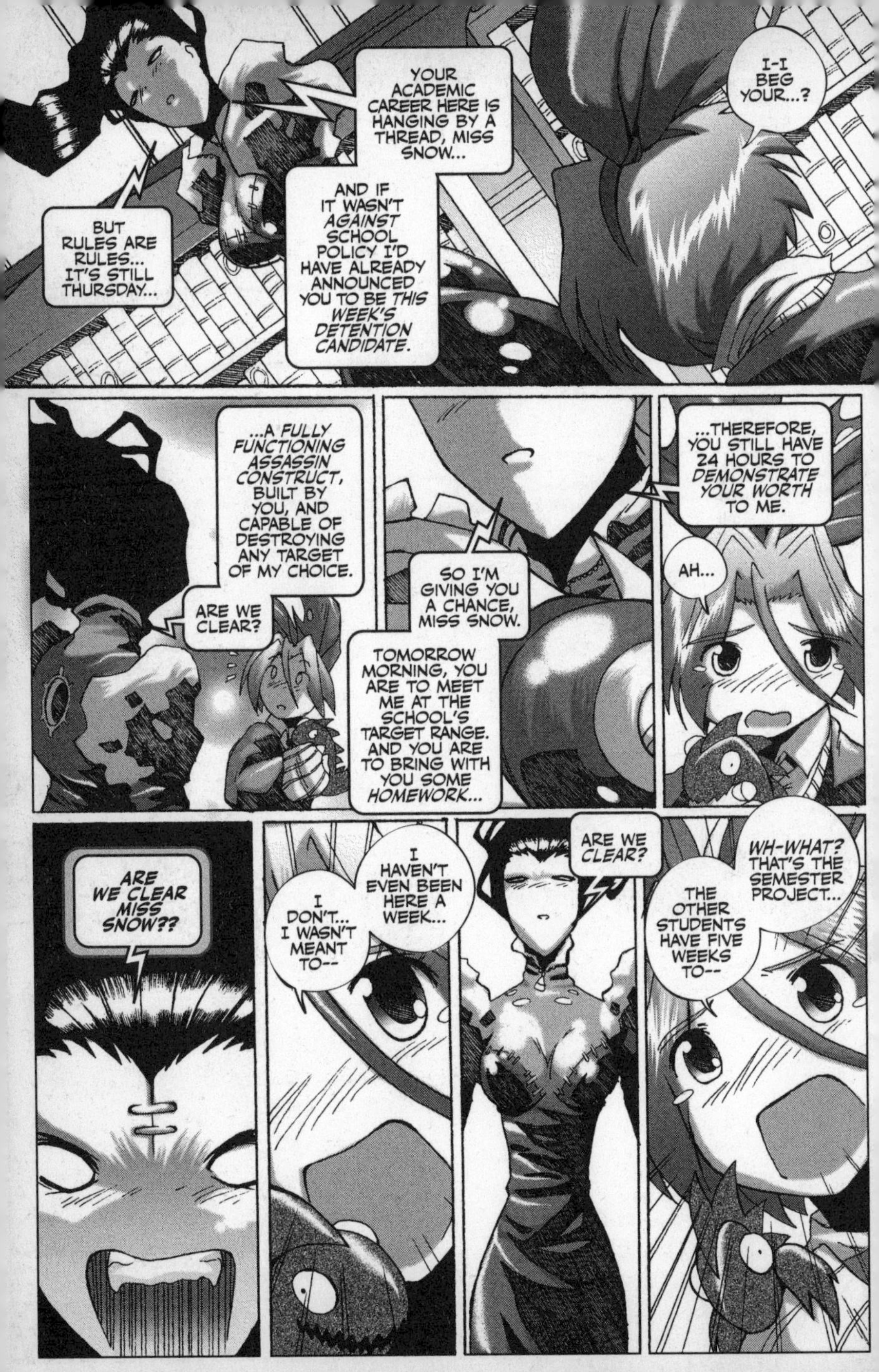
YOUR ACADEMIC CAREER HERE IS HANGING BY A THREAD, MISS SNOW...
I-I BEG YOUR...?
AND IF IT WASN'T *AGAINST* SCHOOL POLICY I'D HAVE ALREADY ANNOUNCED YOU TO BE *THIS WEEK'S DETENTION CANDIDATE.*
BUT RULES ARE RULES... IT'S STILL THURSDAY...
...THEREFORE, YOU STILL HAVE 24 HOURS TO *DEMONSTRATE YOUR WORTH* TO ME.
AH...
SO I'M GIVING YOU A CHANCE, MISS SNOW.
TOMORROW MORNING, YOU ARE TO MEET ME AT THE SCHOOL'S TARGET RANGE. AND YOU ARE TO BRING WITH YOU SOME *HOMEWORK...*
...A *FULLY FUNCTIONING ASSASSIN CONSTRUCT,* BUILT BY YOU, AND CAPABLE OF DESTROYING ANY TARGET OF MY CHOICE.
ARE WE CLEAR?
WH-WHAT? THAT'S THE SEMESTER PROJECT...
THE OTHER STUDENTS HAVE FIVE WEEKS TO--
ARE WE *CLEAR?*
I HAVEN'T EVEN BEEN HERE A WEEK...
I DON'T... I WASN'T MEANT TO--
ARE WE CLEAR MISS SNOW??

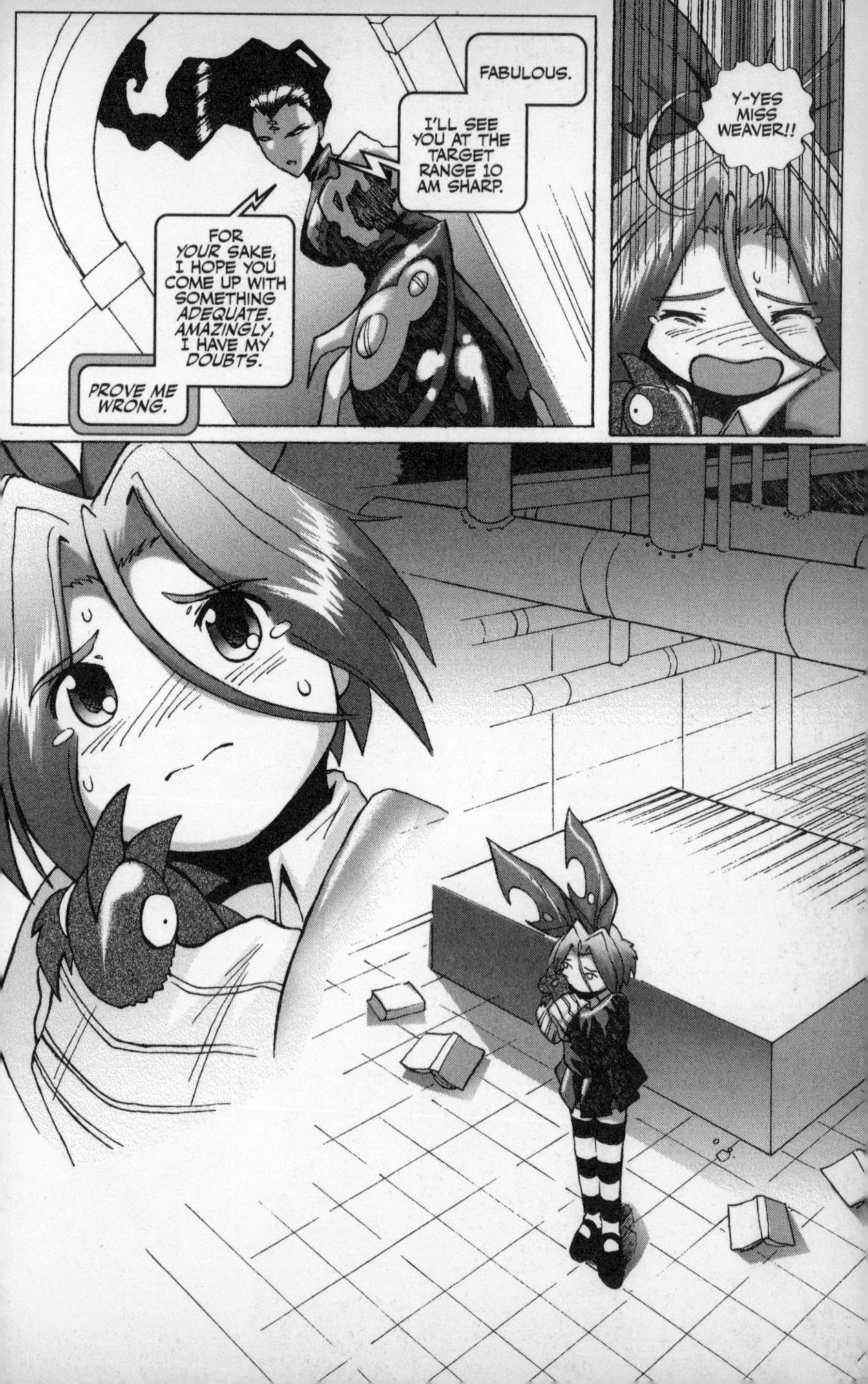
FABULOUS.
I'LL SEE YOU AT THE TARGET RANGE 10 AM SHARP.
FOR *YOUR SAKE*, I HOPE YOU COME UP WITH SOMETHING *ADEQUATE*. *AMAZINGLY*, I HAVE MY *DOUBTS*.
PROVE ME WRONG.
Y-YES MISS WEAVER!!

CHAPTER FOUR
NIGHTMARES AND CLOCKWORK

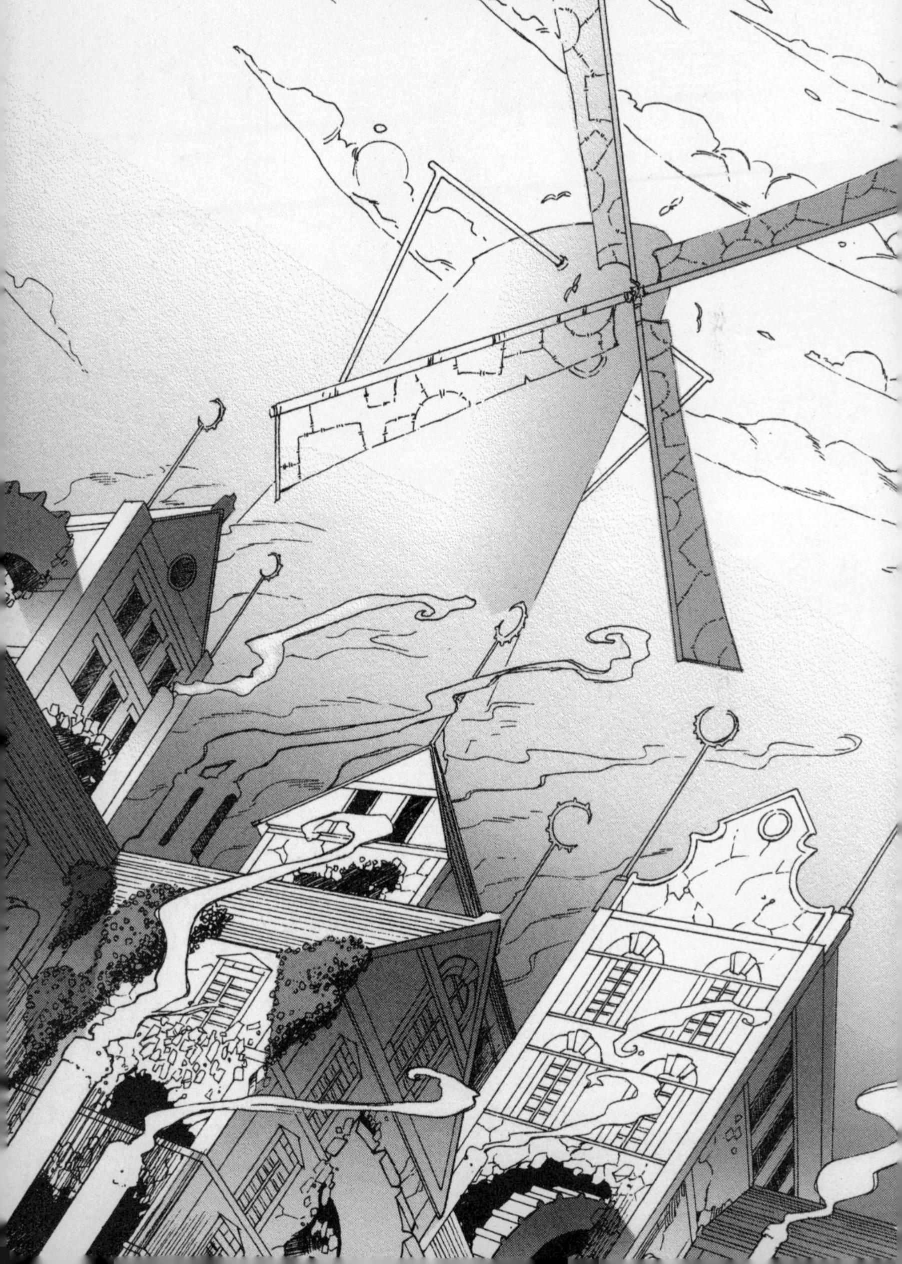

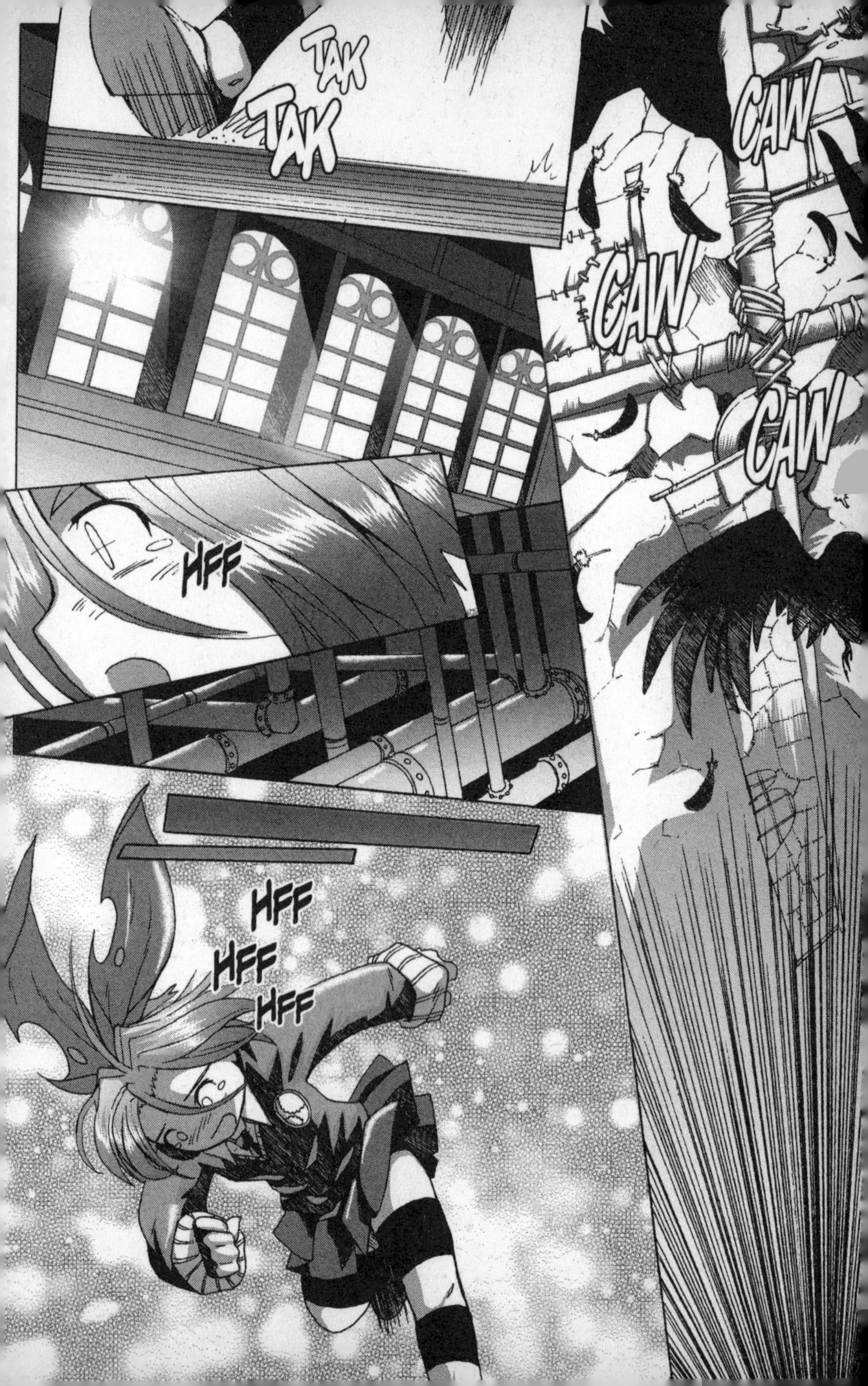
CAW
CAW
CAW
TAK
TAK
HFF
HFF
HFF
HFF

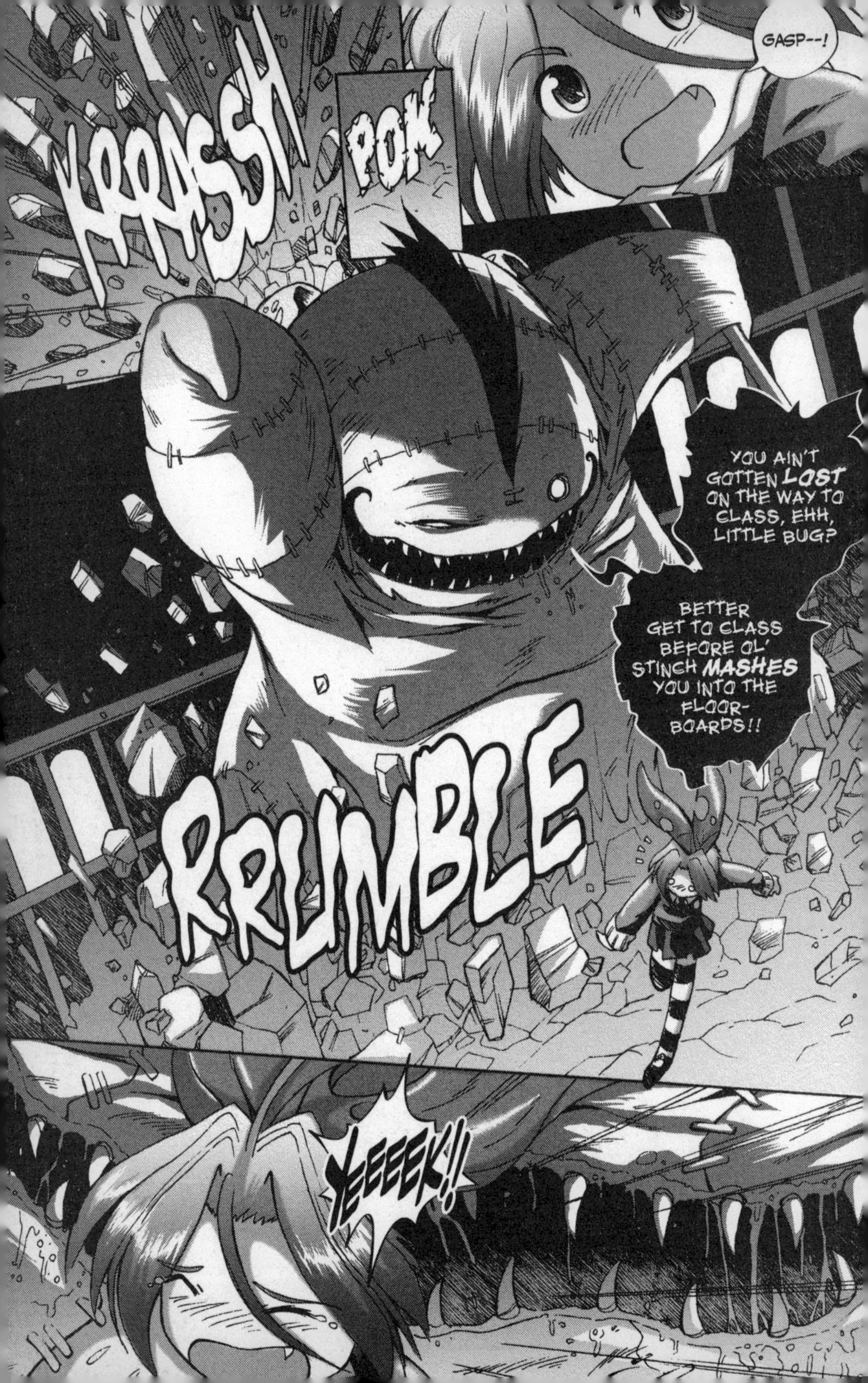
GASP--!
KRRASSH
POK
YOU AIN'T GOTTEN LOST ON THE WAY TO CLASS, EHH, LITTLE BUG?
BETTER GET TO CLASS BEFORE OL' STINCH MASHES YOU INTO THE FLOOR-BOARDS!!
RRUMBLE
YEEEEK!!

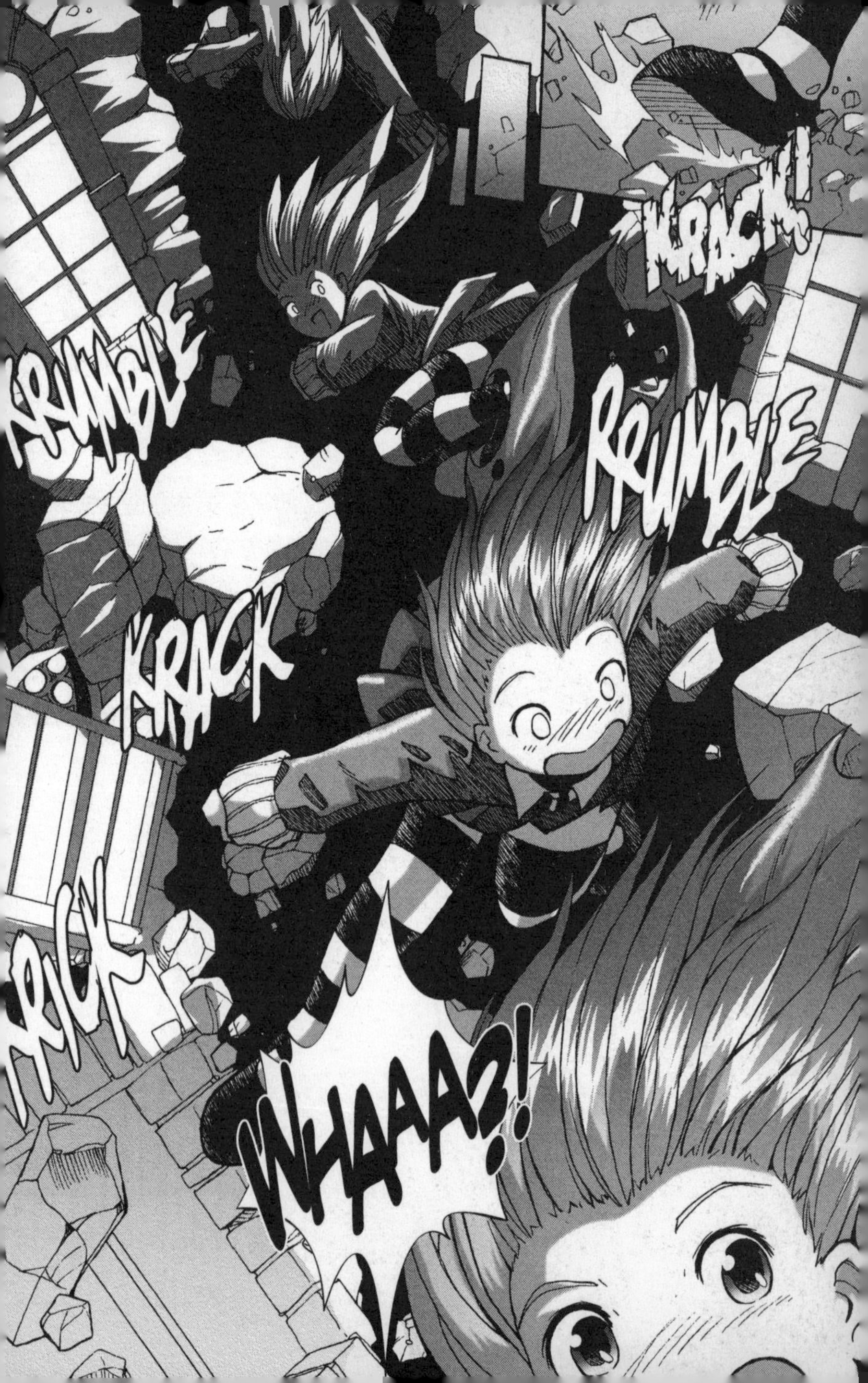

KRACK!
RRUMBLE
RRUMBLE
KRACK
KRICK
WHAAA?!

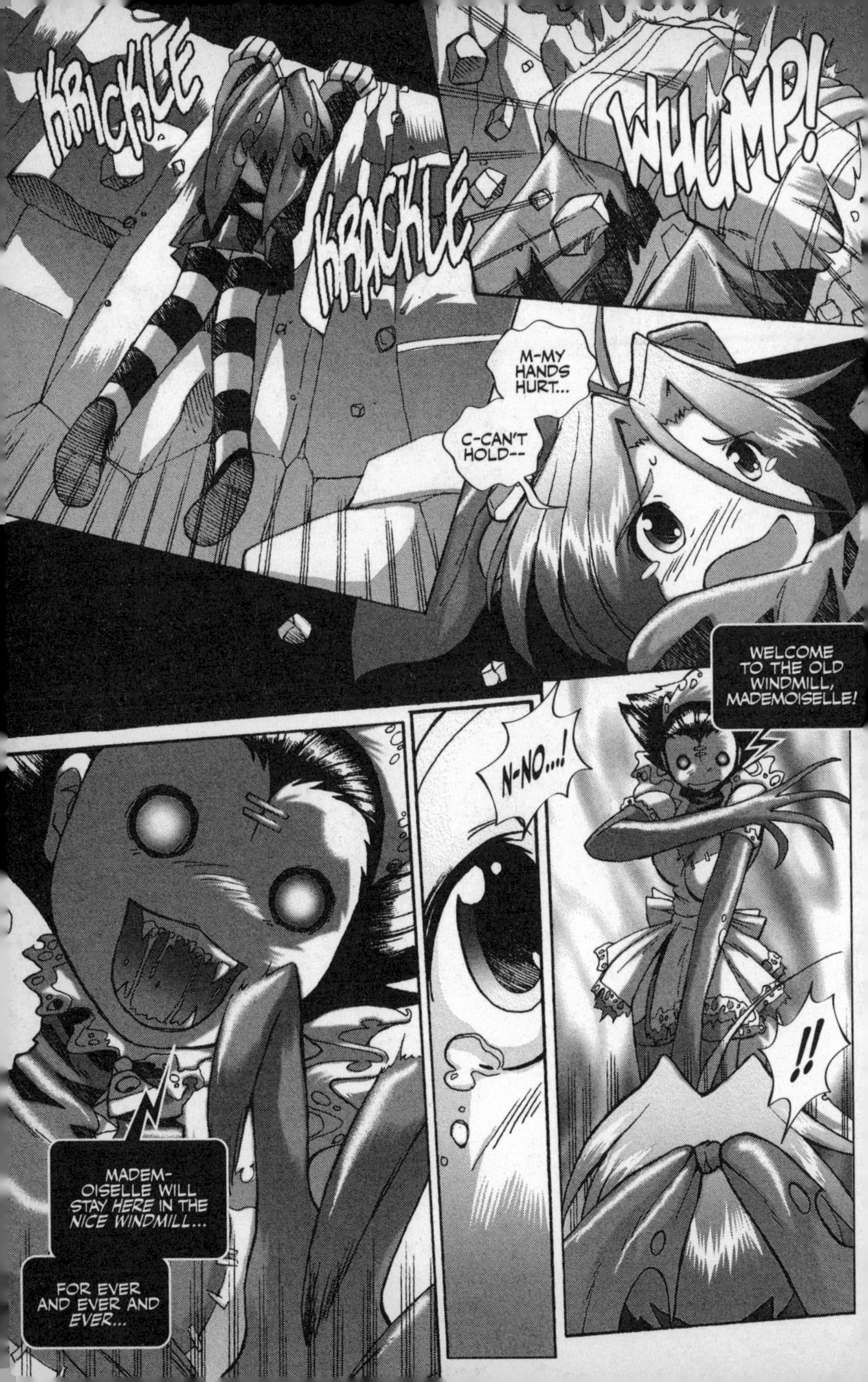
WHUMP!
KRICKLE
KRACKLE
M-MY HANDS HURT...
C-CAN'T HOLD--
WELCOME TO THE OLD WINDMILL, MADEMOISELLE!
!!
N-NO...!
MADEM-OISELLE WILL STAY *HERE* IN THE *NICE WINDMILL*...
FOR EVER AND EVER AND *EVER*...

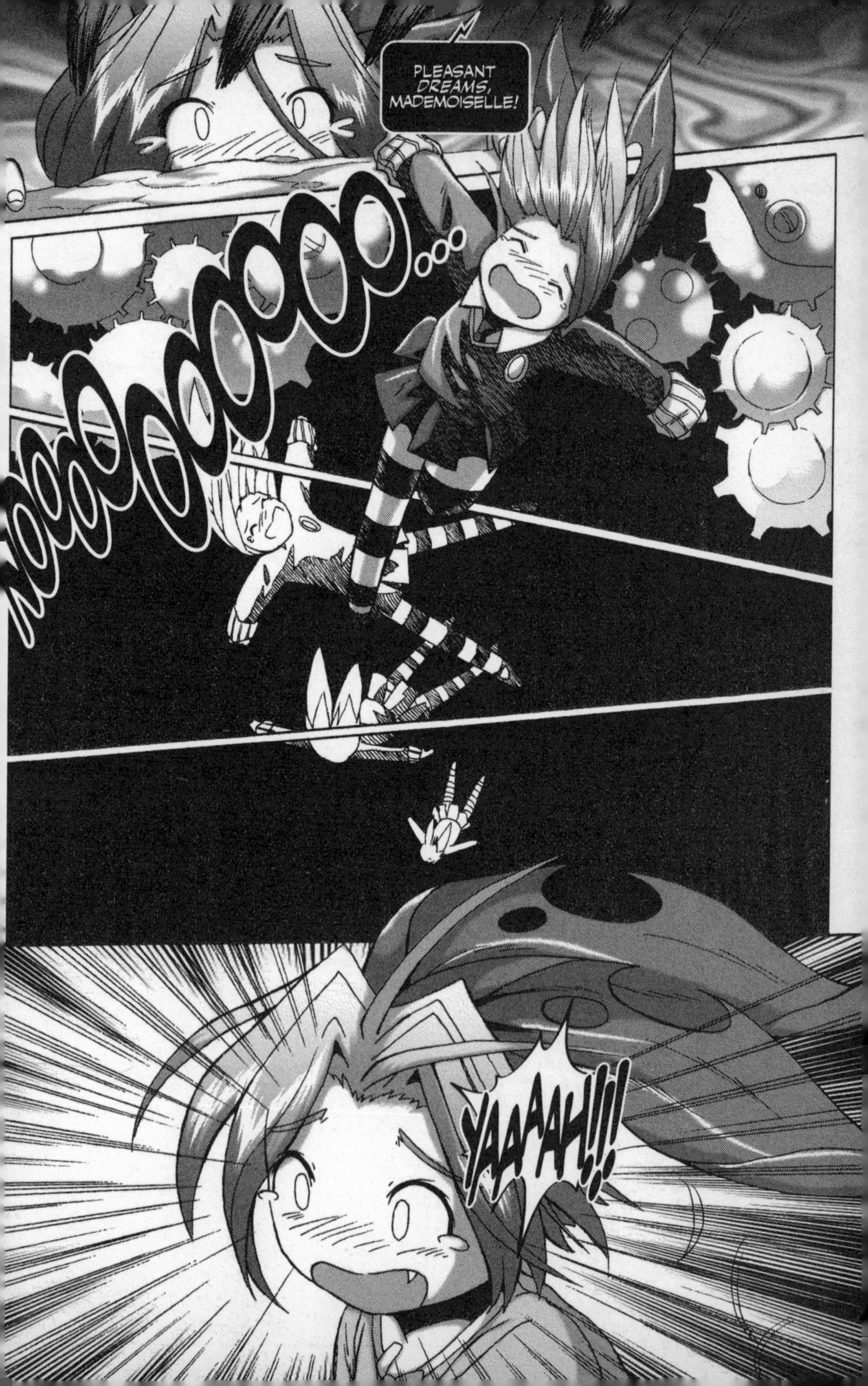
PLEASANT *DREAMS,* MADEMOISELLE!
NOOOOOOOOOOOOO...
YAAAH!!!

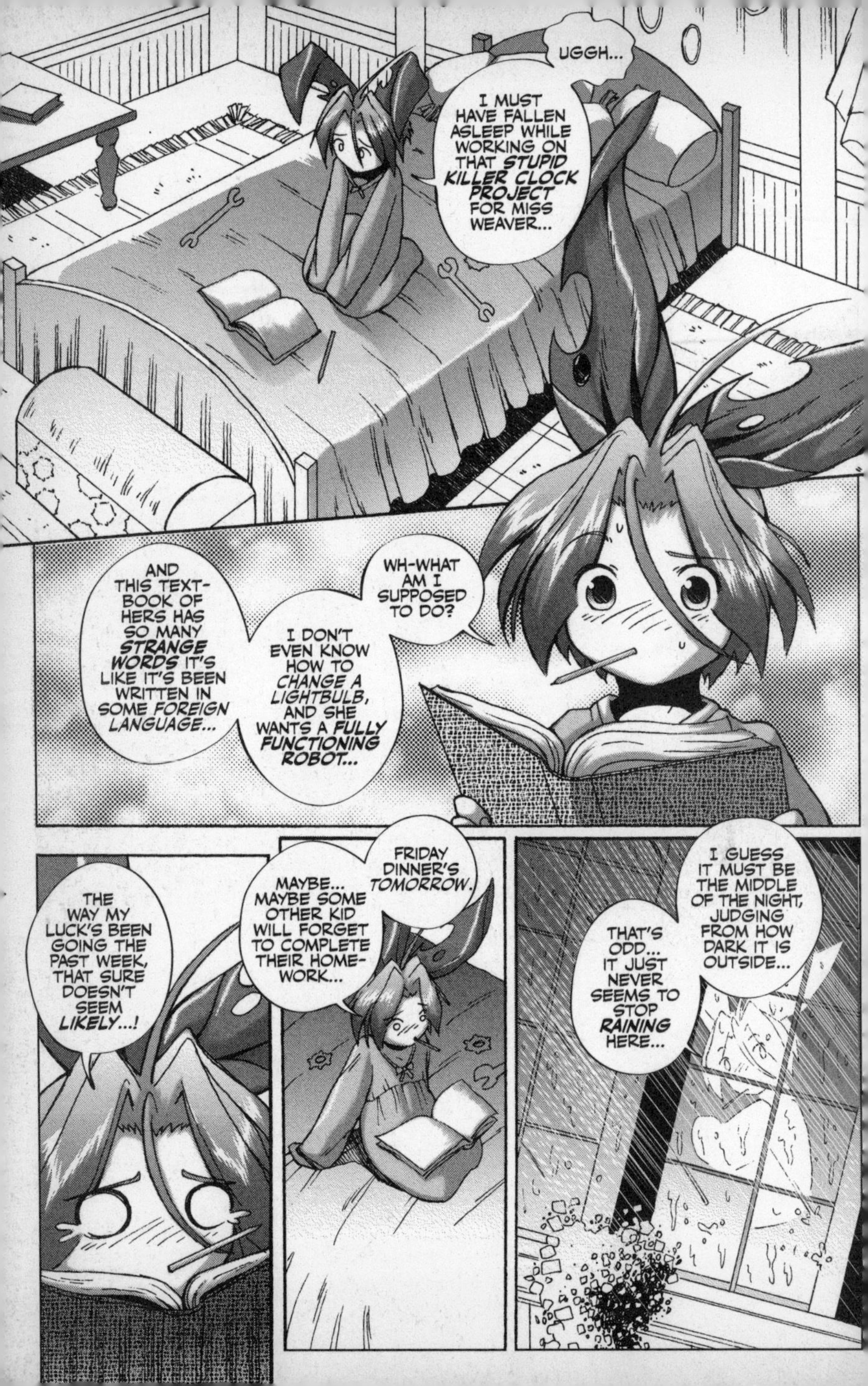
UGGH...
I MUST HAVE FALLEN ASLEEP WHILE WORKING ON THAT STUPID KILLER CLOCK PROJECT FOR MISS WEAVER...
WH-WHAT AM I SUPPOSED TO DO?
I DON'T EVEN KNOW HOW TO CHANGE A LIGHTBULB, AND SHE WANTS A FULLY FUNCTIONING ROBOT...
AND THIS TEXT-BOOK OF HERS HAS SO MANY STRANGE WORDS IT'S LIKE IT'S BEEN WRITTEN IN SOME FOREIGN LANGUAGE...
I GUESS IT MUST BE THE MIDDLE OF THE NIGHT, JUDGING FROM HOW DARK IT IS OUTSIDE...
THAT'S ODD... IT JUST NEVER SEEMS TO STOP RAINING HERE...
FRIDAY DINNER'S TOMORROW.
MAYBE... MAYBE SOME OTHER KID WILL FORGET TO COMPLETE THEIR HOME-WORK...
THE WAY MY LUCK'S BEEN GOING THE PAST WEEK, THAT SURE DOESN'T SEEM LIKELY...!

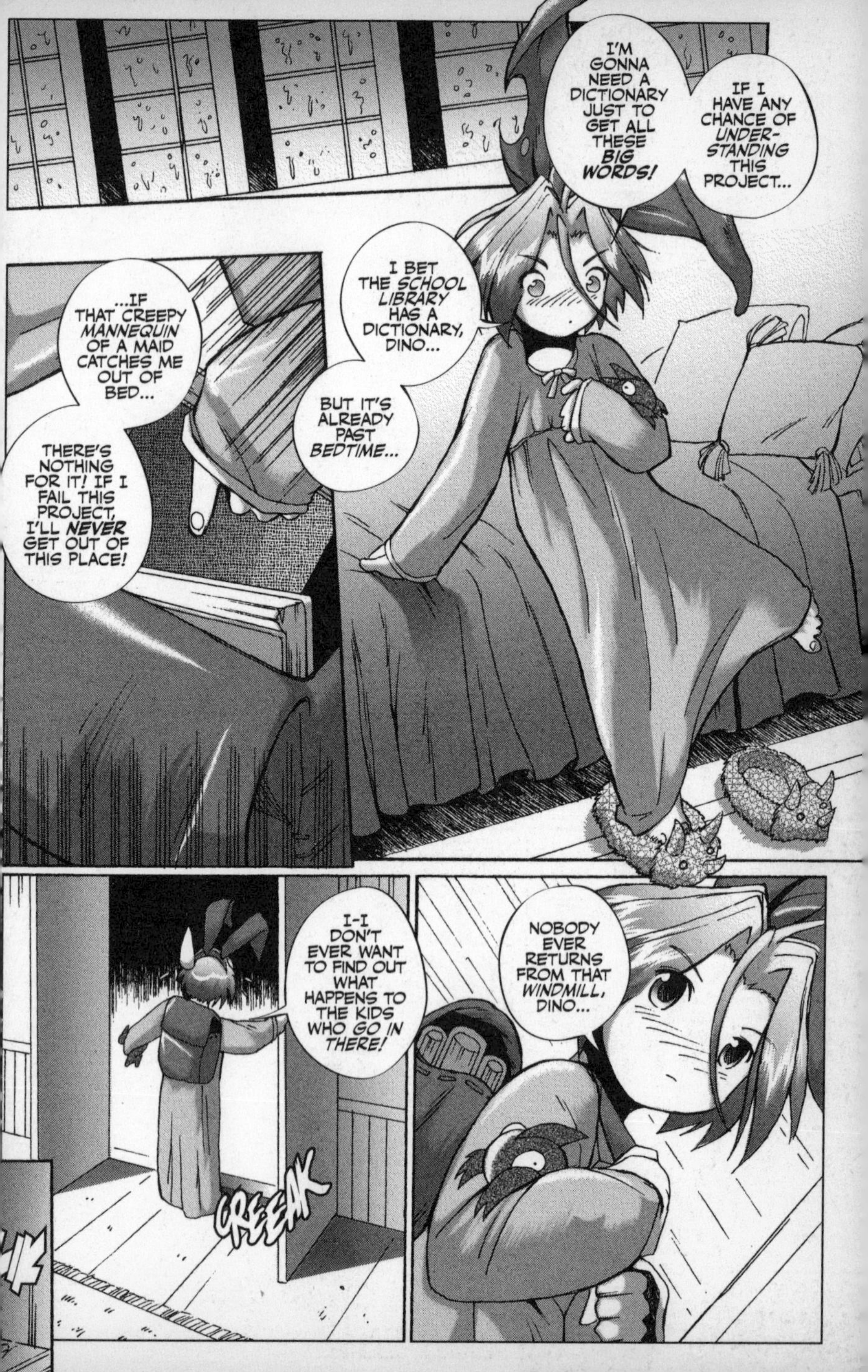
IF I HAVE ANY CHANCE OF UNDER-STANDING THIS PROJECT...
I'M GONNA NEED A DICTIONARY JUST TO GET ALL THESE BIG WORDS!
I BET THE SCHOOL LIBRARY HAS A DICTIONARY, DINO...
BUT IT'S ALREADY PAST BEDTIME...
...IF THAT CREEPY MANNEQUIN OF A MAID CATCHES ME OUT OF BED...
THERE'S NOTHING FOR IT! IF I FAIL THIS PROJECT, I'LL NEVER GET OUT OF THIS PLACE!
NOBODY EVER RETURNS FROM THAT WINDMILL, DINO...
I-I DON'T EVER WANT TO FIND OUT WHAT HAPPENS TO THE KIDS WHO GO IN THERE!
CREEAK

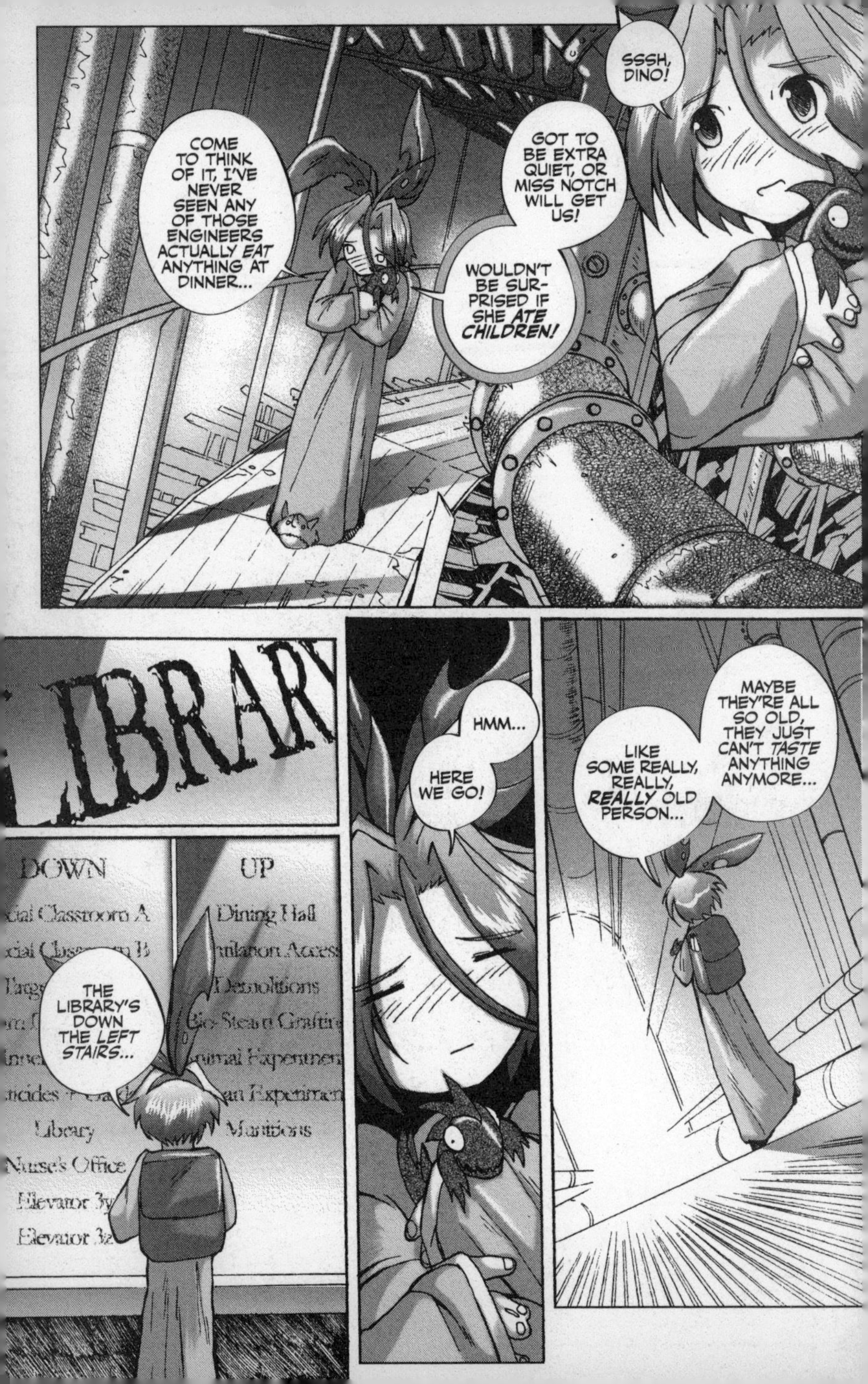
SSSH, DINO!
GOT TO BE EXTRA QUIET, OR MISS NOTCH WILL GET US!
WOULDN'T BE SUR-PRISED IF SHE *ATE CHILDREN!*
COME TO THINK OF IT, I'VE NEVER SEEN ANY OF THOSE ENGINEERS ACTUALLY *EAT* ANYTHING AT DINNER...
MAYBE THEY'RE ALL SO OLD, THEY JUST CAN'T *TASTE* ANYTHING ANYMORE...
LIKE SOME REALLY, REALLY, *REALLY* OLD PERSON...
HMM...
HERE WE GO!
LIBRARY
DOWN
UP
Dining Hall
Demolitions
Library
Munitions
Nurse's Office
THE LIBRARY'S DOWN THE *LEFT STAIRS*...

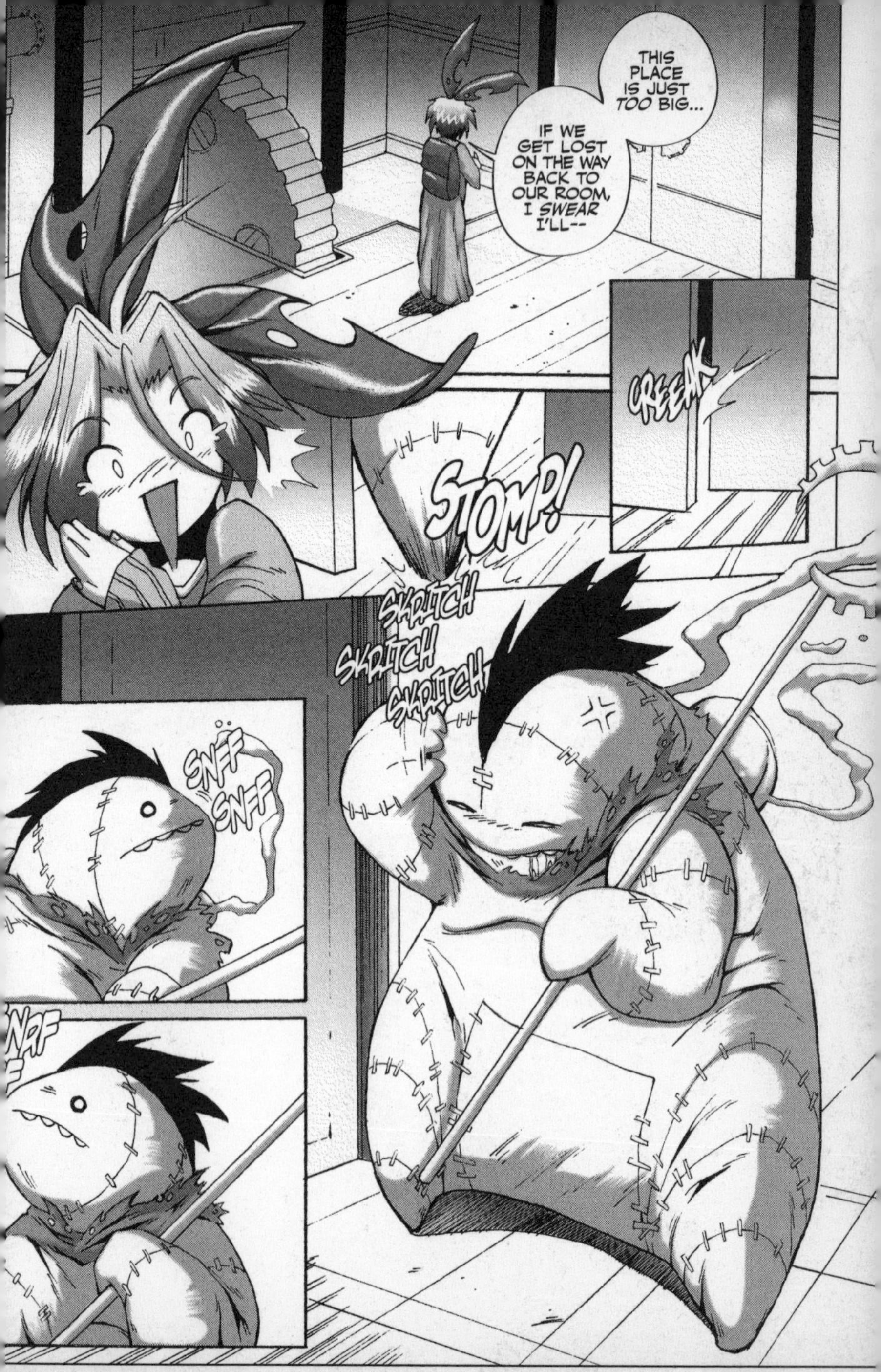
THIS PLACE IS JUST TOO BIG...
IF WE GET LOST ON THE WAY BACK TO OUR ROOM, I SWEAR I'LL--
CREEAK
STOMP!
SKRITCH
SKRITCH
SKRITCH
SNFF
SNFF

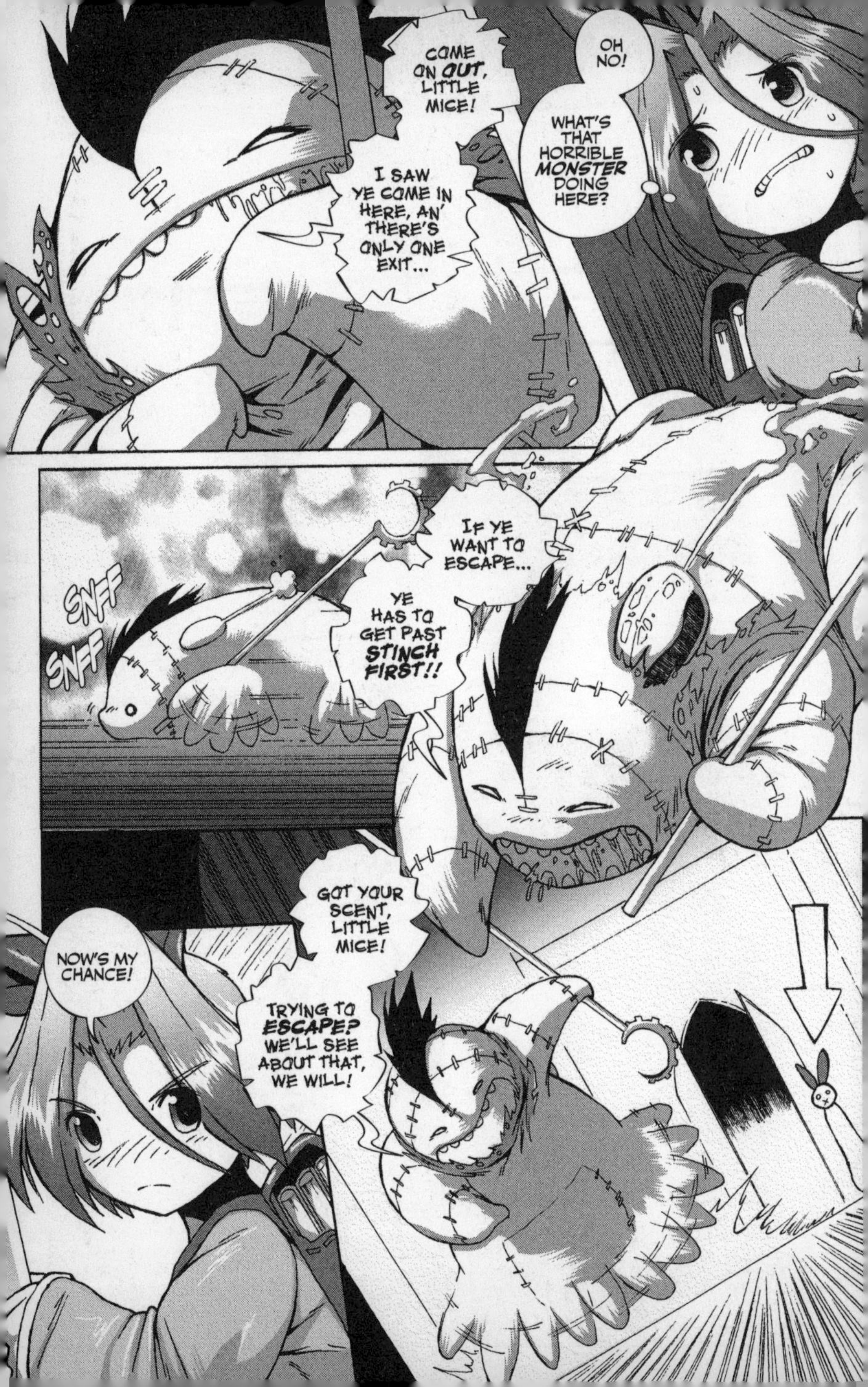
OH NO!
WHAT'S THAT HORRIBLE MONSTER DOING HERE?
COME ON OUT, LITTLE MICE!
I SAW YE COME IN HERE, AN' THERE'S ONLY ONE EXIT...
IF YE WANT TO ESCAPE...
YE HAS TO GET PAST STINCH FIRST!!
SNFF
SNFF
GOT YOUR SCENT, LITTLE MICE!
TRYING TO ESCAPE? WE'LL SEE ABOUT THAT, WE WILL!
NOW'S MY CHANCE!

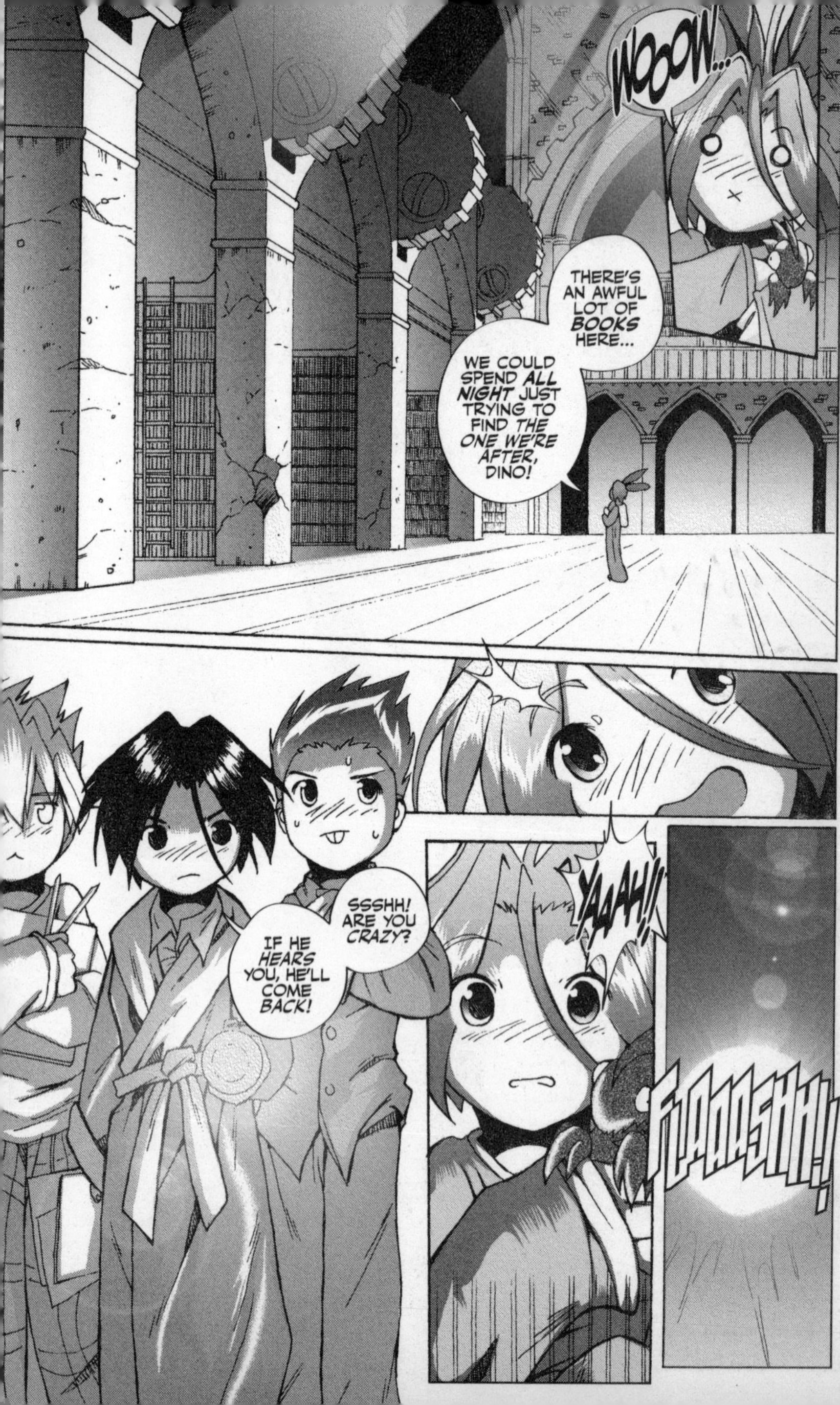
WOOOW...
THERE'S AN AWFUL LOT OF BOOKS HERE...
WE COULD SPEND ALL NIGHT JUST TRYING TO FIND THE ONE WE'RE AFTER, DINO!
SSSHH! ARE YOU CRAZY?
IF HE HEARS YOU, HE'LL COME BACK!
YAAAH!!
FLAAASHH!!

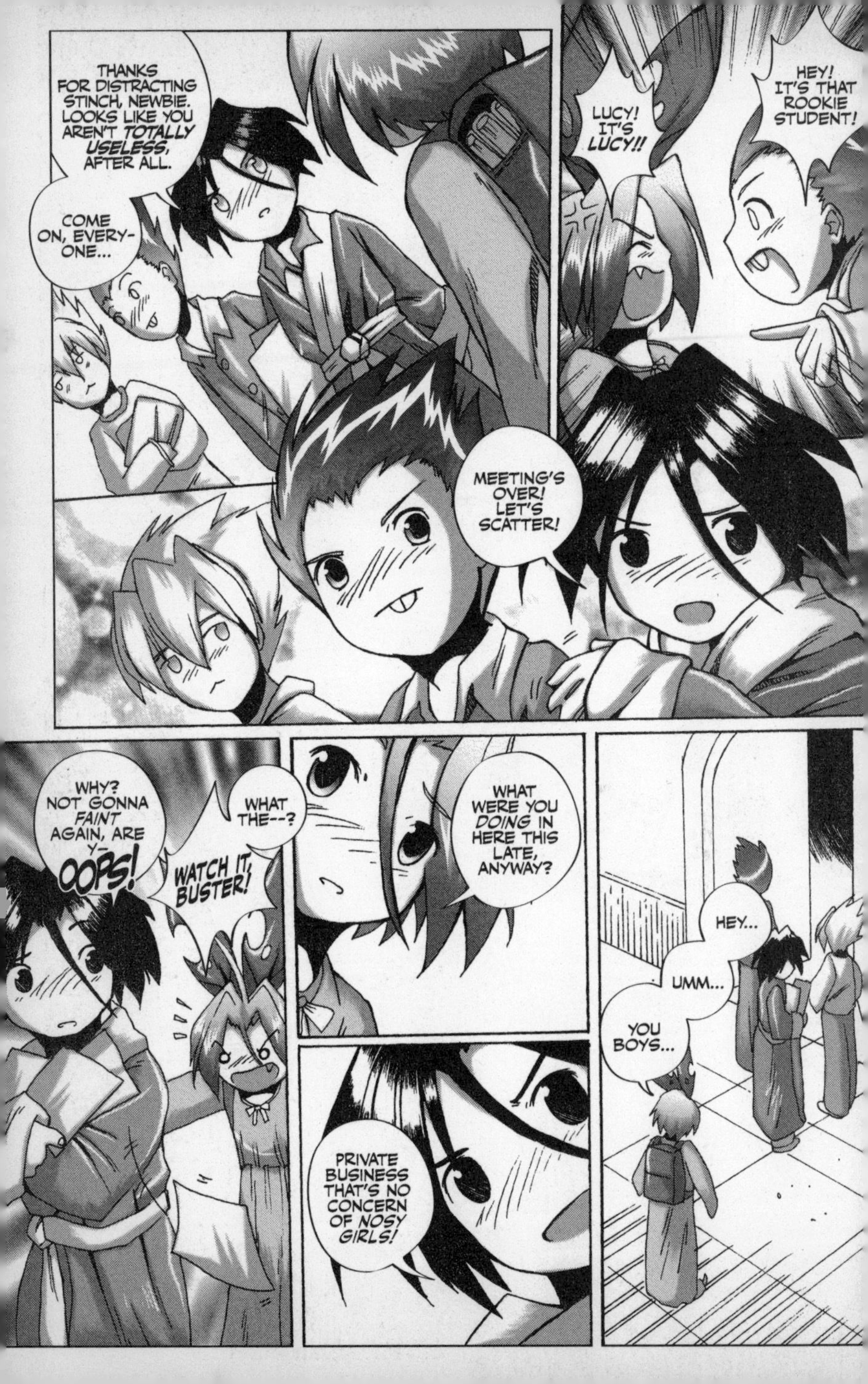
HEY! IT'S THAT ROOKIE STUDENT!
LUCY! IT'S LUCY!!
THANKS FOR DISTRACTING STINCH, NEWBIE. LOOKS LIKE YOU AREN'T TOTALLY USELESS, AFTER ALL.
COME ON, EVERYONE...
MEETING'S OVER! LET'S SCATTER!
HEY...
UMM...
YOU BOYS...
WHAT WERE YOU DOING IN HERE THIS LATE, ANYWAY?
PRIVATE BUSINESS THAT'S NO CONCERN OF NOSY GIRLS!
WHY? NOT GONNA FAINT AGAIN, ARE Y-
OOPS!
WHAT THE--?
WATCH IT, BUSTER!

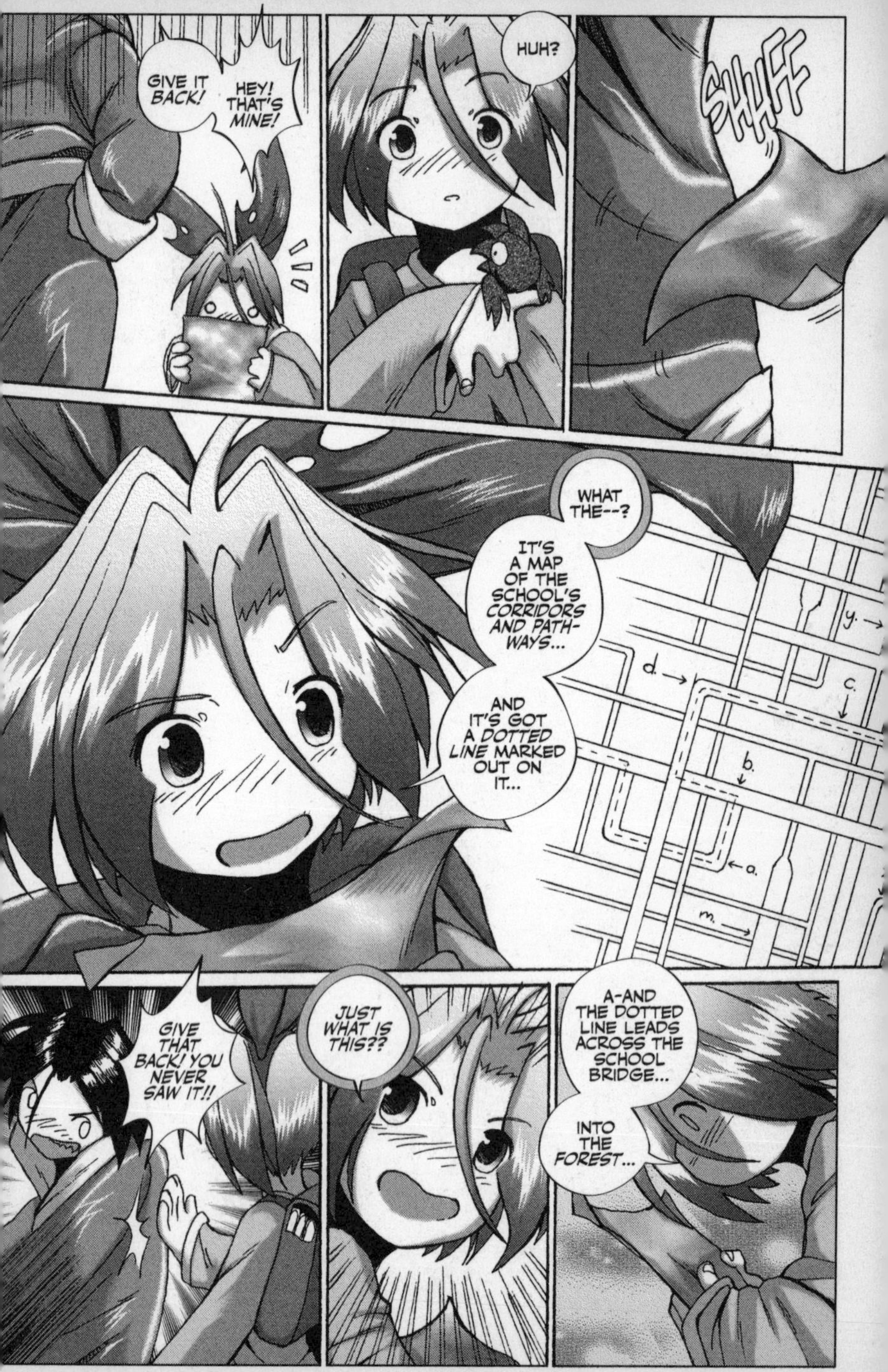
SHUFF
HUH?
HEY! THAT'S MINE!
GIVE IT BACK!
WHAT THE--?
IT'S A MAP OF THE SCHOOL'S CORRIDORS AND PATH-WAYS...
AND IT'S GOT A DOTTED LINE MARKED OUT ON IT...
y.
d.
c.
b.
a.
m.
A-AND THE DOTTED LINE LEADS ACROSS THE SCHOOL BRIDGE...
INTO THE FOREST...
JUST WHAT IS THIS??
GIVE THAT BACK! YOU NEVER SAW IT!!

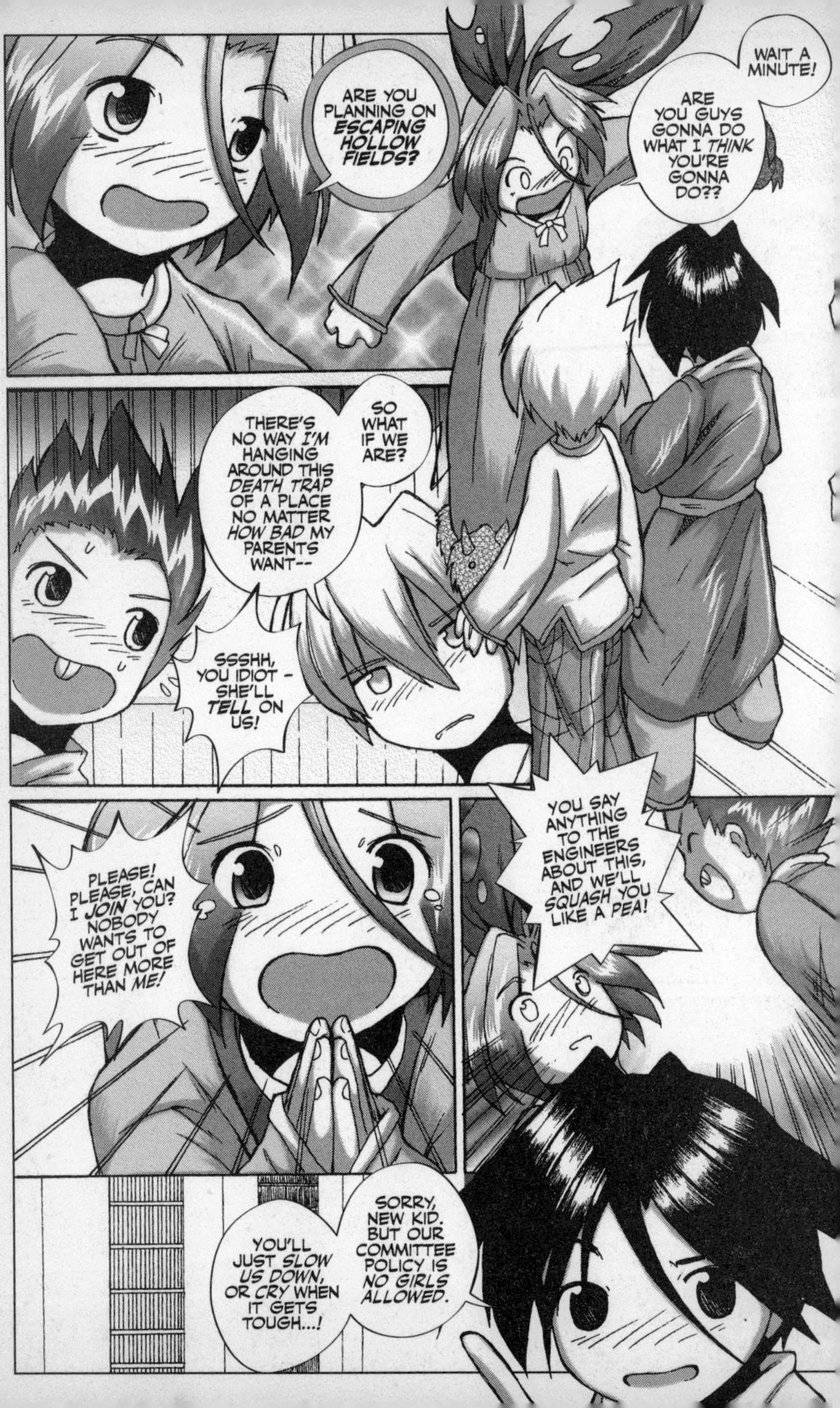
WAIT A MINUTE!
ARE YOU GUYS GONNA DO WHAT I *THINK* YOU'RE GONNA DO??
ARE YOU PLANNING ON *ESCAPING HOLLOW FIELDS?*
SO WHAT IF WE ARE?
THERE'S NO WAY *I'M* HANGING AROUND THIS *DEATH TRAP* OF A PLACE NO MATTER *HOW BAD* MY PARENTS WANT--
SSSHH, YOU IDIOT - SHE'LL **TELL** ON US!
YOU SAY ANYTHING TO THE ENGINEERS ABOUT THIS, AND WE'LL *SQUASH* YOU LIKE A *PEA!*
PLEASE! PLEASE, CAN I *JOIN* YOU? NOBODY WANTS TO GET OUT OF HERE MORE THAN *ME!*
SORRY, NEW KID. BUT OUR COMMITTEE POLICY IS *NO GIRLS ALLOWED.*
YOU'LL JUST *SLOW US DOWN,* OR *CRY* WHEN IT GETS TOUGH...!

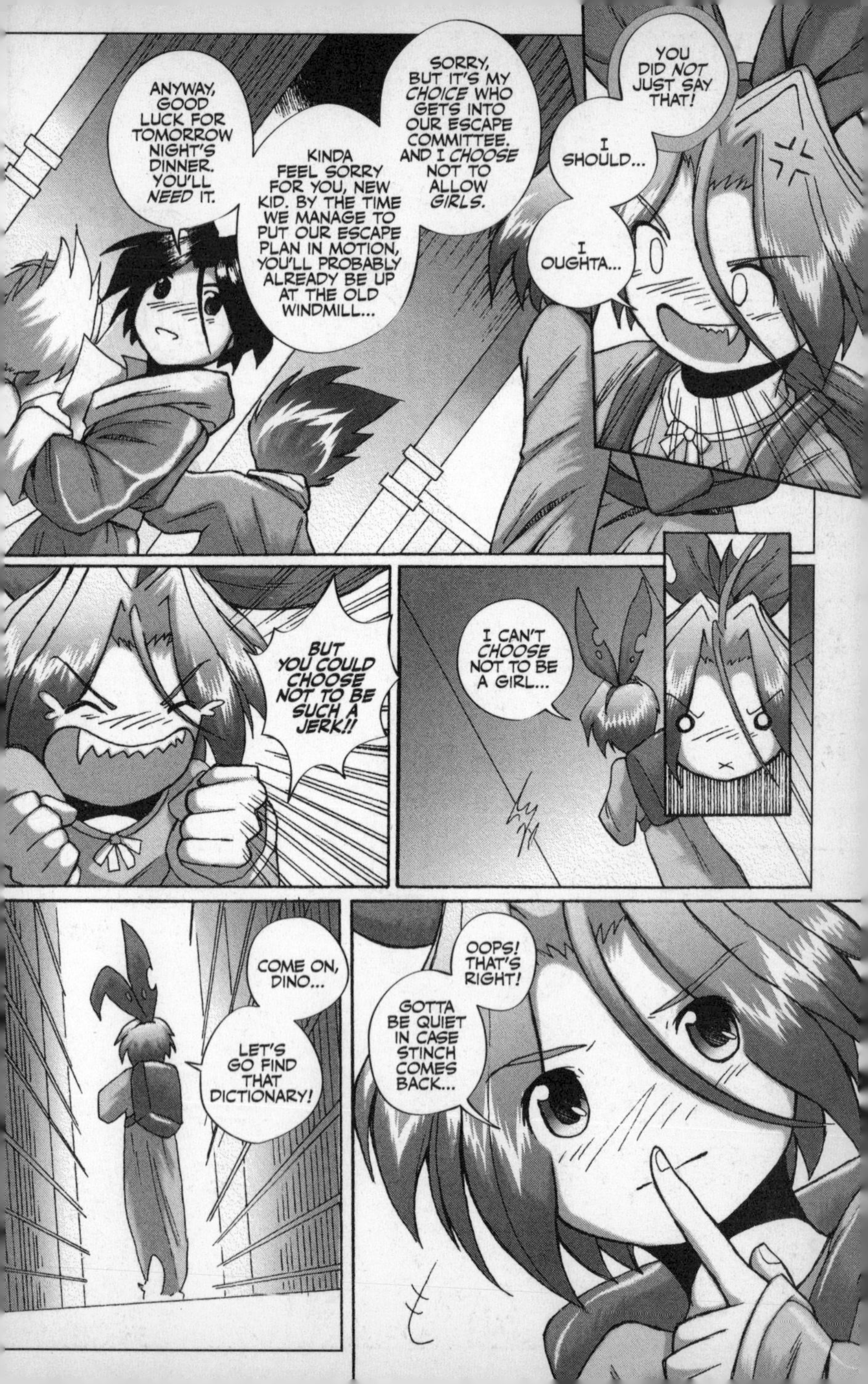
SORRY, BUT IT'S MY CHOICE WHO GETS INTO OUR ESCAPE COMMITTEE. AND I CHOOSE NOT TO ALLOW GIRLS.
KINDA FEEL SORRY FOR YOU, NEW KID. BY THE TIME WE MANAGE TO PUT OUR ESCAPE PLAN IN MOTION, YOU'LL PROBABLY ALREADY BE UP AT THE OLD WINDMILL...
ANYWAY, GOOD LUCK FOR TOMORROW NIGHT'S DINNER. YOU'LL NEED IT.
YOU DID NOT JUST SAY THAT!
I SHOULD...
I OUGHTA...
BUT YOU COULD CHOOSE NOT TO BE SUCH A JERK!!
I CAN'T CHOOSE NOT TO BE A GIRL...
COME ON, DINO...
LET'S GO FIND THAT DICTIONARY!
OOPS! THAT'S RIGHT!
GOTTA BE QUIET IN CASE STINCH COMES BACK...

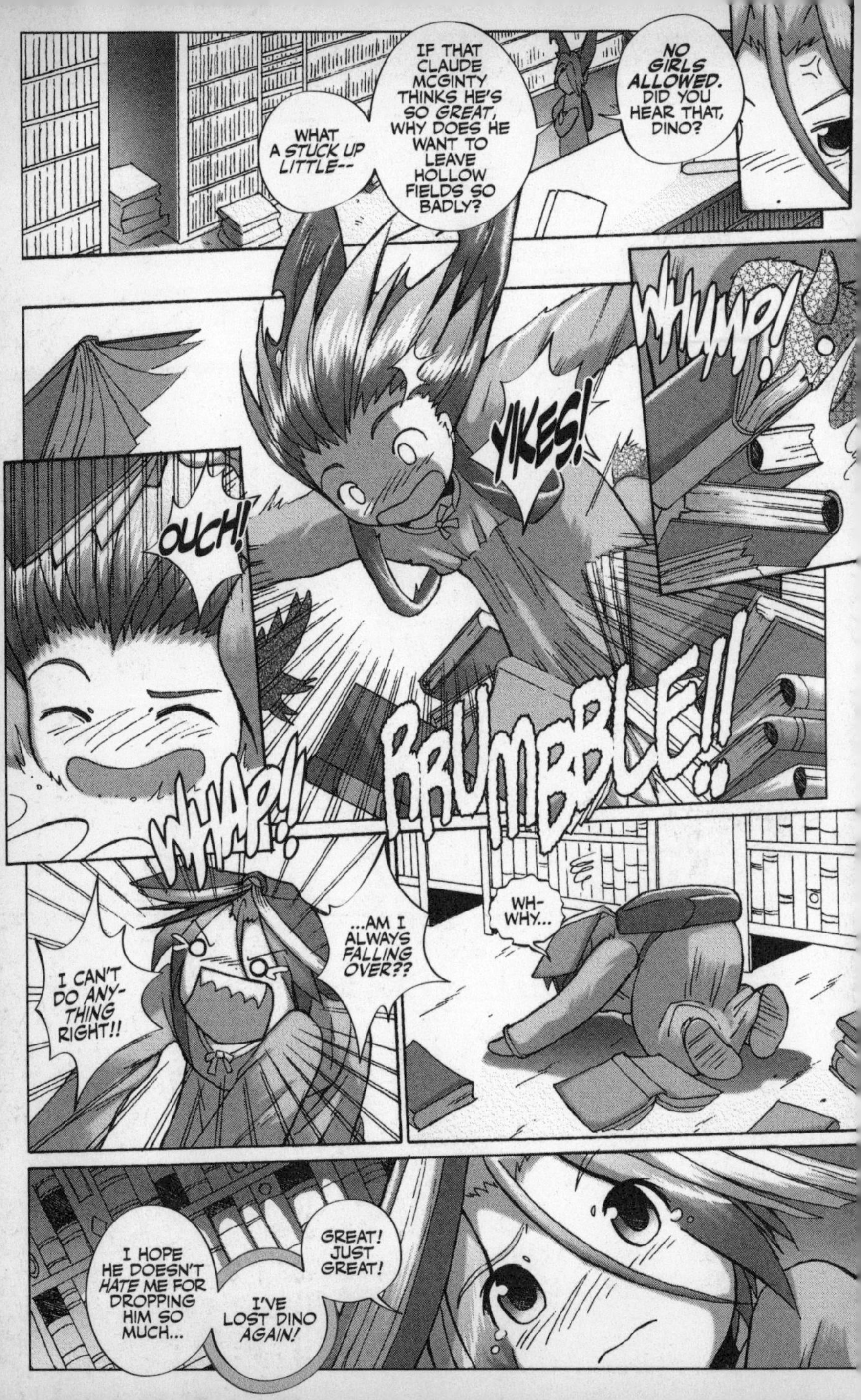
NO GIRLS ALLOWED. DID YOU HEAR THAT, DINO?
IF THAT CLAUDE MCGINTY THINKS HE'S SO GREAT, WHY DOES HE WANT TO LEAVE HOLLOW FIELDS SO BADLY?
WHAT A STUCK UP LITTLE--
WHUMP!
YIKES!
OUCH!
RRUMBBLE!!
WHAP!!
WH-WHY...
...AM I ALWAYS FALLING OVER??
I CAN'T DO ANYTHING RIGHT!!
GREAT! JUST GREAT!
I'VE LOST DINO AGAIN!
I HOPE HE DOESN'T HATE ME FOR DROPPING HIM SO MUCH...

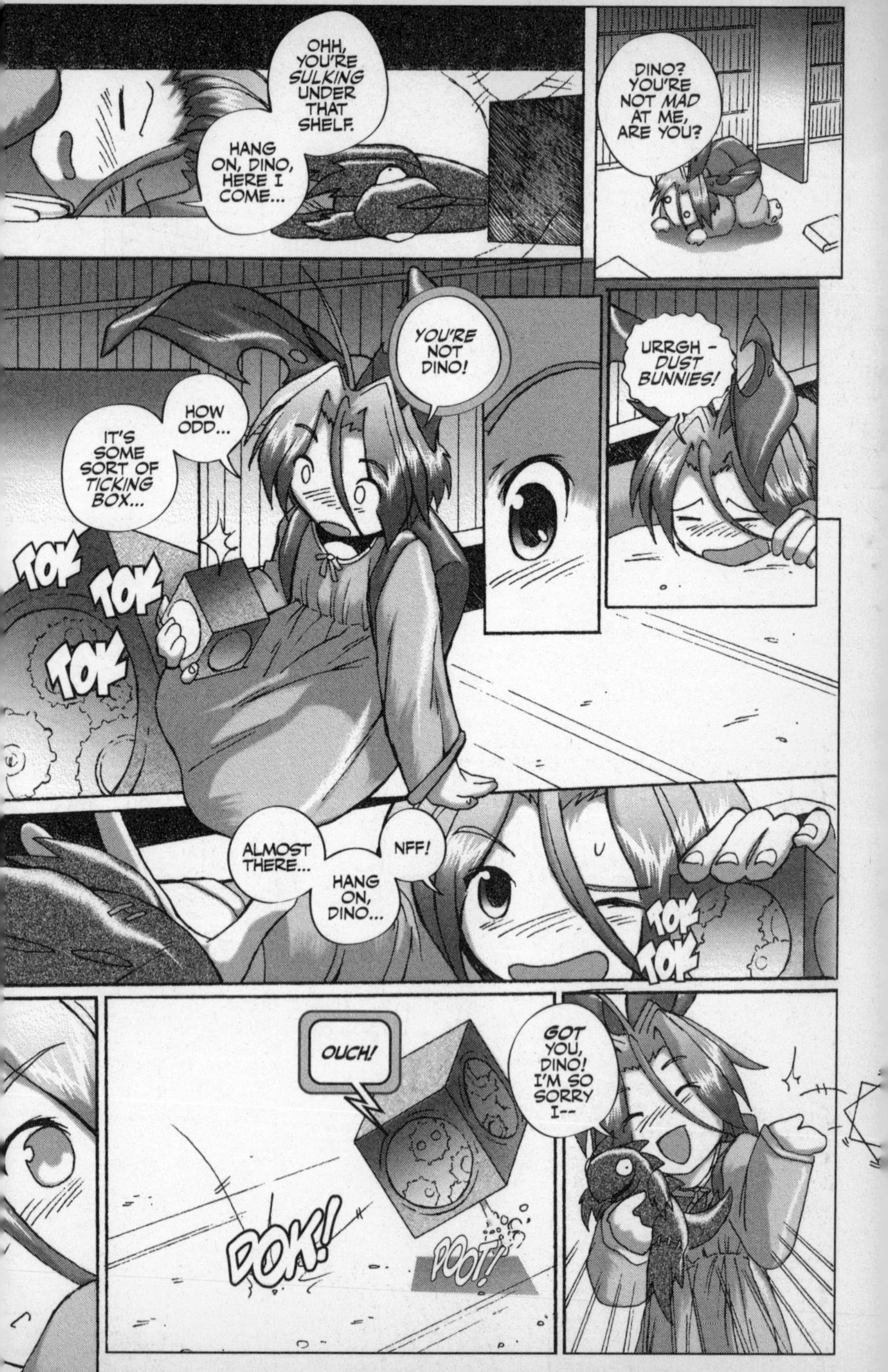
DINO? YOU'RE NOT *MAD* AT ME, ARE YOU?
OHH, YOU'RE *SULKING* UNDER THAT SHELF.
HANG ON, DINO, HERE I COME...
URRGH - *DUST* BUNNIES!
YOU'RE NOT DINO!
HOW ODD...
IT'S SOME SORT OF *TICKING* BOX...
TOK TOK TOK
NFF!
ALMOST THERE...
HANG ON, DINO...
TOK TOK
GOT YOU, DINO! I'M SO SORRY I--
OUCH!
POOT!
DOK!

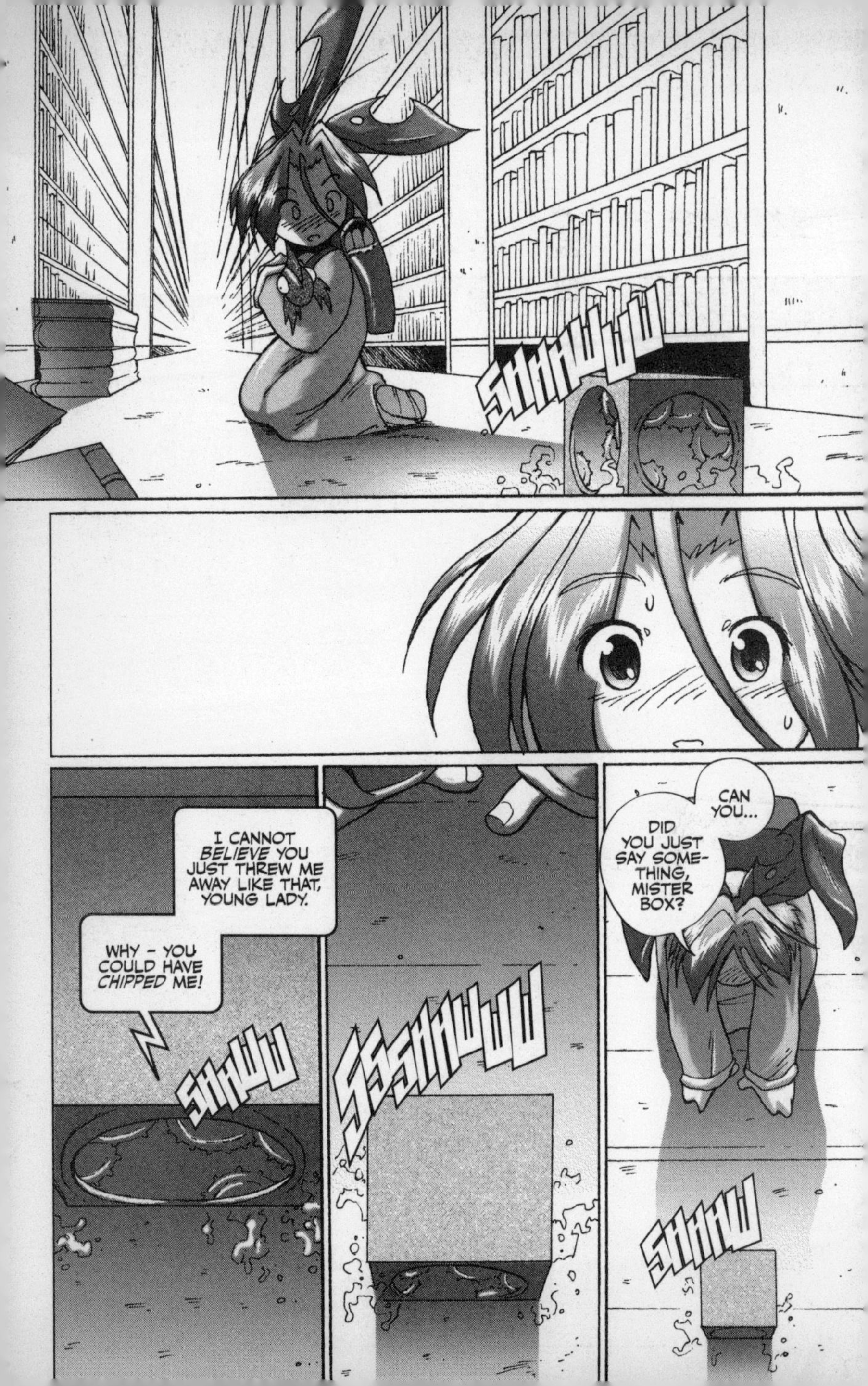
SHAWWW
CAN YOU...
DID YOU JUST SAY SOME- THING, MISTER BOX?
SHAAW
SSSHAWWW
I CANNOT *BELIEVE* YOU JUST THREW ME AWAY LIKE THAT, YOUNG LADY.
WHY - YOU COULD HAVE *CHIPPED* ME!
SHAWW

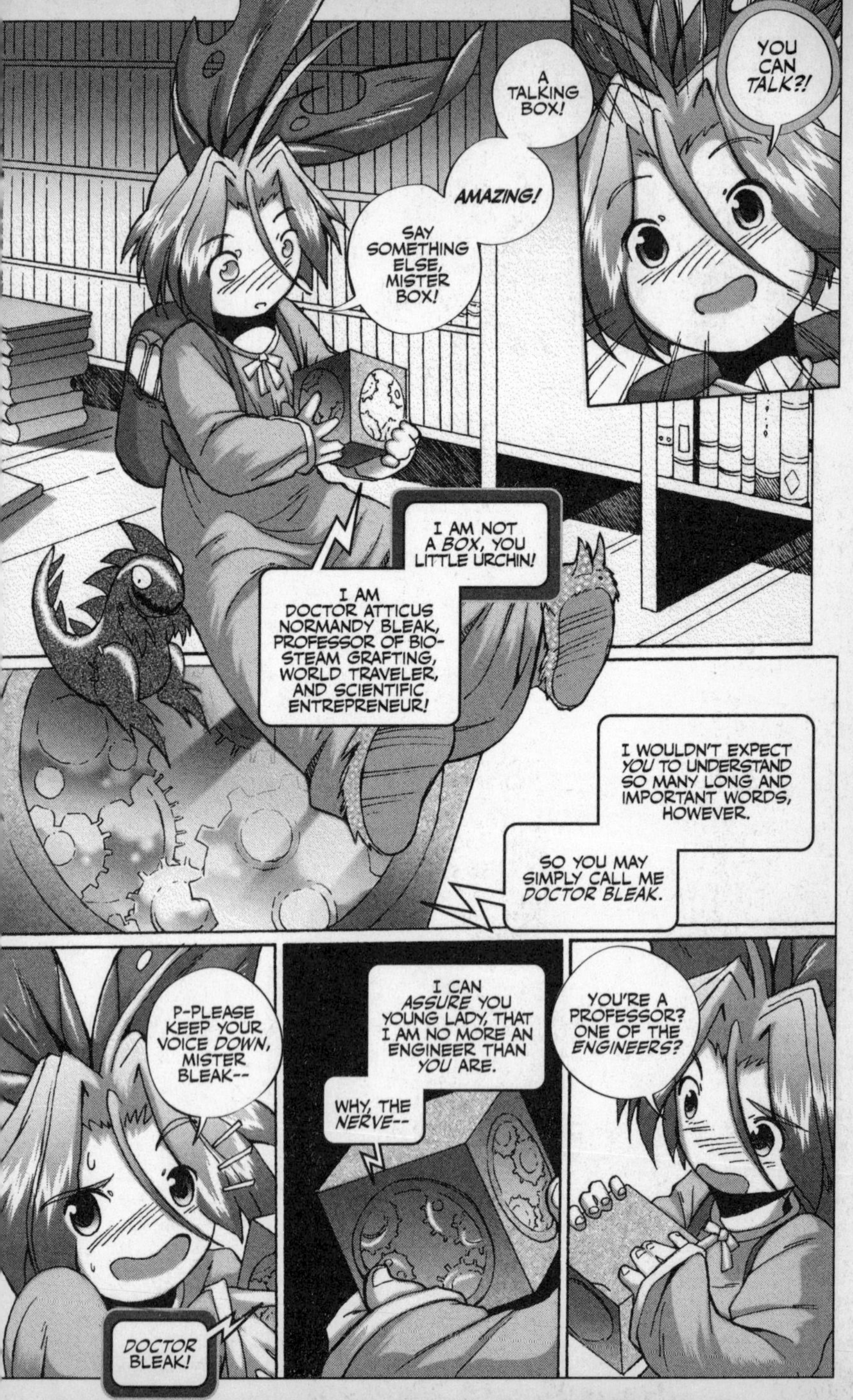
YOU CAN *TALK?!*
A TALKING BOX!
AMAZING!
SAY SOMETHING ELSE, MISTER BOX!
I AM NOT A *BOX*, YOU LITTLE URCHIN!
I AM DOCTOR ATTICUS NORMANDY BLEAK, PROFESSOR OF BIO-STEAM GRAFTING, WORLD TRAVELER, AND SCIENTIFIC ENTREPRENEUR!
I WOULDN'T EXPECT *YOU* TO UNDERSTAND SO MANY LONG AND IMPORTANT WORDS, HOWEVER.
SO YOU MAY SIMPLY CALL ME *DOCTOR BLEAK*.
YOU'RE A PROFESSOR? ONE OF THE *ENGINEERS?*
I CAN *ASSURE* YOU YOUNG LADY, THAT I AM NO MORE AN ENGINEER THAN *YOU* ARE.
WHY, THE *NERVE--*
P-PLEASE KEEP YOUR VOICE *DOWN*, MISTER BLEAK--
DOCTOR BLEAK!

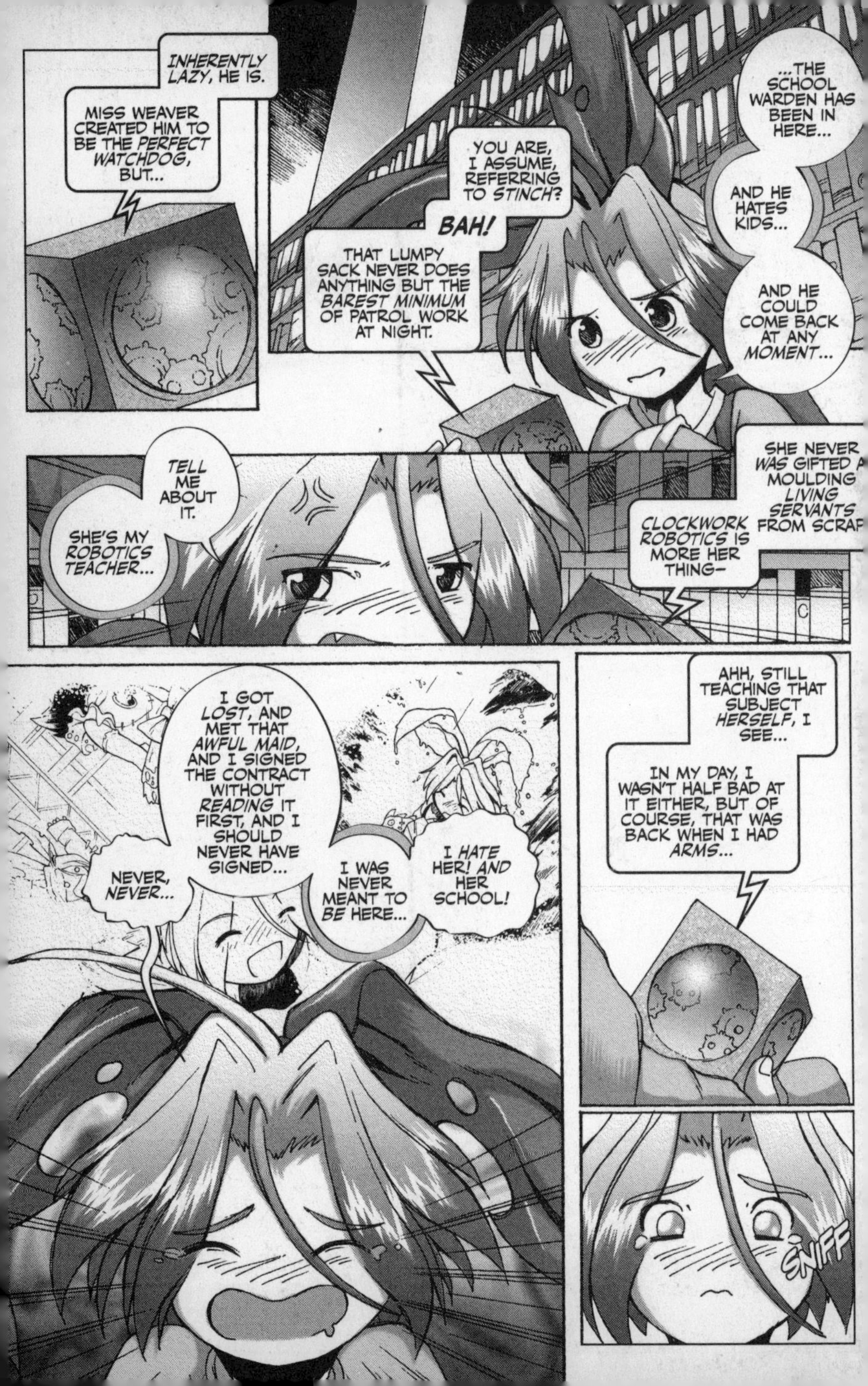
...THE SCHOOL WARDEN HAS BEEN IN HERE...
AND HE HATES KIDS...
AND HE COULD COME BACK AT ANY MOMENT...
YOU ARE, I ASSUME, REFERRING TO STINCH?
BAH!
THAT LUMPY SACK NEVER DOES ANYTHING BUT THE BAREST MINIMUM OF PATROL WORK AT NIGHT.
INHERENTLY LAZY, HE IS.
MISS WEAVER CREATED HIM TO BE THE PERFECT WATCHDOG, BUT...
SHE NEVER WAS GIFTED A MOULDING LIVING SERVANTS FROM SCRAP
CLOCKWORK ROBOTICS IS MORE HER THING—
TELL ME ABOUT IT.
SHE'S MY ROBOTICS TEACHER...
AHH, STILL TEACHING THAT SUBJECT HERSELF, I SEE...
IN MY DAY, I WASN'T HALF BAD AT IT EITHER, BUT OF COURSE, THAT WAS BACK WHEN I HAD ARMS...
SNIFF
I GOT LOST, AND MET THAT AWFUL MAID, AND I SIGNED THE CONTRACT WITHOUT READING IT FIRST, AND I SHOULD NEVER HAVE SIGNED...
NEVER, NEVER...
I WAS NEVER MEANT TO BE HERE...
I HATE HER! AND HER SCHOOL!

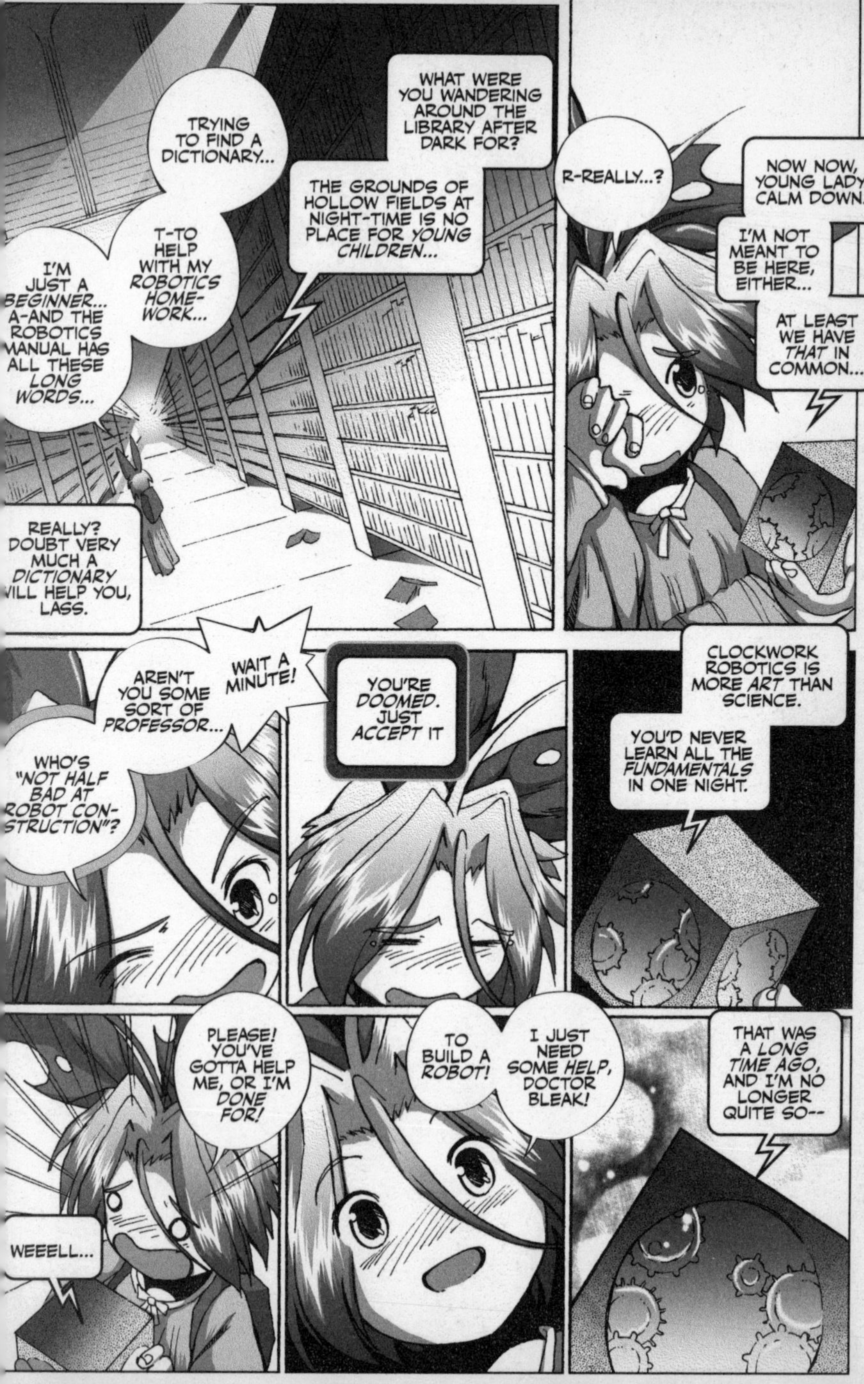
WHAT WERE YOU WANDERING AROUND THE LIBRARY AFTER DARK FOR?
THE GROUNDS OF HOLLOW FIELDS AT NIGHT-TIME IS NO PLACE FOR *YOUNG CHILDREN*...
TRYING TO FIND A DICTIONARY...
T-TO HELP WITH MY *ROBOTICS HOME-WORK*...
I'M JUST A *BEGINNER*... A-AND THE ROBOTICS MANUAL HAS ALL THESE *LONG WORDS*...
REALLY? DOUBT VERY MUCH A *DICTIONARY* WILL HELP YOU, LASS.
R-REALLY...?
NOW NOW, YOUNG LADY. CALM DOWN.
I'M NOT MEANT TO BE HERE, EITHER...
AT LEAST WE HAVE *THAT* IN COMMON...
WAIT A MINUTE!
AREN'T YOU SOME SORT OF *PROFESSOR*...
WHO'S *"NOT HALF BAD AT ROBOT CON-STRUCTION"*?
YOU'RE *DOOMED*. JUST *ACCEPT* IT
CLOCKWORK ROBOTICS IS MORE *ART* THAN SCIENCE.
YOU'D NEVER LEARN ALL THE *FUNDAMENTALS* IN ONE NIGHT.
WEEELL...
PLEASE! YOU'VE GOTTA HELP ME, OR I'M *DONE FOR!*
I JUST NEED SOME *HELP*, DOCTOR BLEAK!
TO BUILD A *ROBOT!*
THAT WAS A *LONG TIME AGO*, AND I'M NO LONGER QUITE SO--

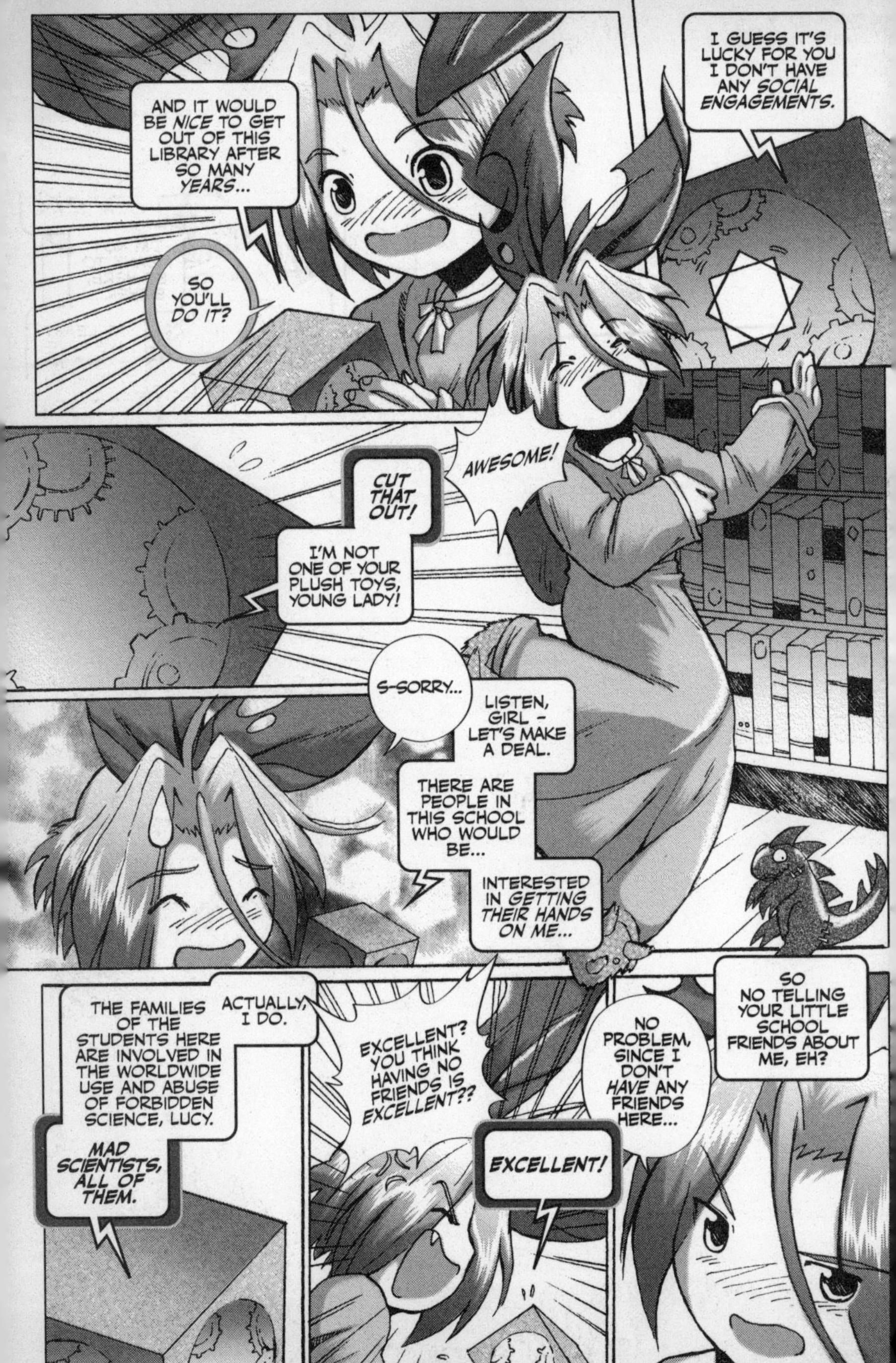
I GUESS IT'S LUCKY FOR YOU I DON'T HAVE ANY *SOCIAL ENGAGEMENTS.*
AND IT WOULD BE *NICE* TO GET OUT OF THIS LIBRARY AFTER SO MANY *YEARS...*
SO YOU'LL *DO* IT?
AWESOME!
CUT THAT OUT!
I'M NOT ONE OF YOUR PLUSH TOYS, YOUNG LADY!
S-SORRY...
LISTEN, GIRL - LET'S MAKE A DEAL.
THERE ARE PEOPLE IN THIS SCHOOL WHO WOULD BE...
INTERESTED IN *GETTING THEIR HANDS* ON ME...
SO NO TELLING YOUR LITTLE SCHOOL FRIENDS ABOUT ME, EH?
NO PROBLEM, SINCE I DON'T *HAVE* ANY FRIENDS HERE...
EXCELLENT!
EXCELLENT? YOU THINK HAVING NO FRIENDS IS *EXCELLENT??*
ACTUALLY, I DO.
THE FAMILIES OF THE STUDENTS HERE ARE INVOLVED IN THE WORLDWIDE USE AND ABUSE OF FORBIDDEN SCIENCE, LUCY.
MAD SCIENTISTS, ALL OF THEM.

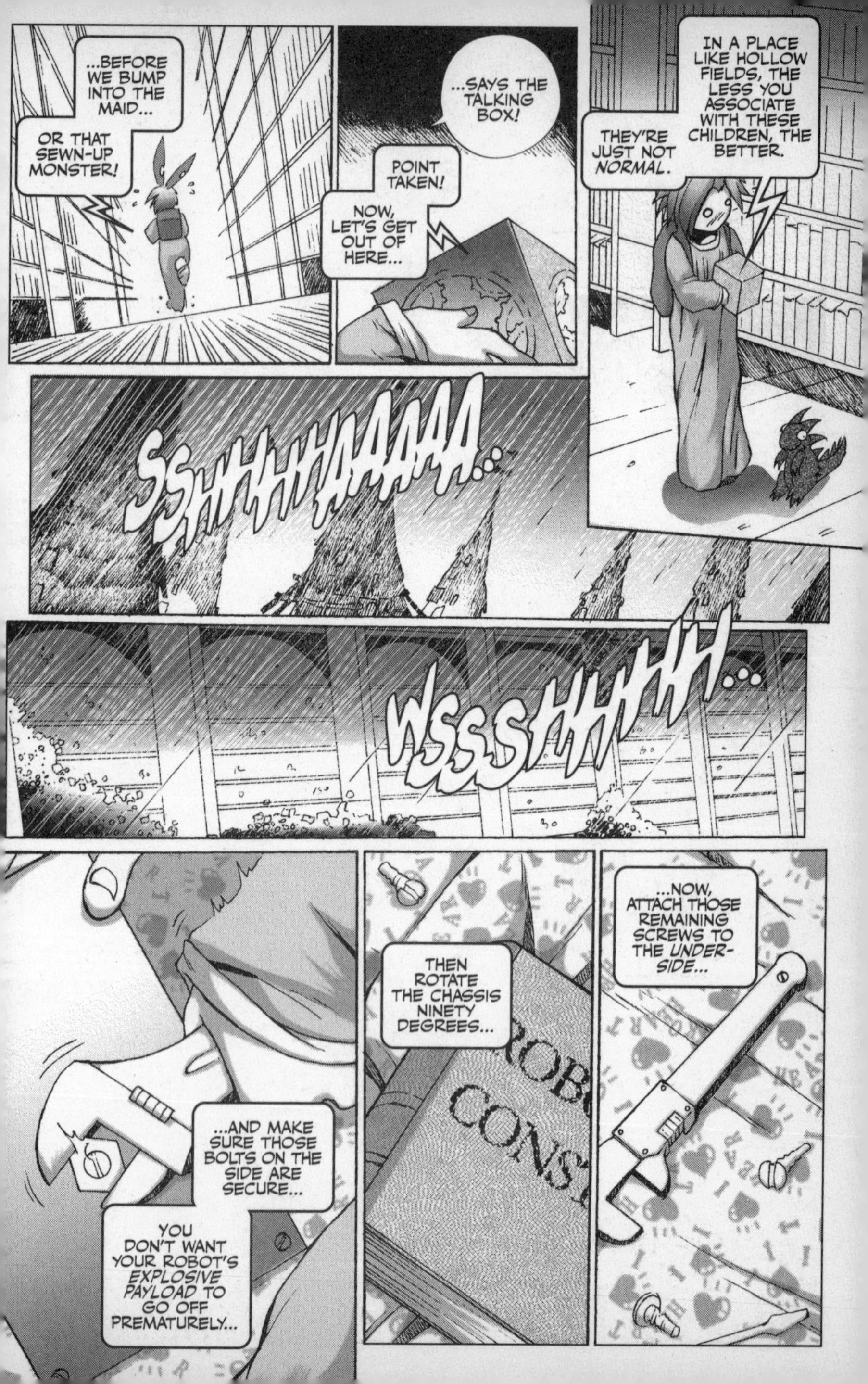
IN A PLACE LIKE HOLLOW FIELDS, THE LESS YOU ASSOCIATE WITH THESE CHILDREN, THE BETTER.
THEY'RE JUST NOT *NORMAL*.
...SAYS THE TALKING BOX!
POINT TAKEN!
NOW, LET'S GET OUT OF HERE...
...BEFORE WE BUMP INTO THE MAID...
OR THAT SEWN-UP MONSTER!
SSHHHHAAAAA...
WSSSHHHHH...
...NOW, ATTACH THOSE REMAINING SCREWS TO THE *UNDER-SIDE*...
THEN ROTATE THE CHASSIS NINETY DEGREES...
...AND MAKE SURE THOSE BOLTS ON THE SIDE ARE SECURE...
YOU DON'T WANT YOUR ROBOT'S *EXPLOSIVE PAYLOAD* TO GO OFF PREMATURELY...

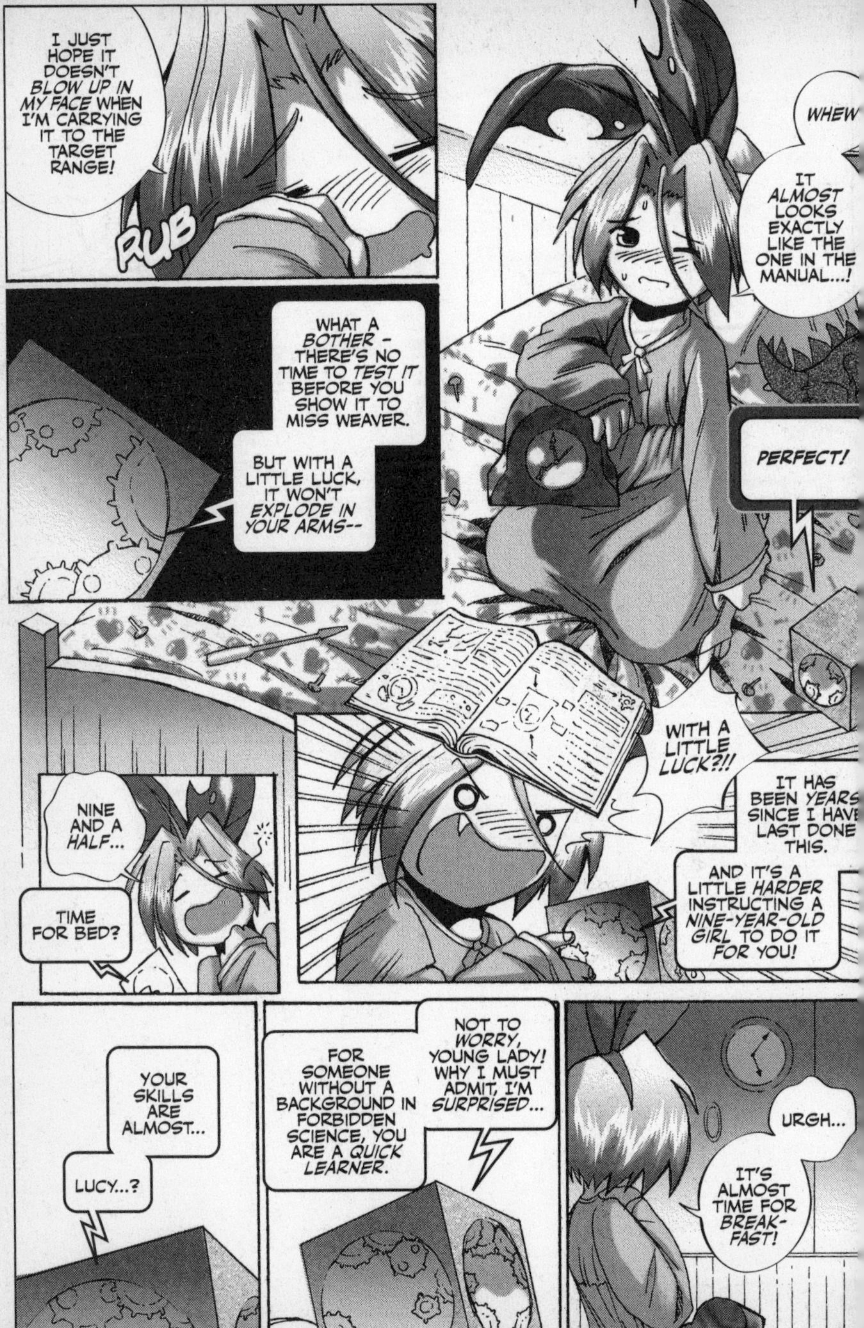
WHEW
IT ALMOST LOOKS EXACTLY LIKE THE ONE IN THE MANUAL...!
PERFECT!
I JUST HOPE IT DOESN'T BLOW UP IN MY FACE WHEN I'M CARRYING IT TO THE TARGET RANGE!
RUB
WHAT A BOTHER - THERE'S NO TIME TO TEST IT BEFORE YOU SHOW IT TO MISS WEAVER.
BUT WITH A LITTLE LUCK, IT WON'T EXPLODE IN YOUR ARMS--
WITH A LITTLE LUCK?!!
IT HAS BEEN YEARS SINCE I HAVE LAST DONE THIS.
AND IT'S A LITTLE HARDER INSTRUCTING A NINE-YEAR-OLD GIRL TO DO IT FOR YOU!
NINE AND A HALF...
TIME FOR BED?
URGH...
IT'S ALMOST TIME FOR BREAK-FAST!
NOT TO WORRY, YOUNG LADY! WHY I MUST ADMIT, I'M SURPRISED...
FOR SOMEONE WITHOUT A BACKGROUND IN FORBIDDEN SCIENCE, YOU ARE A QUICK LEARNER.
YOUR SKILLS ARE ALMOST...
LUCY...?

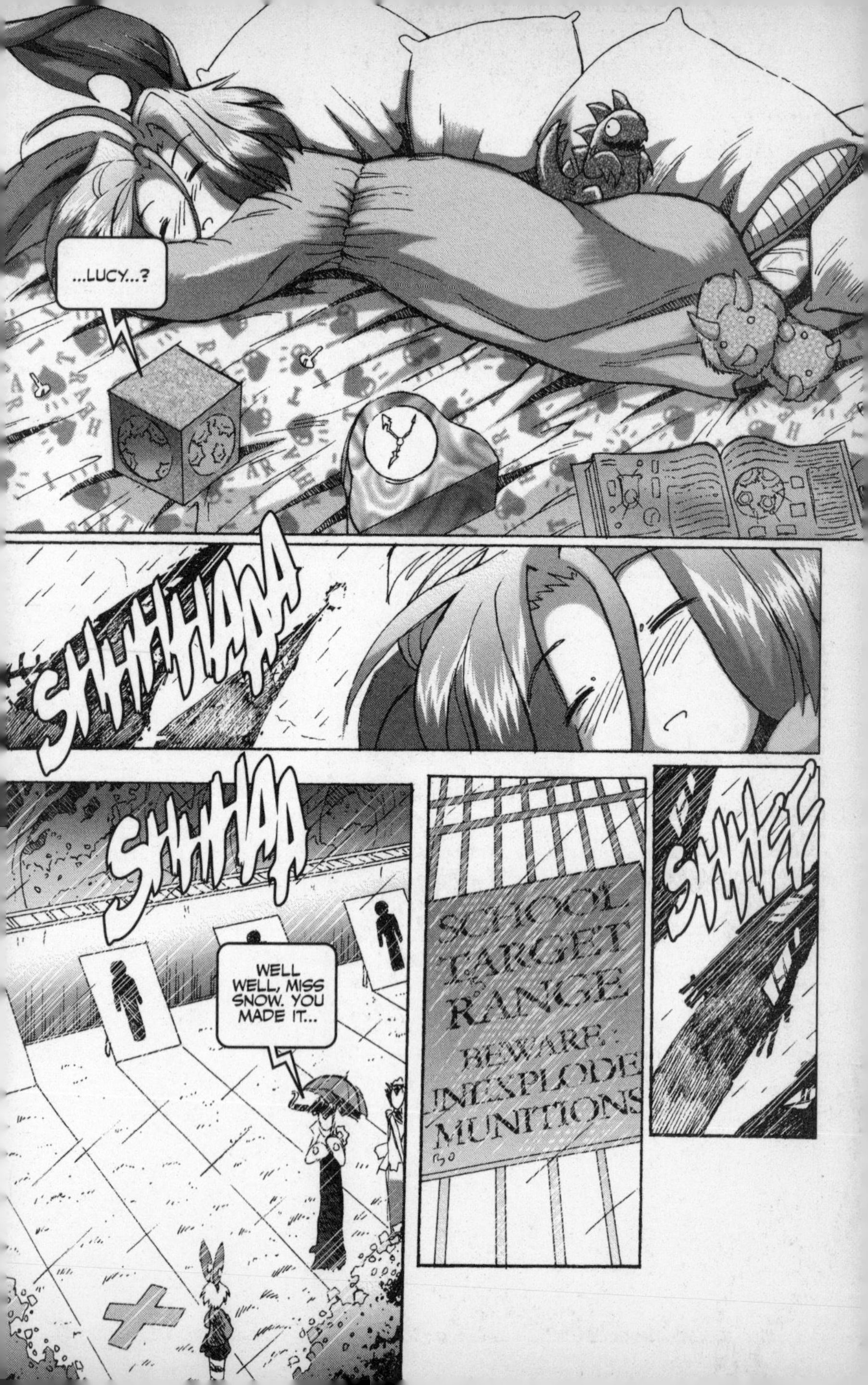
...LUCY...?
SHHHHAAA
SHHEE
SCHOOL TARGET RANGE
BEWARE
UNEXPLODE
MUNITIONS
SHHHAA
WELL WELL, MISS SNOW. YOU MADE IT...

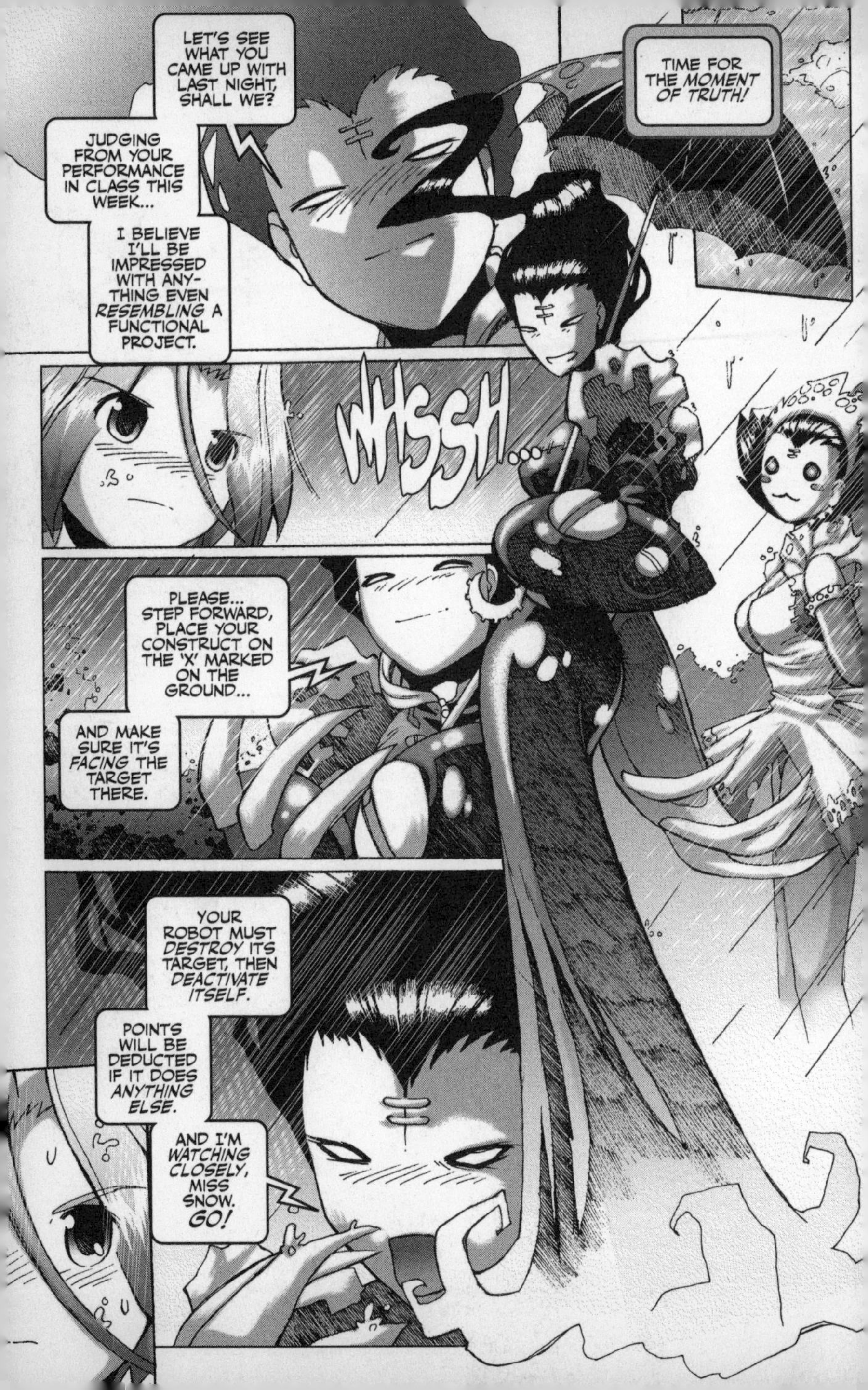
LET'S SEE WHAT YOU CAME UP WITH LAST NIGHT, SHALL WE?
JUDGING FROM YOUR PERFORMANCE IN CLASS THIS WEEK...
I BELIEVE I'LL BE IMPRESSED WITH ANY-THING EVEN *RESEMBLING* A FUNCTIONAL PROJECT.
TIME FOR THE *MOMENT OF TRUTH!*
WHSSH...
PLEASE... STEP FORWARD, PLACE YOUR CONSTRUCT ON THE 'X' MARKED ON THE GROUND...
AND MAKE SURE IT'S *FACING* THE TARGET THERE.
YOUR ROBOT MUST *DESTROY* ITS TARGET, THEN *DEACTIVATE ITSELF*.
POINTS WILL BE DEDUCTED IF IT DOES *ANYTHING ELSE*.
AND I'M *WATCHING CLOSELY*, MISS SNOW. *GO!*

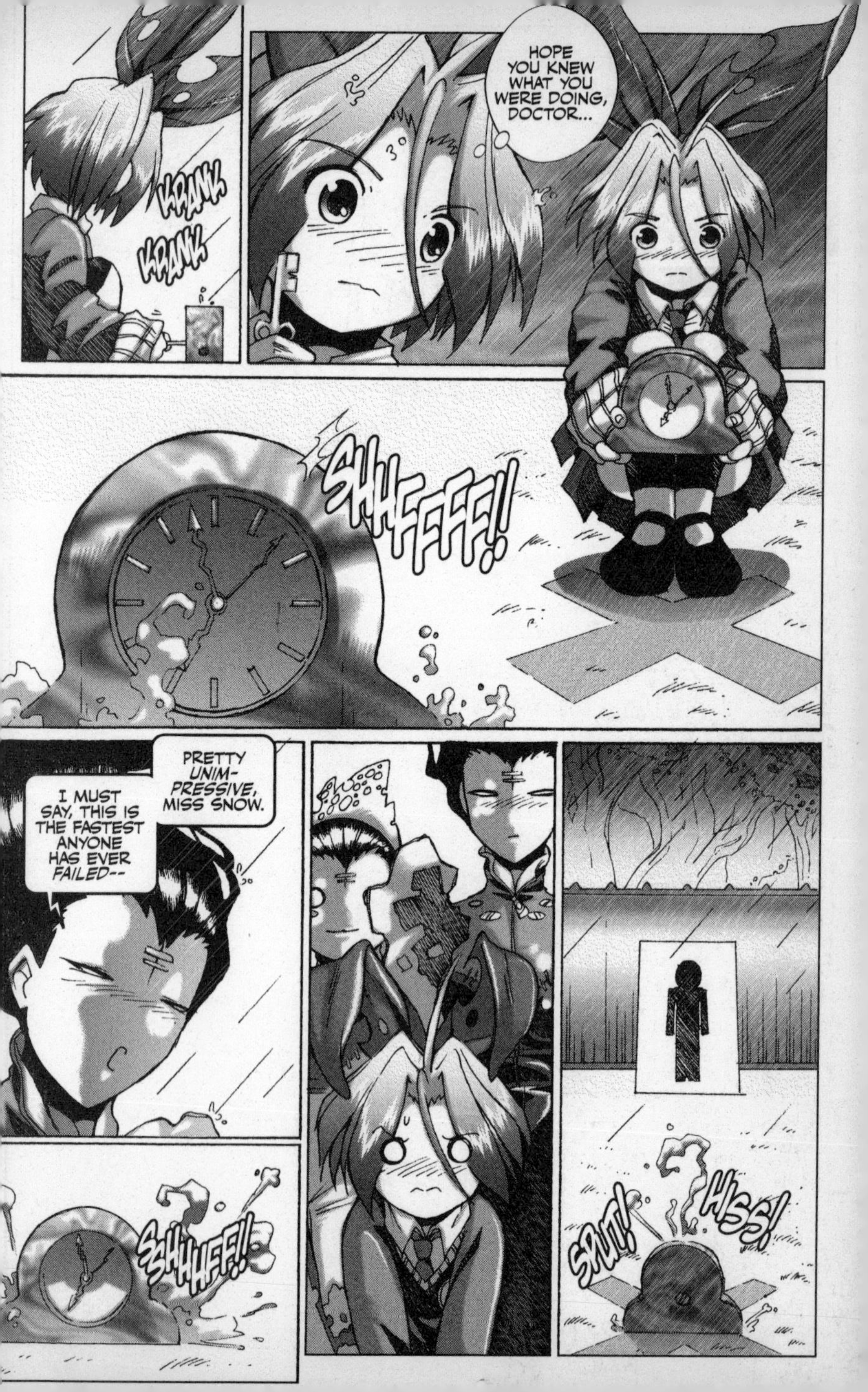
KRANK
KRANK
HOPE YOU KNEW WHAT YOU WERE DOING, DOCTOR...
SHHFFFF!!
I MUST SAY, THIS IS THE FASTEST ANYONE HAS EVER FAILED--
PRETTY UNIMPRESSIVE, MISS SNOW.
SSHHFF!!
SPUT!
HISS!

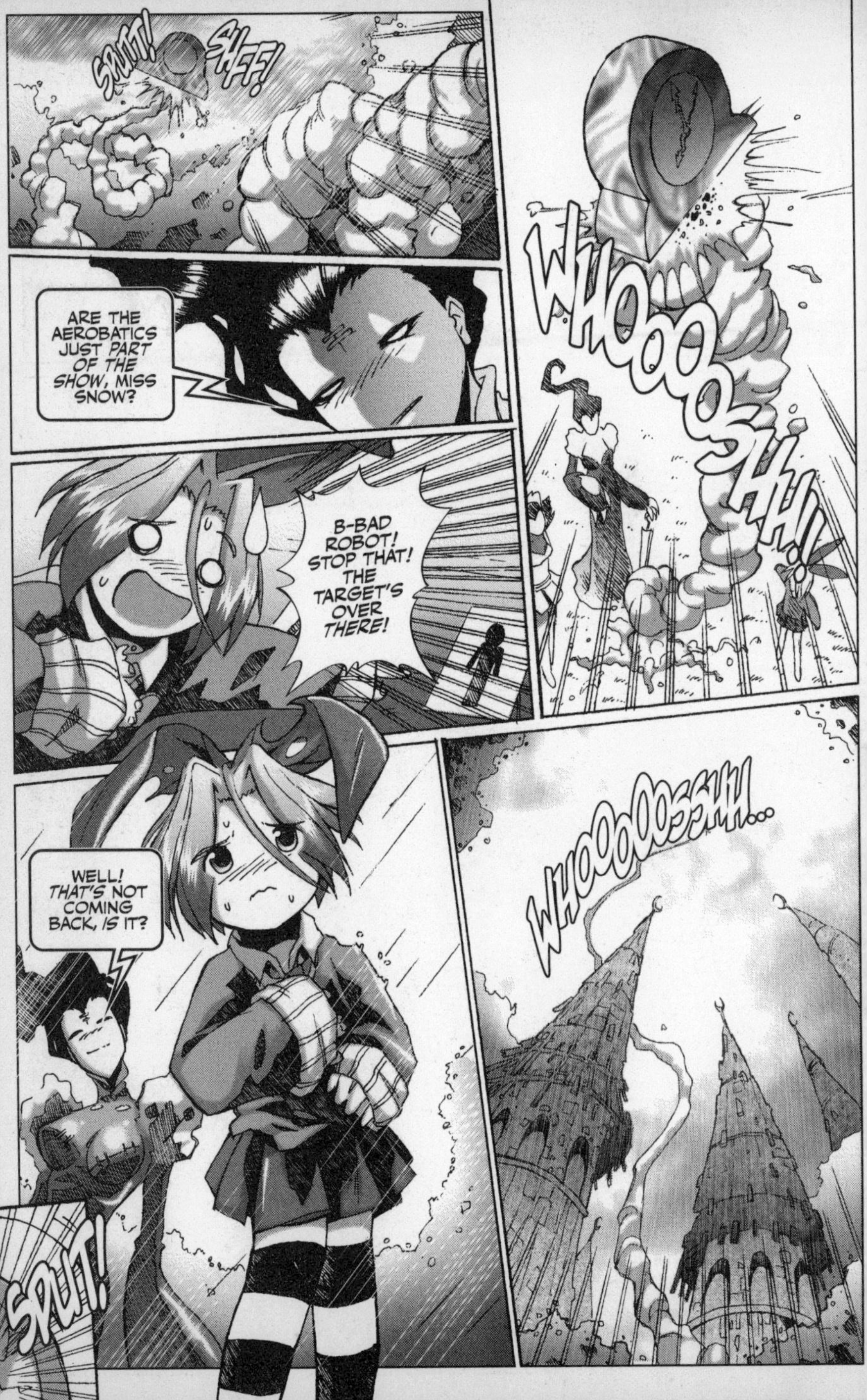
SPLUT!
SHFF!
ARE THE AEROBATICS JUST PART OF THE SHOW, MISS SNOW?
B-BAD ROBOT! STOP THAT! THE TARGET'S OVER THERE!
WHOOOOSHH!!
WELL! THAT'S NOT COMING BACK, IS IT?
SPLUT!
WHOOOOOSSHH...

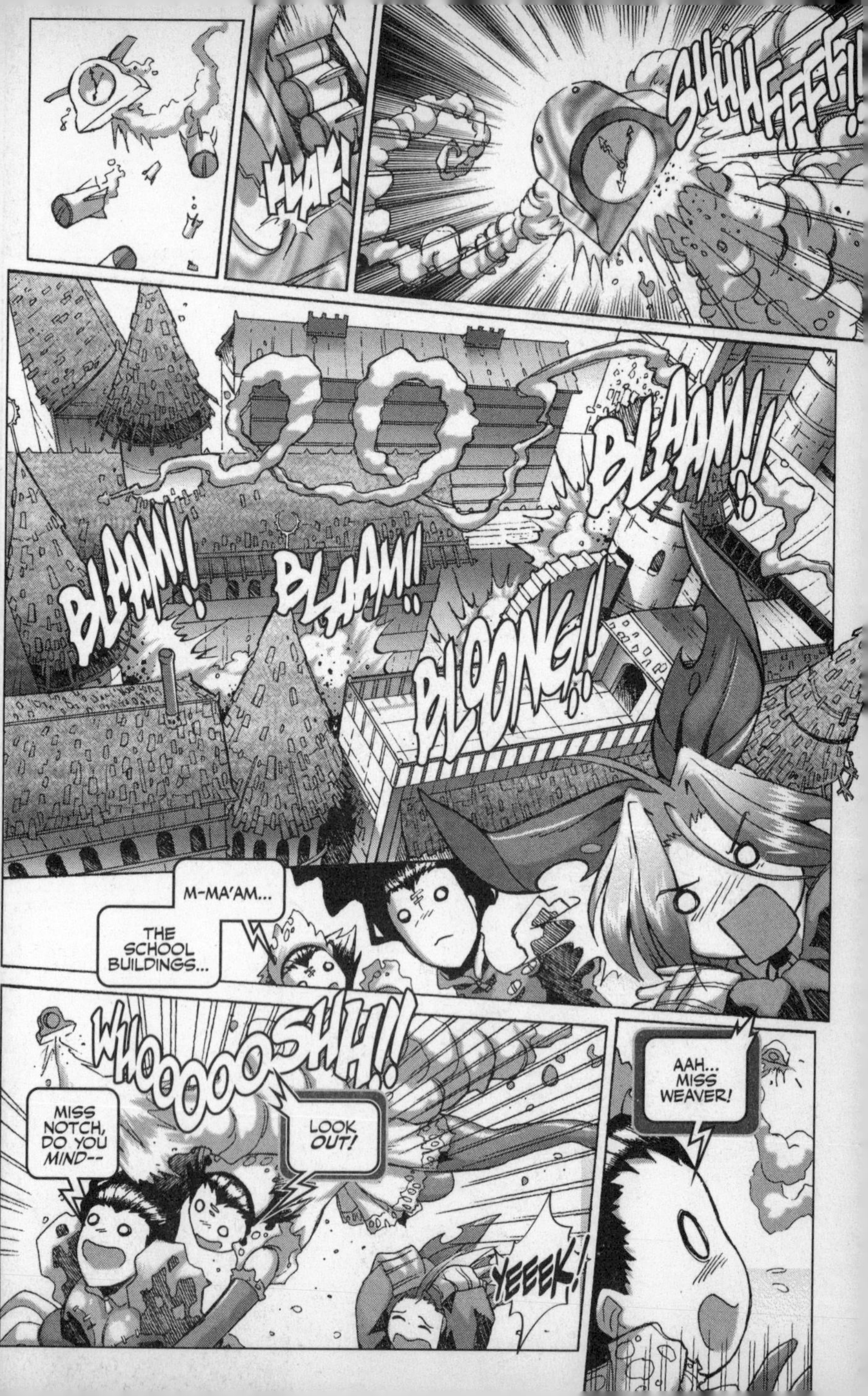

SHUHFFFF!!
KLAK!
BLAAM!!
BLOONG!!
BLAAM!!
BLAAM!!
M-MA'AM...
THE SCHOOL BUILDINGS...
AAH... MISS WEAVER!
WHOOOOOSHH!!
LOOK OUT!
MISS NOTCH, DO YOU MIND--
YEEEK!

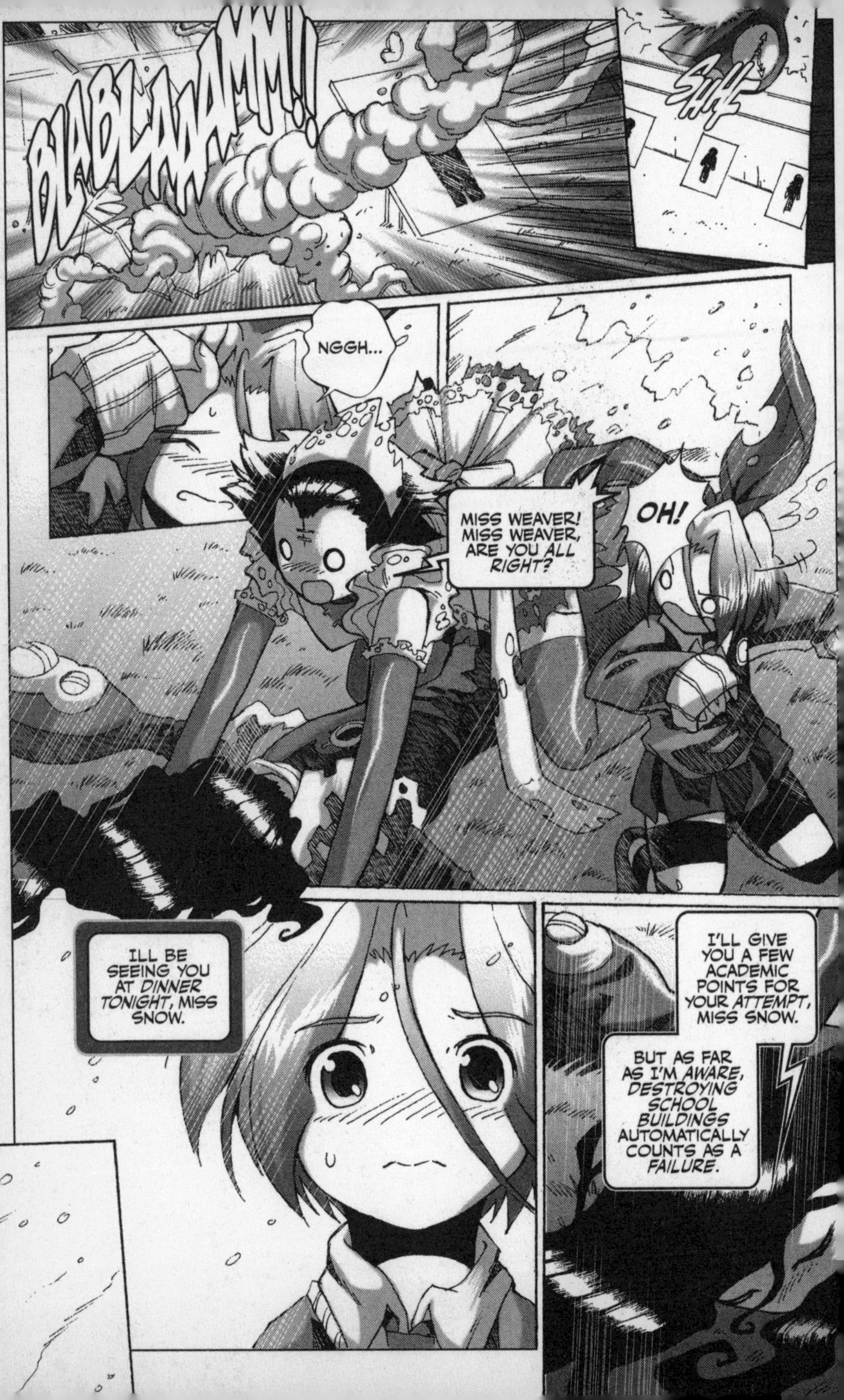
BLABLAAAMM!!
OH!
MISS WEAVER! MISS WEAVER, ARE YOU *ALL RIGHT?*
NGGH...
I'LL GIVE YOU A FEW ACADEMIC POINTS FOR YOUR *ATTEMPT*, MISS SNOW.
BUT AS FAR AS I'M *AWARE*, *DESTROYING SCHOOL BUILDINGS* AUTOMATICALLY COUNTS AS A *FAILURE*.
ILL BE SEEING YOU AT *DINNER TONIGHT*, MISS SNOW.

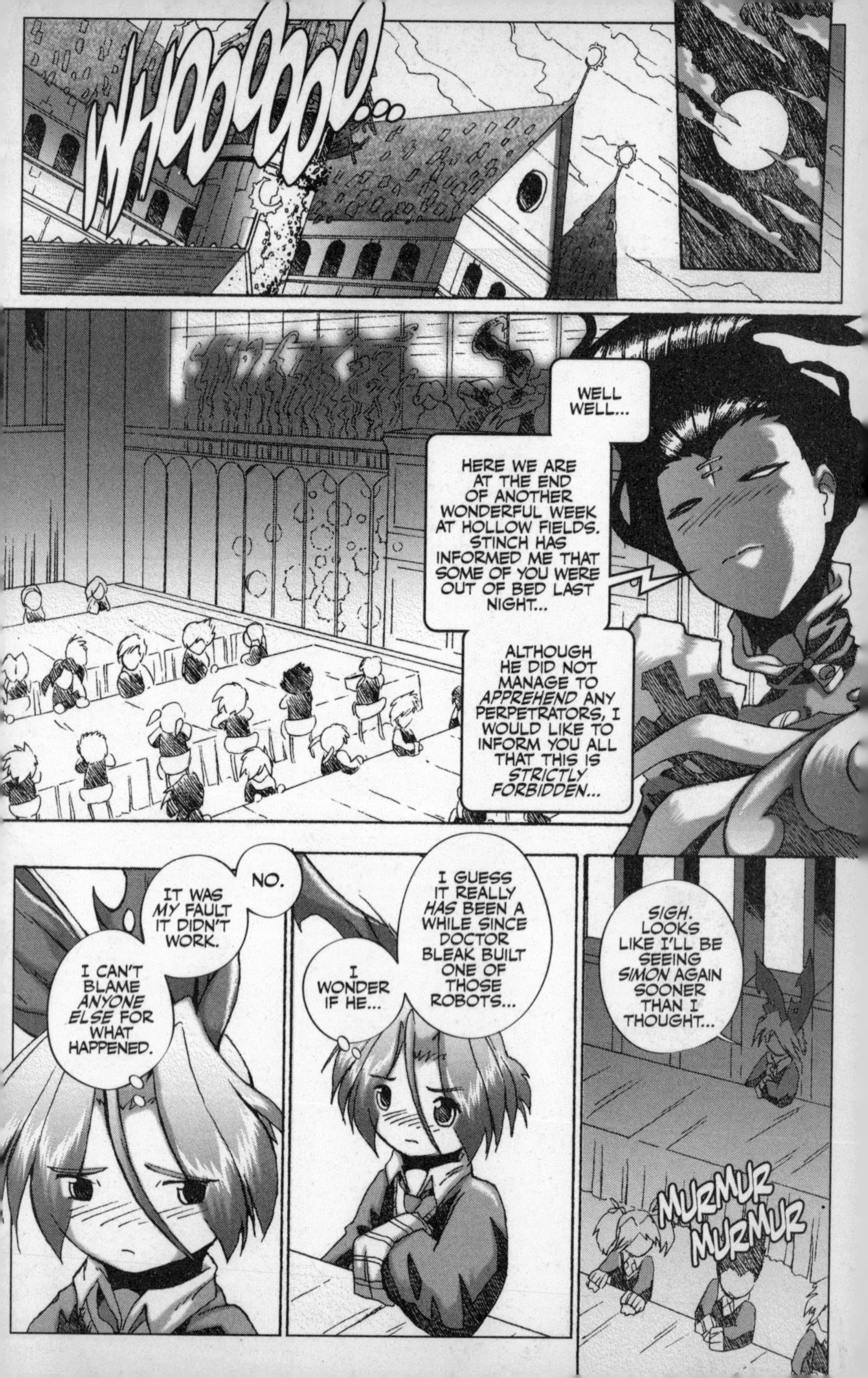
WHOOOOO...
WELL WELL...
HERE WE ARE AT THE END OF ANOTHER WONDERFUL WEEK AT HOLLOW FIELDS. STINCH HAS INFORMED ME THAT SOME OF YOU WERE OUT OF BED LAST NIGHT...
ALTHOUGH HE DID NOT MANAGE TO *APPREHEND* ANY PERPETRATORS, I WOULD LIKE TO INFORM YOU ALL THAT THIS IS *STRICTLY FORBIDDEN*...
NO.
IT WAS *MY* FAULT IT DIDN'T WORK.
I CAN'T BLAME *ANYONE ELSE* FOR WHAT HAPPENED.
I GUESS IT REALLY *HAS* BEEN A WHILE SINCE DOCTOR BLEAK BUILT ONE OF THOSE ROBOTS...
I WONDER IF HE...
SIGH. LOOKS LIKE I'LL BE SEEING *SIMON* AGAIN SOONER THAN I THOUGHT...
MURMUR MURMUR

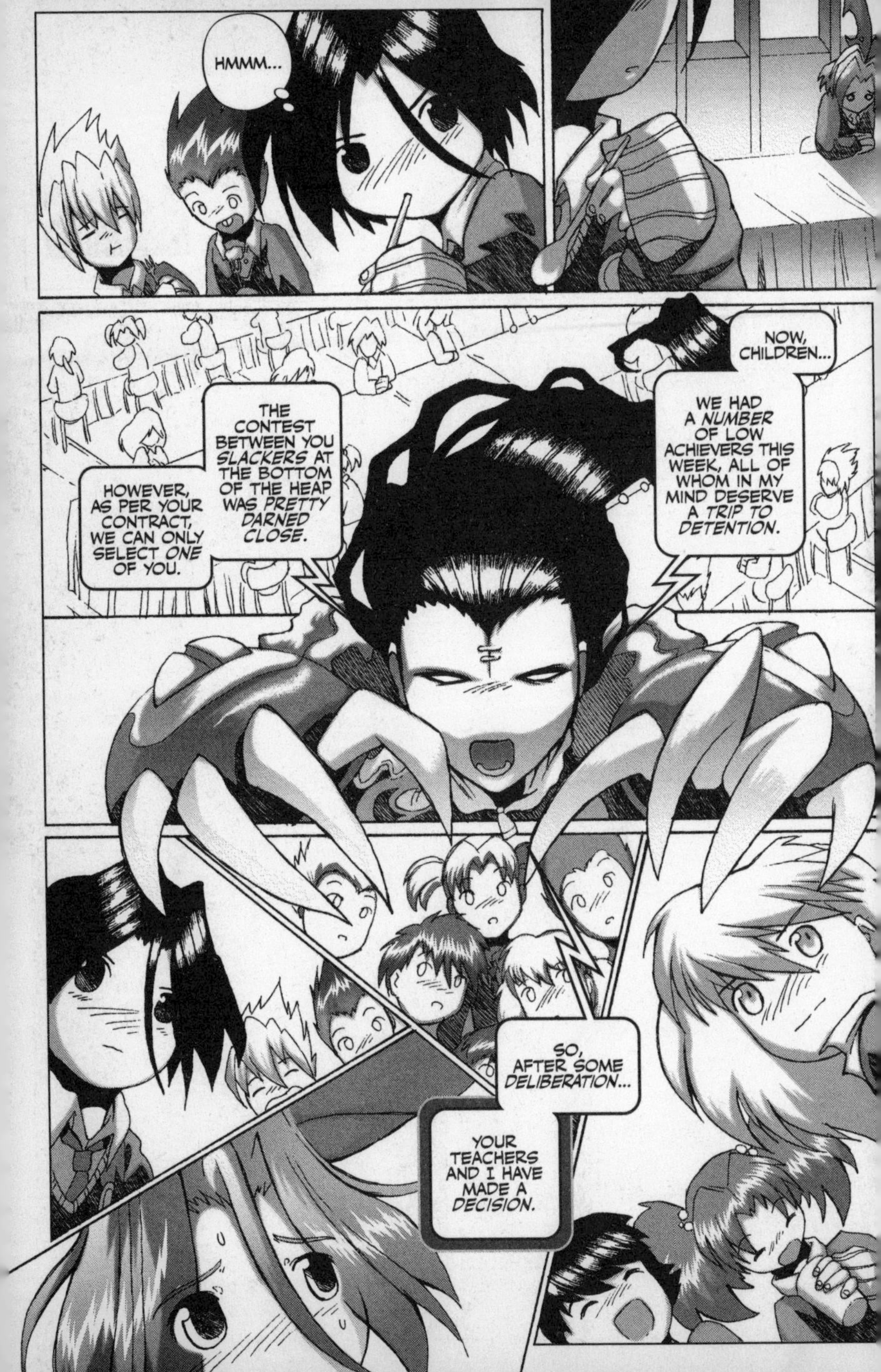
HMMM...
NOW, CHILDREN...
WE HAD A *NUMBER* OF LOW ACHIEVERS THIS WEEK, ALL OF WHOM IN MY MIND DESERVE A *TRIP TO DETENTION*.
THE CONTEST BETWEEN YOU *SLACKERS* AT THE BOTTOM OF THE HEAP WAS *PRETTY DARNED CLOSE*.
HOWEVER, AS PER YOUR CONTRACT, WE CAN ONLY SELECT *ONE* OF YOU.
SO, AFTER SOME *DELIBERATION*...
YOUR TEACHERS AND I HAVE MADE A *DECISION*.

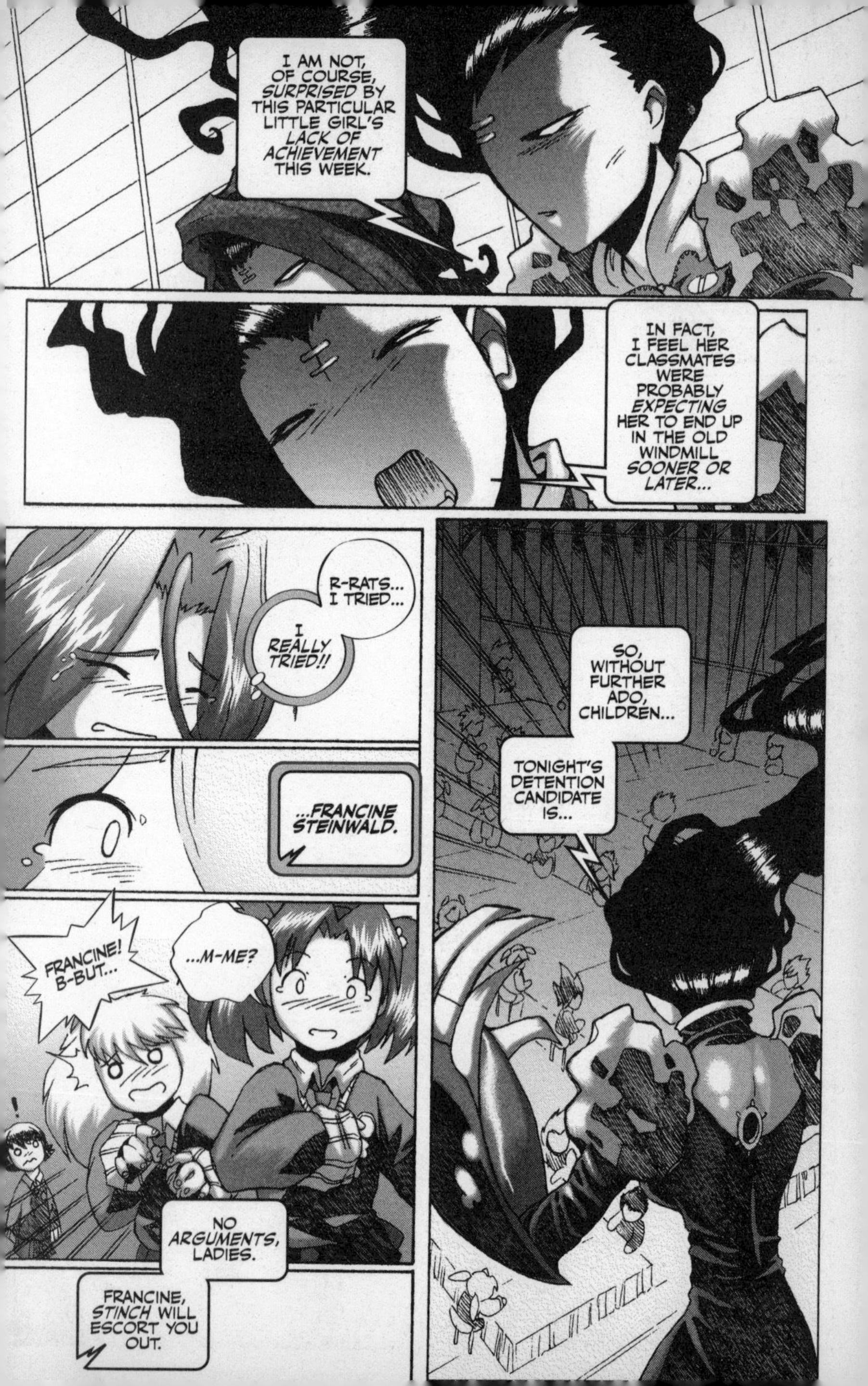
I AM NOT, OF COURSE, SURPRISED BY THIS PARTICULAR LITTLE GIRL'S LACK OF ACHIEVEMENT THIS WEEK.
IN FACT, I FEEL HER CLASSMATES WERE PROBABLY EXPECTING HER TO END UP IN THE OLD WINDMILL SOONER OR LATER...
R-RATS... I TRIED...
I REALLY TRIED!!
SO, WITHOUT FURTHER ADO, CHILDREN...
TONIGHT'S DETENTION CANDIDATE IS...
...FRANCINE STEINWALD.
FRANCINE! B-BUT...
...M-ME?
!
NO ARGUMENTS, LADIES.
FRANCINE, STINCH WILL ESCORT YOU OUT.

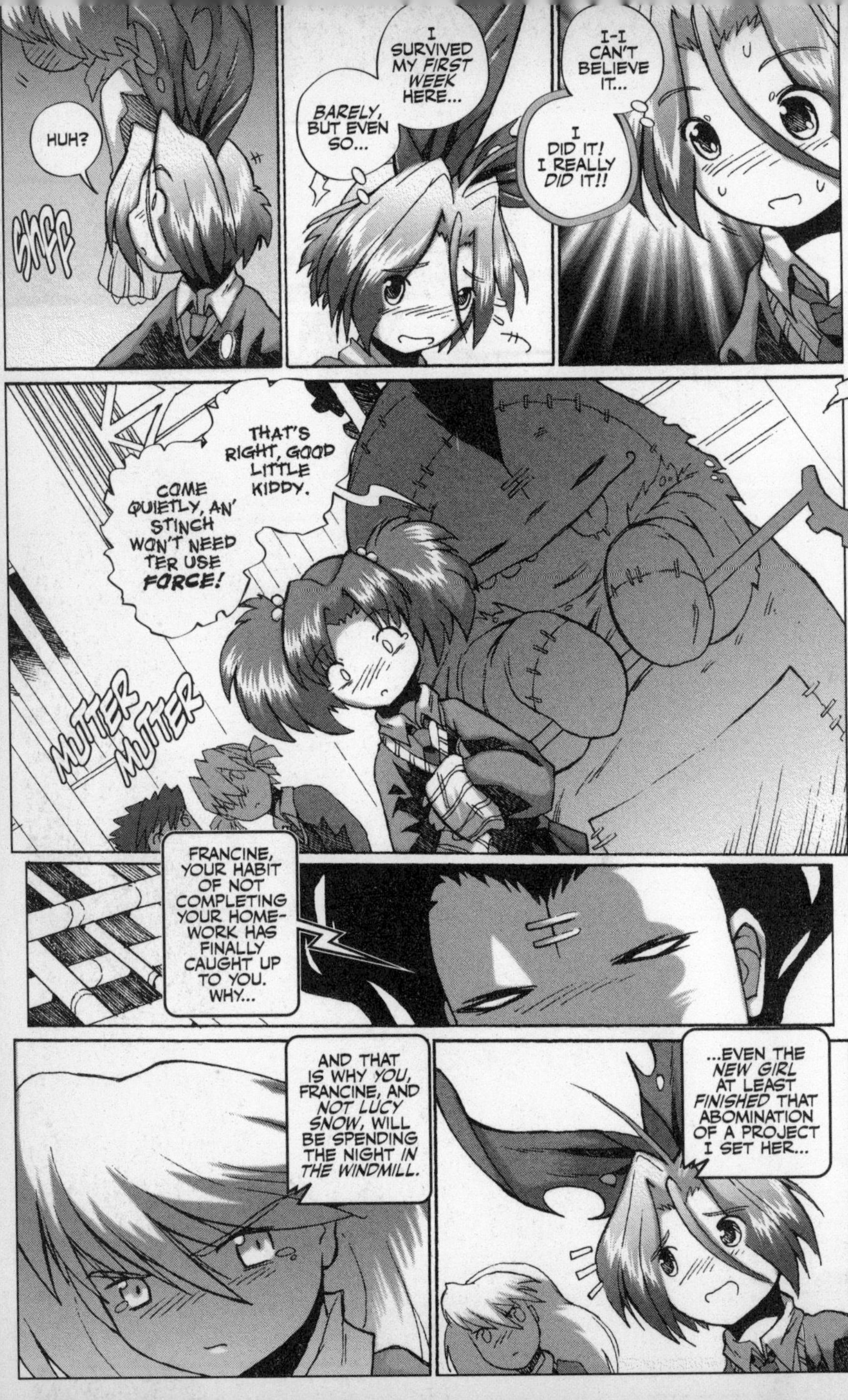
I-I CAN'T BELIEVE IT...
I DID IT! I REALLY *DID* IT!!
I SURVIVED MY *FIRST WEEK* HERE...
BARELY, BUT EVEN SO...
HUH?
SNFF
THAT'S RIGHT, GOOD LITTLE KIDDY.
COME QUIETLY, AN' STINCH WON'T NEED TER USE **FORCE!**
MUTTER MUTTER
FRANCINE, YOUR HABIT OF NOT COMPLETING YOUR HOME-WORK HAS FINALLY CAUGHT UP TO YOU. WHY...
...EVEN THE *NEW GIRL* AT LEAST *FINISHED* THAT ABOMINATION OF A PROJECT I SET HER...
AND THAT IS WHY *YOU,* FRANCINE, AND *NOT LUCY SNOW,* WILL BE SPENDING THE NIGHT *IN THE WINDMILL.*

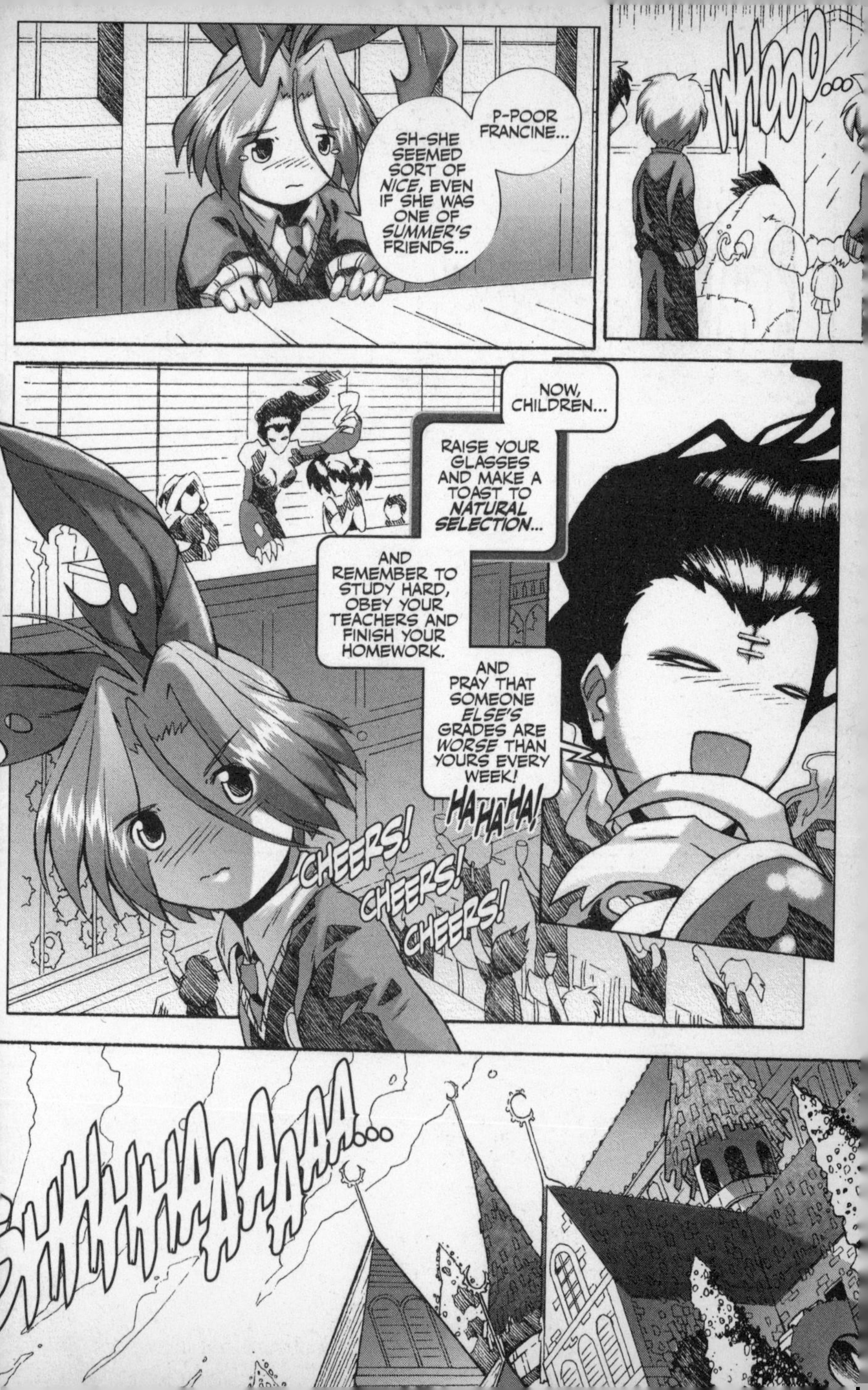
WHOOO...
P-POOR FRANCINE...
SH-SHE SEEMED SORT OF *NICE*, EVEN IF SHE WAS ONE OF *SUMMER'S* FRIENDS...
NOW, CHILDREN...
RAISE YOUR GLASSES AND MAKE A TOAST TO *NATURAL SELECTION*...
AND REMEMBER TO STUDY HARD, OBEY YOUR TEACHERS AND FINISH YOUR HOMEWORK.
AND PRAY THAT SOMEONE *ELSE'S* GRADES ARE *WORSE* THAN YOURS EVERY WEEK!
HAHAHA!
CHEERS! CHEERS! CHEERS!
SHHHHAAAAAA...

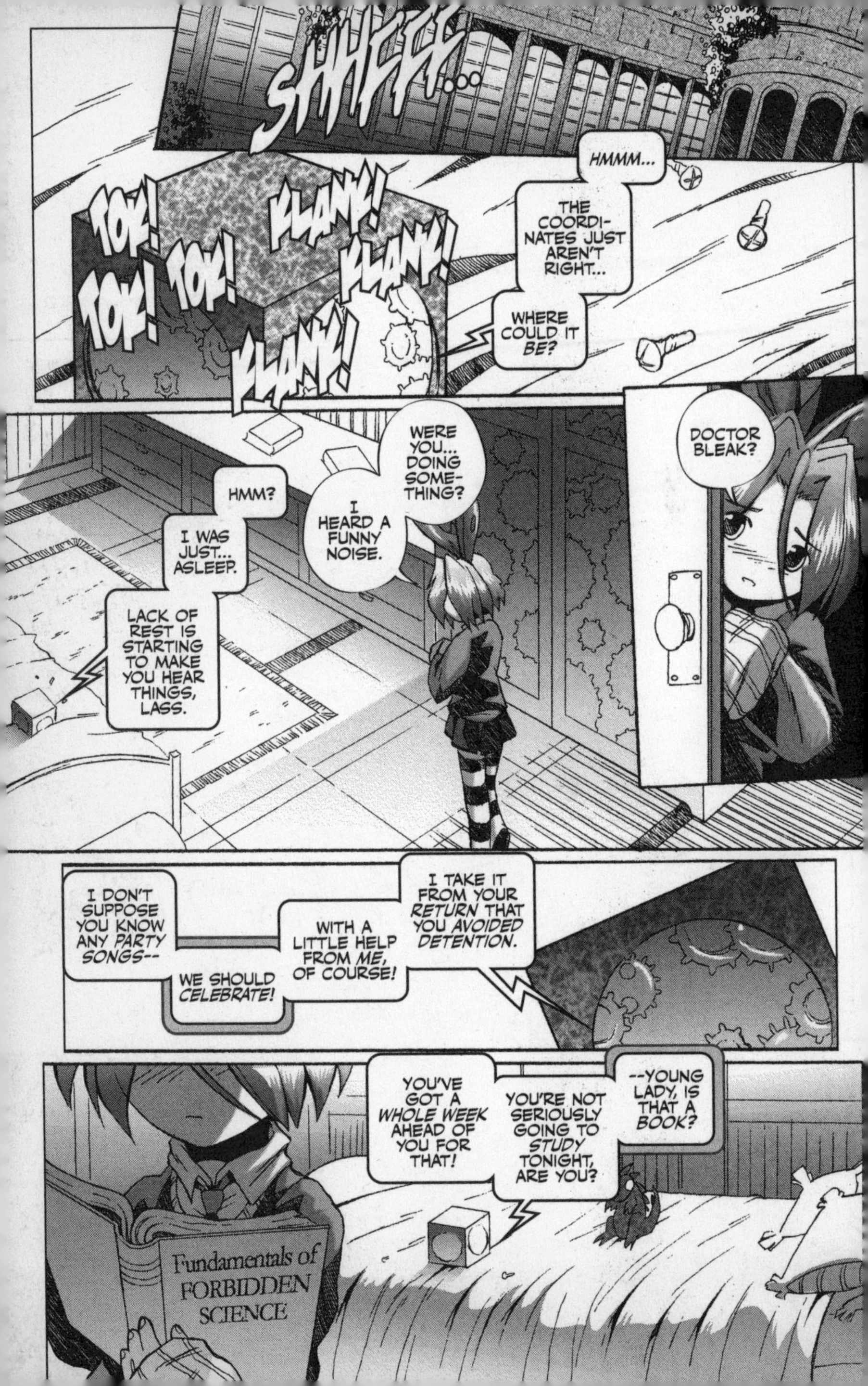
SHHFF...
HMMM...
THE COORDINATES JUST AREN'T RIGHT...
KLANK! KLANK!
TOK! TOK! TOK!
WHERE COULD IT *BE*?
KLANK!
DOCTOR BLEAK?
WERE YOU... DOING SOMETHING?
I HEARD A FUNNY NOISE.
HMM?
I WAS JUST... ASLEEP.
LACK OF REST IS STARTING TO MAKE YOU HEAR THINGS, LASS.
I TAKE IT FROM YOUR *RETURN* THAT YOU *AVOIDED DETENTION*.
WITH A LITTLE HELP FROM *ME*, OF COURSE!
WE SHOULD *CELEBRATE*!
I DON'T SUPPOSE YOU KNOW ANY *PARTY SONGS*--
--YOUNG LADY, IS THAT A *BOOK*?
YOU'RE NOT SERIOUSLY GOING TO *STUDY* TONIGHT, ARE YOU?
YOU'VE GOT A *WHOLE WEEK* AHEAD OF YOU FOR THAT!
Fundamentals of FORBIDDEN SCIENCE

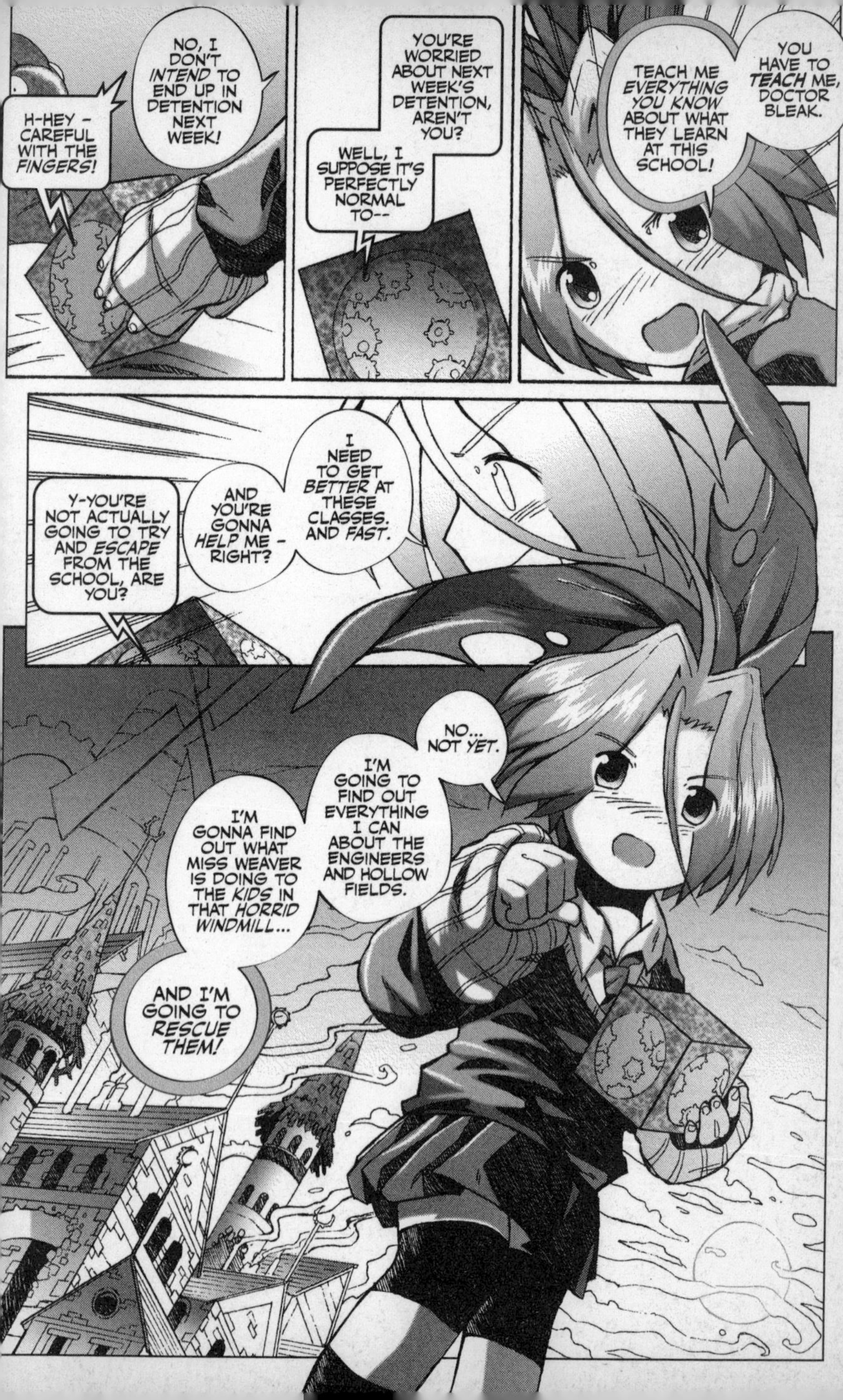
YOU HAVE TO TEACH ME, DOCTOR BLEAK.
TEACH ME EVERYTHING YOU KNOW ABOUT WHAT THEY LEARN AT THIS SCHOOL!
YOU'RE WORRIED ABOUT NEXT WEEK'S DETENTION, AREN'T YOU?
WELL, I SUPPOSE IT'S PERFECTLY NORMAL TO--
NO, I DON'T INTEND TO END UP IN DETENTION NEXT WEEK!
H-HEY - CAREFUL WITH THE FINGERS!
I NEED TO GET BETTER AT THESE CLASSES. AND FAST.
AND YOU'RE GONNA HELP ME - RIGHT?
Y-YOU'RE NOT ACTUALLY GOING TO TRY AND ESCAPE FROM THE SCHOOL, ARE YOU?
NO... NOT YET.
I'M GOING TO FIND OUT EVERYTHING I CAN ABOUT THE ENGINEERS AND HOLLOW FIELDS.
I'M GONNA FIND OUT WHAT MISS WEAVER IS DOING TO THE KIDS IN THAT HORRID WINDMILL...
AND I'M GOING TO RESCUE THEM!

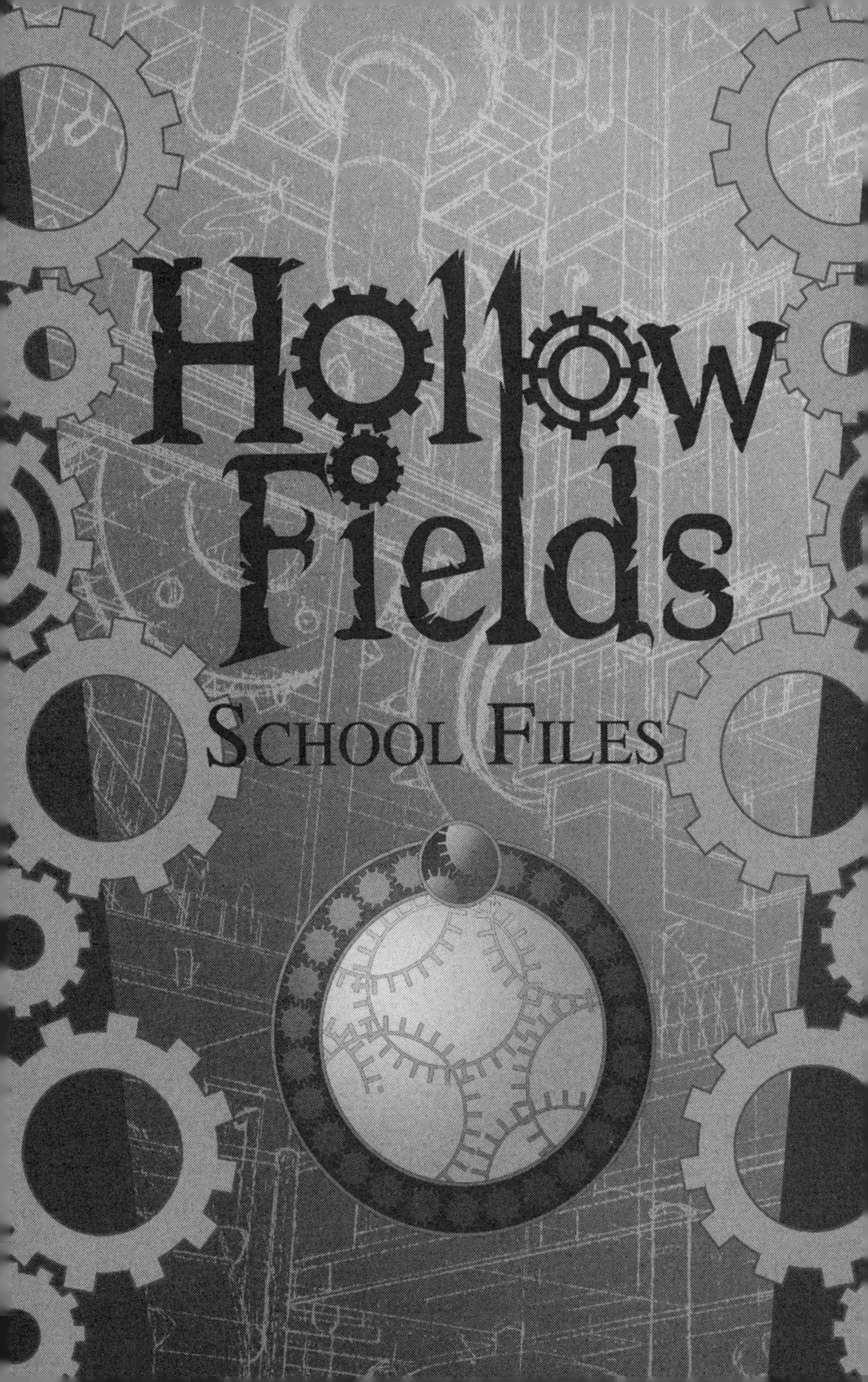
Hollow Fields
School Files

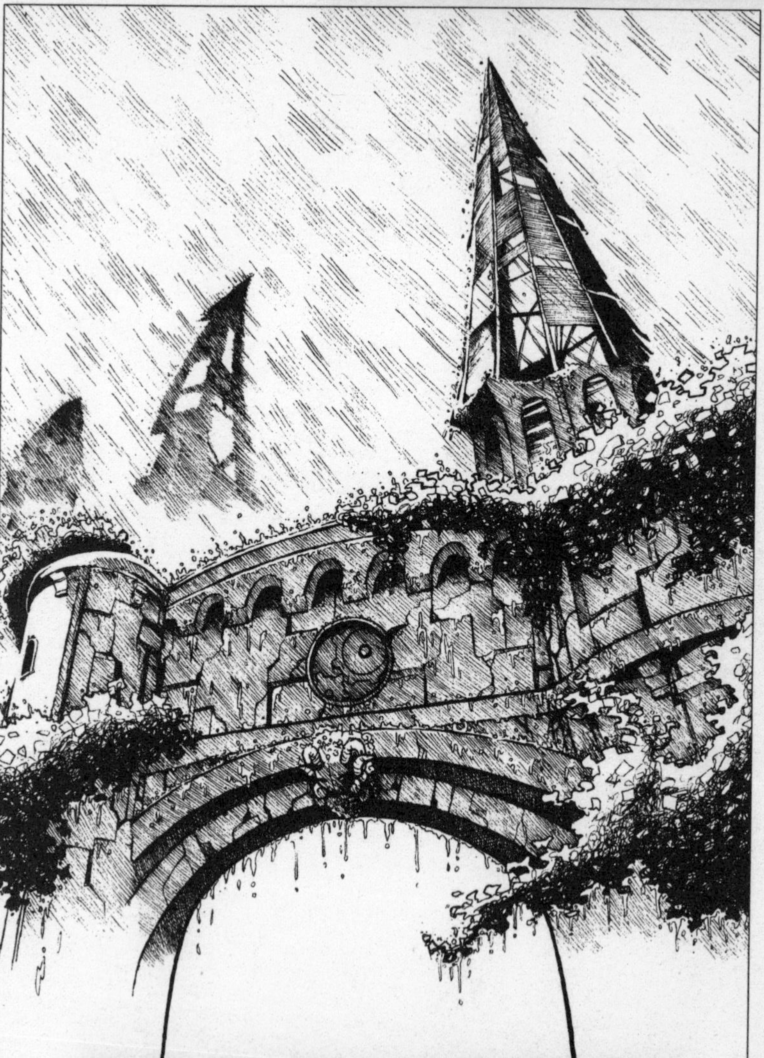

The School

In Hollow Fields, the school itself is the most omnipresent character in the series. It had to be imbued with its own character that set it apart from just being a regular environment in a school-based manga. There's a lot of steam-power and clockwork within its walls, and many of the building exteriors look as if they have been salvaged from different time periods.

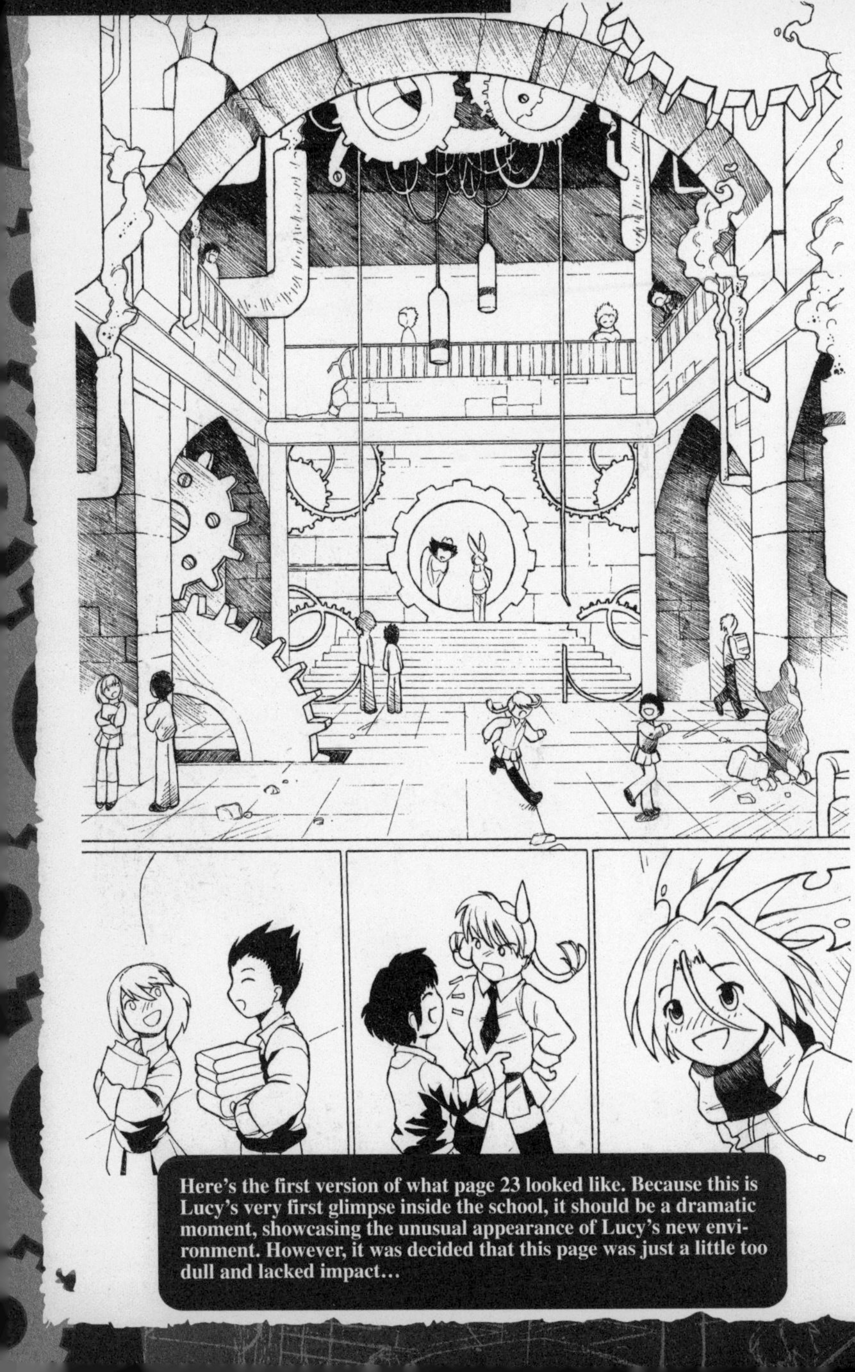

Here's the first version of what page 23 looked like. Because this is Lucy's very first glimpse inside the school, it should be a dramatic moment, showcasing the unusual appearance of Lucy's new environment. However, it was decided that this page was just a little too dull and lacked impact…

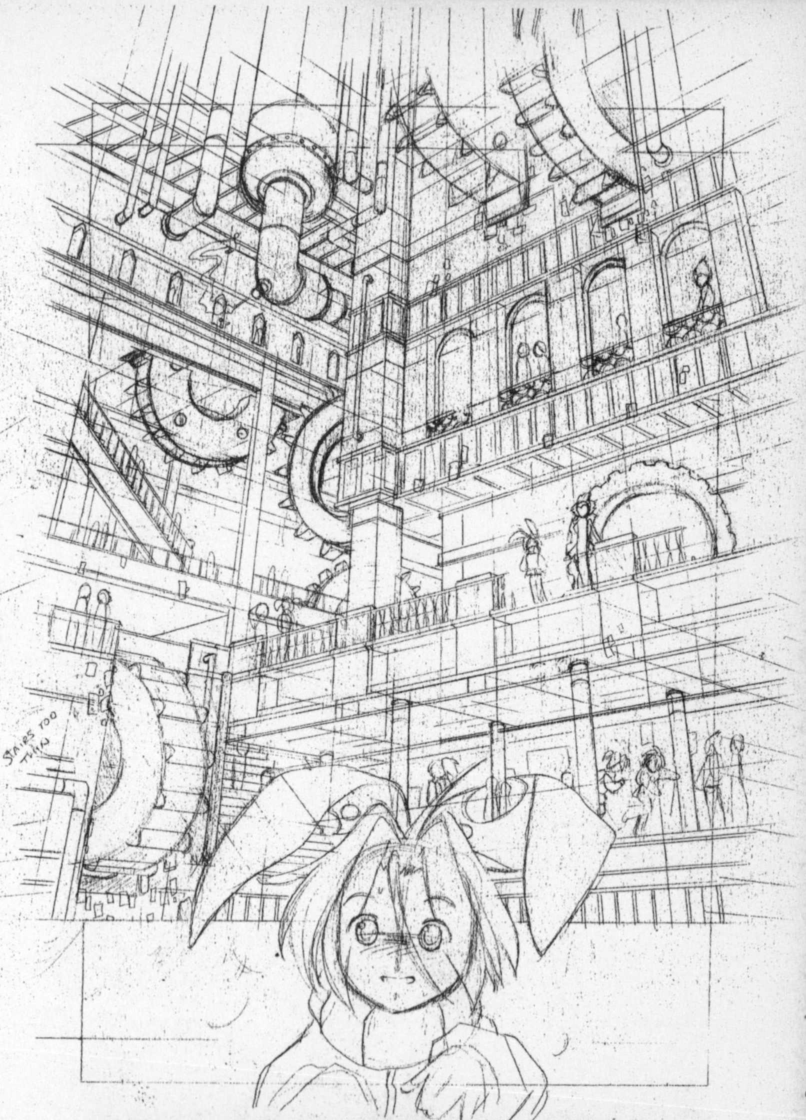
STAIRS TOO THIN

…So it was replaced by a more complicated view. Here, you can see the pencils for the new page 23. The school looks bigger and more menacing – the perfect 'background character' for the story.

• MISS WEAVER •

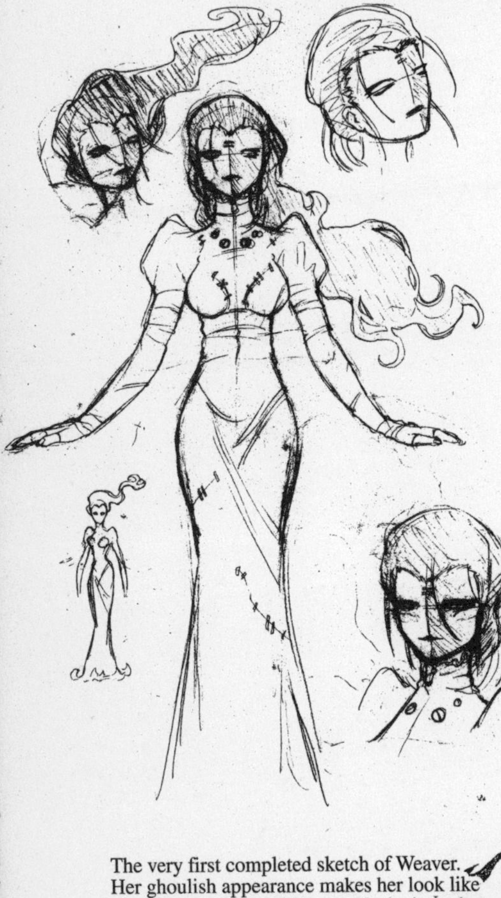

The very first completed sketch of Weaver. Her ghoulish appearance makes her look like one of the undead, which wasn't the intention behind her character.

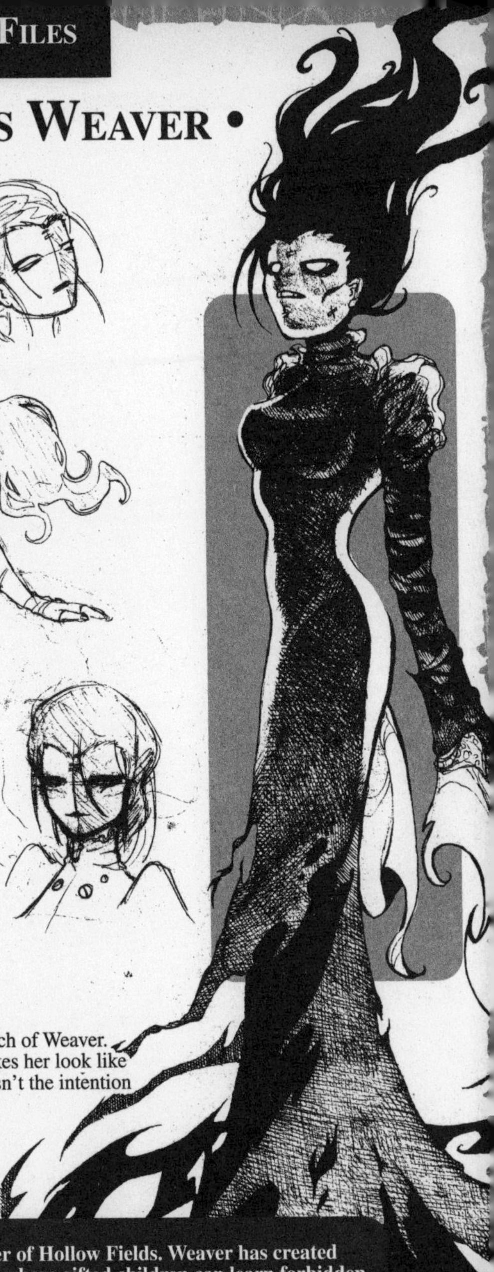

The principal and founder of Hollow Fields. Weaver has created Hollow Fields as a school where gifted children can learn forbidden science and become the next generation of evil geniuses. Tall and imposing, she is extremely domineering towards students and other staff.

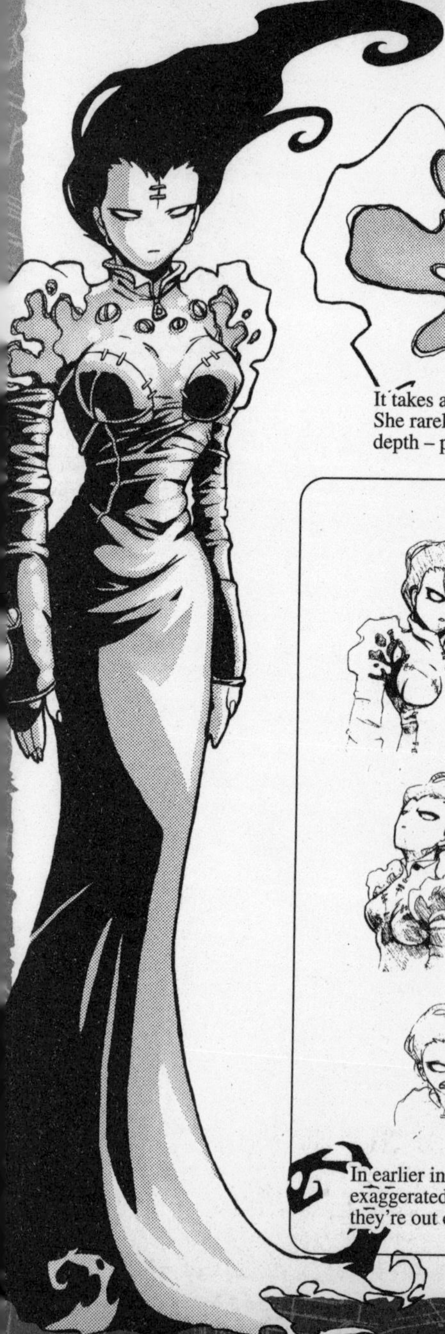

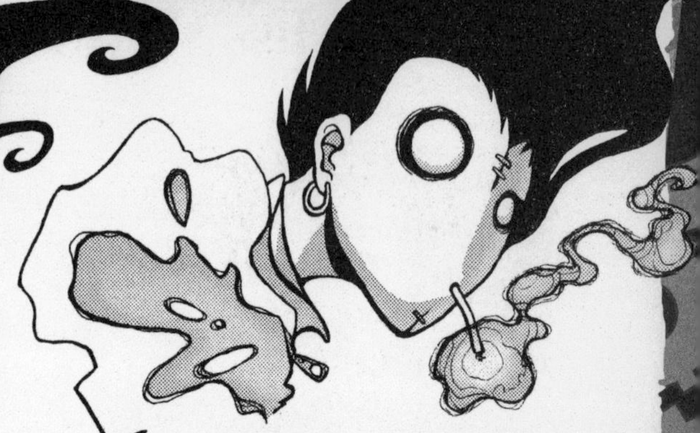

It takes a lot to make Weaver lose her composure. She rarely, if ever, seems threatened or out of her depth – particularly around grade-school children!

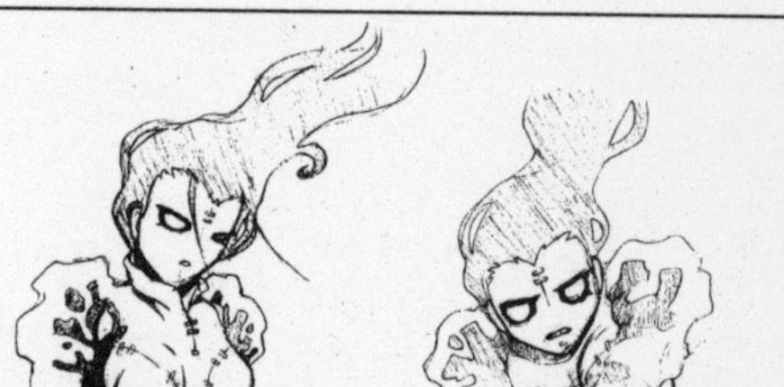

In earlier incarnations, Weaver was capable of more exaggerated, cartoonish expressions. However, they're out of character for her cold-as-ice nature.

• MISS NOTCH •

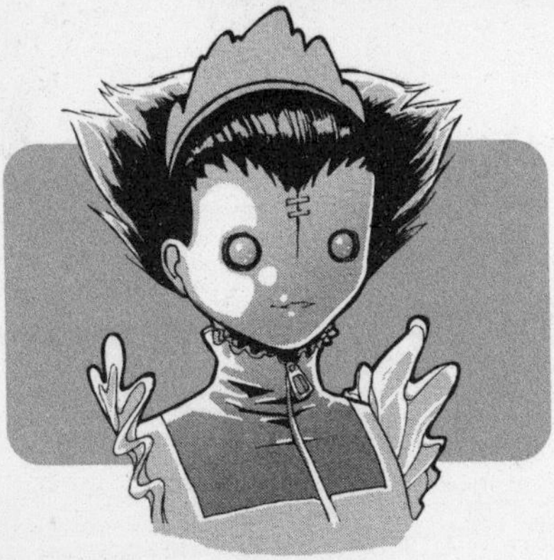

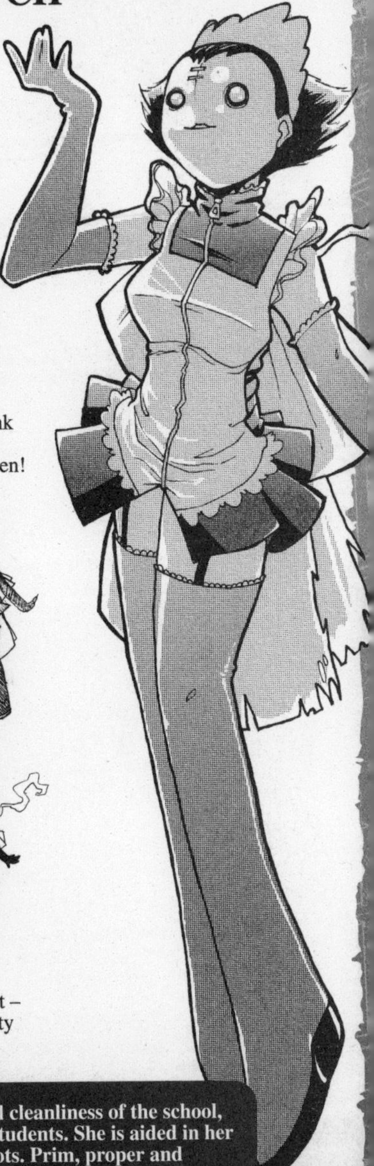

She's a seemingly cheerful busy-bee within the dank surrounds of Hollow Fields. However, she can be coldly efficient when taking care of problem children!

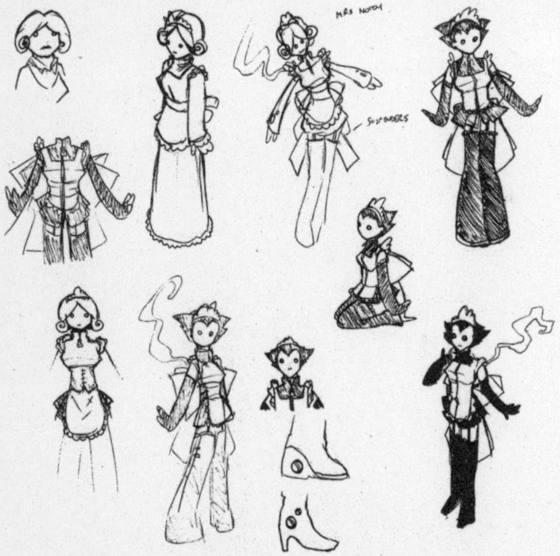
MRS NOTCH

Miss Notch was easy to design from the start – a steam-powered maid with a youthful quality despite her doll-like appearance.

The school maid, she ensures the general cleanliness of the school, as well as overseeing mealtimes for the students. She is aided in her tasks by an army of steam-powered robots. Prim, proper and polite, she never raises her voice to the students, even when threatening them. Very little escapes her attention.

• STINCH •

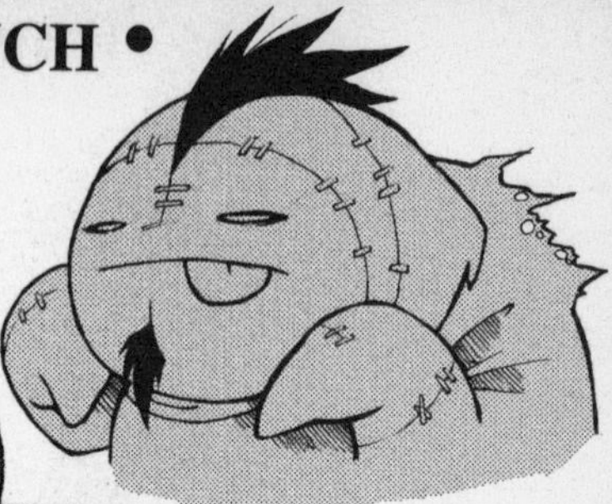

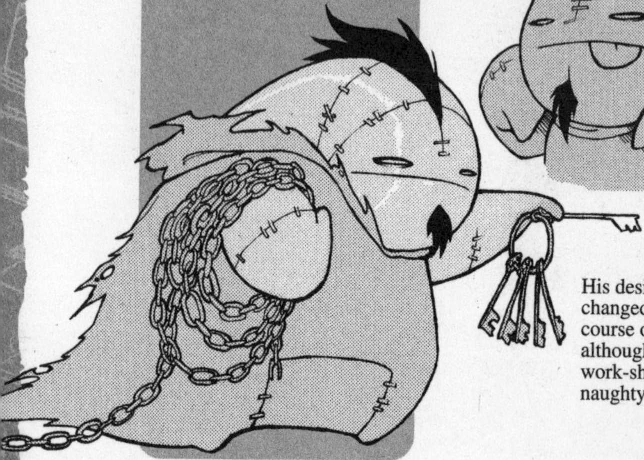

His design has probably changed the least over the course of Hollow Fields – although he now carries a clock-work-shaped crook for yanking naughty children into line!

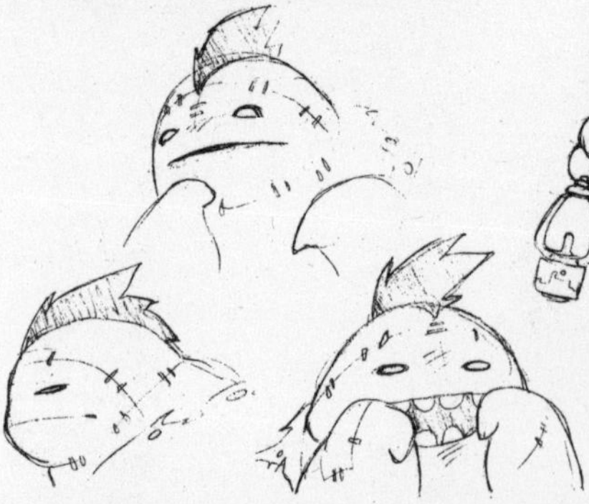

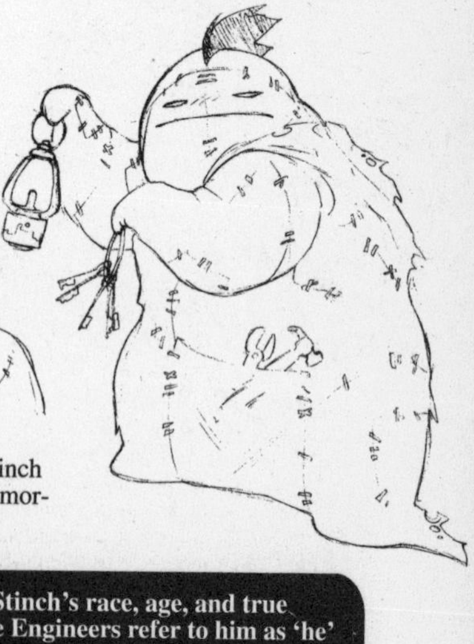

Another straightforward character, Stinch was always going to be a shapeless, amorphous sack of a creature.

The school caretaker and warden. Stinch's race, age, and true gender are all unknown (though the Engineers refer to him as 'he' for convenience). He is believed to be a product of Weaver's bio-medical experiments. His intelligence and vocabulary are fairly limited, and most of his tasks involve ensuring that unwilling children do not escape from school grounds. A hulking, lumbering creature, he exists to do the dirty work of the staff and is always eager to follow orders, particularly when they involve tormenting less talented students.

• MR. CROACH •

Croach doesn't even bother with any pretense of being friendly towards his students. Why then, is he teaching at an elementary school? There's more to him than meets the eye…

Croach is the only adult male character in this volume (since Stinch does not entirely count). So it was easy to make him stand out. Even early designs, such as this, had his trademark sneer.

The school's Graverobbing, Live Taxidermy and Embalming teacher. Anything including stitching skin, preserving flesh and creating unlife, in the form of golems or zombies, is his subject. A tall, lanky, bad-tempered creature with a fondness for his trusty shovel.

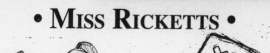

• MISS RICKETTS •

Miss Ricketts changed the most out of any Engineer – from an elderly, bespectacled lady with a fox-fur wrap to the current young, spunky version.

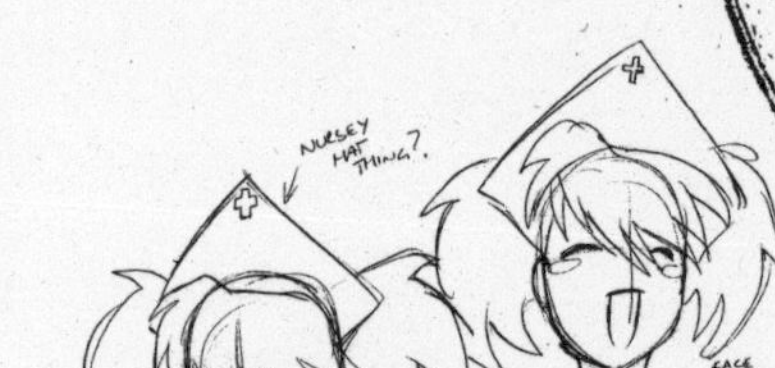

NURSEY HAT THING?

FACE STITCHES HIDDEN?

ARROWS W/ STITCHES

Miss Ricketts is the most approachable teacher, and is a big favorite among the students. She rarely seems ill-tempered or mean.

What kind of elementary teacher would dress like this for work?! She seems sweet as sugar, but how nice can someone who performs ghastly experiments on innocent animals really be?

Hollow Field's school nurse, she also doubles as the Cross-Species Body-Part Transplantation and Bio-Steam Grafting teacher. Any school subject involving taking a foreign part, alive or not, and grafting it onto a living patient is right up Miss Rickett's alley. Her office is the school's hospital wing.

• THE ENGINEERS •

Regardless of their own internal hierarchies, the Engineers reign with an iron first over the young students at Hollow Fields. Even in the early stages of the story, it was apparent their will was never questioned – as this older sketch shows!

I'll admit that when I was first trying to come up with how the Engineers should appear, I had no idea what to do. Here are some of the more bizarre thumbnails.

More light thumbnails – this time, some characters are finally starting to take shape. You can see early versions of Stinch and Mr. Croach in these scribbles.

The staff at Hollow Fields who keep the school running. Their artificial bodies are all steam-powered, resulting in a steady stream of vapour constantly pouring from vents in their backs. They are, for the most part, the teachers at the school; however, some (such as Miss Notch) have special jobs.

• LUCY SNOW •

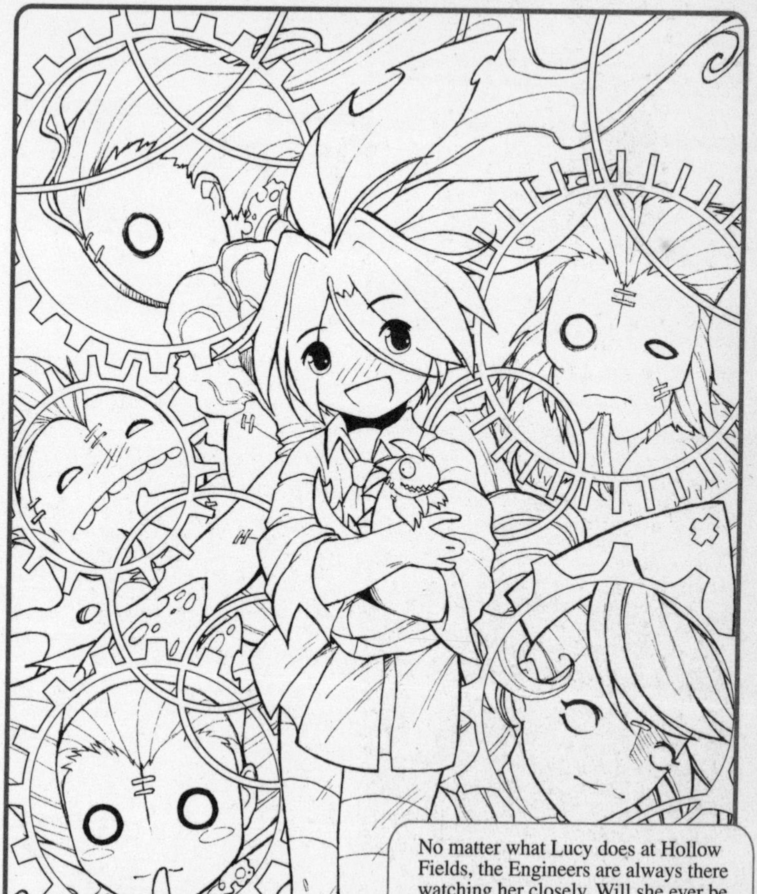

No matter what Lucy does at Hollow Fields, the Engineers are always there watching her closely. Will she ever be able to give them the slip long enough to find out about the schools' dark secrets?

The heroine of the story. She's a friendly nine-and-a-half year old who has until now lived a rather insular, average life. As a result, she is dependent on others, trusting of adults, and naïve about other people, particularly strangers. However, she is a fast learner and enjoys discovering new things. She has a large imagination, and loves any dinosaur-themed toys or books. She is forced to quickly develop some initiative and survival skills over the course of her stay at Hollow Fields.

Lucy has gone through so many different designs it would be difficult to show them all! In the beginning she was a shorter, stockier, more cartoonish character with black, spiky hair (similar to how Miss Notch wears her hair now).

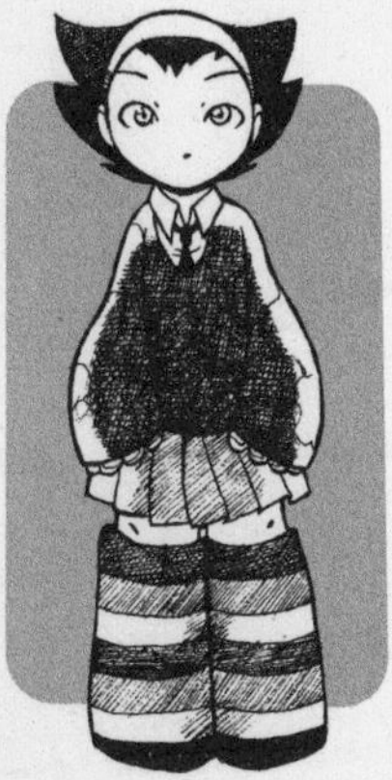

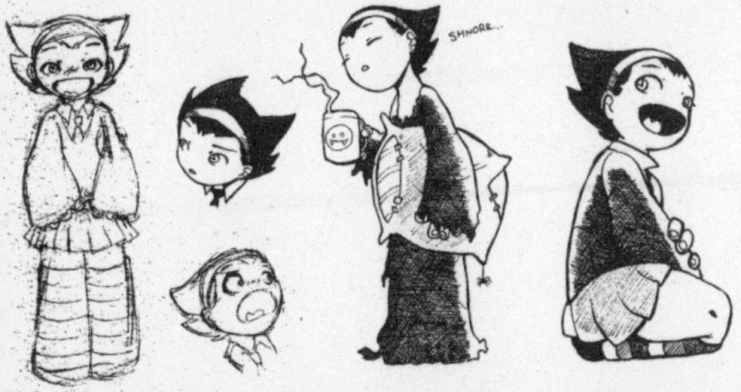
SHNORR...

This old page shows Lucy's earlier version arriving at Hollow Fields, where a stream-drone 'checks in' her bags. Note how, instead of Dino, she's holding a rather well-endowed female doll…

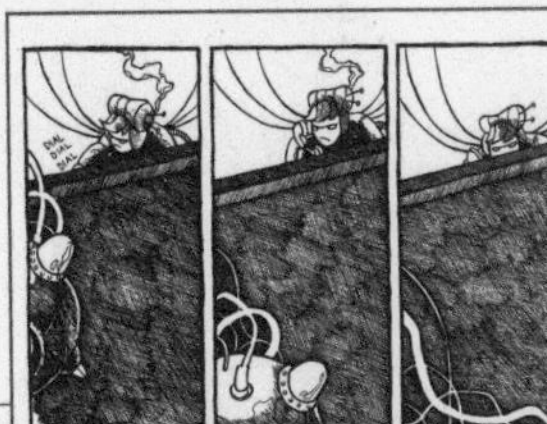
SNIKT!

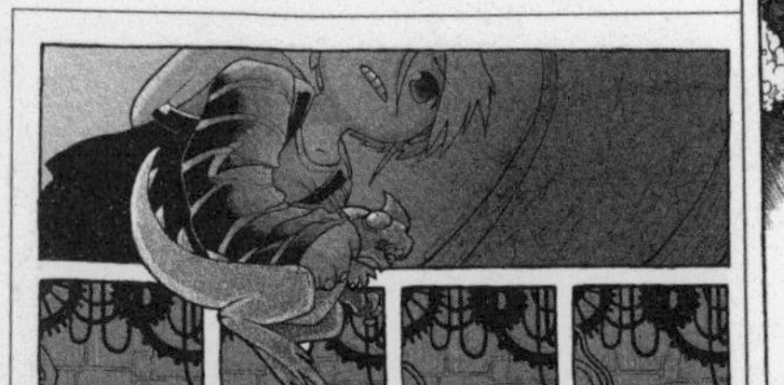
HOLLOW FIELDS DIRECTORY
SURGERY
PROSTHETICS
LIVE ORGAN TRANSPLANTS
TAXIDERMY DEPT.
MORGUE

The same scene drawn in a later version. By now, she has fairer hair, the ubiquitous ribbon, and her toy dinosaur Dino. But what's with those huge feet?

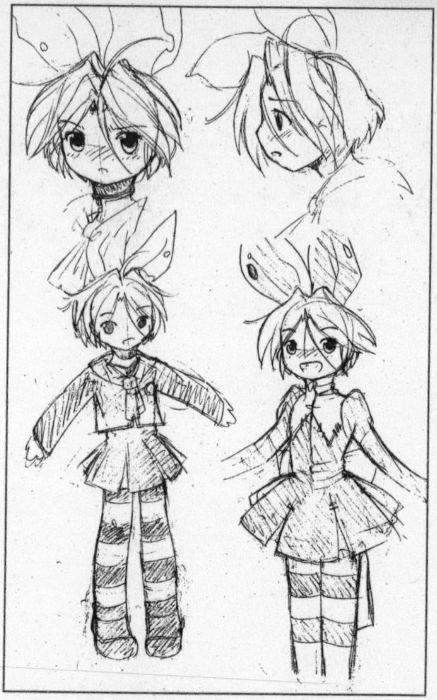

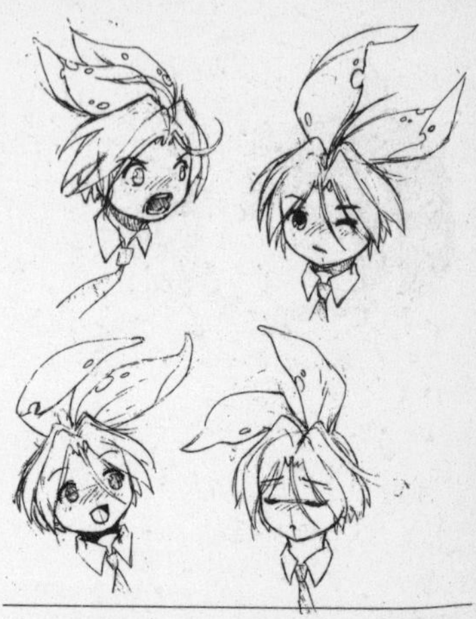

These rough sketches show Lucy's huge range of emotions. She's easily the most expressive character in the series.

Deciding on Hollow Fields' school uniform was almost as tough as deciding on how Lucy should wear her hair! Both these uniform designs were ditched in favor of the shirt-and-tie private school look. However, the striped socks always remained a constant part of her image.

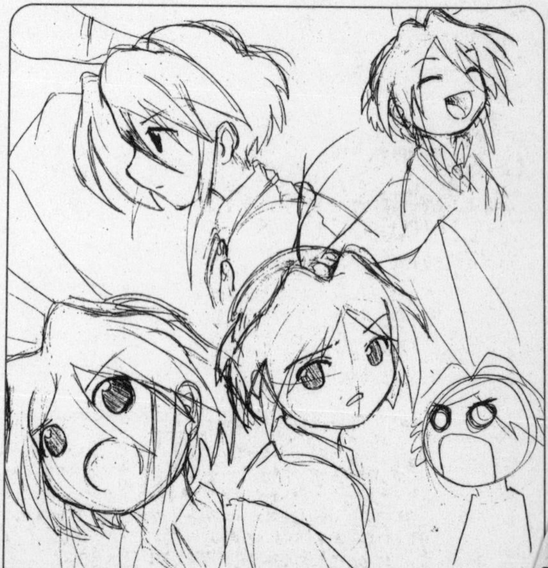

Lucy wears her heart on her sleeve, and her feelings are always easy to read in her facial expressions.

• SUMMER POLANSKI •

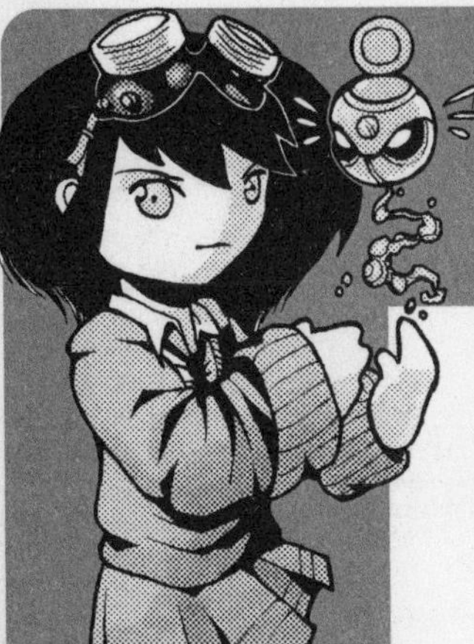

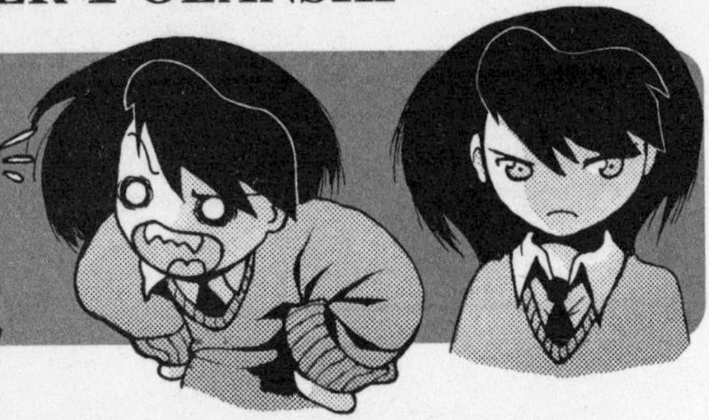

Summer's hair was initially black, then went blonde when I decided there were already too many dark-haired characters in the series, and she needed to 'stand out.' Later on, I felt bad about perpertrating a common school-manga cliche – that blonde-haired girls are always the popular bad-guy characters! So Summer's hair is actually lilac in color.

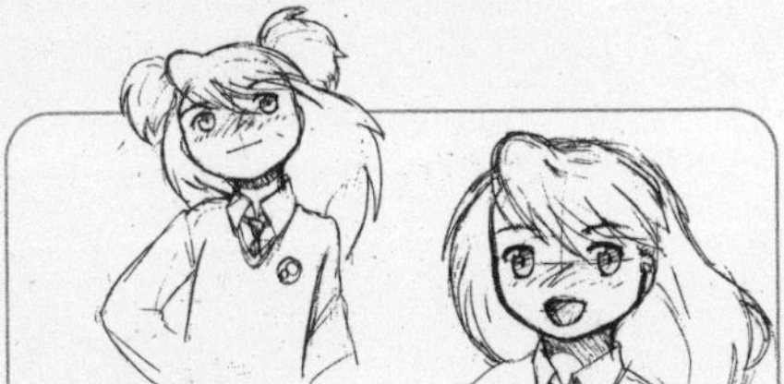

Summer was also easy to design from the start. However, these early sketches almost make her look far too nice to be Hollow Fields' resident mean girl!

Like all the young students at Hollow Fields, Summer is deeply gifted in science – her specialty is Cross-Species Body Part Transplantation. Her father is the CEO of a huge chemical corporation which has been involved in unethical practices in the third world. Summer is officially *"The Most Popular Girl In School."* She is pretty, brilliant, and well-liked by staff, however she has a Machiavellian streak, and will do anything to remain Hollow Fields' top student.

• CLAUDE McGINTY •

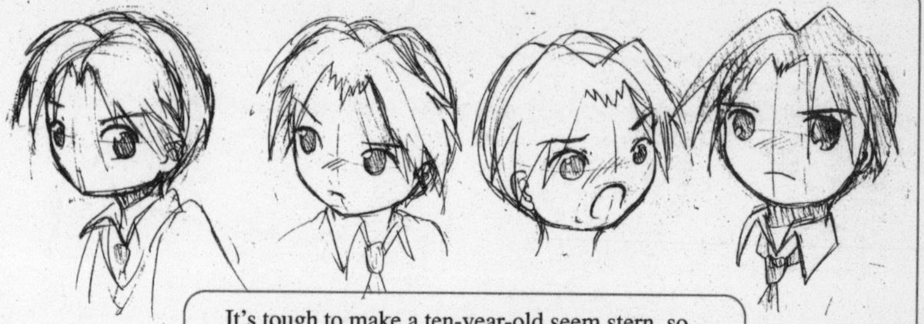

It's tough to make a ten-year-old seem stern, so Claude went through a few basic design changes before he looked 'right.' The face in the right most side is the current version – he's still a child, but his expressions make him look older than he is.

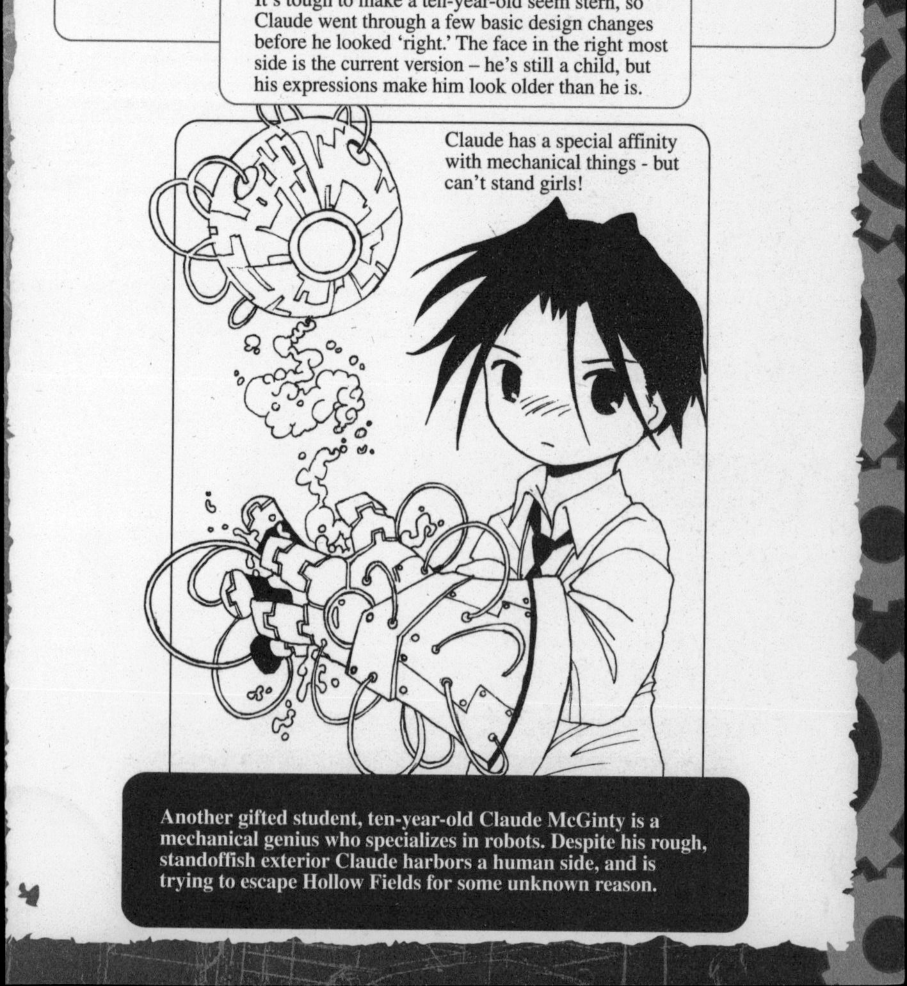

Claude has a special affinity with mechanical things - but can't stand girls!

Another gifted student, ten-year-old Claude McGinty is a mechanical genius who specializes in robots. Despite his rough, standoffish exterior Claude harbors a human side, and is trying to escape Hollow Fields for some unknown reason.

• DOCTOR ATTICUS • NORMANDY BLEAK

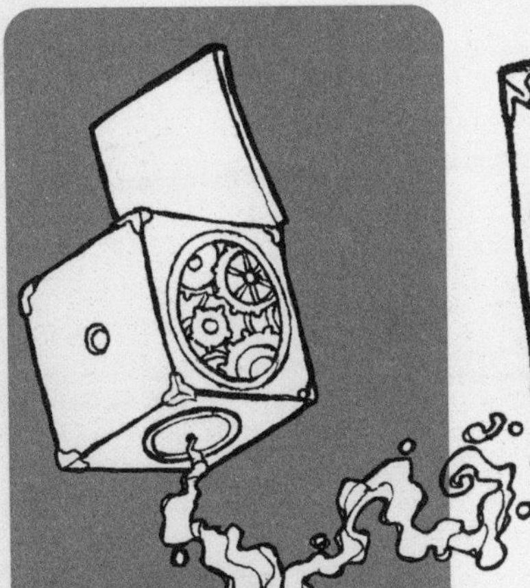

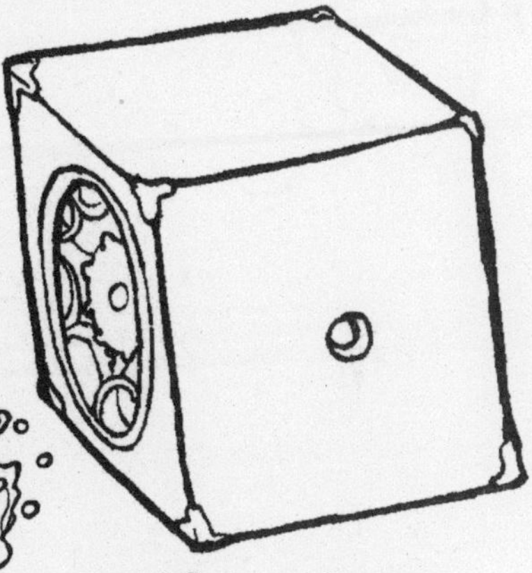

It was difficult to get Doctor Bleak's design wrong – he's just a box with some clockwork designs on him! (If only all the characters looked like this – my job would be much faster…)

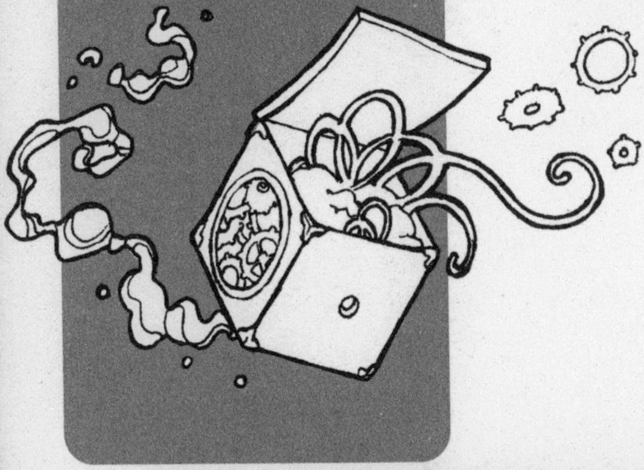

Lucy's unusual sidekick in Hollow Fields is a talking clockwork puzzlebox. A brilliant scientist in his own right, he acts as a sort of mentor and tutor for Lucy as well as a kindly adult influence. His small size allows her to smuggle him around the school in her bag, a process that, as a grown-up, he finds rather demeaning. As yet, Lucy knows nothing of his past.

• Lucy's Classmates •

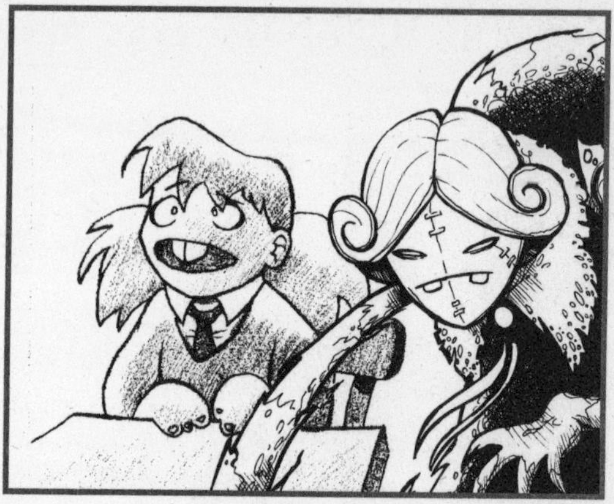

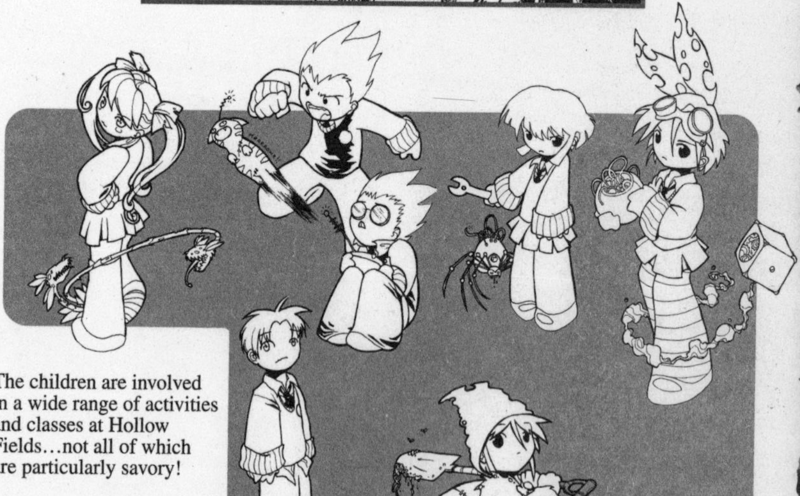

The children are involved in a wide range of activities and classes at Hollow Fields…not all of which are particularly savory!

The students at Hollow Fields all come from a variety of geographical backgrounds; however, by and large their parents are all involved in aspects of forbidden science across the globe. They're highly competitive, and determined to avoid detention at any cost.

Hollow Fields School Files

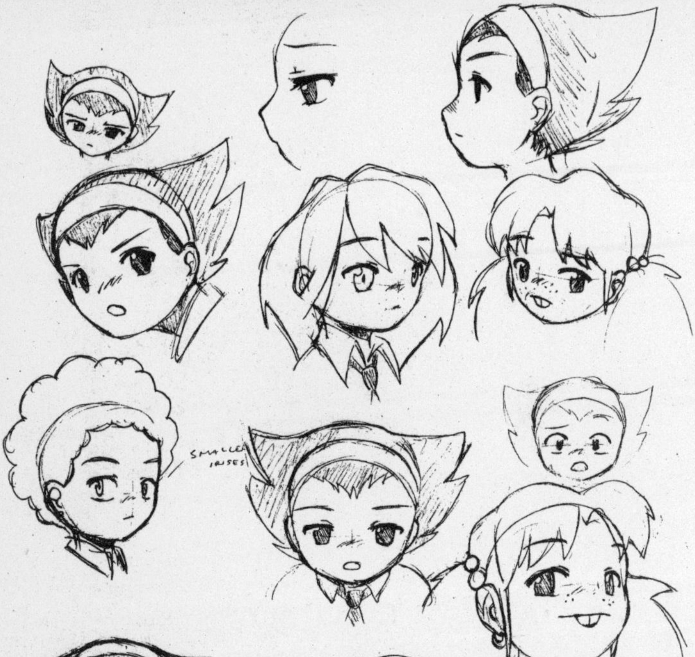
SMALLER IRISES

Lucy and her classmates had to be cute and appealing, to offset the odd appearance of the Engineers. This old set of sketches shows that, even in the early stages of writing and drawing Hollow Fields, Summer was always prone to throwing tantrums…!

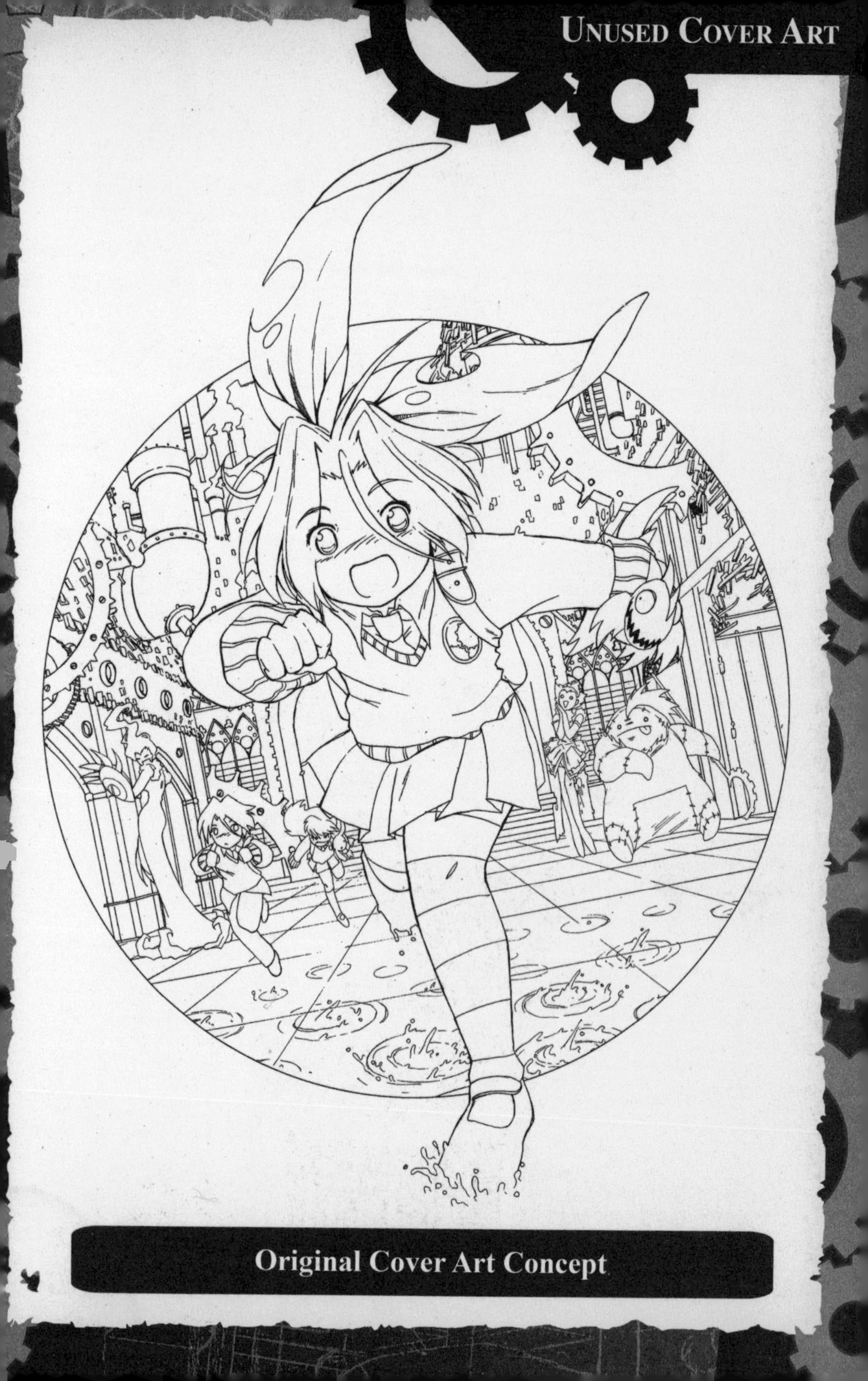

Original Cover Art Concept

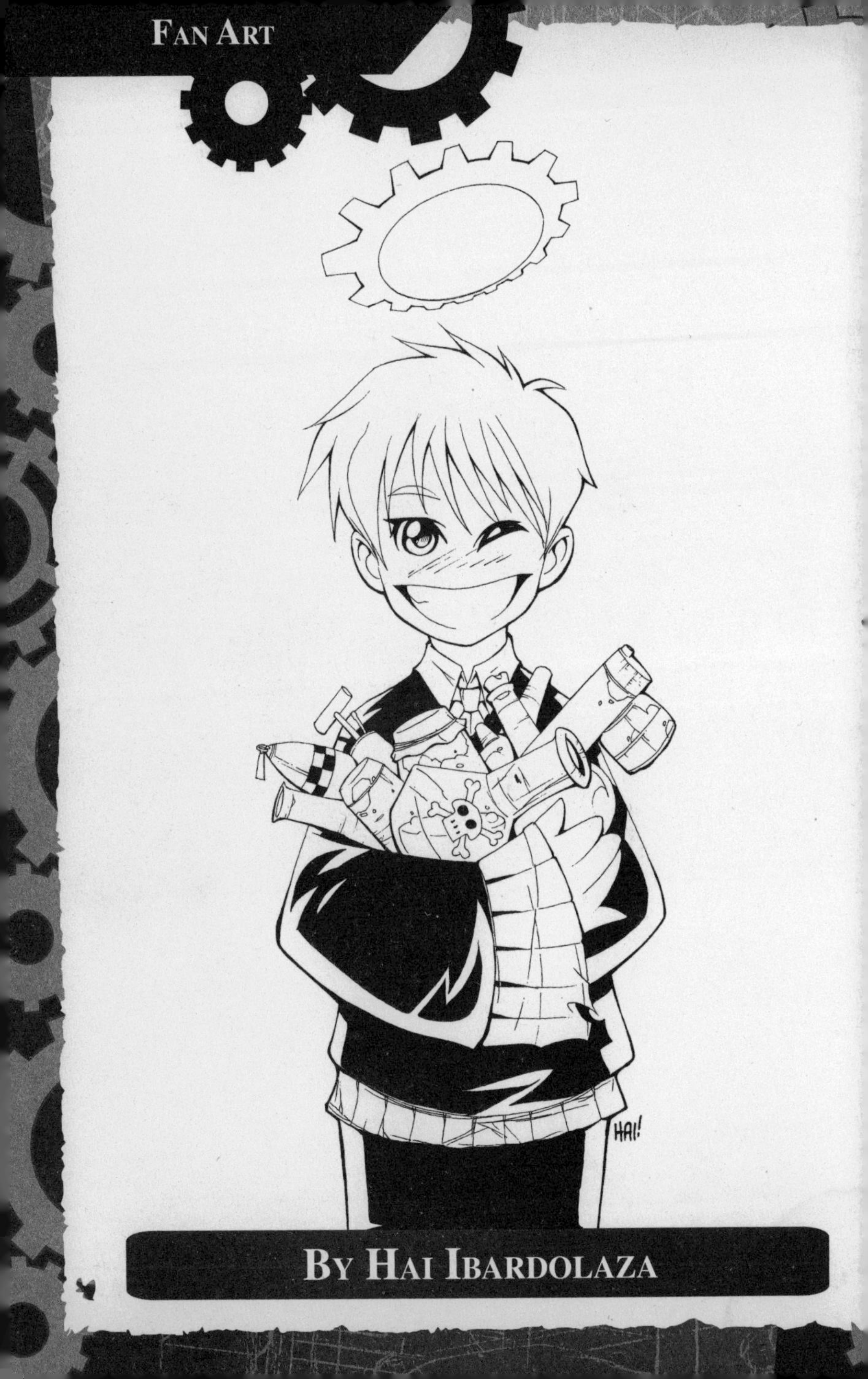
HAI!

BY HAI IBARDOLAZA

About the Author:

Born and raised in Gippsland, Australia, Madeleine Rosca earned her Bachelor of Fine Arts from Monash University before travelling to Melbourne to study multimedia and animation. After being employed as a graphic designer for a number of years, she moved to Tasmania to concentrate on her own creative work. Disappointingly, she has not yet seen a Tasmanian devil in the wild. Her creative influences include Lemony Snickett, Eoin Colfer, Shaun Tan, Daisuke Moriyama and Graeme Base. Hollow Fields, which originally appeared on Wirepop in late 2005, is her first published work.

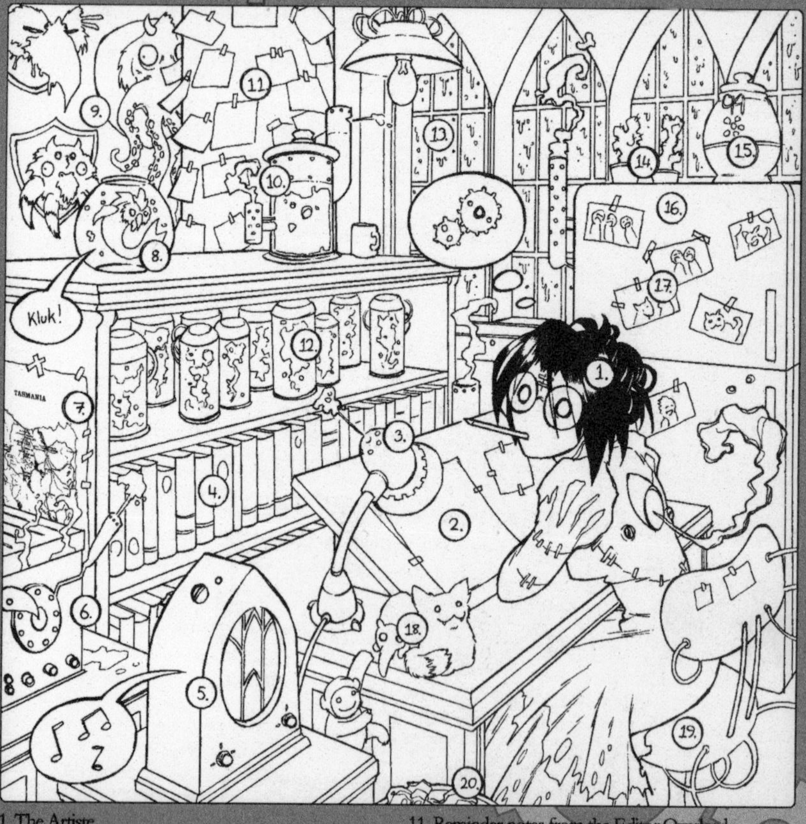

Kluk!
TASMANIA
1.
2.
3.
4.
5.
6.
7.
8.
9.
10.
11.
12.
13.
14.
15.
16.
17.
18.
19.
20.

1. The Artiste.
2. A blank manga page.
3. ZX 2400 steam-powered desk lamp.
4. Reference material (mostly other manga).
5. Clockwork-driven sound machine, for music.
6. RF-8 9B steam-computer, for online correspondence.
7. Map of Tasmania.
8. Chicken-fish, for company.
9. Mounted heads of failed lab experiments.
10. J100S-LB steam-powered Coffeenator.
11. Reminder notes from the Editor Overlord.
12. Creepy specimens sent in by devoted readers.
13. Bars on window preventing escape from deadlines.
14. Neglected cacti.
15. Cookie-jar holding treats for good monster servants.
16. Refridgerator holding nutritious foodstuffs.
17. Photographs of family, pets., successful experiments.
18. Plushies, for more company.
19. MRz09 hydraulic Office Chair Of No Escape.
20. Rubbish bin, for failed manga experiments.

NEXT VOLUME...

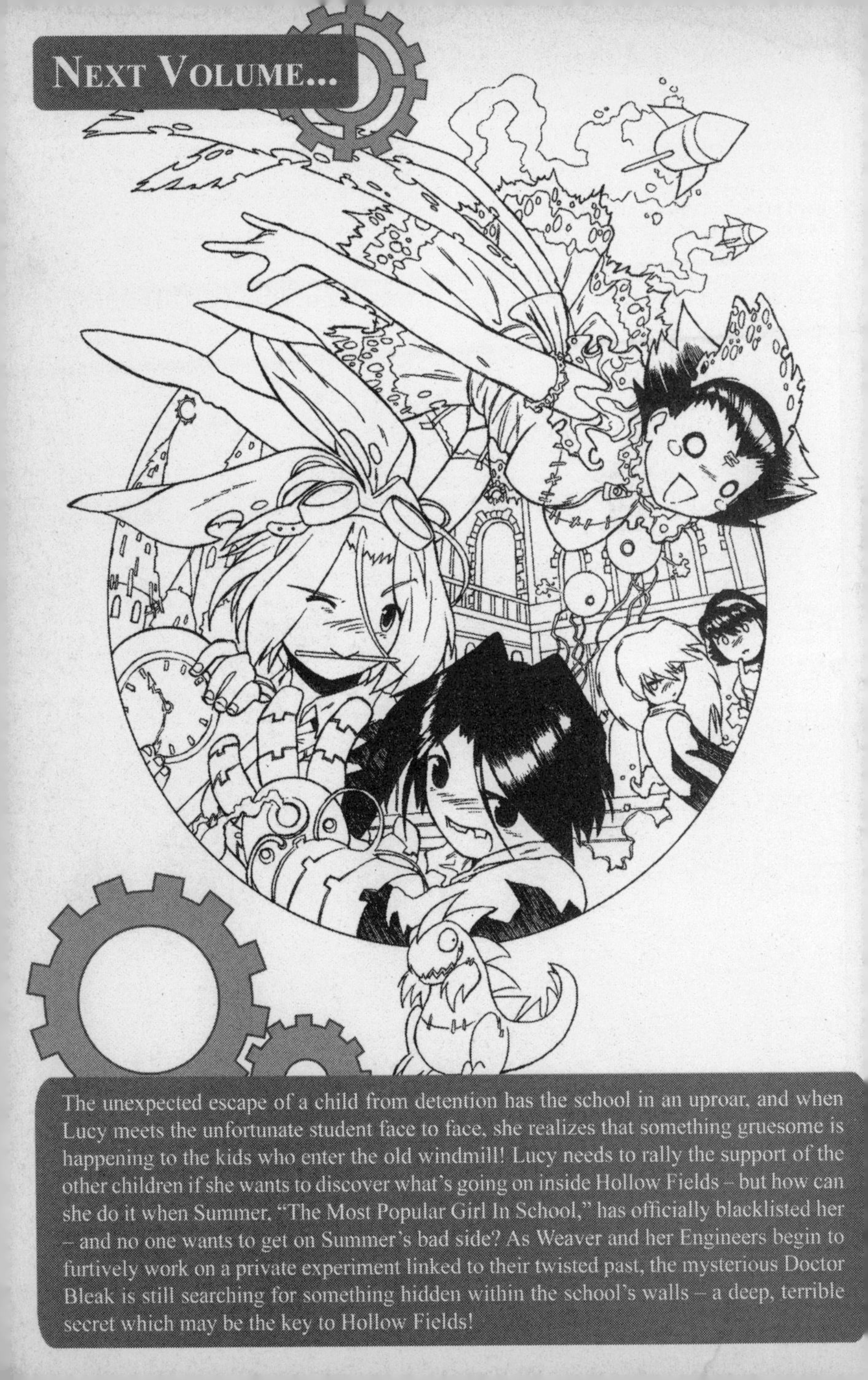

The unexpected escape of a child from detention has the school in an uproar, and when Lucy meets the unfortunate student face to face, she realizes that something gruesome is happening to the kids who enter the old windmill! Lucy needs to rally the support of the other children if she wants to discover what's going on inside Hollow Fields – but how can she do it when Summer, "The Most Popular Girl In School," has officially blacklisted her – and no one wants to get on Summer's bad side? As Weaver and her Engineers begin to furtively work on a private experiment linked to their twisted past, the mysterious Doctor Bleak is still searching for something hidden within the school's walls – a deep, terrible secret which may be the key to Hollow Fields!

INVERLOCH
EARTHSONG
OWN THE NET'S HOTTEST WEBCOMICS!
ON SALE NOW!!!

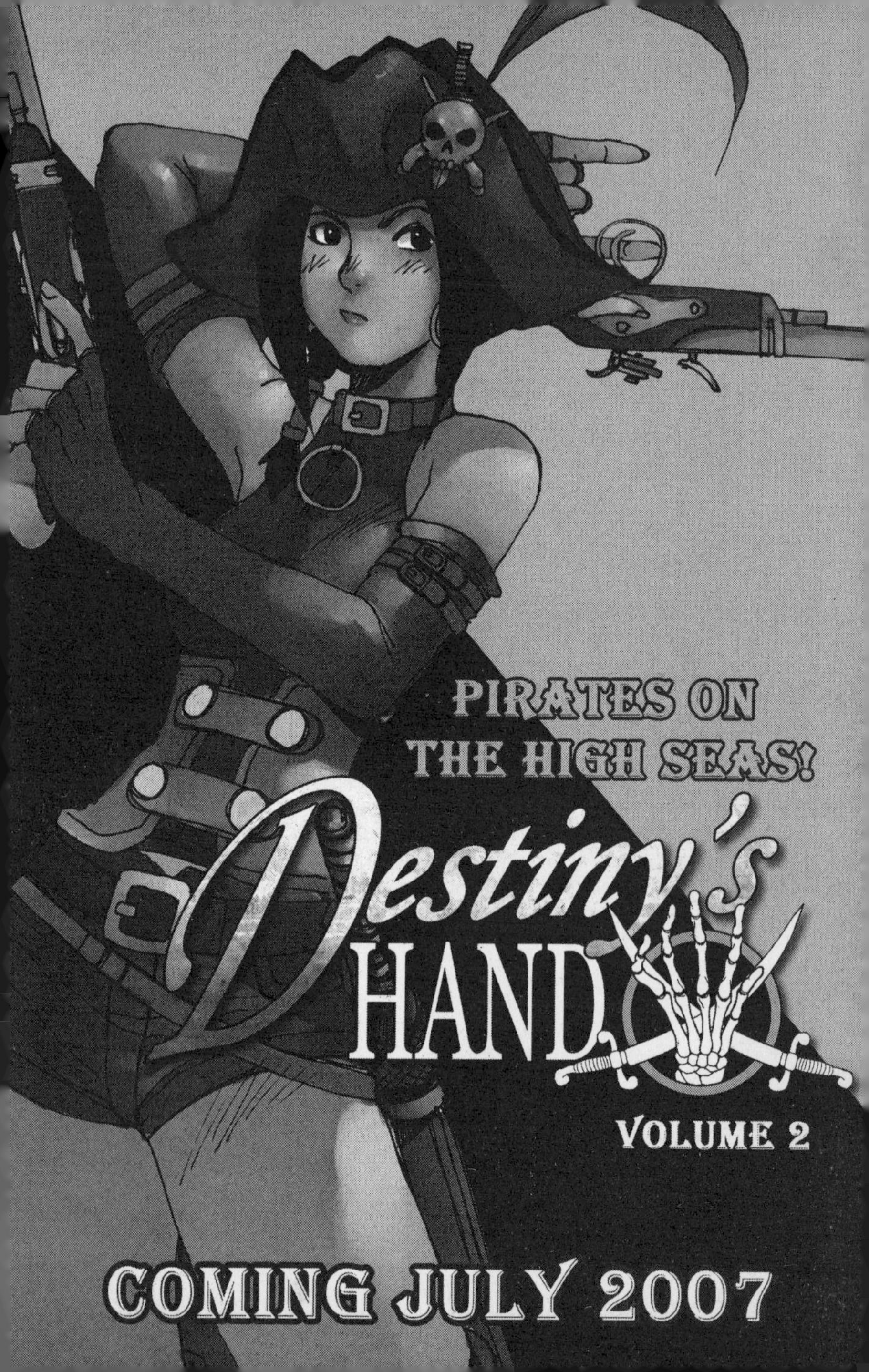
PIRATES ON
THE HIGH SEAS!
Destiny's
HAND
VOLUME 2
COMING JULY 2007

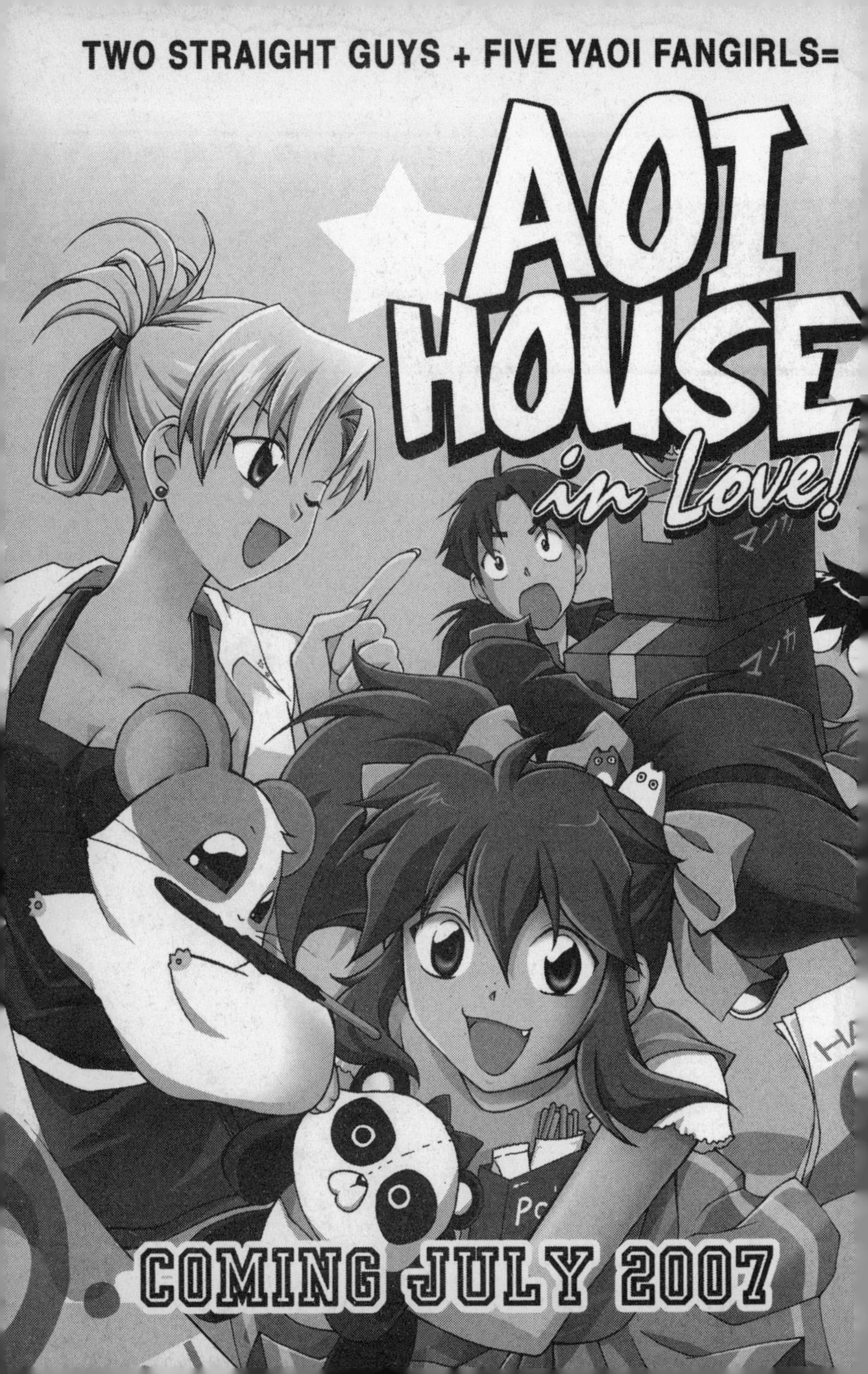
TWO STRAIGHT GUYS + FIVE YAOI FANGIRLS=
AOI HOUSE
in Love!
COMING JULY 2007

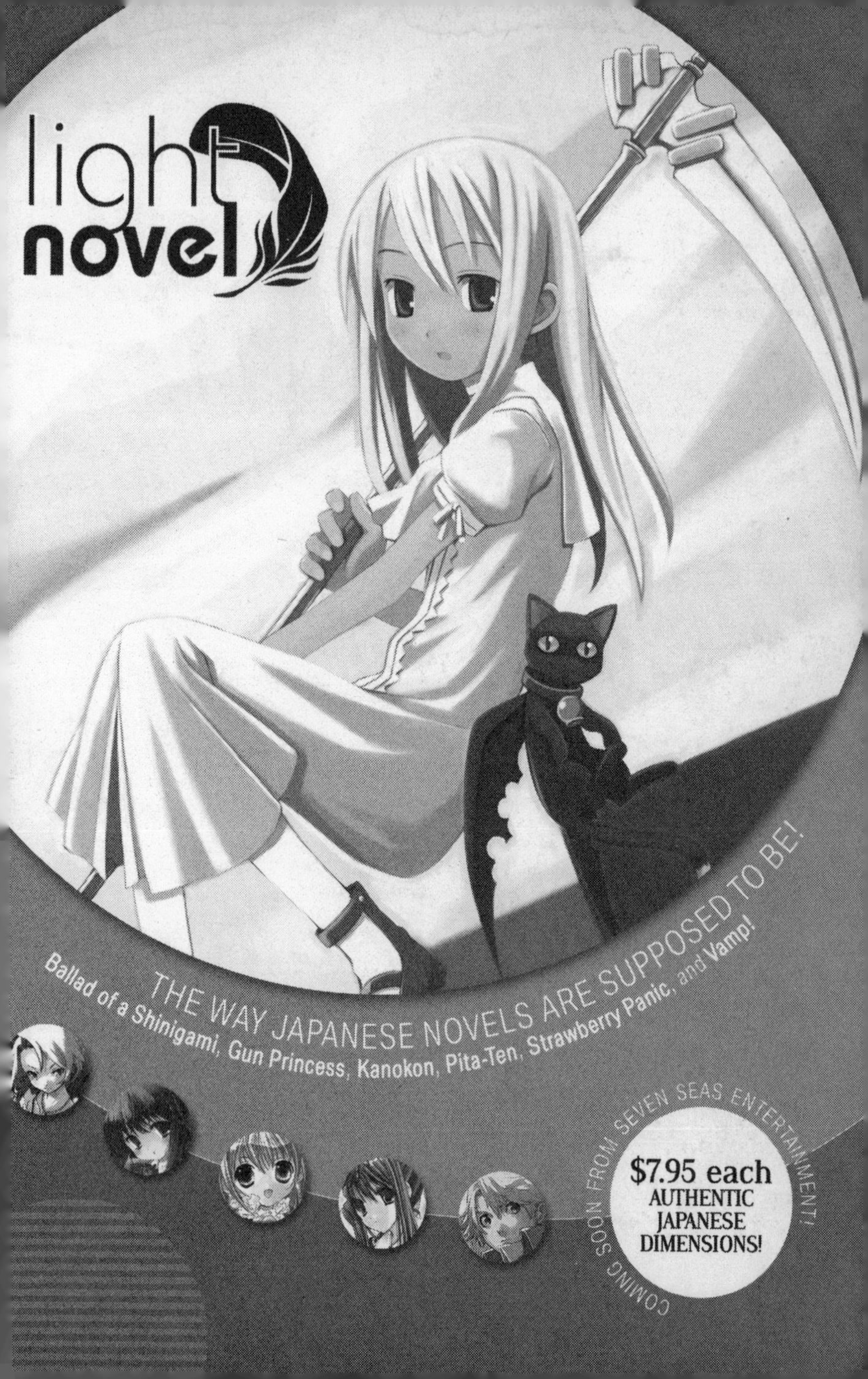
light novel
THE WAY JAPANESE NOVELS ARE SUPPOSED TO BE!
Ballad of a Shinigami, Gun Princess, Kanokon, Pita-Ten, Strawberry Panic, and Vamp!
COMING SOON FROM SEVEN SEAS ENTERTAINMENT!
$7.95 each
AUTHENTIC JAPANESE DIMENSIONS!

THE END

YOU'RE READING THE WRONG WAY

This is the last page of
Hollow Fields Volume 1.

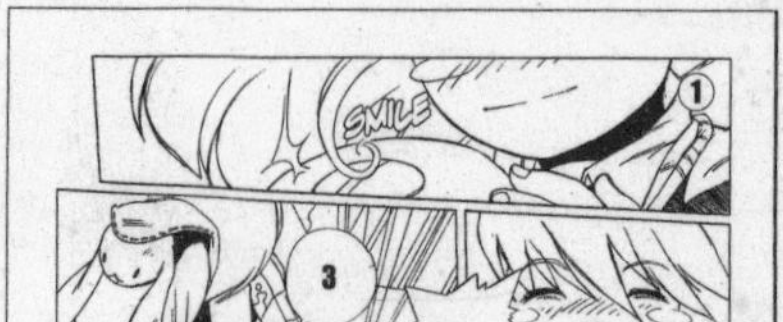
1
SMILE
2
3
4
5
BLOOP!
SUMMER'S HOMEWORK
BLUP!
6
7
MURMUR
MURMUR

This book reads from right to left, Japanese style. To read from the beginning, flip the book over to the other side, start with the top right panel, and take it from there.

If this is your first time reading manga, just follow the diagram. It may seem backwards at first, but you'll get used to it! Have fun!